Lecture Notes in Computer Scie

Commenced Publication in 1973
Founding and Former Series Editors:
Gerhard Goos, Juris Hartmanis, and Jan van Leeuwen

Per Stenström   Michel Dubois
Manolis Katevenis   Rajiv Gupta
Theo Ungerer (Eds.)

High Performance Embedded Architectures and Compilers

Third International Conference, HiPEAC 2008
Göteborg, Sweden, January 27-29, 2008
Proceedings

 Springer

Volume Editors

Per Stenström
Chalmers University of Technology, Dept. of Computer Science and Engineering
412 96 Gothenburg, Sweden
E-mail: pers@chalmers.se

Michel Dubois
University of Southern California, Dept. of Electrical Engineering
3740 McClintock Ave., Los Angeles, CA 90089-2562, USA
E-mail: dubois@paris.usc.edu

Manolis Katevenis
FORTH-ICS
100 Plastira Ave., Vassilika Vouton, 70-013 Heraklion, Crete, Greece
E-mail: kateveni@ics.forth.gr

Rajiv Gupta
University of California, Riverside, Dept. of Computer Science and Engineering
408 Engineering Building II, Riverside, CA 92521, USA
E-mail: gupta@cs.ucr.edu

Theo Ungerer
University of Augsburg, Institute of Computer Science
86135 Augsburg, Germany
E-mail: ungerer@informatik.uni-augsburg.de

Library of Congress Control Number: 2007942570

CR Subject Classification (1998): B.2, C.1, D.3.4, B.5, C.2, D.4

LNCS Sublibrary: SL 1 – Theoretical Computer Science and General Issues

ISSN   0302-9743
ISBN-10   3-540-77559-5 Springer Berlin Heidelberg New York
ISBN-13   978-3-540-77559-1 Springer Berlin Heidelberg New York

Springer is a part of Springer Science+Business Media

springer.com

© Springer-Verlag Berlin Heidelberg 2008
Printed in Germany

Typesetting: Camera-ready by author, data conversion by Scientific Publishing Services, Chennai, India
Printed on acid-free paper   SPIN: 12212101   06/3180   5 4 3 2 1 0

Preface

The first two editions of the HiPEAC conference series in Barcelona (2005) and Ghent (2007) have really demonstrated that the topics covered by HiPEAC attract a lot of interest. In the 2007 conference, about 200 people attended the conference and its satellite events. The third HiPEAC conference was held in Göteborg, the second largest city in Sweden.

The offerings of this conference were rich and diverse. We offered attendees a set of four workshops on topics that are all central to the HiPEAC roadmap: multi-cores, compiler optimizations, reconfigurable computing, and interconnection networks. Additionally, a tutorial on the Sunflower Toolsuite was offered.

The conference program was as rich as in the last years. It featured many important and timely topics such as multi-core processors, reconfigurable systems, compiler optimization, power-aware techniques and more. The conference also offered a keynote speech by Mateo Valero – the Eckert-Mauchly Award winner in 2007. Several social events provided opportunities for interaction and exchange of ideas in informal settings such as a tour at the Universeum – a science exhibition center and aquarium – where the banquet took place as well.

This year we received 77 submissions of which 14 papers were Committee papers. Papers were submitted from 22 different nations (about 40% from Europe, 25% from Asia, 30% from North America and 5% from South America), which is a token of the global visibility of the conference.

We had the luxury of having a strong Program Committee consisting of 37 experts in all areas within the scope of the conference and we kept all reviewing within the Program Committee. Thus, each paper was typically reviewed by four Program Committee members. We collected 301 reviews and we were happy to note that each paper was rigorously reviewed before we made the decisions, despite the fact that we shortened the review phase and that reviewing took place during most reviewers' precious vacation time.

The Program Committee meeting was held in the center of Rome, the ancient capital of Italy. Despite a long trip for many members of the Program Committee, 16 PC members attended the meeting. For virtually all papers, at least two reviewers were present. The PC meeting was preceded by an e-mail discussion of papers among the reviewers. At the PC meeting the papers were discussed in the order of average score also including PC papers. When a paper was discussed where a participating PC member was either a co-author or had conflicts with that paper, that person left the room. We accepted 25 papers of which 4 are PC papers, yielding an acceptance rate of 32%.

The end result of the whole effort was the high-quality program for the HiPEAC 2008 event. We hope that you learn and get much inspiration from this proceedings volume.

The planning of a conference starts way ahead of the actual event. If it were not for the unselfish and hard work of a large number of devoted individuals, this conference would not have been as successful as it was. Let us first thank the authors for their great contributions which constitute the core of the conference. We were very fortunate to collect a great team to power this event and would like to thank all of them: Mats Brorsson (KTH) for putting together an attractive pre-conference program; Ewa Wäingelin (Chalmers) for the enormous effort she invested in the local arrangement; Per Waborg (Chalmers) for a fantastic job in keeping the costs within budget and running the books; Mike O'Boyle (Edinburgh) for timely publicity campaigns; Jörg Mische and Theo Ungerer (Augsburg) for the hard work in putting together the proceedings; Michiel Ronsee (Ghent) for administering the submission and review system; and finally Sylvie Detournay (Ghent) for administering the web. Thanks to all of you!

Finally, we would also like to mention the support from the Sixth Framework Programme of the European Union, represented by project officers Mercè Griera i Fisa and Panagiotis Tsarchopoulos, for sponsoring the event and for the travel grants.

October 2007

Per Stenström
Michel Dubois
Manolis Katevenis
Rajiv Gupta

Organization

Executive Committee

General Co-chairs	Per Stenström
	Chalmers University of Technology, Sweden
	Michel Dubois
	University of Southern California, USA
Program Committee Co-chairs	Manolis Katevenis
	University of Crete / FORTH, Greece
	Rajiv Gupta
	University of California, Riverside, USA
Workshop/Tutorials Chair	Mats Brorsson
	KTH, Sweden
Local Arrangements Chair	Ewa Wäingelin
	Chalmers University of Technology, Sweden
Finance Chair	Per Waborg
	Chalmers University of Technology, Sweden
Publicity Chair	Mike O'Boyle
	University of Edinburgh, UK
Publications Chair	Theo Ungerer
	University of Augsburg, Germany
Submissions Chair	Michiel Ronsse
	Ghent University, Belgium
Web Chair	Sylvie Detournay
	Ghent University, Belgium

Program Committee

Angelos Bilas	FORTH / University of Crete, Greece
Mats Brorsson	KTH, Sweden
Koen De Bosschere	University of Ghent, Belgium
Jack Davidson	University of Virginia, USA
Marc Duranton	NXP Semiconductors, Netherlands
Babak Falsafi	Carnegie Mellon University, USA
Paolo Faraboschi	HP Labs, Spain
Kristian Flautner	ARM, UK
Chris Gniady	University of Arizona, USA
Wen-mei Hwu	University of Illinois, USA
Paolo Ienne	EPFL, Switzerland
Norm Jouppi	HP Labs, USA

Mahmut Kandemir	Pennsylvania State University, USA
Stefanos Kaxiras	University of Patras, Greece
Christos Kozyrakis	Stanford University, USA
Scott Mahlke	University of Michigan, USA
Peter Marwedel	University of Dortmund, Germany
Avi Mendelson	Intel, Israel
Andreas Moshovos	University of Toronto, Canada
Mike O'Boyle	Edinburgh University, UK
Kunle Olukotun	Stanford University, USA
Yunheung Paek	Seoul National Universiry, Korea
Santosh Pande	Georgia Institute of Technology, USA
Yale Patt	University of Texas at Austin, USA
Alex Ramirez	UPC / BSC, Spain
Lawrence Rauchwerger	Texas A&M University, USA
John Regehr	University of Utah, USA
Andre Seznec	INRIA, France
Guri Sohi	University of Wisconsin, USA
Olivier Temam	INRIA, France
Josep Torrellas	University of Illinois, USA
Mateo Valero	UPC / BSC, Spain
David Whalley	Florida State University, USA
Sudhakar Yalamanchili	Georgia Institute of Technology, USA

Steering Committee

Mateo Valero	UPC / BSC, Spain
Anant Agarwal	MIT, USA
Koen De Bosschere	Ghent University, Belgium
Mike O'Boyle	University of Edinburgh, UK
Brad Calder	University of California, USA
Rajiv Gupta	University of California, Riverside, USA
Wen-mei W. Hwu	UIUC, USA
Josep Llosa	UPC, Spain
Margaret Martonosi	Princenton University, USA
Per Stenström	Chalmers University of Technology, Sweden
Olivier Teman	INRIA Futurs, France

Reviewers

Minwook Ahn	Mauricio Breternitz Jr.	Bruce Childers
Mauricio Alvarez	Mats Brorsson	Doosan Cho
Sara Baghsorkhi	Felipe Cabarcas	Michael Chu
Mauro Bianco	Francisco Cazorla	Romain Cledat
Angelos Bilas	Luis Ceze	Michele Co

Albert Cohen
Clark Coleman
Adrian Cristal
Jack Davidson
Koen De Bosschere
Marc Duranton
Ayose Falcon
Babak Falsafi
Kevin Fan
Paolo Faraboschi
Kristian Flautner
Grigori Fursin
Chris Gniady
Daniel Gracia-Perez
Brian Greskamp
Jason Hiser
Wen-mei Hwu
Paolo Ienne
Daniel Jimenez
Jose Joao
Norm Jouppi
Mahmut Kandemir
Stefanos Kaxiras
DaeHo Kim
Hokyun Kim
Wonsub Kim
Yongjoo Kim
Christos Kozyrakis
Manjunath Kudlur
Tushar Kumar
Christopher Kung

Chang Joo Lee
Jongwon Lee
Piotr Lesnicki
Yue Li
Yongmo Liang
Danny Lynch
Scott Mahlke
Peter Marwedel
Mojtaba Mehrara
Avi Mendelson
Rustam Miftakhutdinov
Pablo Montesinos
Miquel Moreto
Andreas Moshovos
Gilles Mouchard
Veynu Narasiman
Mike O'Boyle
Kunle Olukotun
Daniel Ortega
Yunheung Paek
Alex Pajuelo
Santosh Pande
Ioannis Papadopoulos
Hyunchul Park
Sanghyun Park
Yale Patt
Androniki Pazarloglou
Maikel Pennings
Antoniu Pop
Alex Ramirez
Lawrence Rauchwerger

John Regehr
Christopher Rodrigues
Shane Ryoo
Esther Salami
Fermin Sanchez
Oliverio Santana
Andre Seznec
Tim Smith
Guri Sohi
Jaswanth Sreeram
Santhosh Srinath
Samuel Stone
Karin Strauss
M. Aater Suleman
Gabriel Tanase
Olivier Temam
Nathan Thomas
Abhishek Tiwari
Josep Torrellas
Sain-Zee Ueng
Mateo Valero
Javier Vera
David Whalley
Sudhakar Yalamanchili
Sami Yehia
Jonghee Youn
Kun Zhang
Hongtao Zhong

Table of Contents

III   Industrial Processors and Application Parallelization

IV   Power-Aware Techniques

V   High-Performance Processors

VI   Profiles: Collection and Analysis

VII   Optimizing Memory Performance

Invited Program

Supercomputing for the Future, Supercomputing from the Past (Keynote)

Mateo Valero and Jesús Labarta

Barcelona Supercomputing Center and
Universitat Politcnica de Catalunya, Barcelona

Abstract. Supercomputing is a zero billion dollar market but a huge driving boost for technology and systems for the future.

Today, applications in the engineering and scientific world are the major users of the huge computational power offered by supercomputers. In the future, the commercial and business applications will increasingly have such high computational demands.

Supercomputers, once built on technology developed from scratch have now evolved towards the integration of commodity components. Designers of high end systems for the future have to closely monitor the evolution of mass market developments. Such trends also imply that supercomputers themselves provide requirements for the performance and design of those components.

The current technology integration capability is actually allowing for the use of supercomputing technologies within a single chip that will be used in all markets. Stressing the high end systems design will thus help develop ideas and techniques that will spread everywhere. A general observation about supercomputers in the past is their relatively static operation (job allocation, interconnect routing, domain decompositions, loop scheduling) and often little coordination between levels.

Flexibility and dynamicity are some key ideas that will have to be further stressed in the design of future supercomputers. The ability to accept and deal with variance (rather than stubbornly trying to eliminate it) will be important. Such variance may arise from the actual manufacturing/operation mode of the different components (chip layout, MPI internals, contention for shared resources such as memory or interconnect, ...) or the expectedly more and more dynamic nature of the applications themselves. Such variability will be perceived as load imbalance by an actual run. Properly addressing this issue will be very important.

The application behavior typically shows repetitive patterns of resource usage. Even if such patterns may be dynamic, very often the timescales of such variability allows for the application of prediction techniques and matching resources to actual demands. Our foreseen systems will thus have dynamic mechanisms to support fine grain load balancing, while the policies will be applied at a coarse granularity.

As we approach fundamental limits in single processor design specially in terms of the performance/power ratio, multicore chips and massive parallelism will become necessary to achieve the required performance levels. A hierarchical structure is one of the unavoidable approaches to

P. Stenström et al. (Eds.): HiPEAC 2008, LNCS 4917, pp. 3–5, 2008.

future systems design. Hierarchies will show up at all levels from processor to node and system design, both in the hardware and in the software.

The development of programming models (extending current ones or developing new ones) faces a challenge of providing the mechanism to express a certain level of hierarchy (but not too much/detailed) that can be matched by compilers, run times and OSs to the potentially very different underlying architectures. Programmability and portability of the programs (both functional and performance wise, both forward and backwards) is a key challenge for these systems.

The approach to address a massively parallel and hierarchical system with load balancing issues will require coordination between different scheduling/resource allocation policies and a tight integration of the design of the components at all levels: processor, interconnect, run time, programming model, applications, OS scheduler, storage and Job scheduler.

By approaching the way of operation between supercomputers and general purpose, this zero billion dollar market can play a very important role of future unified-computing.

Biography of Mateo Valero

Mateo Valero obtained his PhD at UPC in 1980. He is a professor in the Computer Architecture Department at UPC. His research interests focus on high performance architectures. He has published approximately 400 papers on these topics. He is the director of the Barcelona Supercomputing Center, the National Center of Supercomputing in Spain. Dr. Valero has been honored with several awards. Among them, the Eckert-Mauchly Award in 2007, by the IEEE, Institute of Electrical and Electronics Engineers and the ACM, the Association for Computing Machinery, the King Jaime I in research by the Generalitat Valenciana in 1997 presented by the Queen of Spain, and two Spanish National awards, the Julio Rey Pastor in 2001, to recognize research on IT technologies, and the Leonardo Torres Quevedo in 2006, to recognize research in Engineering, by the Spanish Ministery of Science and Technology, presented by the King of Spain.

In December 1994, Professor Valero became a founding member of the Royal Spanish Academy of Engineering. In 2005 he was elected Correspondant Academic of the Spanish Royal Academy of Science and in 2006, member of the Royal Spanish Academy of Doctors. In 2000 he became a Fellow of the IEEE. In 2002, he became an Intel Distinguished Research Fellow and a Fellow of the ACM, the Association for Computing Machinery. In 1998 he won a Favourite Son Award of his home town, Alfamn (Zaragoza) and in 2006, his native town of Alfamn named their Public College after him.

Biography of Jess Labarta

Jess Labarta is full professor on Computer Architecture at the Technical University of Catalonia (UPC) since 1990. Since 1981 he has been lecturing on computer architecture, operating systems, computer networks and performance evaluation. His research interest has been centered on parallel computing, covering areas from multiprocessor architecture, memory hierarchy, parallelizing compilers, operating systems, parallelization of numerical kernels, performance analysis and prediction tools.

Since 1995 till 2004 he was director of CEPBA (European Center of Parallelism of Barcelona) where he has been highly motivated by the promotion of parallel computing into industrial practice, and especially within SMEs. Since 2000 he has been strongly committed in carrying out and promoting productive research cooperation with IBM as part of the CEPBA-IBM Research Institute. Since 2005 he is responsible of the parallel computing research team within the Barcelona Supercomputing Center (BSC).

His major directions of current work relate to performance analysis tools, programming models (OpenMP for SMPs and clusters, CellSuperscalar for the Cell processor and Grid Superscalar for distributed environments) and resource management. His team distributes the CEPBA tools (Paraver and Dimemas).

Part I

Multithreaded and Multicore Processors

MIPS MT: A Multithreaded RISC Architecture for Embedded Real-Time Processing

Kevin D. Kissell

MIPS Technologies Inc.
39 chemin des Martelles, 06620 Le Bar sur Loup, France
Tel.: +33 4.93.42.45.15; Fax: +33 4.93.42.45.13.
kevink@acm.org
http://www.mips.com/

Abstract. The MIPS® MT architecture is a fine-grained multithreading extension to the general-purpose MIPS RISC architecture. In addition to the classical multithreaded provision for explicit exploitation of cuncurrency as a mechanism for latency tolerance, MIPS MT has unique features to address the problems of real-time and embedded computing in System-on-a-Chip environments. This paper provides an overview of the MIPS MT architecture and how it can variously be exploited to improve computational bandwidth, real time quality of service, and response time to asynchronous events.

1 Multithreading and Embedded Processors

Most of the work that has been done in multithreaded processor architecture over the years [1] has been motivated by the demands of high-performance on computational workloads. However, from the very beginning, starting with the multithreaded peripheral processor of the CDC 6600 [2], multithreading has been recognized as a valuable architectural tool for real-time and embedded processing. In recent years, specialized multithreaded processor architectures for network data-plane processing have been proposed and deployed with some success [3][4], but their adoption has been limited because of the non-standard instruction sets, software tools, and environments.

In late 2002, the author's group at MIPS Technologies Inc. began the investigation of the extension of the standard MIPS32® RISC architecture to encompass explicit multithreading as a superset extension. The resulting multithreading architecture, MIPS MT, has been instantiated in a synthesizable processor, the MIPS32 34K™ core, which has served as a platform for verification and research.

The development of the MIPS MT architecture was constrained by a set of philosophical principles:

1. *Scalability.* The architecture must be implementable and useful on processor implementations spanning orders of magnitude in size and complexity, from microcontrollers to numerical supercomputer nodes.
2. *Run-time Efficiency.* Basic operations of thread creation and destruction, and of inter-thread communication and synchronization, must be realizable in a minimal number of clock cycles, and without OS intervention in the most probable cases.

P. Stenström et al. (Eds.): HiPEAC 2008, LNCS 4917, pp. 9–21, 2008.

3. *Virtualizability*. The physical resources which support multithreading must be invisible or abstracted to user-mode software, such that an application which consumes more resources than are physically implemented on a given MIPS MT platform can nevertheless execute correctly, given appropriate OS support.
4. *Migratability*. The architecture must allow threads to migrate from processor to processor to balance load, and be amenable to multithreaded/multi-core implementations.
5. *Scheduling Agnosticism*. The architecture must allow for a broad variety of thread scheduling models, while isolating these models from user-mode software.

2   The Hierarchy of Multithreaded Entities

MIPS MT defines two levels of multithreading, the VPE (Virtual Processing Element), which is a virtual processor implementing the full MIPS instruction set and privileged resource architecture, and the TC (for Thread Context), which is a lighter-weight "microthread" entity. This was largely dictated by the fact that the MIPS privileged resource architecture provides direct software access to a TLB and other resources that are relatively expensive to instantiate in a small design. However, it also provides a rich framework for dynamic multithreading under software control. A VPE can have a variable number of TCs bound to it, sharing its privileged resources.

2.1   VPEs as Exception Domains

A MIPS MT VPE can be thought of as an exception domain. A single MMU and a single set of system coprocessor registers for exception management exists per VPE, shared by as many TC microthreads as may be bound to the VPE. There is, for example, a single exception program counter register to indicate where execution should be resumed at the end of exception service. It thus becomes essential that, when an exception is dispatched, thread scheduling within the VPE be suspended until software can sample the relevant privileged resource state and acknowledge the exception. In the base MIPS architecture, the exception entry state is already indicated by a privileged resource architecture state bit (EXL), which is cleared automatically on a return from exception. In MIPS MT, that bit is instantiated per-VPE, and acts as an inhibitor of multithreaded issue.

Synchronous exceptions, such as TLB and floating-point exceptions, are serviced by the microthread which caused them. Asynchronous interrupt exceptions, however, are asserted at the VPE level and serviced opportunistically by any available TC bound to the VPE. A TC can be excluded from the interrupt service pool of its associated VPE by setting a per-TC "interrupt exemption" bit. While only one interrupt exception may be dispatched at a time in a VPE, once the critical state has been captured by the exception vector, interrupts can be re-enabled, allowing multiple interrupt service routines to execute concurrently within a VPE.

2.2   VPEs as Scheduling Domains

Privileged software can atomically enable and disable multithreaded execution within a VPE without directly affecting other VPEs of the same processor core. The MIPS MT architecture is scheduling-agnostic, but defines a software interface to the implementation-specific hardware thread scheduling logic. This interface is implemented hierarchically, at both the level of the VPE and the level of the TC. This is discussed further in section 5.

3   Thread Creation and Destruction

One of the design objectives of MIPS MT was to allow for lightweight creation and destruction of concurrent threads of execution, since the overhead of thread creation and destruction can create a lower bound on the granularity of parallelism that can be exploited. In MIPS MT, a microthread can be created and assigned to a TC using the FORK instruction, and conditionally terminated using the YIELD instruction.

3.1   Thread Creation with FORK

The MIPS MT FORK instruction causes a new microthread to begin execution, provided that the hardware resources are available to do so. While other architectures have proposed fork instructions with semantics similar to that of the traditional UNIX *fork()* system call, where the operation replicates the full software-visible state of the thread context [5], the MIPS MT FORK instruction follows the basic rules of the MIPS RISC instruction set: It requires no more than 2 general-purpose register reads and 1 GPR write, so that it can be fully pipelined in a straightforward design. A starting instruction fetch address and an arbitrary register value are read from the FORKing thread's registers, and the arbitrary value is written to the specified register of the FORKed TC. If more than a single register value needs to be transmitted to the new microthread, the necessary values are passed via memory - in most cases the primary data cache.

Unlike dynamic thread creation in the Tera MTA[6][7], which is a two-phase process involving RESERVE and CREATE operations to allocate and, if the allocation was successful, launch a new thread, the MIPS MT FORK is "optimistic". Either a dynamically allocatable TC is free to be FORKed, and the operation succeeds, or the FORK instruction throws a *thread overflow* exception to be caught by the operating system. The OS can then determine whether to swap out some TCs state and make it available to the restarted FORK, to emulate the operation by creating a new OS-level thread to time-share in the system, or to signal an error. FORK is thus "virtualizable".

It is worth noting that a successful FORK provides no "handle" to the FORKing thread by which it might reference the thread it created. In part, this is due to the GPR write port rule alluded to above, but there is also a philosophical argument. While it would be trivial to provide an ephemerally valid value, such as the index into the physical array of TCs, the software thread created might be interrupted, swapped out, or migrated at any time. A persistent hardware handle that would follow a software thread for its entire lifetime would be of some utility, but the complexity associated with creating and maintaining such a handle does not seem to be warranted in an architecture that needs to scale down to microcontroller-class implementations.

3.2   Thread Termination with YIELD

The YIELD instruction serves several purposes in MIPS MT. Some of these will be described below in section 5, but one important one is that of terminating a dynamically allocated thread. If the input argument to YIELD is zero, the TC associated with the instruction stream changes state from being active to being "free", and available for use by a subsequent FORK.

If the last active TC within a VPE executes a YIELD $0 instruction, so that all execution would stop on the VPE, a *thread underflow* condition exists, and an exception is taken. It is up to the operating system to determine the correct action to take.

4   Inter-thread Synchronization

The efficiency of inter-thread synchronization is another key factor that limits the granularity of concurrency that can be exploited by a multithreaded architecture. The standard synchronization mechanism in the MIPS architecture is the load-linked/store-conditional operator pair. This mechanism must work on MIPS MT processors, for compatibility, but spin-lock semantics are highly undesirable on a multithreaded processor. The act of spinning and retrying a lock consumes issue and memory bandwidth that would better be used by the thread holding it, to make progress towards its release.

While the power and generality of extending memory load/store semantics with the notion of empty/full synchronization has been demonstrated in systems like the Denelcor HEP[8], the Tera MTA and the Alewife machine[9], the simplicity of the concept belies the costs of implementation. Designers of cost-sensitive embedded systems-on-chips are not willing to pay the price to provide a main memory with empty/full attributes.

Rather than require empty/full support for all of memory, the MIPS MT architecture defines the notion of *gating storage*, which is some subset of the physical address space which has the property that loads and stores to it can block for unbounded periods of time, and can be aborted and restarted without any side-effects. A specific variety of gating storage defined by MIPS MT is the "ITC" (Inter-thread Communication) store. The ITC store is broken up into *cells*, each of which has a set of *views*, which are distinguished by low-order address bits. To software, an ITC cell looks like a data structure in memory, but instead of having distinct and independent data in each element of the data structure, loads and stores to different elements of a cell operate on the same data, but with different semantics. A C language description might be:

```
typedef volatile long long viewtype;
typedef struct {
     viewtype bypass;  /* Non-blocking read/write */
     viewtype control; /* Exposes Empty/Full state, etc. */
     viewtype ef_sync; /* Empty/Full blocking load/store */
```

```
    viewtype ef_try;    /* Empty/Full non-blocking poll */
    viewtype pv_sync;   /* PV Semaphore blocking load/store */
    viewtype pv_try;    /* PV Semaphore non-blocking poll */
    viewtype reserved[10]; /* Reserved for future views */
} itc_cell;
```

For example, the *ef_sync* cell view provides classical blocking empty/full semantics, such that if itc_ptr is a pointer to an *itc_cell* in an "empty" state, then

```
    x = itc_ptr->ef_sync;
```

will cause the executing thread to be suspended until such time as some other instruction stream performs an operation like

```
    itc_ptr->ef_sync = y;
```

at which point the first thread's x variable will pick up the value of y, and it will resume execution.

The *pv_sync* view provides a more complex primitive, that of a counting, or PV semaphore[10]. Stores which reference this view cause the value of the cell to be atomically incremented, regardless of the register value stored, while loads return the value and perform a post-decrement if it is non-zero. If the pre-load value is zero, the load blocks until a *pv_sync* store is done.

The "try" views allow for non-blocking synchronization, using either the empty/full or the P/V paradigm. In the *pv_try* case, loads return the cell data value, even if zero, performing an auto-decrement only if the pre-load value was non-zero. In the *ef_try* case, loads references return zero if the cell is empty, regardless of the last data value written, and stores may be attempted using the MIPS32 SC (store conditional) instruction, which will indicate failure if the cell is full. Whereas the *ef_sync* view allows arbitrary data to be passed through the cell, the use of a zero value to indicate the failure of a load from an *ef_try* view implies that a word value of zero cannot be passed. In the most frequent use case, however, it is pointers that are passed between threads via the ITC cell, and a null pointers and non-pointers from an empty cell can be treated alike.

5   Hybrid Scheduling Control

Most of the study and application of multithreaded processor architecture has focused on multithreading as a latency tolerance technique, a means of keeping fast functional units busy in the face of long operand delays. This is of value in computationally intensive embedded applications, but in many cases, it is the ability to provide latency *avoidance*, rather than latency tolerance, where mulithreading provides an advantage in such systems[11]. MIPS MT provides architectural support for this in several ways, allowing processor hardware, system and application software, and external logic to jointly control the scheduling of instruction streams.

5.1   Zero-Latency Event Service Using YIELD Instructions

The use of the YIELD instruction for thread termination was described in section 3.2 above, but the YIELD instruction is in fact a general tool for controlling the execution of a thread. A processor implementing MIPS MT has up to 31 yield qualifier inputs, to be connected to indicators of events external to the core. When a YIELD instruction is issued with a positive input operand value, that value is interpreted as a vector of orthogonal bits corresponding to the yield qualifier inputs. If none of the qualifier inputs corresponding to the operand value are asserted, execution of the thread is suspended until such time as one of them goes active.

The ability to suspend execution based on a particular yield qualifier can be controlled by the operating system, using a privileged mask register. If a program issues a YIELD where the input value has a set bit that is not set in the mask register, an exception is delivered on the YIELD. This allows operating systems to prevent unauthorized programs using input state as a covert channel, and allows virtualization, whereby a program executing on a VPE to which a particular yield qualifier input is not connected can have the YIELD operation emulated by the OS, in response to the illegal qualifier exception.

Event service gated by YIELD instructions has potentially less latency than interrupts, even those handled by dedicated interrupt threads or shadow register files, because in addition to eliminating the need to save and restore context, there is no control transfer to a vector, which would typically require a pipeline flush, and no decode of state to determine where to resume event processing. In the case of the 34K-family cores, which have a per-TC instruction buffer (IB), the instruction following the YIELD is generally already in the IB, ready to issue once the YIELD ceases to be blocked.

5.2 Hierarchically Programmable Scheduling

In MIPS MT, each VPE and each TC has two registers of privileged resource state associated with its scheduling; a control register and a feedback register. The scheduling control registers allow software to express dynamic information, such as priority or a TDMA schedule, to a hardware scheduling policy manager, while the scheduling feedback registers allow the scheduling hardware to provide feedback, such as the number of instructions issued or retired by the VPE or TC.

The 34K processor core design features a modular scheduling policy manager that can be replaced or modified to suit the quality-of-service requirements of a particular application.

5.3 Gating Storage as a Peripheral Interface

In addition to its primary function of providing inter-thread synchronization for software, I/O FIFOs can be mapped into the gating storage space, so that threads can be programmed to consume or produce data in an open loop. Their execution will then be governed by the ability of the peripherals connected to the FIFOs to consume or produce data.

6   Virtualization of MIPS MT Resources

In order to better support the portability of applications across different MIPS MT implementations, the new user-visible resources defined by the architecture: FORKed threads, ITC cells, and YIELD qualifiers, are all virtualizable.

6.1   Thread Context Virtualization

User-mode code has no knowledge of which physical TC it is using, nor which physical TC is allocated by a successful FORK instruction. All interaction between concurrently executing threads is done via shared memory or memory-like storage, and there is no architectural assumption made about whether it is the "parent" or "child" which executes first after a FORK.

When a FORK instruction is issued, it is transparent to the application whether a TC was allocated and launched, or whether a thread overflow exception was taken instead. In response to the thread overflow exception, an operating system has the option of treating it as a fatal application error, treating it as an exception to be raised to the application, or emulating the operation.

Emulation of a FORK implies hybrid scheduling, wherein the multithreaded processor schedules among the threads resident in N TCs, while system software multiplexes $M>N$ software threads across those N TCs. The MIPS MT architecture facilitates this with MFTR (Move From Thread Register) and MTTR (Move To Thread Register) instructions, which allow a privileged thread running on one TC to halt another TC and manipulate its contents, and with the per-TC scheduling feedback registers that allow the forward progress of each thread to be monitored.

TCs which are blocked on ITC references or YIELD instructions may be halted and swapped-out without any side-effect on the software-visible state of the thread or of the ITC storage.

6.2   ITC Storage Virtualization

ITC storage is a special case of physical memory, and can be mapped and protected by the MIPS32 MMU. Unlike physical memory, ITC storage cannot be swapped in or out with direct I/O operations. System software must extract and restore both the cell data and the cell control state, via the bypass and control views, respectively.

6.3   YIELD Qualifier Virtualization

The MIPS MT architecture exposes a new set of physical inputs, the YIELD qualifiers, to user-mode software. To allow for trap and emulation of qualified YIELD operations, each VPE has a privileged mask register to selectively enable the YIELD qualifiers. If an application's YIELD instruction attempts to wait on an input that has not been enabled in the associated mask, an exception is taken. The operating system can then implement an appropriate policy of termination, raising of a software exception, or emulation of the YIELD with a software suspension of the thread.

7   Software Use Models

The flexibility of the MIPS MT architecture as a multithreading framework has been demonstrated in the development of four different operating system models. All of them proved usable, and each has its distinct advantages.

7.1   Asymmetric Multiple Virtual Processors (AMVP)

In this model, different operating systems execute on different VPEs of the same processor core. Typically, this consists of a feature-rich multi-tasking OS such a Linux on one VPE and a low-level real-time OS on the other(s). Such a configuration exploits the independence of the VPE scheduling domains and allows a single processor core to handle a mix of hard-real-time and high-level user interface functions that would normally require multiple processors.

7.2   Symmetric Multiple Virtual Processors (SMVP)

As each VPE of a MIPS MT processor implements the full MIPS privileged resource architecture, it is trivial to adapt an SMP operating system to treat each VPE as a CPU. The level of concurrency available to applications is limited to the number of VPEs. In the case of a single-core system, if caches are common to all VPEs, interprocessor cache coherence support can be optimized out.

7.3   Symmetric Multiple TC (SMTC)

An SMTC OS extends SMP processor management to the TC level, so that a MIPS MT TC appears to the user to be a full CPU in an SMP system, allowing a higher degree of concurrency to be exploited. Since TCs do not implement the full privileged resource architecture, some features must be emulated by the OS, at some cost in complexity and performance.

7.4   The ROPE Kernel

The ROPE kernel is an experimental Linux kernel for MIPS MT processors. Rather than being based on an SMP configuration, the ROPE kernel is a uniprocessor kernel in which each kernel "thread" is itself potentially multithreaded. Each context switch saves the state of all active TCs of the kernel thread being switched-out, and restores the state of as many active TCs as were saved for the kernel thread being switched-in. On a trap or system call, multi-threaded issue is suspended until user-mode execution is resumed. The fact that the kernel model is single-threaded is thus not a problem.

Whereas the SMVP and SMTC kernels activate at boot time all TCs that are to be used by Linux processes, the ROPE kernel allows for dynamic thread creation/destruction without OS intervention, using the FORK and YIELD instructions. If more FORKs are performed than there are allocatable TCs, a Linux signal is sent to the FORKing process. While SMVP and SMTC OS models allow thread-level concurrency between unrelated threads and processes, and for both application and OS execution, the ROPE kernel supports only application-level concurrency, and only in explicitly multithreaded programs.

Source code for AMVP, SMVP, and SMTC Linux kernels for the 34K processor has been accepted by the kernel maintainers and is available from the source repositories at www.linux-mips.org and www.kernel.org.

8   Experimental Results

The following are experimental results obtained on an FPGA implementation of the 34K processor with 5TCs, running on the MIPS Malta™ development board, using the ROPEbench framework developed by Jacob Leverich of Stanford. Each benchmark is run for a constant large number of iterations, divided among some number of software threads. The results are the calculated cycles-per-iteration.

On a uniprocessor configuration, each software thread is a *pthread*, time-sharing a single virtual CPU. In the SMTC configurations, each pthread represents a kernel thread scheduled according to standard SMP algorithms across 5 virtual CPUs. In the ROPE configuration, each pthread represents a ROPE microthread, of which the kernel has no direct knowledge. The uniprocessor and "SMTC-PT" systems use the pthread mutex implementation of the Linux glibc 2.4. The "SMTC-ITC" and ROPE systems use an experimental library using MIPS MT ITC cells mapped into the program's address space.

8.1   Synchronization

The "Ferris wheel" benchmark measures synchronization costs between threads, where N threads are organized as a logical ring, each repeatedly acquiring a lock that must first be released by its predecessor. It's inner loop is:

```
for (i = 0; i < count; i++) {
    lock(wheel, me);
    unlock(wheel, next);
}
```

Table 1. Ferris Wheel

Cycles/ Iteration	1 Thread	2 Threads	3 Threads	4 Threads	5 Threads
Uniprocessor	414	2046	2494	2792	3004
SMTC-PT	572	2052	11833	13556	14451
SMTC-ITC	27	19	19	19	19
ROPE	26	18	18	18	18

There are two noteworthy phenomena here. One is that the classical software pthread implementation degrades significantly as SMP threads are added. In the uniprocessor case, it is only by a rare accident of pre-emption that there will be contention for a low-level lock, but with multiple concurrent instruction streams active, such contention becomes increasingly likely.

The second phenomenon worth noting is that using the MIPS MT ITC store to implement the mutex in hardware is more than an order of magnitude faster, and does not suffer from the same scaling problems.

8.2   Thread Creation/Destruction

The "Split/Join" benchmark creates threads which promptly exit, and synchronizes with their termination. The inner loop looks like:

```
for (i = 0; i < count; i++) {
    thread_t th;
    thread_create(&th, slave, NULL);
    thread_join(th);
}
```

Table 2. Split/Join

Cycles/ Iteration	1 Thread	2 Threads	3 Threads	4 Threads	5 Threads
Uniprocessor	34990	31790	31361	33042	33070
SMTC-PT	38193	29978	29736	30276	29730
SMTC-ITC	39150	31125	29473	29450	30660
ROPE	583	404	-	-	-

Note that the inner loop is itself executed concurrently by each of the test threads, so the maximum number of threads executing is twice the number of test threads. As the 34K test platform was equipped with only 5 TCs, the ROPE kernel could not support more than 2 test threads. As noted in section 3.1, failing FORK instructions can be trapped and emulated by an OS, but this was not implemented in the ROPE kernel prototype.

Within the limitations of hardware, however, the ROPE runtime's use of the MIPS MT FORK instruction is at least 60 times as efficient, at the system level, as the standard pthread library and SMP OS.

8.3   Latency Tolerance

The type and degree of latency tolerance that can be realized with a MIPS MT processor is very much a function of the microarchitecture of the particular processor. The MIPS32 34K has a relatively simple single-issue, in-order pipeline, but can switch threads on a cycle-by-cycle basis to fill memory and functional unit stalls.

8.3.1   Memory Latency

The effectiveness of multithreading in tolerating memory latency can be observed in comparing the results of two memory benchmarks, one of which issues load every 8 instructions which hits in the cache, the other of which differs only in that the address calculation always results in a cache miss.

Table 3. Load Cache Hit

Cycles/ Iteration	1 Thread	2 Threads	3 Threads	4 Threads	5 Threads
Uniprocessor	9.1	9.0	9.1	9.1	9.0
SMTC-PT	9.6	8.5	8.4	8.2	8.2
SMTC-ITC	9.7	8.5	8.4	8.2	8.2
ROPE	9.1	8.0	8.1	8.0	8.1

Table 4. Load Cache Miss

Cycles/ Iteration	1 Thread	2 Threads	3 Threads	4 Threads	5 Threads
Uniprocessor	95	95	95	95	95
SMTC-PT	99	54	42	37	35
SMTC-ITC	88	53	43	37	35
ROPE	83	51	41	37	34

The interleaving of execution with load stall time more than doubles the throughput of this particular test, so long as 3 or more TCs are active.

Memory latency affects not only data references, but also instruction fetches. The 34K processor core fills stall cycles due to instruction cache misses, provided that there are instructions in some other IB that can be issued. But if the processor is experiencing a large number of instruction cache misses, by definition, the number of available instructions in the IBs is reduced, limiting the opportunity for multithreaded issue.

The experiment for measuring the effects of multithreading on instruction cache miss-intensive code consists of a set of linear instruction sequences, one for each thread, each larger than the instruction cache of the processor. Each sequence consists of a series of 5000 jumps forward to the next cache line. As the 34K processor's cache line size is four words, the sequence looks like the following.

```
      ...
labelN:
      j    labelNplus1
      nop
      nop
      nop
labelNplus1:
      j    labelNplus2
      . . .
```

Table 5. Instruction Cache Miss

Cycles/Jump	1 Thread	2 Threads	3 Threads	4 Threads	5 Threads
Uniprocessor	45	45	45	45	45
SMTC-PT	48	31	31	34	37
SMTC-ITC	48	31	30	34	38
ROPE	45	30	30	34	38

The 34K processor implementation used in this experiment has only two memory transaction buffers for instruction cache fills, with pre-arbitration and reservation of a buffer for the first thread to be stalled on the instruction fill resource. The experimental data reflects these implementation details: Runs with two and three threads show some significant overlap of fetch miss stalls, but adding more threads beyond the first 3 adds additional resource contention without any corresponding increase in hardware concurrency.

8.3.2   Functional Unit Latency

The 34K microarchitecture also exploits scheduling opportunities created by functional unit stalls for operations with more than a single-cycle latency. The following loop compiles to 7 instructions, 5 of which are targeted multiplies.

```
for (i = 0; i < count; i++) {
    r1 *= 239875981;
    r2 *= r1;
    r3 *= r2;
    r4 *= r3;
    r5 *= r4;
}
```

Table 6. Integer Multiplication

Cycles/ Iteration	1 Thread	2 Threads	3 Threads	4 Threads	5 Threads
Uniprocessor	21	21	21	21	21
SMTC-PT	22	14	11	9	8
SMTC-ITC	22	14	11	9	8
ROPE	21	13	10	9	8

As was the case with the cache miss benchmark, the effective multiply throughput is more than doubled when 3 or more threads are used.

9   Conclusions

The MIPS MT architecture represents another case of supercomputer architecture techniques of the 20th century finding application in the embedded systems of the 21st century. The effectiveness of multithreading for latency tolerance is demonstrable in small-scale systems. The effectiveness of multithreading for latency avoidance, given the architectural support of MIPS MT, is less hostage to other system design parameters, and at least as relevant to practical application in real-time and embedded domains.

References

[1] Ungerer, T., et al.: A Survey of Processors with Explicit Multithreading. ACM Computing Surveys 35(1), 29–63 (2003)

[2] Thornton, J.E.: Design of a Computer: The CDC 6600. Foresman and Company, Scott (1970)

[3] El-Haj-Mahmoud, Rotenberg: Safely Exploiting Multithreaded Processors to Tolerate Memory Latency in Real-Time Systems. In: Proceedings of CASES 2004, pp. 2-13 (2004)

[4] Ubicom, Inc. The Ubicom IP3023 Wireless Network Processor (2003), Available from http://www.ubicom.com/pdfs/whitepapers/WP-IP3023WNP-01.pdf

[5] Papadopoulos, Traub: Multithreading: A Revisionist View of Dataflow Architectures. In: Proceedings of ISCA 1991, pp. 342–351 (1991)

[6] Alverson, G., et al.: The Tera Computer System. In: Proceedings of the 1990 International Conference on Supercomputing, Amsterdam, The Netherlands, pp. 1–6 (1990)

[7] Alverson, G., et al.: Exploiting Heterogeneous Parallelism on a Multithreaded Multiprocessor. In: Proceedings of the 6th International Conference on Supercomputing, pp. 188–197 (1992)

[8] Hwang, Briggs: Computer Architecture and Parallel Processing, pp. 679–680. McGraw Hill, New York (1984)

[9] Agarwal, A., et al.: The MIT Alewife Machine: Architecture and Performance. In: Proceedings of ISCA 1995, pp. 2–13 (1995)

[10] Dijkstra, E.W.: Cooperating Sequential Processes. In: Genuys, F. (ed.) Programming Languages, pp. 43–112 (1968)

[11] Hoover, G., et al.: A Case Study of Multi-Threading in the Embedded Space. In: Proceedings of the 2006 International Conference on Compilers, Architecture, and Synthesis for Embedded Systems, pp. 357–367 (2006)

rMPI: Message Passing on Multicore Processors with On-Chip Interconnect

James Psota and Anant Agarwal

Massachusetts Institute of Technology, Cambridge, MA 02139, USA

Abstract. With multicore processors becoming the standard architecture, pro-grammers are faced with the challenge of developing applications that capitalize on multicore's advantages. This paper presents rMPI, which leverages the on-chip networks of multicore processors to build a powerful abstraction with which many programmers are familiar: the MPI programming interface. To our knowl-edge, rMPI is the first MPI implementation for multicore processors that have on-chip networks. This study uses the MIT Raw processor as an experimentation and validation vehicle, although the findings presented are applicable to multi-core processors with on-chip networks in general. Likewise, this study uses the MPI API as a general interface which allows parallel tasks to communicate, but the results shown in this paper are generally applicable to message passing com-munication. Overall, rMPI's design constitutes the marriage of message passing communication and on-chip networks, allowing programmers to employ a well-understood programming model to a high performance multicore processor ar-chitecture.

This work assesses the applicability of the MPI API to multicore processors with on-chip interconnect, and carefully analyzes overheads associated with com-mon MPI operations. This paper contrasts MPI to lower-overhead network inter-face abstractions that the on-chip networks provide. The evaluation also compares rMPI to hand-coded applications running directly on one of the processor's low-level on-chip networks, as well as to a commercial-quality MPI implementation running on a cluster of Ethernet-connected workstations. Results show speedups of 4x to 15x for 16 processor cores relative to one core, depending on the appli-cation, which equal or exceed performance scalability of the MPI cluster system. However, this paper ultimately argues that while MPI offers reasonable perfor-mance on multicores when, for instance, legacy applications must be run, its large overheads squander the multicore opportunity. Performance of multicores could be significantly improved by replacing MPI with a lighter-weight communica-tions API with a smaller memory footprint.

1 Introduction

Next-generation microprocessors will increasingly rely on parallelism, as opposed to frequency scaling, for improvements in performance scalability. Microprocessor de-signers are attaining such parallelism by placing multiple processing cores on a single piece of silicon, a feat now achievable thanks to the technology scaling described by Moore's Law [2]. Most multicore processors such as the POWER5 and AMD Opteron 800 force interprocessor communication to go through the memory system, which can

P. Stenström et al. (Eds.): HiPEAC 2008, LNCS 4917, pp. 22–37, 2008.

be slow, but some offer first-class on-chip inter-core network support. Technology scaling is enabling such network-interconnected parallel systems to be built on a chip, offering users extremely low latency networks. The MIT Raw processor [33], [31], [30], [32] builds on this idea and provides a prototype to evaluate these ideas. Raw includes first-class instruction set architecture (ISA) support for inter-processor communication, enabling orders of magnitude improvement in communication latency.

This paper investigates the merits of tightly integrated on-chip networks, especially in light of their programmability and performance. This paper introduces rMPI, which provides a scalable interface that allows transparent migration of the large extant legacy code base which will have to run on multicores. rMPI leverages the on-chip network of the Raw multicore processor to build an abstraction with which many programmers are familiar: the Message Passing Interface (MPI). The processor cores that constitute chip multicores (CMPs) such as Raw are tightly coupled through fast integrated on-chip networks, making such CMPs quite different from more traditional heavily-decoupled parallel computer systems. Additionally, some CMPs eliminate many layers of abstraction between the user program and underlying hardware, allowing programmers to directly interact with hardware resources. Because of the removal of these layers, CMPs can have extremely fast interrupts with low overhead. Removing standard computer system layers such as the operating system both represents an opportunity for improved performance but also places an increased responsibility on the programmer to develop robust software. These and other novel features of multicore architectures motivated designing rMPI to best take advantage of the tightly-coupled networks and direct access to hardware resources that many CMPs offer. rMPI offers the following features: 1) robust, deadlock-free, and scalable programming mechanisms; 2) an interface that is compatible with current MPI software; 3) an easy interface for programmers already familiar with high-level message passing paradigms; 4) and fine-grain control over their programs when automatic parallelization tools do not yield sufficient performance.

Multicores with low-latency on-chip networks offer a great opportunity for performance and energy savings [29], [33]. However, this opportunity can be quickly squandered if programmers do not structure their applications and runtime systems in ways that leverage the aforementioned unique aspects of multicores. Multicores with on-chip networks and small on-chip memories usually perform best when data are communicated directly from core to core *without accessing off-chip memory*, encouraging *communication-centric algorithms*[33]. Multcores also perform well when the underlying networks provide the ability to send fine-grain messages between cores within a few cycles. MPI was originally developed 15 years ago assuming coarser-grain communication between cores and communication overhead usually included operating system calls and sockets overhead. rMPI allows investigation into how well MPI, given its assumptions about system overheads, maps to multicore architectures with on-chip networks.

The evaluation of rMPI presented in this paper attempts to understand how well it succeeds in offering the above-mentioned features, and if MPI is still an appropriate API in the multicore domain. rMPI is evaluated in comparison to two references. To develop a qualitative intuition about the scaling properties of rMPI, it is compared against LAM/MPI, a highly optimized commercial MPI implementation running on a cluster of workstations. Additionally, it is compared against hand-coded and hand-orchestrated applications running on one of Raw's low-level on-chip dynamic networks on top of which rMPI was built. The comparison against the Raw network is an attempt to determine the overhead imposed by features that rMPI offers, which include the MPI programming interface, removal of sub-application-level deadlock potential, and automatic message packetization/reassembly. The sources of rMPI's overhead are determined by analyzing where cycles are spent in enacting both a send and a receive using MPI function calls for both short and long messages. Overall, we show that rMPI running on Raw can provide performance scalability that is comparable to a commercial MPI implementation running on a cluster of workstations by leveraging the underlying network architecture of the Raw processor. However, rMPI's overhead relative to the GDN varies from 5% to nearly 500%.

The rest of this paper is organized as follows. Section 2 provides an overview of the Raw architecture, focusing on the resources that are especially relevant to rMPI's design and operation. Section 3 discusses rMPI's design at a high level, and describes some of its optimizations. Section 4 provides detailed results. Section 5 discusses other work related to message passing on parallel computer systems. Finally, Section 6 concludes the paper.

2 Background

RAW PROCESSOR. Before investigating rMPI's design and implementation, a brief overview of the Raw processor must be given. The Raw processor consists of 16 identical tiles, which each contain a processing core and network components that allow for interprocessor communication. The processing cores each have an 8-stage in-order single-issue MIPS-style processing pipeline and a 4-stage single-precision pipelined FPU. The Raw chip also has four register-mapped on-chip networks which are exposed to the programmer through the Raw ISA. Additionally, tiles contain 32KB of hardware-managed data cache, 32KB of software-managed instruction cache, and 64KB of software-managed switch instruction memory. The Raw prototype was implemented in hardware with an ASIC process, and has been shown to perform well on a variety of application types [33].

Raw's software-exposed ISA allows programmers to directly control all of the chip's resources, including gates, wires, and pins. Programmers of Raw have the ability to carefully orchestrate data transfer between tiles simply by reading and writing registers. Raw has four 32-bit full-duplex on-chip networks, two static (routes specified at compile time) and two dynamic (routes specified dynamically at run time). rMPI leverages one of Raw's dynamic networks, the General Dynamic Network (GDN), for all communication between tiles prompted by an MPI communication routine.

rMPI relies on several key features of the GDN that necessitate elaboration. The GDN is a dimension-ordered wormhole routed network on which messages containing 32-bit header words are sent. In addition to containing routing information. The maximum GDN message size is 32 words, including the header, and the network guarantees that GDN messages arrive at the destination tile atomically and in-order. GDN messages from different senders sent to the same receiver may be interleaved and received in a different order relative to the absolute time when each was sent. The GDN's atomicity constraint does guarantee, though, that the contents of individual GDN messages from different sources will not be interleaved with each other.

If the sending tile must communicate more than 32 words, it must break the message into pieces, which then must be re-assembled by the receiver. Managing many senders and many receivers in an all-to-all communication pattern clearly becomes challenging using the low-level GDN. Additionally, it is trivial to construct a communication pattern on the GDN which deadlocks the network—the GDN's input and output network ports are both blocking, and contain space for only four words and sixteen words of data, respectively. Thus, the programmer must construct programs which manage buffer space and communication patterns carefully to avoid deadlock. Raw also offers programmers fast interrupts that take less than 60 clock cycles of overhead for both call and return. This facility is exploited by rMPI to handle receiving messages from the network in an interrupt-driven manner.

MPI. In the parallel computing domain, MPI has become the *de-facto* standard for writing parallel applications. MPI is not an implementation or a language, but a standard with which implementations on different parallel computers must comply. Thus, programs written using MPI are portable: they can be moved from one parallel system to another, assuming both systems offer a valid MPI implementation. Overall, such portability is a key goal of MPI, providing a virtual computing model that hides many architectural details of the underlying parallel computer. MPI implementations exist for most high performance parallel computer systems, with LAM/MPI [6], [28] and MPICH [15], [34] being two of the most popular.

The MPI standard [10], [9] includes primitives for blocking and non-blocking point-to-point communications, collective operations (*e.g.*, broadcast, scatter and gather), process groups, communication topologies, and bindings for C, C++, and Fortran. The MPI standard is large, containing over 200 function calls. rMPI implements the blocking point-to-point communication routines (but not the non-blocking routines), collective operations, MPI datatypes, process groups, and communication topologies for C programs. More information about MPI is available in [27], [14], [26], [24].

3 Design

This section describes the design, architecture, and implementation of rMPI from a high level. rMPI is a runtime system that enables users to run MPI programs on Raw. rMPI leveraged many ideas from well-known open source MPI libraries, such as MPICH [34] and LAM/MPI [6], [28], but also attempted to implement the MPI standard in a way that leverages the unique resources that Raw provides. Indeed, multi-core processors with low-latency on-chip networks and fast interrupts serve as very different hardware platforms compared to a cluster of workstations interconnected via TCP/IP, and rMPI reflects these differences. rMPI consists of over 75,000 lines of code, written mostly in ANSI C. Much more detail on rMPI's implementation can be found in [25].

Figure 1 shows rMPI's system architecture. Upon invoking an MPI routine, the user's program calls into the high-level MPI layer, which implements the public MPI API

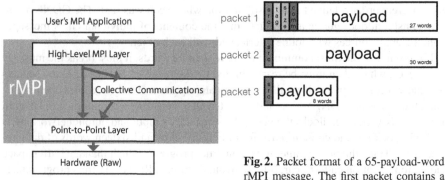

Fig. 1. The rMPI system architecture

Fig. 2. Packet format of a 65-payload-word rMPI message. The first packet contains a full rMPI header, while the later two packets only contain the sender ID.

functions. This layer is responsible for preparing the MPI request for processing by lower layers and handles tasks such as argument checking and data buffer management. This top layer also determines how to best utilize the low level communication routines, and directly invokes them for point-to-point communication. The point-to-point layer implements basic communication primitives through which all communication takes place. This layer interacts directly with Raw's hardware mechanisms, including reading and writing from the GDN network ports. The collective communication layer is invoked by the high-level MPI layer for collective communications operations. This layer implements high-level collective communication algorithms such as broadcast and scatter/gather, and ultimately also calls down into the point-to-point layer for communication. The high-level MPI layer and collective communication layer leverage some of the code base from the LAM/MPI implementation, although much of it was re-implemented for rMPI.

The collective communications layer implements high-level communication primitives such as broadcast and scatter/gather. This layer is called directly by the user program, and ultimately performs the communication operations by calling into the point-to-point layer. More implementation detail can be found in [25].

The point-to-point layer interacts with Raw directly, and is responsible for sending and receiving all data between tiles. As alluded to in Section 2, rMPI takes care of breaking up messages larger than 32 words into packets that are sequentially injected into the network as GDN messages. It does this by prepending an *rMPI header* to each packet to encode metadata required by the MPI standard (*e.g.,* tag, size, etc.) and also so the receiver can associate incoming packets with logical MPI messages. Figure 2 shows how a logical message with 65 payload words is broken up into three packets, each with appropriate headers as just described. Each receiving tile registers all outstanding receive requests, and is therefore able to reassemble messages using the minimal rMPI headers. The rMPI header length was heavily optimized to improve effective network bandwidth for message payloads; the first packet of any logical MPI message includes a four-word header (source, tag, length, communication context), and subsequent packets just contain a one-word header which encodes the source of the message. Such small headers attempt to mitigate MPI overhead for short messages, and maximize the benefit of Raw's low-latency on-chip networks.

Messages are received in the point-to-point layer by using Raw's fast interrupt handler routine. That is, when a message arrives on the GDN input port of a tile, an interrupt fires, and the receiving tile's control flow immediately jumps into the interrupt handler. The interrupt handler proceeds to drain the GDN network into temporary dynamically-allocated buffers, keeping track of header information and sorting packet payloads appropriately. The on-chip cache and off-chip DRAM is used for the temporary storage; large amounts of temporary storage require extra time to buffer, as they are stored in off-chip DRAM, unless they are consumed immediately by the receiver in a streaming manner. The interrupt handler is arguably the most complex component in rMPI. As packets can be received over multiple invocations of the interrupt handler, and packets from multiple senders can be interleaved, the interrupt hander must carefully sort them out and keep track of the status of each incoming message. Further, the interrupt handler must share some of its data structures with the rest of the system, as the user-level thread must be able to access the buffer where the handler stores messages.

An interrupt-driven design was chosen over a standard blocking receive design for a number of reasons. First, an interrupt-driven design allows MPI programs to make asynchronous progress on both communication and computation. Messages are received as soon as they arrive, and otherwise each processor can continue computation. The interrupt-driven design also reduces the potential for network congestion, since Raw's internal network buffering is minimal (4 words per input and output port per tile) and sends are blocking. Because of this, deadlock could easily occur in a blocking receive design. Since the interrupt handler always drains the network of its contents immediately, deadlock can not occur at the network level. The interrupt-driven design may not have made sense in some other contexts where interrupts must go through the operating system and are therefore slow, but Raw's interrupts take on the order of 60 cycles of overhead, and therefore made sense in this context. Finally, the interrupt-driven design was straightforward from an algorithmic standpoint; all tiles are able to continue computing unless data is available to be received, thereby always allowing forward progress to be made.

A number of optimizations in the interrupt handler improved the overall performance of rMPI. In the case where a particular message arrives at a tile before the MPI receive call for that message was called by the user program, the interrupt handler must buffer the message contents. However, when the user program requests a message before it arrives, rMPI registers a *posted receive entry* with the user's buffer address. When the message finally arrives, the interrupt handler places the payload directly into the user's buffer instead of storing it into temporary memory, thereby eliminating a memory copy operation, which can be quite expensive for very large messages. This optimization yields the following speedups (averaged over multiple messages) over the non-optimized system: $2.47\times$ for a 1-word message; $1.80\times$ for a 100-word message; $1.18\times$ for a 10,000-word message. Note that this optimization significantly improves performance of small messages because the receiver does not have to instantiate the data structures and bookkeeping mechanisms that are normally necessary to buffer an unexpected message. Larger messages also benefit from not having to perform a memory copy operation. Raw's direct access to low-level hardware resources made such optimizations straightforward to implement. rMPI also optimizes for the case where a process sends to itself by circumventing the typical data structures and network hardware that are normally traversed.

4 Evaluation and Analysis

METHODOLOGY. This section presents experimental results that show rMPI provides reasonably good performance for the Raw architecture, but points out a number of places where the MPI abstraction imposes overly large overheads. It discusses various performance metrics such as latency, bandwidth, and performance scalability on a number of kernel benchmarks and applications. The evaluations use two bases for comparison in evaluating rMPI: hand-programmed native GDN, running on Raw, and LAM/MPI, running on a Beowulf cluster of workstations. While tedious and time-consuming to implement, hand-coded GDN programs generally provide a performance upper-bound for a given algorithm that uses the Raw GDN. Thus, experiments comparing rMPI programs to native GDN programs offer an assessment of rMPI's overhead and performance scalability. The experiments that compare rMPI programs to MPI programs running on a cluster of Ethernet-interconnected workstations also give insight into the scalability of rMPI, but relative to a drastically different hardware platform using a different MPI implementation.

As described in [33], Raw's instruction cache is managed by software. While this caching system provides an array of benefits and much flexibility, it has not yet been optimized, and therefore had a degrading effect on the performance of rMPI programs because of the rMPI library's large size. Thus, the results presented in this section were collected using the Raw simulator with a 256kB instruction cache (as opposed to Raw's normal instruction cache size of 32kB), large enough to mitigate the effects of Raw's software instruction caching system. The effect that the instruction cache size has on performance is discussed later in this section.

One of the most common parallel processing platforms today that is used to run MPI programs is a "Beowulf" cluster: a collection of workstations interconnected by some commodity interconnect such as Ethernet. This section compares the scalability of MPI programs running on rMPI and on LAM/MPI. The results presented here were collected on a cluster containing 128 nodes, each containing 2 2GHz 64-bit AMD Opteron processors. Each node contains 4GB of memory, and they are connected using 10GB/sec Ethernet over TCP/IP. For this experiment, only one processor from each node was used at any given time, forcing inter-node communication to always occur over the Ethernet connection. The speedups of four MPI applications were computed relative to a single processor on each respective platform running a serial implementation of each application. The same serial and MPI source codes were run on both platforms, and the speedups were calculated using cycle counts. Normalizing each platform by a single processor of itself essentially removed many system-dependent variables such as processor clock frequency and memory system performance, so the evaluation could focus on the scalability of the systems' interconnects and software.

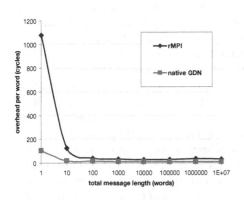

Fig. 3. rMPI overhead for a send/receive pair between adjacent tiles for various message sizes. Results relative to hand-coded GDN, and expressed as overhead in cycles per transmitted word.

MPI_Send Call	1 word	10000 words
Argument Checking	67.26%	0.09%
Envelope Construction	5.52%	0.01%
Sending headers and payload, packetization	27.22%	99.90%

MPI_Receive Call	1 word	10000 words
Reading data from network	7.29%	36.16%
Call into and out of interrupt handler	7.75%	0.02%
Argument Checking, function call overhead	32.82%	0.09%
Bookkeeping and packet sorting	52.14%	63.74%

Fig. 4. Cycle breakdowns for an MPI_Send and MPI_Recv for 1 and 10000 words

END-TO-END OVERHEAD ANALYSIS. Figure 3 shows the overhead of rMPI for messages of length 1 word to 10 million words transmitted from one tile on the Raw chip to an adjacent tile that continuously consumes the incoming message data. The overhead was calculated using total latency of the rMPI send/receive pair relative to a hand-coded send/receive pair on the native GDN. "Overhead cycles" include the total time, in cycles, from transferring a memory buffer from the sending core to a memory buffer in the receiving core, not counting the 1 cycle per word network latency. The rMPI overhead for very short messages is quite large—it takes 1080 cycles of overhead to send a 1-word message, and 126 cycles of overhead per word for a ten-word message. As the message size grows from 10 to 100 words, the difference of end-to-end latencies narrows; rMPI's overhead is 30 cycles per word for a 10000-word message, compared to 12 cycles per word for the native GDN version. Given that multicores will likely be frequently programmed with finer-grain communication patterns, MPI's significant overhead for short messages squashes the benefit of multicore. For larger message sizes, MPI's overhead is more palatable.

To further understand the cause of rMPI's overhead, experiments were run to capture where rMPI spends its time during an MPI_Send and MPI_Recv for the same single-sender, single-receiver latency test, seen in Table 4. For the 1-word case, 67% of cycles are spent on argument checking (to preserve MPI semantics) and function call overhead, and another 5.5% is spent constructing the rMPI message envelope. However, both of these actions only occur once in any MPI_Send call. Hence, virtually all of the time in sending a 10000-word message is spent breaking the messages into packets and pushing them out to the GDN. Thus, the fixed overhead due to MPI_Send is amortized for large message sends, explaining the overhead drop from 1080 cycles for a one-word message to 30 cycles for a 10000-word message.

Table 4 also shows the same analysis for MPI_Recv. In the 1-word case, 33% of the cycles are spent calling into the rMPI library and checking arguments, and over 50% were spent managing bookkeeping data structures and sorting packets. About 8% of the time was spent calling into the interrupt handler, and only 7% of the time was spent actually receiving and storing data from the network. Contrasting this to the 10000-word message case, it is once again clear that some of the overhead is fixed argument checking and calling in and out of the interrupt handler accounts for about 0.1% of the total cycles. Over 1/3 of the time is spent receiving data from the network, and nearly two-thirds of the cycles are spent managing the packet sorting and data structure bookkeeping. In fact, only 0.02% of cycles were spent managing data structures before the data was available, and only 0.04% of cycles were spent managing data structures after the message was completely received. Thus, sorting and demultiplexing packets while they are arriving consumes a relatively large portion of the time in an MPI_Recv.

While the GDN's "to-the-metal" access to underlying network resources enables it to achieve extremely efficient communication, it is sufficiently challenging to program that programmers would not want to use it directly in most cases. MPI provides easy-to-use high-level abstractions, but such high overheads for small messages, that it wastes much of the benefits (*e.g.,* low-latency inter-core communication) that multicore provides. Thus, *neither low-level GDN programming nor high-level MPI programming provides the appropriate balance of performance and programmability for multicore.* While this work does not investigate new programming models for multicore, the overhead analysis can be used to help direct designers of future lightweight multicore programming interfaces. For instance, one of the aspects of the GDN that makes it so hard to program is that large messages must be broken into packets, and re-assembled by the receiver *in software by the user program.* Furthermore, the receiver must also sort packets from different senders in software. A lightweight API that provides simple facilities for sending large messages and sorting them appropriately would be quite beneficial to the programmer. The API should also help prevent deadlock by keeping track of network buffering, and alert the user program when buffer space is full. This middle ground between direct GDN programming and MPI would hopefully offer most of the programmability of MPI, without the extra overhead of significant argument checking and many layers of function call overhead.

PERFORMANCE SCALING. This section analyzes four applications run on rMPI, the native GDN, and LAM/MPI.

Jacobi Relaxation. The jacobi relaxation algorithm was evaluated on all three platforms. While programming this application using the native GDN directly was tedious and time-consuming, it is seen as an upper bound for performance scalability because of its extremely low overhead for sending and receiving. The algorithm was run on 2-dimensional floating point matrices with sizes ranging from 16×16 to 2048×2048. Figure 5 shows the results for the 16×16 case. With very small input data sizes, the low overhead GDN is the only configuration that actually yields a speedup. rMPI and LAM/MPI are both slower than the serial version of the code for this input data size. In fact, LAM/MPI slows down even more when 8 and 16 processors are used. The slowdown for rMPI and LAM/MPI is caused by the low computation-to-communication

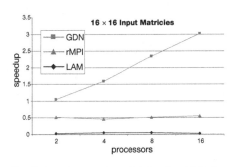

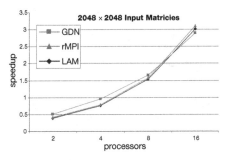

Fig. 5. Speedup (cycle ratio) for Jacobi Relaxation (16×16 input matrix)

Fig. 6. Speedup (cycle ratio) for Jacobi Relaxation (2048×2048 input matrix)

ratio; there is simply not enough computation to effectively amortize the cost imposed by the MPI semantics. On the other hand, the extremely low overhead of the GDN can achieve a non-trivial speedup despite the small input matrix.

For an input matrix size of 2048×2048, the three configurations scale very similarly, as seen in Figure 6. This is congruent with intuition: the low-overhead GDN outperforms both MPI implementations for small input data sizes because its low overhead immunizes it against low computation-to-communication ratios. However, the MPI overhead is amortized over a longer running program with larger messages in this case. rMPI even outperforms the GDN in the 16 processor case, which is most likely a due to memory access synchronization on the GDN, as the GDN algorithm is broken into phases in which more than one processor accesses memory at the same time. Contrastingly, the interrupt-driven approach used in rMPI effectively staggers memory accesses, and in this case, such staggering provides a win for rMPI.

Figure 7 summarizes the speedup characteristics for the GDN, rMPI, and LAM/MPI. Again, the GDN achieves a 3x speedup immediately, even for small input data sizes. On the other hand, both MPI implementations have slowdowns for small data sizes, as their overhead is too high and does not amortize for low computation to communication ratios. rMPI starts to see a speedup before LAM/MPI, though, with an input data matrix of size 64×64. One potential reason rMPI exhibits more speedup is its fast interrupt mechanism and lack of operating system layers.

One clearly interesting input data size for the GDN and rMPI graphs is 512×512: both show a significant speedup spike. Figure 8, which shows the throughput (computed elements per clock cycle) of the serial jacobi implementation running on Raw, sheds some light on why this speedup jump occurs. Up until the 512×512 input size, the entire data set fit into the Raw data cache, obviating the need to go to DRAM. However, the 512×512 data size no longer fit into the cache of a single Raw tile. Hence, a significant dip in throughput occurs for the serial version for that data size. On the other hand, since the data set is broken up for the parallelized GDN and rMPI versions, this cache bottleneck does not occur until even larger data sizes, which explains the jump in speedup. It should be noted that this distributed cache architecture evident in many multicore architectures can be generally beneficial, as it allows fast caches to be tightly coupled with nearby processors.

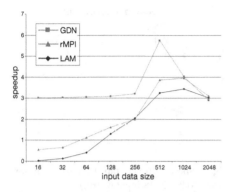

Fig. 7. Speedup for Jacobi. x-axis shows N, where the input matrix is N×N.

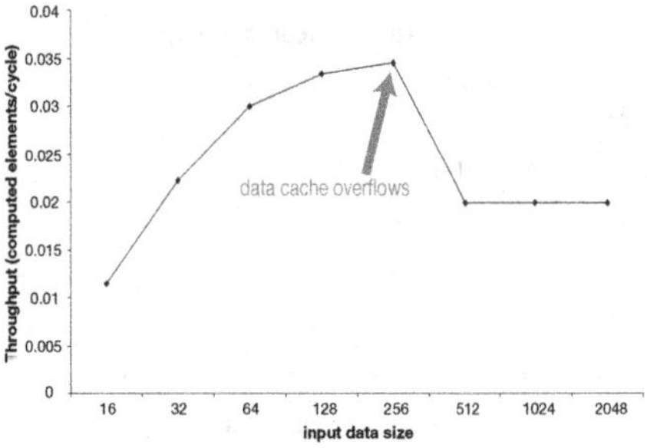

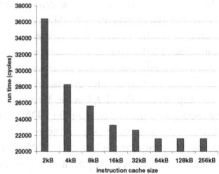

Fig. 8. Throughput (computations/cycle) for Jacobi (on Raw). Cache overflows at 512×512 input size.

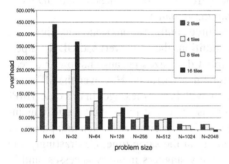

Fig. 9. Overhead of rMPI for Jacobi Relaxation relative to a GDN implementation for various input sizes. Overhead computed using cycle counts.

Fig. 10. Performance of jacobi with varying instruction cache size. Lower is better.

Figure 3 characterizes the overhead of rMPI for a simple send/receive pair of processors on the Raw chip. To characterize rMPI's overhead for real applications, which may have complex computation and communication patterns, the overhead of rMPI was measured for jacobi. The experiment measured the complete running time of jacobi experiments for various input data sizes and numbers of processors for both the GDN and rMPI implementations. Figure 9 shows the results of this experiment. Here, rMPI overhead is computed as $overhead_{rMPI} = (cycles_{rMPI} - cycles_{GDN})/(cycles_{GDN})$.

As can be seen, rMPI's overhead is quite large for small data sets. Furthermore, its overhead is particularly high for small data sets running on a large number of processors, as evidenced by the 16×16 case for 16 processors, which has an overhead of nearly 450%. However, as the input data set increases, rMPI's overhead drops quickly. It should also be noted that for data sizes from 16×16 through 512×512, adding processors *increases* overhead, but for data sizes larger than 512×512, adding processors *decreases* overhead. In fact, the 1024×1024 data size for 16 processors has just a 1.7% overhead. The 2048×2048 for 16 processors actually shows a speedup beyond the GDN

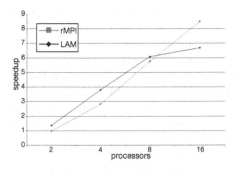

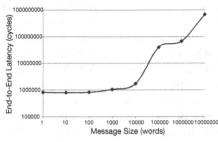

Fig. 11. rMPI and LAM/MPI speedups for matrix multiplication

Fig. 12. Latency for send/receive pairs between two nodes on cluster (LAM/MPI)

implementation. This is most likely due to memory access synchronization, as described above, and does not generally hold true for all applications.

Instruction Cache Size Sensitivity. As mentioned in Section 1, many multicore designers are opting for fairly simple cores in order to fit many of them on a single chip. Likewise, the cores of such systems will likely have a smaller amount of on-chip memory than monolithic processors such as the Pentium 4 have. As such, it is important that the memory footprint of multicore programs be small enough that instruction cache misses do not significantly hurt performance. The rMPI library, however, is large, containing over 200 top-level MPI API calls with a total text segment size of 160kB. In order to measure the effect of instruction cache misses on multicores, jacobi was run with various instruction cache sizes using a standard hardware instruction cache model. Figure 10 shows that performance improves by 40% as the per-core instruction cache size grows from 2kB to 64kB. At that point, increasing the cache size further has no impact on performance. For more complex MPI programs that use much more of the API than the jacobi benchmark does, the impact on performance of small instruction caches would be even more severe (this implementation of jacobi only makes use of 6 MPI calls).

This experiment reinforces the notion that MPI is most likely too large and heavyweight for multicore processors. A ligher-weight alternative that fits entirely in the instruction cache for multicores with small instruction memories would be better suited to multicores' constraints.

Scalability of Other Applications. In an attempt to further characterize the performance scalability of rMPI, three other applications were evaluated. The applications were run using both rMPI on Raw and LAM/MPI on the cluster. As before, the sequential versions of each application were run on each respective architecture to determine baseline performance. Note that a GDN version of these applications was not evaluated, as developing non-trivial applications on the GDN is quite time-consuming and tedious, and the above experiments with jacobi served as a solid comparison. The three applications used in this evaluation are matrix multiplication, trapezoidal integration, and pi estimation. The matrix multiply benchmark uses a standard 2-dimensional matrix multiplication algorithm that is parallelized in a master-slave configuration. The results for the matrix multiplication experiment multiplying a 640×150 floating point matrix by a 150×700 floating point matrix can be seen in Figure 11. As can be seen, LAM/MPI outperforms rMPI in terms of speedup for the experiments that used 2, 4, and 8 processors, while rMPI has a larger speedup for the 16 processor case.

One potential reason rMPI has greater speedup relative to LAM/MPI for larger numbers of processors has to do with the shape of rMPI's and LAM/MPI's latency curves for increasing message sizes. As seen in Figure 3, the latency for a send/receive pair for rMPI increases proportionately as message sizes increase for message sizes larger than 10 words. As mentioned above, the end-to-end latency for a one-word message send/receive is roughly 1000 cycles on rMPI. However, the shape of the LAM/MPI latency curve is notably different, as can be seen in Figure 12. First of all, the overhead for sending a single-word message from one process to another on LAM/MPI is quite high, taking almost 1 million cycles to complete. This can be attributed to the many software layers that LAM/MPI must go through to access the network. Additionally, the latency to send and receive a 10000-word message is roughly the same as sending a 1-word message. Not until message sizes reach 100000-words and above does the round trip latency grow.

This empirical result explains why rMPI's speedup is greater than LAM/MPI's speedup for large numbers of processors. In the 16 processor case, the system had to send 8 times as many messages compared to the 2 processor case. rMPI's latency increases proportionately with increasing message sizes, so it scaled well as more processors were introduced. However, the latency for sending smaller messages on LAM/MPI is not much different than the latency for sending 10000-words. Thus, while rMPI reaps the savings of smaller messages which ensue in the 16 processor case, LAM/MPI's large fixed overhead is the same and therefore does not benefit from smaller messages.

Figure 13 and Figure 14 show the speedups for a parallelized trapezoidal integration application and a parallelized pi estimation algorithm, respectively. Both applications are similar in terms of their computation-to-communication ratios, which are both quite large relative to jacobi relaxation. As can be seen in the figures, LAM/MPI generates a larger speedup for a small number of processors, but rMPI has larger speedups for larger numbers of processors. rMPI's performance on trapezoidal with 16 processors is over double LAM/MPI's speedup. This result can again be explained by the argument given

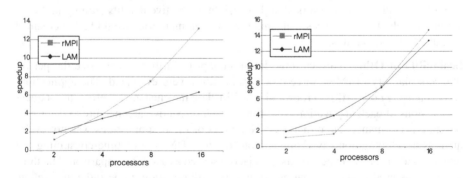

Fig. 13. Trapezoidal integration speedup for rMPI and LAM/MPI

Fig. 14. Matrix multiply speedup for rMPI and LAM/MPI

above for the matrix multiplication application. In these cases, the messages are quite small (20 words or less), so sending many more, as in the 16 processor case, affects LAM/MPI's performance more drastically than it does rMPI's.

In general, though, both applications achieve speedups ranging from approximately 6x – 14.5x on both rMPI and LAM/MPI. These speedups are larger than that of matrix multiply and jacobi, which algorithmically have significantly lower computation-to-communication ratios. The results for all four applications evaluated agree with intuition: rMPI and LAM/MPI both exhibit better performance scalability for applications with larger computation-to-communication ratios.

5 Related Work

A large number of other message passing work have influenced this work. The iWarp system [5], [16] attempted to integrate a VLIW processor and fine-grained communication system on a single chip. The INMOS transputer [4] had computing elements that could send messages to one another. The MIT Alewife machine [19] also contained support for fast user-level messaging. Other multicore microprocessors include VIRAM [18], Wavescalar [29], TRIPS [23], Smart Memories [21], [22], and the Tarantula [7] extension to Alpha. Some commercial chip multiprocessors include the POWER 4 [8] and Intel Pentium D [1]. This work is applicable to many newer architectures that are similar to Raw in that they contain multiple processing elements on a single chip.

This paper primarily concentrated on Raw's dynamic network, but much work has been done using Raw's static network, which operates on scalar operands. Prior work [33], [12] shows considerable speedups can result using the static network for stream computation. Additionally, there exist a number of compiler systems for Raw that automatically generate statically-scheduled communication patterns. CFlow [13], for instance, is a compiler system that enables statically-scheduled message passing between programs running on separate processors. Raw's rawcc [20] automatically parallelize C programs, generating communication instructions where necessary.

While this paper showed that MPI can be successfully ported to a multicore architecture, its inherent overhead causes it to squander the multicore opportunity. The Multicore Association's CAPI API [3] offers a powerful alternative—a lightweight API for multicore architectures that is optimized for low-latency inter-core networks, and boasts a small memory footprint that can fit into in-core memory. There also exist a number of MPI implementations for a variety of platforms and interconnection devices, including MPICH [34], LAM/MPI [6], and OpenMPI [11]. [17] discusses software overhead in messaging layers.

6 Conclusion

This paper presented rMPI, an MPI-compliant message passing library for multi-core architectures with on-chip interconnect. rMPI introduces robust, deadlock-free, mechanisms to program multicores, offering an interface that is compatible with current MPI software. Likewise, rMPI gives programmers already familiar with MPI an easy interface with which to program Raw which enables fine-grain control over their programs.

rMPI was designed to leverage the unique architectural resources that a multicore processor architecture with on-chip networks and direct access to hardware resources such as Raw provides.

A number of evaluations using the rMPI implementation show that its overhead, especially for applications with many short messages on multicores such as Raw, illustrates that MPI is likely not the optimal interface for multicores with on-chip interconnect, as it imposes significant overhead on all communication. Furthermore, rMPI's large memory footprint makes it less well-suited for multicore's generally smaller on-chip instruction caches. Overall, this work shows that MPI is too heavyweight for multicores with on-chip networks such as Raw, and suggests that a lighter-weight multicore programming interface that takes advantage of low latency networks and has a smaller memory footprint be developed. The authors hope that this work provides guidance and useful insights to application developers of future multicore processors containing on-chip interconnect.

References

1. Intel pentium d,
   http://www.intel.com/products/processor/pentium_d/
2. Moore's law 40th anniversary,
   http://www.intel.com/technology/mooreslaw/index.htm
3. The multicore association communications api,
   http://www.multicore-association.org/workgroup/ComAPI.html
4. Transputer reference manual. Prentice Hall International (UK) Ltd. Hertfordshire, UK (1998)
5. Borkar, S., Cohn, R., Cox, G., Gleason, S., Gross, T., Kung, H.T., Lam, M., Moore, B., Peterson, C., et al.: iwarp: An integrated solution to high-speed parallel computing. In: Proceedings of Supercomputing (1998)
6. Burns, G., Daoud, R., Vaigl, J.: LAM: An Open Cluster Environment for MPI. In: Proceedings of Supercomputing Symposium, pp. 379–386 (1994)
7. Espasa, et al.: Tarantula: A Vector Extension to the Alpha Architecture. In: ISCA, pp. 281–292 (2002)
8. T.J., et al.: POWER4 system microarchitecture. IBM Journal of Research and Development 46(1), 5–25 (2002)
9. Forum, M.: A message passing interface standard. Technical report, University of Tennessee, Knoxville (1994)
10. Forum, M.P.I.: Mpi: A message-passing interface standard (1995),
    http://www.mpi-forum.org/docs/mpi-11-html/mpi-report.html
11. Gabriel, E., Fagg, G.E., Bosilca, G., Angskun, T., Dongarra, J.J., Squyres, J.M., Sahay, V., Kambadur, P., Barrett, B., Lumsdaine, A., Castain, R.H., Daniel, D.J., Graham, R.L., Woodall, T.S.: Open MPI: Goals, concept, and design of a next generation MPI implementation. In: Proceedings, 11th European PVM/MPI Users' Group Meeting, Budapest, Hungary, pp. 97–104 (September 2004)
12. Gordon, M.I., Thies, W., Karczmarek, M., Lin, J., Meli, A.S., Lamb, A.A., Leger, C., Wong, J., Hoffmann, H., Maze, D., Amarasinghe, S.: A Stream Compiler for Communication-Exposed Architectures. In: Conference on Architectural Support for Programming Languages and Operating Systems, pp. 291–303 (2002)
13. Griffin, P.: CFlow. Master's thesis, Lab for Computer Science, MIT (2005)

14. Gropp, W., Huss-Lederman, S., et al.: MPI: The Complete Reference, vol. 2. The MIT Press, Cambridge (1998)
15. Gropp, W.D., Lusk, E.: User's Guide for mpich, a Portable Implementation of MPI. In: ANL-96/6. Mathematics and Computer Science Division, Argonne National Laboratory (1996)
16. Hinrichs, S., Kosak, C., O'Hallaron, D., Stricker, T., Take, R.: An architecture for optimal all-to-all personalized communication. In: Proceedings of Symposium on Parallelism in Algorithms and Architectures (1994)
17. Karamcheti, V., Chien, A.A.: Software overhead in messaging layers: Where does the time go? In: Proceedings of the Sixth International Conference on Architectural Support for Programming Languages and Operating Systems, San Jose, California, pp. 51–60 (1994)
18. Kozyrakis, C.E., Patterson, D.: A new direction for computer architecture research. Journal of the ACM (1997)
19. Kubiatowicz, J.: Integrated Shared-Memory and Message-Passing Communication in the Alewife Multiprocessor. PhD thesis, MIT (1998)
20. Lee, W., Barua, R., Frank, M., Srikrishna, D., Babb, J., Sarkar, V., Amarasinghe, S.: Space-Time Scheduling of Instruction-Level Parallelism on a Raw Machine. In: Proceedings of the Eighth ACM Conference on Architectural Support for Programming Languages and Operating Systems, San Jose, CA, pp. 46–57 (October 1998)
21. Mai, K., Paaske, T., Jayasena, N., Ho, R., Dally, W., Horowitz, M.: Smart memories: A modular reconfigurable architecture. In: Proceedings of the 27th International Symposium on Computer Architecture, pp. 161–170 (2000)
22. Mai, et al.: Smart Memories: A Modular Reconfigurable Architecture. In: ISCA (2000)
23. Nagarajan, R., Sankaralingam, K., Burger, D., Keckler, S.W.: A design space evaluation of grid processor architectures. In: International Symposium on Microarchitecture (MICRO) (2001)
24. Pacheco, P.S.: Parallel Programming with MPI. Morgan Kaufmann Publishers, San Francisco (1997)
25. Psota, J.: rMPI: An MPI-Compliant Message Passing Library for Tiled Architectures. Master's thesis, Lab for Computer Science, MIT (2005), http://cag.lcs.mit.edu/jim/publications/ms.pdf
26. Quinn, M.J.: Parallel Programming in C with MPI and OpenMP. McGraw Hill, New York (2004)
27. Gropp, W., Huss-Lederman, S., et al.: MPI: The Complete Reference. The MIT Press, Cambridge (1998)
28. Squyres, J.M., Lumsdaine, A.: A Component Architecture for LAM/MPI. In: Dongarra, J.J., Laforenza, D., Orlando, S. (eds.) EuroPVM/MPI 2003. LNCS, vol. 2840, pp. 379–387. Springer, Heidelberg (2003)
29. Swanson, S., Michelson, K., Schwerin, A., Oskin, M.: Wavescalar. In: In the 36th Annual International Symposium on Microarchitecture (MICRO-36) (2003)
30. Taylor, M.B.: The Raw Processor Specification, ftp://ftp.cag.lcs.mit.edu/pub/raw/documents/RawSpec99.pdf
31. Taylor, et al.: The Raw Microprocessor: A Computational Fabric for Software Circuits and General-Purpose Programs. IEEE Micro, 25–35 (March 2002)
32. Taylor, et al.: Scalar Operand Networks: On-Chip Interconnect for ILP in Partitioned Architectures. In: HPCA (2003)
33. Taylor, et al.: Evaluation of the Raw Microprocessor: An Exposed-Wire-Delay Architecture for ILP and Streams. In: ISCA (2004)
34. William Gropp, A.S., Lusk. E.: A high-performance, portable implementation of the mpi message passing interface standard, http://www-unix.mcs.anl.gov/mpi/mpich/papers/mpicharticle/paper.html

Modeling Multigrain Parallelism on Heterogeneous Multi-core Processors: A Case Study of the Cell BE

Filip Blagojevic, Xizhou Feng,
Kirk W. Cameron, and Dimitrios S. Nikolopoulos

Center for High-End Computing Systems
Department of Computer Science
Virginia Tech
{filip,fengx,cameron,dsn}@cs.vt.edu

Abstract. Heterogeneous multi-core processors invest the most significant portion of their transistor budget in customized "accelerator" cores,
while using a small number of conventional low-end cores for supplying
computation to accelerators. To maximize performance on heterogeneous
multi-core processors, programs need to expose multiple dimensions of
parallelism simultaneously. Unfortunately, programming with multiple
dimensions of parallelism is to date an ad hoc process, relying heavily on
the intuition and skill of programmers. Formal techniques are needed to
optimize multi-dimensional parallel program designs. We present a model
of multi-dimensional parallel computation for steering the parallelization
process on heterogeneous multi-core processors. The model predicts with
high accuracy the execution time and scalability of a program using conventional processors and accelerators simultaneously. More specifically,
the model reveals optimal degrees of multi-dimensional, task-level and
data-level concurrency, to maximize performance across cores. We use
the model to derive mappings of two full computational phylogenetics
applications on a multi-processor based on the IBM Cell Broadband
Engine.

1 Introduction

To overcome the performance and power limitations of conventional general-
purpose microprocessors, many high-performance systems off-load computation
to special-purpose hardware. These computational accelerators come in many
forms, ranging from SIMD co-processors to FPGA boards to chips with multiple
specialized cores. We consider a computational accelerator as any programmable
device that is capable of speeding up a computation. Examples of high-end
systems utilizing computational accelerators are the Cell Broadband Engine from
IBM/Sony/Toshiba [1], Cray's XD1 [2], the Starbridge Hypercomputer [3], and
SGI's FPGA-based NUMA node [4].

The migration of parallel programming models to accelerator-based architectures raises many challenges. Accelerators require platform-specific programming

P. Stenström et al. (Eds.): HiPEAC 2008, LNCS 4917, pp. 38–52, 2008.

interfaces and re-formulation of parallel algorithms to fully exploit the additional hardware. Furthermore, scheduling code on accelerators and orchestrating parallel execution and data transfers between host processors and accelerators is a non-trivial exercise [5].

Consider the problem of identifying the most appropriate programming model and accelerator configuration for a given parallel application. The simplest way to identify the best combination is to exhaustively measure the execution time of all of the possible combinations of programming models and mappings of the application to the hardware. Unfortunately, this technique is not scalable to large, complex systems, large applications, or applications with behavior that varies significantly with the input. The execution time of a complex application is the function of many parameters. A given parallel application may consist of N phases where each phase is affected differently by accelerators. Each phase can exploit d dimensions of parallelism or any combination thereof such as ILP, TLP, or both. Each phase or dimension of parallelism can use any of m different programming and execution models such as message passing, shared memory, SIMD, or any combination thereof. Accelerator availability or use may consist of c possible configurations, involving different numbers of accelerators. Exhaustive analysis of the execution time for all combinations requires at least $N \times d \times m \times c$ trials with any given input.

Models of parallel computation have been instrumental in the adoption and use of parallel systems. Unfortunately, commonly used models [6,7] are not directly portable to accelerator-based systems. First, the heterogeneous processing common to these systems is not reflected in most models of parallel computation. Second, current models do not capture the effects of multi-grain parallelism. Third, few models account for the effects of using multiple programming models in the same program. Parallel programming at multiple dimensions and with a synthesis of models consumes both enormous amounts of programming effort and significant amounts of execution time, if not handled with care. To overcome these deficits, we present a model for multi-dimensional parallel computation on heterogeneous multi-core processors. Considering that each dimension of parallelism reflects a different degree of computation granularity, we name the model MMGP, for **M**odel of **M**ulti-**G**rain **P**arallelism.

MMGP is an analytical model which formalizes the process of programming accelerator-based systems and reduces the need for exhaustive measurements. This paper presents a generalized MMGP model for accelerator-based architectures with one layer of host processor parallelism and one layer of accelerator parallelism, followed by the specialization of this model for the Cell Broadband Engine.

The input to MMGP is an explicitly parallel program, with parallelism expressed with machine-independent abstractions, using common programming libraries and constructs. Upon identification of a few key parameters of the application derived from micro-benchmarking and profiling of a sequential run, MMGP predicts with reasonable accuracy the execution time with all feasible mappings of the application to host processors and accelerators. MMGP is fast

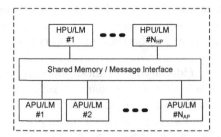

Fig. 1. A hardware abstraction of an accelerator-based architecture with two layers of parallelism. Host processing units (HPUs) supply coarse-grain parallel computation across accelerators. Accelerator processing units (APUs) are the main computation engines and may support internally finer grain parallelism. Both HPUs and APUs have local memories and communicate through shared-memory or message-passing. Additional layers of parallelism can be expressed hierarchically in a similar fashion.

and reasonably accurate, therefore it can be used to quickly identify optimal operating points, in terms of the exposed layers of parallelism and the degree of parallelism in each layer, on accelerator-based systems. Experiments with two complete applications from the field of computational phylogenetics on a shared-memory multiprocessor with two Cell BEs, show that MMGP models parallel execution time of complex parallel codes with multiple layers of task and data parallelism, with mean error in the range of 1%–5%, across all feasible program configurations on the target system. Due to the narrow margin of error, MMGP predicts accurately the optimal mapping of programs to cores for the cases we have studied so far.

In the rest of this paper, we establish preliminary background and terminology for introducing MMGP (Section 2), we develop MMGP (Section 3), and we validate MMGP using two computational phylogenetics applications (Section 4). We discuss related work in Section 5 and conclude the paper in Section 6.

2 Modeling Abstractions

In this section we identify abstractions necessary to allow us to define a simple, accurate model of multi-dimensional parallel computation for heterogeneous multi-core architectures.

2.1 Hardware Abstraction

Figure 1 shows our abstraction of a heterogeneous, accelerator-based parallel architecture. In this abstraction, each node consists of multiple host processing units (HPU) and multiple accelerator processing units (APU). Both the HPUs and APUs have local and shared memory. Multiple HPU-APU nodes form a cluster. We model the communication cost for i and j, where i and j are HPUs,

APUs, and/or HPU-APU pairs, using a variant of *LogP* [6] of point-to-point communication:

$$C_{i,j} = O_i + L + O_j, \tag{1}$$

where $C_{i,j}$ is the communication cost, O_i, O_j is the overhead of send and receive respectively, and L is communication latency.

2.2   Program Abstraction

Figure 2 illustrates the program abstraction used by MMGP. We model programs using a variant of the Hierarchical Task Graph (HTG [8]). An HTG represents multiple layers of concurrency with progressively finer granularity when moving from outermost to innermost layers. We use a phased HTG, in which we partition the application into multiple phases of execution and split each phase into nested sub-phases, each modeled as a single, potentially parallel task. The degree of concurrency may vary between tasks and within tasks.

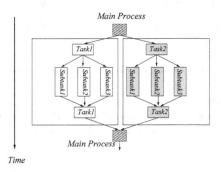

Fig. 2. Program abstraction for two parallel tasks with nested parallelism

Mapping a workload with nested parallelism as shown in Figure 2 to an accelerator-based multi-core architecture can be challenging. In the general case, any task of any granularity could be mapped to any type combination of HPUs and APUs. The solution space under these conditions can be unmanageable. We confine the solution space by making some assumptions about the program and the hardware. First, we assume that the application exposes all available layers of inherent parallelism to the runtime environment, without however specifying how to map this parallelism to parallel execution vehicles in hardware. Second, we assume hardware configurations consist of a hierarchy of nested resources, even though the actual resources may not be physically nested in the architecture. For instance, the Cell Broadband Engine can be considered as 2 HPUs and 8 APUs, where the two HPUs correspond to the PowerPC dual-thread SMT core and APUs to the synergistic (SPE) accelerator cores. This assumption is reasonable since it represents faithfully current accelerator architectures, where front-end processors off-load computation and data to accelerators. This assumption simplifies modeling of both communication and computation.

3   Model of Multi-grain Parallelism

This section provides theoretical rigor to our approach. We begin by modeling sequential execution on the HPU, with part of the computation off-loaded to a single APU. Next, we incorporate multiple APUs in the model, followed by multiple HPUs.

3.1   Modeling Sequential Execution

As the starting point, we consider an accelerator-based architecture that consists of one HPU and one APU, and a program with one phase decomposed into three sub-phases, a prologue and epilogue running on the HPU, and a main accelerated phase running on the APU, as illustrated in Figure 3. Off-loading computation

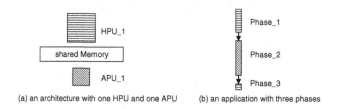

(a) an architecture with one HPU and one APU   (b) an application with three phases

Fig. 3. The sub-phases of a sequential program are readily mapped to HPUs and APUs. In this example, sub-phases 1 and 3 execute on the HPU and sub-phase 2 executes on the APU. HPUs and APUs communicate via shared memory.

incurs additional communication cost, for loading code and data, in the case of a software-managed APU memory hierarchy, and committing results calculated from the APU. We model each of these communication costs with a latency and an overhead at the end-points, as in Equation 1. We assume that APU's accesses to data during the execution of a procedure are streamed and overlapped with APU computation. This assumption reflects the capability of current streaming architectures, such as the Cell and Merrimac, to aggressively overlap memory latency with computation, using multiple buffers. Due to overlapped memory latency, communication overhead is assumed to be visible only during loading the code and arguments of a procedure on the APU and during committing the result of an off-loaded procedure to memory, or sending the result of an off-loaded procedure from the APU to the HPU. We note that this assumption does not prevent us from incorporating a more detailed model that accurately estimates the non-overlapped and overlapped communication operations in MMGP. We leave this issue as a subject of future work. Communication overhead for off-loading the code and arguments of a procedure and signaling the execution of that procedure on the APU are combined in one term (O_s), while the overhead for returning the result of a procedure from the APU to the HPU and committing intermediate results to memory are combined in another term (O_r).

The execution time for the off-loaded sequential execution for sub-phase 2 in Figure 3, can be modeled as:

$$T_{offload}(w_2) = T_{APU}(w_2) + O_r + O_s \qquad (2)$$

where $T_{APU}(w_2)$ is the time needed to complete sub-phase 2 without additional overhead. We can write the total execution time of all three sub-phases as:

$$T = T_{HPU}(w_1) + T_{APU}(w_2) + O_r + O_s + T_{HPU}(w_3) \qquad (3)$$

To reduce complexity, we replace $T_{HPU}(w_1) + T_{HPU}(w_3)$ with T_{HPU}, $T_{APU}(w_2)$ with T_{APU}, and $O_s + O_r$ with $O_{offload}$. We can now rewrite Equation 3 as:

$$T = T_{HPU} + T_{APU} + O_{offload} \qquad (4)$$

The program model in Figure 3 is representative of one of potentially many phases in a program. We further modify Equation 4 for a program with N phases:

$$T = \sum_{i=1}^{N} (T_{HPU,i} + T_{APU,i} + O_{offload}) \qquad (5)$$

3.2   Modeling Parallel Execution on APUs

Each off-loaded part of a phase may contain fine-grain parallelism, such as task-level parallelism in nested procedures or data-level parallelism in loops. This parallelism can be exploited by using multiple APUs for the offloaded workload. Figure 4 shows the execution time decomposition for execution using one APU and two APUs. We assume that the code off-loaded to an APU during phase i, has a part which can be further parallelized across APUs, and a part executed sequentially on the APU. We denote $T_{APU,i}(1,1)$ as the execution time of the further parallelized part of the APU code during the ith phase. The first index 1 refers to the use of one HPU thread in the execution. We denote $T_{APU,i}(1,p)$ as the execution time of the same part when p APUs are used to execute this part during the ith phase. We denote as $C_{APU,i}$ the non-parallelized part of APU code in phase i. Therefore, we obtain:

$$T_{APU,i}(1,p) = \frac{T_{APU,i}(1,1)}{p} + C_{APU,i} \qquad (6)$$

Given that the HPU off-loads to APUs sequentially, there exists a latency gap between consecutive off-loads on APUs. Similarly, there exists a gap between receiving or committing return values from two consecutive off-loaded procedures on the HPU. We denote with g the larger of the two gaps. On a system with p APUs, parallel APU execution will incur an additional overhead as large as $p \cdot g$. Thus, we can model the execution time in phase i as:

$$T_i(1,p) = T_{HPU,i} + \frac{T_{APU,i}(1,1)}{p} + C_{APU,i} + O_{offload} + p \cdot g \qquad (7)$$

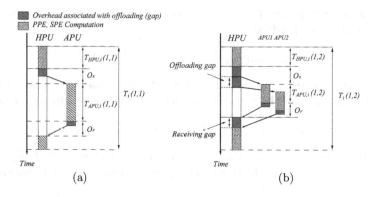

Fig. 4. Parallel APU execution. The HPU (leftmost bar in parts a and b) offloads computations to one APU (part a) and two APUs (part b). The single point-to-point transfer of part a is modeled as overhead plus computation time on the APU. For multiple transfers, there is additional overhead (g), but also benefits due to parallelization.

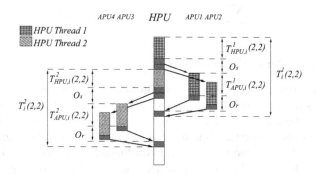

Fig. 5. Parallel HPU execution. The HPU (center bar) offloads computations to 4 APUs (2 on the right and 2 on the left).

3.3   Modeling Parallel Execution on HPUs

Since the compute intensive parts of an application are off-loaded to APUs, HPUs are expected to be idle for extended intervals. Therefore, HPU multithreading can be used to reduce idle time on the HPU and provide more sources of work for APUs.

Figure 5 illustrates the execution timeline when two threads share an HPU, and each thread off-loads parallel code on two APUs. We use different shade patterns to represent the workload of different threads.

For m concurrent HPU threads, where each thread uses p APUs for distributing a single APU task, the execution time of a single off-loading phase can be represented as:

$$T_i^k(m,p) = T_{HPU,i}^k(m,p) + T_{APU,i}^k(m,p) + O_{offload} + p \cdot g \qquad (8)$$

where $T_i^k(m, p)$ is the completion time of the kth HPU thread during the ith phase. Similarly to Equation 6, we can write the APU time of the k-th thread in phase i in Equation 8 as:

$$T_{APU,i}^k(m, p) = \frac{T_{APU,i}(m, 1)}{p} + C_{APU,i} \qquad (9)$$

The execution time of each HPU thread is affected by architecture and software factors. For a multi-threaded HPU where threads share on-chip execution resources, these factors include contention between HPU threads for shared resources, context switch overhead related to resource scheduling, and global synchronization between dependent HPU threads. Considering all three factors, we can model the i-th phase of an HPU thread as:

$$T_{HPU,i}^k(m, p) = \alpha_m \cdot T_{HPU,i}(1, p) + T_{CSW} + O_{COL} \qquad (10)$$

In this equation, T_{CSW} is context switching time on the HPU and O_{COL} is the time needed for global synchronization. The parameter α_m is introduced to account for contention between threads that share resources on the HPU. On SMT and CMP HPUs, such resources typically include one or more levels of the on-chip cache memory. On SMT HPUs in particular, shared resources include also TLBs, branch predictors and instruction slots in the pipeline. Contention between threads often introduces artificial load imbalance due to occasionally unfair hardware policies of allocating resources between threads.

Combining Equations (8)-(10) and summarizing all phases, we can write the execution time for MMGP as:

$$T(m, p) = \alpha_m \cdot T_{HPU}(1, 1) + \frac{T_{APU}(1, 1)}{m \cdot p}$$
$$+ C_{APU} + N \cdot (O_{Offload} + T_{CSW} + O_{COL} + p \cdot g) \qquad (11)$$

Due to limited hardware resources (i.e. number of HPUs and APUs), we further constrain this equation to $m \times p \leq N_{APU}$, where N_{APU} is the number of available APUs. As described later in this paper, we can either measure directly or estimate all parameters in Equation 11 from micro-benchmarks and a profile of a sequential run of the program. Given a parallel program, MMGP can be applied using the following process:

1. Estimate $O_{Offload}$, α_m, T_{CSW} and O_{COL} using micro-benchmarks.
2. Profile a run of the sequential program, with annotations of parallelism included, to estimate $T_{HPU}(1)$, $T_{APU}(1, 1)$ and C_{APU}.
3. Solve a special case of Equation 11 (e.g. 7) to find the optimal mapping between application concurrency and available HPUs and APUs.

4 Experimental Validation and Results

We use MMGP to derive multi-dimensional parallelization schemes for two bioinformatics applications, RAxML and PBPI, on an IBM QS20 BladeCenter with two Cell BEs. RAxML and PBPI construct evolutionary trees from DNA or AA sequences, using different optimality criteria for approximating the best trees.

4.1   Parameter Approximation

MMGP has six free parameters, C_{APU}, $O_{offload}$, g, T_{CSW}, O_{COL} and α_m. We estimate four of the parameters using micro-benchmarks. α_m captures contention between processes or threads running on the PPE. This contention depends on the scheduling algorithm on the PPE. We estimate α_m under an event-driven scheduling model which oversubscribes the PPE with more processes than the number of hardware threads supported for simultaneous execution on the PPE, and switches between processes upon each off-loading event on the PPE [5]. The reason for using oversubscribing is the potential imbalance between supply and demand of computation between the PPE and SPEs.

To estimate α_m, we use a parallel micro-benchmark that computes the product of two $M \times M$ arrays of double-precision floating point elements. Matrix-matrix multiplication involves $O(n^3)$ computation and $O(n^2)$ data transfers, thus stressing the impact of sharing execution resources and the L1 and L2 caches between processes on the PPE. We used several different matrix sizes, ranging from 100×100 to 500×500, to exercise different levels of pressure on the thread-shared caches of the PPE. In the MMGP model, we use α_m=1.28, computed from these experiments. We should point out that α_m is not a constant in the general case. However, α_m affects only a small portion of the code (executed on the HPU). Therefore, approximating α_m with a constant is a reasonable choice which results in fairly accurate MMGP predictions, as shown later in this section.

PPE-SPE communication is optimally implemented through DMAs on Cell. In PBPI and RAxML, the off-loaded code remains in the local storage during the entire execution of the application. Also, the arguments for the off-loaded functions are fetched directly from the main memory by the SPE thread. Therefore, the only PPE-SPE communication ($O_{offload}$) is PPE $\rightarrow$ SPE *trigger* signal, and the signal sent back by each SPE after finishing the off-loaded work. We devised a ping-pong micro-benchmark using DMAs to send a single integer from the PPE to one SPE and backwards. We measured PPE$\rightarrow$SPE$\rightarrow$PPE round-trip communication overhead for a single 4-byte packet to 70 ns. To measure the overhead caused by various collective communications we used *mpptest* [9] on the PPE. Using a micro-benchmark that repeatedly executes the *sched_yield()* system call, we estimate the overhead caused by the context switching (T_{CSW}) on the PPE to 2 μs.

C_{APU} and the gap g between consecutive DMAs on the PPE are application-dependent and can not be approximated easily with a micro-benchmark. To estimate these parameters, we use a profile of a sequential run of the code, with tasks off-loaded on one SPE.

4.2   PBPI Outline

PBPI [10,11] is a parallel Bayesian phylogenetic inference implementation, which constructs phylogenetic trees from DNA or AA sequences using a Markov chain Monte Carlo sampling method. The method exploits the multi-dimensional data parallelism available in Bayesian phylogenetic inference (across the sequence and within the likelihood computations), to achieve scalability on large-scale distributed memory systems, such as the IBM BlueGene/L [12]. The algorithm used in PBPI can be summarized as follows:

1. Markov chains are partitioned into chain groups and the data set is split into segments along the sequences.
2. Virtual processors are organized in a two-dimensional grid; each chain group is mapped to one row on the grid, and each segment is mapped to one column on the grid.
3. During each generation, the partial likelihood across all columns is computed using all-to-all communication to collect the complete likelihood values from all virtual processors on the same row.
4. When there are multiple chains, two chains are randomly chosen for swapping using point-to-point communication.

PBPI is implemented in MPI. We ported PBPI to Cell by off-loading the computationally expensive functions that perform the likelihood calculation on SPEs and applied a sequence of Cell-specific optimizations on the off-loaded code.

4.3   PBPI with One Dimension of Parallelism

We compare the PBPI execution times modeled by MMGP to the actual execution times obtained on real hardware, using various degrees of PPE and SPE parallelism, the equivalents of HPU and APU parallelism on Cell. For these experiments, we used the arch107_L10000 input data set. This data set consists of 107 sequences, each with 10000 characters. We run PBPI with one Markov chain for 20000 generations. Using the time base register on the PPE and the decrementer register on one SPE, we were able to profile the sequential execution of the program. We obtained the following model parameters for PBPI: $T_{HPU} = 1.3s$, $T_{APU} = 370s$, $g = 0.8s$ and $C_{APU} = 1.72s$.

Figure 6 (a),(b), compares modeled and actual execution times for PBPI, when PBPI only exploits one-dimensional PPE (HPU) parallelism in which each PPE thread uses one SPE for off-loading. We execute the code with up to 16 MPI processes, which off-load code to up to 16 SPEs on two Cell BEs. Referring to Equation 11, we set $p = 1$ and vary the value of m from 1 to 16. The X-axis shows the number of processes running on the PPE (i.e. HPU parallelism), and the Y-axis shows the modeled and measured execution times. The maximum prediction error of MMGP is 5%. The arithmetic mean of the error is 2.3% and the standard deviation is 1.4. The largest gap between MMGP prediction and the real execution time occurs when the number of processes is larger than 10, (Figure 6 (b)). The reason is contention caused by context switching and MPI communication, when a large number of processes is multiplexed on 2 PPEs. Nevertheless, the maximum prediction error even in this case is close to 5%.

Figure 6 (c),(d), illustrates modeled and actual execution times when PBPI uses one dimension of SPE (APU) parallelism. Referring to Equation 11, we set $m = 1$ and vary p from 1 to 16. MMGP remains accurate, the mean prediction

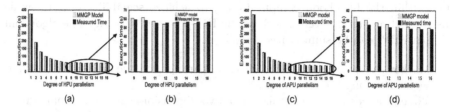

Fig. 6. MMGP predictions and actual execution times of PBPI, when the code uses one dimension of PPE-HPU, ((a), (b)), and SPE-APU ((c), (d)) parallelism

error is 4.1% and the standard deviation is 3.2. The maximum prediction error in this case is 10%. We measured the execution time necessary for solving Equation 11 for $T(m, p)$ to be 0.4μs. The overhead of the model is therefore negligible.

4.4 PBPI with Two Dimensions of Parallelism

Figure 7 shows the modeled and actual execution times of PBPI for all feasible combinations of two-dimensional parallelism under the constraint that the code does not use more than 16 SPEs, i.e. the maximum number of SPEs on the experimental platform. MMGP's mean prediction error is 3.2%, the standard deviation of the error is 2.6 and the maximum prediction error is 10%. The important observation in these results is that MMGP matches the experimental outcome in terms of the degrees of PPE and SPE parallelism to use in PBPI for maximizing performance. In a real program development scenario, MMGP would point the programmer in the direction of using two layers of parallelism with a balanced allocation of PPE contexts and SPEs between the two layers.

In principle, if the difference between the optimal and nearly optimal configurations of parallelism are within the margin of error of MMGP, MMGP may not predict the optimal configuration accurately. In the applications we tested, MMGP never mispredicts the optimal configuration. We also anticipate that due to high accuracy, potential MMGP mispredictions should generally lead to configurations that perform marginally lower than the actual optimal configuration.

4.5 RAxML Outline

RAxML uses an embarrassingly parallel master-worker algorithm, implemented with MPI. In RAxML, workers perform two tasks: (i) calculation of multiple inferences on the initial alignment in order to determine the best known Maximum Likelihood tree, and (ii) bootstrap analyses to determine how well supported are some parts of the Maximum Likelihood tree. From a computational point of view, inferences and bootstraps are identical. We use an optimized port of RAxML on Cell, described in further detail in [5].

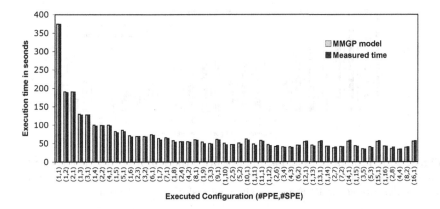

Fig. 7. MMGP predictions and actual execution times of PBPI, when the code uses two dimensions of SPE (APU) and PPE (HPU) parallelism. Performance is optimized with a layer of 4-way PPE parallelism and a nested layer of 4-way SPE parallelism.

4.6   RAxML with Two Dimensions of Parallelism

We compare the execution time of RAxML to the time modeled by MMGP, using a data set that contains 10 organisms, each represented by a DNA sequence of 50,000 nucleotides. We set RAxML to perform a total of 16 bootstraps using different parallel configurations. The MMGP parameters for RAxML, obtained from profiling a sequential run of the code are $T_{HPU} = 8.8s, T_{APU} = 118s, C_{APU} = 157s$. The values of other MMGP parameters are negligible compared to T_{APU}, T_{HPU}, and C_{APU}, therefore we disregard them for RAxML. We observe that a large portion of the off-loaded RAxML code cannot be parallelized across SPEs (C_{APU} - 57% of the total SPE time). Due to this limitation, RAxML does not scale with one-dimensional parallel configurations that use more than 8 SPEs. We omit the results comparing MMGP and measured time in RAxML with one dimension of parallelism due to space limitations. MMGP remains highly accurate when one dimension of parallelism is exploited in RAxML, with mean error rates of 3.4% for configurations with only PPE parallelism and 2% for configurations with only SPE parallelism.

Figure 8 shows the actual and modeled execution times in RAxML, when the code exposes two dimensions of parallelism to the system. Regardless of execution time prediction accuracy, MMGP is able to pin-point the optimal parallelization model thanks to the low prediction error. Performance is optimized in the case of RAxML with task-level parallelization and no further data-parallel decomposition of tasks between SPEs. There is very little opportunity for scalable data-level parallelization in RAxML. MMGP remains very accurate, with mean execution time prediction error of 2.8%, standard deviation of 1.9, and maximum prediction error of 7%.

Although the two codes tested are similar in their computational objective, their optimal parallelization model is at the opposite ends of the design spectrum.

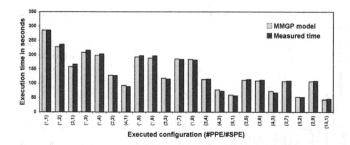

Fig. 8. MMGP predictions and actual execution times of RAxML, when the code uses two dimensions of SPE (APU) and PPE (HPU) parallelism. Performance is optimized by oversubscribing the PPE and maximizing task-level parallelism.

MMGP accurately reflects this disparity, using a small number of parameters and rapid prediction of execution times across a large number of feasible program configurations.

5   Related Work

Traditional parallel programming models, such as BSP [13], LogP [6], and derived models [14,15] developed to respond to changes in the relative impact of architectural components on the performance of parallel systems, are based on a minimal set of parameters, to capture the impact of communication overhead on computation running across a homogeneous collection of interconnected processors. MMGP borrows elements from LogP and its derivatives, to estimate performance of parallel computations on heterogeneous parallel systems with multiple dimensions of parallelism implemented in hardware. A variation of LogP, HLogP [7], considers heterogeneous clusters with variability in the computational power and interconnection network latencies and bandwidths between the nodes. Although HLogP is applicable to heterogeneous multi-core architectures, it does not consider nested parallelism. It should be noted that although MMGP has been evaluated on architectures with heterogeneous processors, it can also support architectures with heterogeneity in their communication substrates.

Several parallel programming models have been developed to support nested parallelism, including extensions of common parallel programming libraries such as MPI and OpenMP to support nested parallel constructs [16,17]. Prior work on languages and libraries for nested parallelism based on MPI and OpenMP is largely based on empirical observations on the relative speed of data communication via cache-coherent shared memory, versus communication with message passing through switching networks. Our work attempts to formalize these observations into a model which seeks optimal work allocation between layers of parallelism in the application and optimal mapping of these layers to heterogeneous parallel execution hardware.

Sharapov et. al [18] use a combination of queuing theory and cycle-accurate simulation of processors and interconnection networks, to predict the performance of hybrid parallel codes written in MPI/OpenMP on ccNUMA architectures. MMGP uses a simpler model, designed to estimate scalability along more than one dimensions of parallelism on heterogeneous parallel architectures.

6   Conclusions

The introduction of accelerator-based parallel architectures complicates the problem of mapping algorithms to systems, since parallelism can no longer be considered as a one-dimensional abstraction of processors and memory. We presented a new model of multi-dimensional parallel computation, MMGP, which we introduced to relieve users from the arduous task of mapping parallelism to accelerator-based architectures. We have demonstrated that the model is fairly accurate, albeit simple, and that it is extensible and easy to specialize for a given architecture. We envision three uses of MMGP: i) As a rapid prototyping tool for porting algorithms to accelerator-based architectures. ii) As a compiler tool for assisting compilers in deriving efficient mappings of programs to accelerator-based architectures automatically. iii) As a runtime tool for dynamic control of parallelism in applications. Extensions of MMGP which we will explore in future research include accurate modeling of non-overlapped communication and memory accesses, accurate modeling of SIMD and instruction-level parallelism within accelerators, integration of the model with runtime performance prediction and optimization techniques, and application of the model to emerging accelerator-based parallel systems.

Acknowledgments

This research is supported by the National Science Foundation (Grant CCF-0346867, CCF-0715051), the U.S. Department of Energy (Grants DE-FG02-05ER25689, DE-FG02-06ER25751), the Barcelona Supercomputing Center, and the College of Engineering at Virginia Tech.

References

1. IBM Corporation. Cell Broadband Engine Architecture, Version 1.01. Technical report, (October 2006)
2. Fahey, M., Alam, S., Dunigan, T., Vetter, J., Worley, P.: Early Evaluation of the Cray XD1. In: Proc. of the 2005 Cray Users Group Meeting (2005)
3. Starbridge Systems. A Reconfigurable Computing Model for Biological Research: Application of Smith-Waterman Analysis to Bacterial Genomes. Technical report (2005)
4. Chamberlain, R., Miller, S., White, J., Gall, D.: Highly-Scalable Recondigurable Computing. In: Proc. of the 2005 MAPLD International Conference, Washington, DC (September 2005)

5. Blagojevic, F., Nikolopoulos, D., Stamatakis, A., Antonopoulos, C.: Dynamic Multigrain Parallelization on the Cell Broadband Engine. In: Proc. of the 2007 ACM SIGPLAN Symposium on Principles and Practice of Parallel Programming, San Jose, CA, pp. 90–100 (March 2007)
6. Culler, D., Karp, R., Patterson, D., Sahay, A., Scauser, K., Santos, E., Subramonian, R., Von Eicken, T.: LogP: Towards a Realistic Model of Parallel Computation. In: PPoPP 1993. Proc. of the 4th ACM SIGPLAN Symposium on Principles and Practice of Parallel Programming (May 1993)
7. Bosque, J., Pastor, L.: A Parallel Computational Model for Heterogeneous Clusters. IEEE Transactions on Parallel and Distributed Systems 17(12), 1390–1400 (2006)
8. Girkar, M., Polychronopoulos, C.: The Hierarchical Task Graph as a Universal Intermediate Representation. International Journal of Parallel Programming 22(5), 519–551 (1994)
9. Gropp, W., Lusk, E.: Reproducible Measurements of MPI Performance Characteristics. In: Proc. of the 6th European PVM/MPI User's Group Meeting, Barcelona, Spain, pp. 11–18 (September 1999)
10. Feng, X., Cameron, K., Buell, D.: PBPI: a high performance Implementation of Bayesian Phylogenetic Inference. In: Proc. of Supercomputing 2006, Tampa, FL (November 2006)
11. Feng, X., Buell, D., Rose, J., Waddell, P.: Parallel algorithms for bayesian phylogenetic inference. Journal of Parallel Distributed Computing 63(7-8), 707–718 (2003)
12. Feng, X., Cameron, K., Smith, B., Sosa, C.: Building the Tree of Life on Terascale Systems. In: Proc. of the 21st International Parallel and Distributed Processing Symposium, Long Beach, CA (March 2007)
13. Valiant, L.: A bridging model for parallel computation. Communications of the ACM 22(8), 103–111 (1990)
14. Cameron, K., Sun, X.: Quantifying Locality Effect in Data Access Delay: Memory LogP. In: Proc. of the 17th International Parallel and Distributed Processing Symposium, Nice, France (April 2003)
15. Alexandrov, A., Ionescu, M., Schauser, C., Scheiman, C.: LogGP: Incorporating Long Messages into the LogP Model: One Step Closer towards a Realistic Model for Parallel Computation. In: Proc. of the 7th Annual ACM Symposium on Parallel Algorithms and Architectures, Santa Barbara, CA, pp. 95–105 (June 1995)
16. Cappello, F., Etiemble, D.: MPI vs. MPI+OpenMP on the IBM SP for the NAS Benchmarks. In: Reich, S., Anderson, K.M. (eds.) Open Hypermedia Systems and Structural Computing. LNCS, vol. 1903, Springer, Heidelberg (2000)
17. Krawezik, G.: Performance Comparison of MPI and three OpenMP Programming Styles on Shared Memory Multiprocessors. In: Proc. of the 15th Annual ACM Symposium on Parallel Algorithms and Architectures (2003)
18. Sharapov, I., Kroeger, R., Delamater, G., Cheveresan, R., Ramsay, M.: A Case Study in Top-Down Performance Estimation for a Large-Scale Parallel Application. In: Proc. of the 11th ACM SIGPLAN Symposium on Pronciples and Practice of Parallel Programming, New York, pp. 81–89 (March 2006)

Part IIa

Reconfigurable - ASIP

BRAM-LUT Tradeoff on a Polymorphic DES Design

Ricardo Chaves[1,2], Blagomir Donchev[2], Georgi Kuzmanov[2], Leonel Sousa[1],
and Stamatis Vassiliadis[2]

[1] Instituto Superior Técnico/INESC-ID. Rua Alves Redol 9, 1000-029 Lisbon, Portugal
http://sips.inesc-id.pt/
[2] Computer Engineering Lab, TUDelft. Postbus 5031, 2600 GA Delft,
The Netherlands
http://ce.et.tudelft.nl/

Abstract. A polymorphic implementation of the DES algorithm is presented.
The polymorphic approach allows for a very fast integration of the DES hardware
in existing software implementations, significantly reducing the time to marked
and the development costs associated with hardware integration. The tradeoff between implementing the DES SBOXs in LUT or in BRAMs is the focus of the
study presented in this paper. The FPGA implementation results suggest LUT
reduction in the order of 100 slices (approximately 37%) for the full DES core,
at the expense of 4 embedded memory blocks (BRAM). Even with this delay
increase, the usage of BRAMs allows for an improvement of the Throughput
per Slice ratio of 20%. The proposed computational structure has been implemented on a Xilinx VIRTEX II Pro (XC2VP30) prototyping device, requiring
approximately 2% of the device resources. Experimental results, at an operating
frequency of 100 MHz, suggest for the proposed polymorphic implementation a
throughput of 400 Mbit/s for DES and 133 for 3DES. When compared with the
software implementation of the DES algorithm, a speed up of 200 times can be
archived for the kernel computation.

1 Introduction

In present days, most of the communication systems requires secure data transfer in
order to maintain the privacy of the transmitted message; this message can be a simple
email or a billion euro transaction between banks. In order to maintain the security of
the communication channels, several encryption standards and algorithms exist, such
as public key ciphers, symmetric ciphers and hash functions. For ciphering the bulk
of data, symmetrical ciphering algorithms are used. Even though new emerging algorithms for symmetrical encryption have been appearing, the Data Encryption Standard
(DES) [1] is still widely used, especially in banking application and monetary transactions, due to backward compatibility and legacy issues. In 1998 [2] the DES algorithm
and its 54 bit key, have been deemed unsafe and replace by 3DES, which basically consists in performing the DES computation three times with three different keys, having
a 112 bits equivalent key. With the increase of embedded application requiring DES
(and 3DES), like RFID and bank cards, efficient hardware implementations of DES are
demanded. In this paper a polymorphic implementation of the DES algorithm is proposed. This approach allows the hardware implemented DES core to be invoked in the

P. Stenström et al. (Eds.): HiPEAC 2008, LNCS 4917, pp. 55–65, 2008.

same manner as has the equivalent software function, making its usage transparent to the software developer. This allows for a lower development cost and a much faster time to market. This paper also studies the advantages and disadvantages of using embedded memories for the implementation of the DES S-BOXs.

The FPGA implementation results suggest that a significant LUT reduction in the order of 100 slices (approximately 37%) for the full DES core, at the expense of 4 embedded memory blocks (BRAM). Even with this delay increase, the usage of BRAMs allows for an improvement of the Throughput per Slice ratio of 20%.

Experimental results for the polymorphic implementation, obtained from a prototype developed using a Xilinx VIRTEX II pro 30 prototyping FPGA, suggest:

- Speedups up to 200 times compared to the pure software implementations;
- Minimal software integration costs;
- Throughput of 400 Mbit/s for DES and 133 Mbits for 3DES, with 2% device usage.

The paper is organized as follows: Section 2 presents an overview on the DES algorithm. The implemented hardware structure is presented in section 3. Section 4 describes the proposed polymorphic DES organization and its usage in existing applications. Section 5 presents the obtained experimental results and compares them to related DES state-of-the-art. Section 6 concludes this paper with some final remarks.

2   DES Computation

Nowadays, the field of cryptography is growing up very intensively and many others algorithms are presented to meet the requirements of modern electronic systems. Since the time when the DES algorithm was introduce (in 1976), there are many devices and systems in which this algorithm is the bases into their security level. The high performance solutions are based on ASIC technologies and the reconfigurable ones are based on FPGA technologies. In both of the cases for each new solution is necessary to keep the compatibility with devices which are already available on the market. In our paper, an implementation of DES algorithm as a part of dynamic reconfigurable system based on FPGA technology is presented.

In DES, 64 bit data blocks are encrypted using a 54 bit Key (obtained from an input key with 64 bits). The intermediate ciphered values are processed as two 32-bit words (L_i and R_i), which are manipulated in 16 identical rounds as depicted in Figure 1. This manipulation consists of substitution, permutation, and bitwise XOR operation, over the 64-bit data block. The DES algorithm also has an Initial bit Permutation (IP) at the beginning of a block ciphering. To conclude the ciphering of a block, a final permutation is performed, which corresponds to the inverse of the initial permutation (IP^{-1}). The main computation is performed in 16 round designated by Feistel network, named after cryptographer Horst Feistel. In each round a different sub-key is used, generated form the main key expansion. The round computation or Feistel network is depicted in Figure 2.

The Feistel network is composed be the 3 main operation in symmetrical ciphering, namely key addition, confusion, and diffusion [3]. The first half of the round block is expanded from 32 to 48 bits and added to the 48-bits of the current sub-key. While the

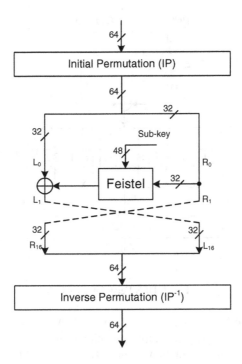

Fig. 1. DES computation

data expansion can be hardwired in the computation logic, the key addition requires XOR gates for the computation. The Key addition operation is followed by the confusion operation, performed by SBOXs. In this operation the value resulting from the addition is grouped in 8 blocks of 6 bits each. Each 6 bits are replaced by a different set of 8 groups of 4 bits, resulting in 32 different bits. The diffusion operation is performed by a final permutation. After the 16 rounds have been computed, a final permutation (IP^{-1}) is performed over the 64 bit data block.

The DES computational structure has the advantage that the decryption computation is identical to the encryption computation, only requiring the reversal of the key schedule.

3   Proposed DES Structure

As depicted in Figures 1 and 2 the core computation of DES can be summed up to XOR operations, the SBOXs, permutations and word expansions. Since the permutations and expansions can be performed by routing, only the XORs, SBOXs, and some glue logic require computational logic. In order to create a compact DES computational core, a fully folded design has been implemented. In each clock cycle one round of the DES 16 rounds are computed, thus 16 clock cycles are required to compute a 64-bit data block. The used structure is presented in Figure 3. In this folded design some additional logic is required for multiplexing and additional round control.

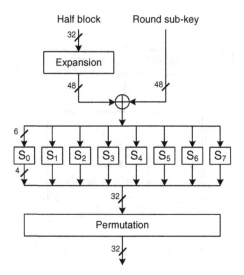

Fig. 2. DES Feistel network

Given that, this DES core is to be used on a FPGA device, two major computational structures can chosen for the implementation of the SBOXs. The first and most commonly used is the implementation of the SBOX using the FPGA Look Up Tables (LUT). In this approach distributed memory blocks are created for each of the 32 bits of the word resulting from the SBOXs. Since most of the used Xilinx FPGAs have 4 input LUTs, the 6 bit SBOX requires at least 2 LUTs for each output bit. From this, it can be estimated that at least 64 LUT are required having a critical path of at least 2 LUTs, as depicted in Figure 4.

Taking into account that current FPGAs have embedded memory blocks (BRAMs), an alternative implementation of the SBOXs can be used. These BRAMs can be used as

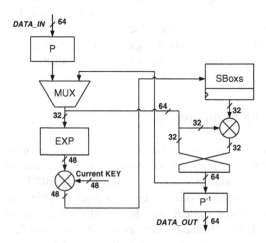

Fig. 3. DES computational structure

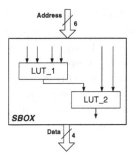

Fig. 4. LUT based SBOXs

ROM blocks, to implement a full SBOX table. Since these BRAMs have output ports with at leat 4 bits, one BRAM can be used to replace at leat $2 \times 4 = 8$ LUTs. Moreover, modern FPGAs have embedded dual port BRAMs with more that $(2 \times 2^6 =)$ 128 words, thus, two SBOXs can be computed in each BRAM, as depicted in Figure 5. With this,

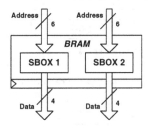

Fig. 5. BRAM based SBOXs

only 4 BRAMs need to be used, instead of at least 64 LUTs. Due to the fact that existing BRAMs have registered output ports the round register must be located at the end of the SBOXs, limiting the options of the designer where to place the round registers.

In the DES algorithm the encryption and decryption of data differs only in the order in which the key expansion is performed. The key expansion consists of fixed permutations and rotate operations. While the permutation operations can be performed by routing, the rotation requires dedicated hardware. The rotation can be of 1 or 2 positions and, depending on the operation (encryption or decryption), to the left or to the right. The implemented structure is depicted in Figure 6.

In order to simplify the computational structure and the key expansion, only the DES algorithm is performed in hardware. To compute the 3DES algorithm, the DES hardware is called 3 times with the 3 different keys, thus performing the 3DES calculation.

4 Polymorphic Implementation

In order to efficiently use the DES core with a low development cost to the programmer, the MOLEN [4,5] computational paradigm is used. The MOLEN paradigm is based on the coprocessor architectural paradigm, allowing the usage of reconfigurable custom designed hardware units. In this computational approach, the non critical part of the software code is executed on a General Purpose Processor (GPP), while the main DES algorithm, is executed on the Custom Computing Unit (CCU). The DES core is seen by the programmer in the same manner as a software implemented function. The decision where the function is executed is made at compile time. At microarchitectural level the arbiter, depicted in Figure 7, redirects each instruction either to the GPP (a PowerPC in our case) or to the cryptographic units.

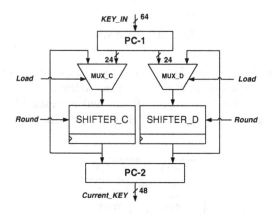

Fig. 6. DES key expansion

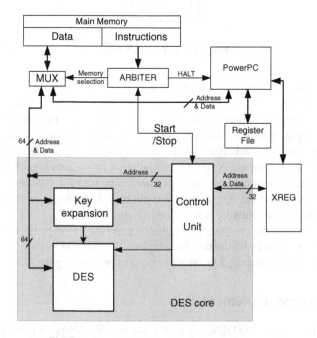

Fig. 7. Polymorphic processor internal structure

In a software function, the parameter passing is done through the stack. In the Molen processor, when a hardware function is invoked the parameters are passed through a dedicated register bank, designated by eXchange REGisters (XREG).

Given that the dedicated computational units are also connected to the main data memory, only initialization parameters are passed to the DES computational unit via the XREG. These parameter are the private key, memory pointers to the data to be ciphered, and the operation modes, e.g. encrypt or decrypt. The data to be processed is directly retrieved and send to the main data memory, via a shared memory mechanism.

In order to illustrate the data flow, the encryption operation for a 64 bit data block is described. When the DES cipher function is called, a few software instructions are executed, namely instructions that move the function parameters from the GPP internal registers to the XREG, followed by an execute instruction. When an execute instruction is detected by the arbiter, the later starts addressing the microcode memory, giving control of the data memory to the DES core, and signals it to start the computation via the *start* signal depicted in Figure 7.

Once the DES core receives the *start* signal, it starts retrieving the values from the XREG. The first value read is the operation mode, which indicates which operation will be performed. Continuously, the start and end memory addresses for the data to cipher are retrieved from the XREG. While the first data block is read from the memory, the key is read from the XREG and stored in the DES internal registers. After this initialization phase, the DES core enters a loop where, while the data is being ciphered, the next 64-bit data block is read from the memory. In the end of each loop, the ciphered data is written back into the data memory. When the current memory address coincides with the data end address, the computation loop is broken and the *stop* signal is sent to the arbiter. Upon receiving this stop signal, the arbiter returns the memory control to the GPP.

To indicate which function performs the DES encryption computed in hardware, a pragma annotation is used in the C code, as depicted in Figure 8.

```
#pragma DES
DES (key, &data[0], &data[end], mode){
    \* implemented in HW *\
}
```

Fig. 8. Usage of the pragma notation

This pragma annotation is recognized by the compiler which automatically generates the required instructions sequence [4]. This pragma addition and recompilation are the only operation required to use the hardware implemented DES, instead of the software implemented version. With this mechanism, any application using DES or 3DES can be accelerated by the DES core, with a reduced time market and a very low development cost.

5   Performance Analysis

To evaluate the advantages and disadvantages of using BRAMs on DES computational structures and the polymorphic DES implementation, a Xilinx VIRTEX II Pro 30 prototyping FPGA device has been used. The FPGAs embedded PowerPC is used as the core GPP [4].The PowerPC is running at 300 MHz, with a main data memory running at 100 MHz. The DES co-processor runs at the same frequency as the data memory, 100 MHz.

In Table 1, the two implemented DES computational structures, with and without BRAMs, are compared. In this table related DES stand-alone art is also presented. Note that these figures are for the DES kernel computation only.

Table 1. Stand-alone DES performances

	Our-BRAM	Our-LUT	Wee [6]	Rouv [7]	Our-BRAM	Our-LUT	CAST [8]	Our-BRAM	Our-LUT
Device	V1000E	V1000E	V2-4	V2-5	V2-5	V2-5	V2P2-7	V2P30-7	V2P30-7
Freq. (MHz)	81	138	179	274	152	202	261	218	287
Slices	174	277	382	**189**	**175**	**278**	**255**	**175**	**278**
BRAMs	4	0	0	0	4	0	0	4	0
Thrput (Mb/s)	354	551	716	974	609	808	1044	872	1148
Latency	16	16	16	18	16	16	16	16	16
TP/S	2.03	1.99	1.87	5.15	3.48	2.91	**4.09**	**4.98**	**4.13**

From the implementation results of Our DES core with and without BRAMs on the VIRTEX-2 and VIRTEX-2 Pro FPGA technologies it can be concluded that a significant reduction on the required slices (37%), at the expense of 4 BRAMs, can be achieved. However, as a consequence, the critical path increases about 32%. This delay increase is due to the fact that a BRAM has a critical path equivalent to about 3 Look Up Tables (LUT), and the critical path of a LUT implemented SBOX is of 2 LUTs. Nonetheless, an improvement of 20% to the Throughput per Slice (TP/S) efficiency metric can be achieved. In these technologies and for the BRAM based structures, the slice occupation (2%) is the same as the BRAM usage (2%), thus an adequate utilization of the available resources in the device is achieved. In older technologies, where BRAMs are not so fast, like the VIRTEX-E, the penalty on the delay is higher. In this case, practically no improvement to the TP/S is achieved (only 2%).

When compared with related art, that use the unmodified DES algorithm structure, the proposed core has an equivalent Throughput per Slice as the commercial core from CAST, when compared with the proposed LUT based DES structure. The TP/S metric improves to 22% when compared with the BRAM based DES structure. When compared with [6] a TP/S metric improvement of 86% and 57% is achieved for the proposed structure with and without BRAMs, respectively.

In [7], the authors propose a modification to the DES computational algorithm, which allows for the efficient use of a pipeline computation, resulting in a very efficient computational structure. This improvement comes at the expense of a higher latency and a potentially lower resistance to side-channel attacks, since the same key is added at two locations, instead of one [9, 10]. This algorithmic alteration also makes the usage of side-channel defences more difficult [11, 12]. Nevertheless, when no side-channel concerns exist, this structure is quite advantageous.

Taking into account that, the computational block used to perform the SBOXs operation is exactly the same in both papers; the same tradeoff between LUTs and BRAMs can still be applied to the design proposed in [7]. As a result, the 64 slices [7] required for the SBOXs can be replaced by 4 BRAMs, further improving the Throughput per Slice efficiency metric, as suggested by the results in Table 1. In the proposed usage of the DES core, as a polymorphic processor, the operating frequency is constituted by the memory not by the core itself. This means that the higher latency and pipeline depth makes the proposed structure [7] less advantageous.

For the experimental results a VIRTEX-2 Pro FPGA on a Xilinx University Program (XUPV2P) board. The comparative results for a pure software implementation and for the polymorphic usage are presented in Table 2. This table also presents the speedup

Table 2. DES polymorphic performances

Bits	Hardware ThrPut	Software ThrPut	Kernel SpeedUp
64	89 Mbit/s	0.92 Mbit/s	97
128	145 Mbit/s	1.25 Mbit/s	116
4k	381 Mbit/s	1.92 Mbit/s	198
64k	399 Mbit/s	1.95 Mbit/s	205

achieved for the kernel computation of the DES algorithm. In these results, a difference in the ciphering throughput can be seen, for different block sizes. This is due to the initialization cost of the of DES CCU, which includes the loading of the key and the transfer of the data addresses from the XREG to the DES core. This initialization overhead becomes less significant as the amount of data to be ciphered increases, becoming negligible for data blocks above 4 kbits. A speedup of 200x can be attained, achieving a ciphering throughput of 399 Mbit/s, working at the memory frequency of 100 Mbit/s.

Table 3 presents the figures for the proposed polymorphic DES core and for related art, using DES hardware acceleration. It can be seen that the proposed DES processor is able to outperform the related art in terms of throughput by 30% with less than 40% FPGA usage. This results in a Throughput per Slice improvement of 117%. Another advantage of this polymorphic computational approach is the capability to easily integrate existing software application in this embedded system, since existing applications just have to be recompiled, in order to used the dedicated DES hardware, as depicted in Figure 8.

Table 3. DES processors

	Chodo [13]	Our-LUT	Our-BRAM
Device	V1000	V1000E	V2P30-7
Freq. (MHz)	57	100	100
FPGA usage	5%	3%	2%
DES (Mbit/s)	306	399	399
3DES (Mbit/s)	102	133	133

6 Conclusions

In this paper, a hybrid hardware/software implementation of the DES algorithm was presented, using a polymorphic computational paradigm. The tradeoffs of using BRAMs to implement the DES SBOXs are also studied in this paper. Implementation results suggest that the Throughput per Slice metric can be improved by 20% with the use of BRAMs. The use of the BRAM implies a decrease on the maximum frequency, compensated by a significant reduction on amount of required slices. Implementation results suggest that for the complete DES core, the employed polymorphic paradigm and the tightly coupled organization between the General Purpose Processor (GPP) and the dedicated DES core, allow for a short development cycle and substantial performance improvement. Given that the DES core can directly access the main data memory and the usage of the exchange register to transfer the initialization parameters, the hardware implemented DES algorithm can be invoked in the same manner as the software implemented function. The parameter passing via the exchange register is performed by the compiler, thus making the usage of the DES core transparent for the programmer. Experimental results of the proposed processor on a VIRTEX II Pro FPGA, indicate that for data blocks of larger that 4 kbits a speedup of 200x for the DES algorithm can be attained, achieving a throughput of 400 Mbit/s for DES and 133 Mbit/s for 3DES. This performance improvement is achieved with a significantly low cost in terms of reconfigurable area, approximately 2% of the used device (328 slices and 4 BRAMS), and with a minimal development cost, since the integration of the dedicated hardware is performed by the compiler. In conclusion, with this polymorphic implementation of the DES algorithm, existing software application that demand high ciphering rates can be embedded with DES hardware implementations with a low development cost and without large reconfigurable resources.

Evaluation Prototype

An evaluation prototype for the XUP prototyping board of the hybrid DES processor is available for download at http://ce.et.tudelft.nl/MOLEN/applications/DES

Acknowledgments

This work has been partially supported by the Portuguese FCT–Fundacão para a Ciência e Tecnologia, the Dutch Technology Foundation STW, applied science division of NWO and the Technology Program of the Dutch Ministry of Economic Affairs (project DCS. 7533).

References

1. NIST, Data encryption standard (DES), FIPS 46-2 ed, tech. rep., National Institute of Standards and Technology (December 1993)
2. NIST, Data encryption standard (DES), FIPS 46-3 ed, tech. rep., National Institute of Standards and Technology (1998)

3. Shannon, C.E.: Communication theory of secrecy systems. Bell Systen Technicl Journal 28, 656–715 (1949)
4. Vassiliadis, S., Wong, S., Gaydadjiev, G.N., Bertels, K., Kuzmanov, G., Panainte, E.M.: The Molen polymorphic processor. In: IEEE Transactions on Computers, pp. 1363–1375 (November 2004)
5. Vassiliadis, S., Wong, S., Cotofana, S.D.: The Molen $\rho\mu$-coded Processor. In: Brebner, G., Woods, R. (eds.) FPL 2001. LNCS, vol. 2147, pp. 275–285. Springer, Heidelberg (2001)
6. Wee, C.M., Sutton, P.R., Bergmann, N.W.: An FPGA network architecture for accelerating 3DES –CBC. In: International Conference on Field Programmable Logic and Applications, pp. 654–657 (August 2005)
7. Rouvroy, G., Standaert, F.-X., Quisquater, J.-J., Legat, J.-D.: Design strategies and modified descriptions to optimize cipher FPGA implementations: fast and compact results for DES and triple-DES. In: FPGA 2003: Proceedings of the 2003 ACM/SIGDA eleventh international symposium on Field programmable gate arrays, pp. 247–247. ACM Press, New York (2003)
8. CAST, DES Cryptoprocessor Core – XILINX FPGA Results, http://www.cast-inc.com/ (2007)
9. Kocher, P., Jaffe, J., Jun, B.: Introduction to differential power analysis and related attacks, http://www.cryptography.com/dpa/technical (1998)
10. Akkar, M.-L., Goubin, L.: A generic protection against high-order differential power analysis. In: Johansson, T. (ed.) FSE 2003. LNCS, vol. 2887, pp. 192–205. Springer, Heidelberg (2003)
11. Goubin, L., Patarin, J.: DES and differential power analysis (the "duplication" method). In: Koç, Ç.K., Paar, C. (eds.) CHES 1999. LNCS, vol. 1717, pp. 158–172. Springer, Heidelberg (1999)
12. Akkar, M.-L., Giraud, C.: An implementation of DES and AES, secure against some attacks. In: Koç, Ç.K., Naccache, D., Paar, C. (eds.) CHES 2001. LNCS, vol. 2162, pp. 309–318. Springer, Heidelberg (2001)
13. Chodowiec, P., Gaj, K., Bellows, P., Schott, B.: Experimental testing of the gigabit IPSec-compliant implementations of rijndael and triple DES using SLAAC-1V FPGA accelerator board. In: Davida, G.I., Frankel, Y. (eds.) ISC 2001. LNCS, vol. 2200, pp. 220–234. Springer, Heidelberg (2001)

Architecture Enhancements for the ADRES Coarse-Grained Reconfigurable Array

Frank Bouwens[1,2], Mladen Berekovic[1,2], Bjorn De Sutter[1],
and Georgi Gaydadjiev[2]

[1] IMEC vzw, DESICS
Kapeldreef 75, B-3001 Leuven, Belgium
{bouwens,berekovic,desutter}@imec.be
[2] Delft University of Technology, Computer Engineering
Mekelweg 4, 2628 CD, Delft, The Netherlands
g.n.gaydadjiev@its.tudelft.nl

Abstract. Reconfigurable architectures provide power efficiency, flexibility and high performance for next generation embedded multimedia devices. ADRES, the IMEC Coarse-Grained Reconfigurable Array architecture and its compiler DRESC enable the design of reconfigurable 2D array processors with arbitrary functional units, register file organizations and interconnection topologies. This creates an enormous design space making it difficult to find optimized architectures. Therefore, architectural explorations aiming at energy and performance trade-offs become a major effort. In this paper we investigate the influence of register file partitions, register file sizes and the interconnection topology of ADRES. We analyze power, performance and energy delay trade-offs using IDCT and FFT as benchmarks while targeting 90nm technology. We also explore quantitatively the influences of several hierarchical optimizations for power by applying specific hardware techniques, i.e. clock gating and operand isolation. As a result, we propose an enhanced architecture instantiation that improves performance by 60 - 70% and reduces energy by 50%.

1 Introduction

Power and performance requirements for next generation multi-media mobile devices are becoming more relevant. The search for high performance, low power solutions focuses on novel architectures that provide multi-program execution with minimum non-recurring engineering costs and short time-to-market. IMEC's coarse-grained reconfigurable architecture (CGRA) called *Architecture for Dynamically Reconfigurable Embedded Systems* (ADRES) [1] is expected to deliver superior energy eficiency of 60MOPS/mW based on 90nm technology.

Several CGRAs are proposed in the past and applied in a variety of fields. The KressArray [2] has a flexible architecture and is ideal for pure dataflow organizations. SiliconHive [3] provides an automated flow to create reconfigurable architectures. Their architectures can switch between *standard DSP mode* and *pure dataflow*. The DSP mode fetches several instructions in parallel, which requires a wide program memory. In pure dataflow mode these instructions are executed in a single cycle. PACT XPP [4]

P. Stenström et al. (Eds.): HiPEAC 2008, LNCS 4917, pp. 66–81, 2008.

is a commercial reconfigurable architecture designed for multi-media and telecommunication applications. The architecture is fixed to 64 ALUs, which means the kernel mapping is constrained by these ALUs. MorphoSys [5] is a typical CGRA consisting of 8x8 basic units split-up into 4 tiles of 4x4 reconfigurable cells. Each cell in a tile is connected to all cells in the same row and column. There are also connections between the different tiles. The array speeds up the kernel, while a TinyRISC is utilized for the control section of the code. A more extensive overview of CGRAs is provided by Hartenstein in [6].

The ADRES template enables the designer to configure the architecture based on a variable number of functional units, register files and interconnections allowing advanced power and performance optimizations. Finding the optimal architecture for the customizable processor is not trivial task as there is a huge space of possible design points. Architectural explorations are mandatory to empirically find the architecture that best balances power, performance and cost characteristics.

Previous architectural explorations of ADRES were performed [7], [8] to find an optimal interconnection scheme for a good performance and power ratio. The architecture template obtained in [8] will function as the starting point of this work. This base template consists of a 4x4 array of FUs and local data register files. All these components are vertically, horizontally and diagonally interconnected.

The architecture in [8] showed the importance of not only interconnections, but also the register files of the coarse-grained array (CGA) of ADRES as these have a significant influence on power and performance. Kwok et al. [9] performed initial analysis of architectural explorations for the register file (RF) sizes and under utilization of the CGA, which motivated the drastic RF size reduction. As the DRESC CGA compiler and ADRES architectural template evolved the CGA utilization improved considerably making Kwok's results outdated for the latest compiler version (DRESC2.x).

This paper elaborates on the results of [8] on the interconnect and component level optimizations as the data sharing among functional units and register files can be improved significantly. We show the relevance of explorations to derive an efficient design for two widely used wireless and multi-media kernels (FFT and IDCT). We also show the fallacy that a system with distributed, fully interconnected register files is the best in terms of energy-delay. Our ADRES architectural proposal is modified by decreasing the sizes of the local register files.

The main contributions of this paper are:

- Careful architectural exploration of the register file distribution, interconnection topology and register file sizes for the CGRA;
- Empirical study of power, performance and energy-delay of all proposed intermediate and the final architectures;
- Quantitative evaluation of specific optimizations such as clock gating, operand isolation and pipelining;
- Determination of an energy optimized architecture for IDCT and FFT;
- Array size modifications of the proposed architecture for energy-delay analysis.

This paper is organized as follows. Section 2 briefly describes the ADRES architecture and the programming model. Section 3 presents the utilized tool flow during the explorations. Three different optimizations are described and benchmarked in Section 4 to select the final architecture based on power and energy-delay results. Section 5 presents the intermediate and final implemented results of the created architecture instances. The conclusions section finalizes this paper.

2   ADRES Base Architecture and Programming Model

The ADRES architecture based on its template [1] is a tightly-coupled architecture that can operate in either VLIW or CGA mode. Figure 1 shows the selected 4x4 ADRES base architecture of [8] including data and instruction memories. When the architecture is operating in VLIW mode the performance is improved due to instruction level parallelism. In CGA mode performance is improved by parallelizing loops on the array (loop level parallelism). ADRES based systems are programmed in ANSI-C language. Any existing ANSI-C program can be modified to suit the ADRESS CGA by modifying the if-conversions and removing all nested loops as described in [1]. No additional instructions in the source code are needed for the compiler to map the loops to the CGA. Code that could not be mapped on the array is executed on the VLIW relying only on instruction level parallelism.

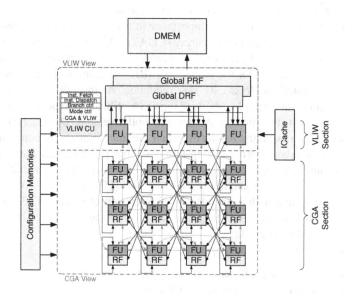

Fig. 1. ADRES Instance example

The VLIW control unit (CU) controls the program counter (PC) and is responsible for fetching instructions from the instruction cache. The switch between VLIW and CGA modes is directed by the same VLIW CU by fetching a CGA instruction in VLIW mode. The configuration memories (CM) are addressed by a control unit and provide instructions and routing data for the entire array during CGA operation.

Communication between the two modes goes via the multi-port global Data Register File (DRF) or data memory (DMEM). The VLIW functional units (FU) communicate through the global DRF with eachother. The CGA FUs communicate through the global DRF, local data and predicate register files (PRF) and the dedicated interconnections. The predicate register files or busses handle branches, loop prologue and epilogue for proper control flow.

The VLIW section of the base architecture has a four instructions issue width, while the CGA section has an issue width of 4 by 3 (12) instructions. The template consists of mesh, mesh plus and diagonal interconnections [8] between FUs and local DRFs. This resulted in good routing capabilities in the array, but can be improved as researched in this paper.

3   Tool Flow

The tool flow used in this architecture exploration study is the same as used in [8]. It provides the necessary results in terms of performance, power and energy usage. A simplified representation of this flow is depicted in Figure 2.

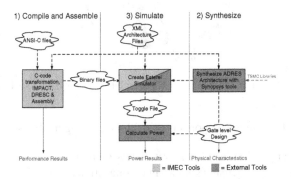

Fig. 2. Simple representation of Tool Flow

All three steps in the figure (Compile and Assemble, Synthesize and Simulate) use the same ADRES XML architecture file as input. The first step, *Compile and Assemble*, maps ANSI-C code on either the CGA or the VLIW architecture views. This step generates the program binary files needed for the HDL simulation stage, but also provides the number of instructions and cycles. The latter are used to calculate performance using high-level simulations of the applications on a given architectural instance.

The second step, *Synthesize*, translates the XML file into a top-level VHDL file and synthesizes the architecture using 90nm TSMC libraries. Physical characteristics are obtained from the gate-level architecture with 90nm, regular-Vt (1V, 25°C) general purpose libraries. The final architecture is also placed and routed to obtain the circuit layout.

The third step, *Simulation*, utilizes either the enhanced Esterel [10] or the ModelSim v6.0a simulator for HDL verification and analysis. The Esterel simulator provides faster results compared to ModelSim without significant loss of accuracy [8]. Annotating the captured switching activity of the HDL simulations onto the gate-level design results in power figures.

4   Architectural Explorations

The architecture explorations in the following sections start from the base architecture presented in Figure 1 that was analyzed for energy efficiency in [8]. The power distribution of the base architecture for IDCT are depicted in Figure 3. The components with the highest consumption (primary targets for improvement) are the configuration memories (CMs: 37.22%), the FUs (19.94%) and the DRFs (14.80%) of the CGA.

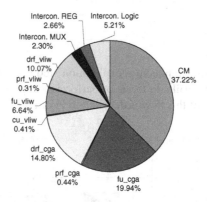

Fig. 3. Power distribution of our base architecture for IDCT: 80.45mW

We optimize these three components using the following methods:

CM: Create an array with less configuration bits by reducing the number of architecture components or by using simpler interconnections;

FU_CGA: Improve the FU design from non-pipelined to pipelined (VHDL modifications) and optimize the routing of the CGA array (XML architecture description update);

DRF_CGA: Reduce the register file sizes, apply clock gating and use register file sharing.

Sharing data between the FUs and the local DRFs and PRFs is important for the power consumption and performance of the architecture as these influence the CMs, FUs and the local DRFs in power and performance. Therefore we will focus the explorations on routing and the register files. We only utilize IDCT and FFT kernels for architecture explorations due to the fact that simulating complete applications such as MPEG2 would result in prohibitively long simulation times. We will perform the following experiments for the explorations:

Local DRF distribution: Determine the influences of the RFs in the array by exploring the distribution of the local data register files;

Interconnection Topology: Determine the influence of additional interconnections. More interconnections improve routing, but increases the power consumption and vice-versa;

Register File Size Reduction: Determine what is the minimum size of the local DRFs and PRFs. This results in local register file size optimally fitting the array increasing the performance vs. power ratio.

Our exploration and comparison starts from the result architecture obtained in [8] and shown in Figure 1. All explored architectures have a CGA dimension of 4x4, 32-bit data bus and are non-pipelined. Pipelining of the FUs is of little relevance for our study as the performance vs. power ratio remains constant. However, pipelining will be applied to the selected architecture in Section 5 and analyzed with different array sizes. Furthermore, the VLIW DRF and PRF have 64 words of which 14 are rotating for the DRF and 32 for the PRF. The local DRFs and PRFs have 16 words created as rotating register files. The configuration memories have 128 words and vary in width depending on the CGA organization.

4.1 Distributing Local Data Register Files

This section investigates the influence of the local DRFs and PRFs on power and performance for the array. This study is based on a fixed mesh plus interconnection topology between the FUs with vertical and horizontal connections [8]. Among the FUs we explore variable register file distributions proposed in [11] which are also depicted in Figure 4. There are eight FUs with multiplication and four FUs with memory LD/ST capabilities.

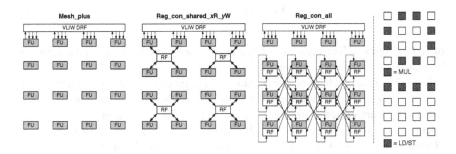

Fig. 4. Distribution of the Local DRFs

The three different architectures have a local PRF for each FU that can be replaced by predicated busses (noted with suffix _pd in Table 1). The capability of storing and later processing is not possible with the busses that is a potential performance bottleneck.

The simplest architecture *mesh_plus* does not have local DRFs and completely rely on the available data busses for all data transfers. Only the first row of FUs is connected to the global DRF. The architecture *reg_con_shared_xR_yW* shares its inputs and outputs of the RFs to decrease the area of the RFs and share data more efficiently. For the shared RF architecture we investigate the influence of the number of ports for the local RFs. More precisely we simulated instances with 2, 4 and 8 read ports. The most complex architecture *reg_con_all* has a DRF for each FU in the array and is similar to the one

Table 1. Distributed DRFs Names

Original	Renamed	Original	Renamed
4x4_mesh_plus	arch_1	4x4_mesh_plus_pred_bus	arch_1_pb
4x4_reg_con_shared_2R_1W	arch_2	4x4_reg_con_shared_2R_1W_pred_bus	arch_2_pb
4x4_reg_con_shared_4R_2W	arch_3	4x4_reg_con_shared_4R_2W_pred_bus	arch_3_pb
4x4_reg_con_shared_8R_4W	arch_4	4x4_reg_con_shared_8R_4W_pred_bus	arch_4_pb
4x4_reg_con_all	arch_5	4x4_reg_con_all_pred_bus	arch_5_pb

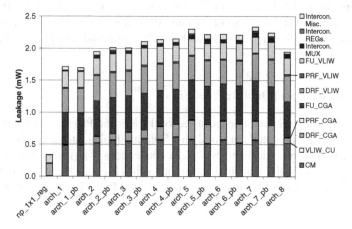

Fig. 5. Leakage Power

depicted in Figure 1. The created architectures are noted in Table 1 and the names are abbreviated for ease of explanation.

All results presented here and in Section 4.2 are placed together in Figures 5 and 7 - 10. The leakage results are depicted in Figure 5 and the power results at 100MHz of IDCT and FFT are presented in Figures 7 and 8, respectively. The energy-delay results are depicted in Figures 9 and 10. We will discuss the results presented here first.

Removing the local DRFs in the first two architectures (arch_1 and arch_1_pb) result in a low energy consumption, but decreased performance as depicted in Figures 9 and 10. This indicates the DRFs are beneficial during CGA operation. Replacing the PRFs with a bus increases energy consumption by (FFT: 10 - 46%, IDCT: 5 - 37%) except for arch_5. This experiment shows that storing predicate results of previous operations in local PRFs is essential for overall power consumption in cases with few local DRFs or no DRF at all.

The experiment in this section showed that register file sharing creates additional routing for the DRESC compiler that improves scheduling density of the array. Interconnection complexity is reduced requiring less configuration bits, hence decreasing the size of the configuration memories. Replacing four RFs with only one reduced leakage and IDCT/FFT power consumption of the local DRFs. Local RFs with 1 write and 2 read ports in arch_2 outperforms in terms of power and energy-delay the fully distributed RFs architecture arch_5 for both, FFT and IDCT, kernels.

4.2   Interconnection Topology

This section explores the impact of additional interconnections on power and performance. This enhancement has a fixed *reg_con_all* RF distribution similar to the base architecture in [8]. The three different interconnection topologies are depicted in Figure 6. The resources and LD/ST units are distributed in the same way as in Figure 4.

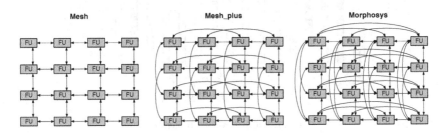

Fig. 6. Interconnection Topologies

We apply the same methodology as in Section 4.1 by replacing the local PRFs with busses. The different architectures explored are listed in Table 2 and their results are merged with the results of Section 4.1 and depicted in Figures 5 to 10. Combining the Mesh_plus architecture with the reg_con_all base architecture in Figure 6 would result in *arch_5* in Table 1, hence it is omitted in Table 2. The Morphosys interconnection is based on the Morphosys architecture [5] that fully interconnects the array in both row and column directions. The final *arch_8* architecture will be explained at the end of this section.

By considering only the architectures noted in Table 2 we notice that additional interconnections in the base architecture are beneficial for energy-delay [9]. This is especially noticeable with the Morphosys architecture (*arch_7*). Figures 7 and 8 show that replacing the local PRFs by predicate busses decreases the overall power and energy consumption. Although the architecture *arch_5* is better than *arch_7_pb* in both power and energy, the additional Morphosys connection would be useful for larger arrays e.g. 8x8 and more. Therefore, we selected the *arch_7_pb* as the best fit for IDCT and FFT.

When the results of Sections 4.1 and 4.2 are combined, the *arch_8* architecture with shared DRFs, Morphosys connections and local PRFs is created as depicted in Figure 11. The predicate busses are omitted as they showed not to improve power and performance of the architecture with shared register files. Figure 9 and 10 show *arch_2* is energy and delay appropriately, however it lacks the Morphosys interconnection that

Table 2. Interconnection Topologies Names

Original	Renamed	Original	Renamed
4x4_reg_con_all_mesh	arch_6	4x4_reg_con_all_mesh_pred_bus	arch_6_pb
4x4_reg_con_all_morphosys	arch_7	4x4_reg_con_all_morphosys_pred_bus	arch_7_pb
4x4_reg_con_shared_2R_1W_morphosys	arch_8		

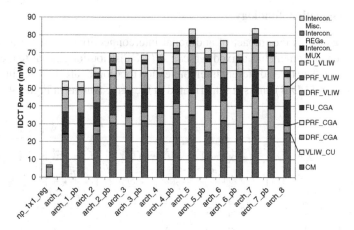

Fig. 7. IDCT Power @ 100MHz

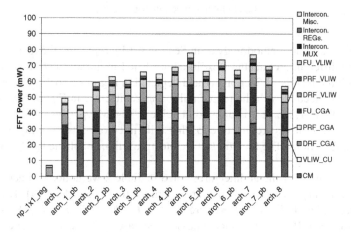

Fig. 8. FFT Power @ 100MHz

is beneficial for larger arrays. Table 3 notes the improvements of *arch_8* over the base architecture in Figure 1. The results clearly show an improvement in performance (MIPS/mW) of 14 - 16%. Power consumption was decreased by 22%, however, energy improved only by 1.6% as additional execution cycles are required for the applications due to the reduced local DRFs and PRFs sizes. Minimizing the number of local DRFs has a beneficial effect on area resulting in 14.4% reduce. We select the *arch_8* architecture for further optimizations and explorations.

4.3   Register File Size Modification

In this section we evaluate the selected architecture *arch_8* of Section 4.2 with variable local DRF and PRF sizes to improve power while maintaining performance of the architecture for kernels considered here. The global DRF and PRF can not modified and

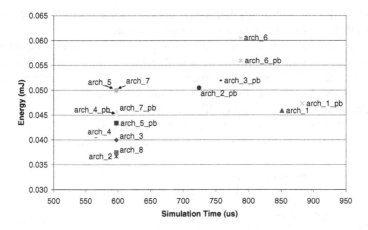

Fig. 9. IDCT Energy-Delay @ 100MHz

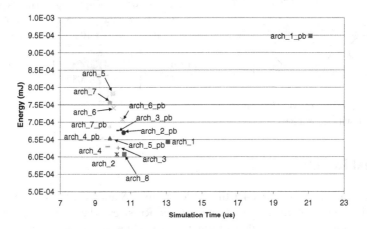

Fig. 10. FFT Energy-Delay @ 100MHz

Table 3. Base vs. arch_8 for IDCT & FFT @ 100MHz

Benchmark	MIPS/mW	mW/MHz	Power (mW)	Energy (uJ)	Area mm^2
IDCT					
base	17.51	0.81	80.45	37.72	1.59
arch_8	20.00	0.63	62.68	37.46	1.36
Improvement	14.22%	22%	22%	0.6%	14.4%
FFT					
base	9.40	0.72	73.28	0.62	
arch_8	10.95	0.57	57.05	0.61	
Improvement	16.5%	20.8%	22.1%	1.6%	

fixed at 64 words. The global DRF has 8 read and 4 write ports, which are 32-bits wide. The global PRF has 4 read and write ports each 1-bit wide.

The results in Table 4 show that 4 registers provide the least amount of instructions and cycles with an optimal instructions per cycle (IPC) for an 4x4 array. The registers that are not used will be clock gated reducing the negative impact on power. Interesting to note is the decrease of IPC with increasing RF sizes. This was unexpected as IPC usually saturates with increasing RF sizes. Nevertheless, our tests showed that the scheduler of DRESC2.x improved over time [9] as the IPC increased with better usage of the local DRFs, but the number of utilized registers is still relatively low.

Reg_con_shared_2R_1W_morphosys

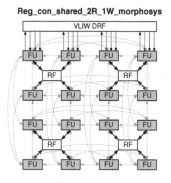

Fig. 11. Proposed ADRES architecture with shared RFs

Table 4. Reducing Register File Size arch_8

Application	Local Register File Size			
	2	4	8	16
IDCT				
Instructions	974632	923940	923980	923960
Cycles	62924	59755	59762	59757
IPC	9.69	10.21	10.21	10.21
FFT				
Instructions	11364	10532	11040	11060
Cycles	1087	1035	1063	1065
IPC	2.48	2.73	2.57	2.58

5   Final Results

The optimizations in Sections 4.1 till 4.3 led to *arch_8* architecture with shared local DRFs, Morphosys interconnections and reduced RF sizes. The architecture discussed is a non-pipelined version with no further optimizations of the architecture and data path. We apply three additional optimizations for the architecture and data path in this section: clock gating, operand isolation and pipelining. *Clock gating* targets the register files by reducing their switching activity. This feature is implemented automatically by Synopsys *Power Compiler*. Empirical results show a power reduction of the register file between 50 - 80%. A pipelined version of the same architecture shows 20 - 25% power improvement in overall. *Operand Isolation* targets the data path of a FU reducing switching activity of unused components. It is implemented manually as the automated version built in the design tools used only reduced the power by 1%. Our manual implementation using OR-based isolation [12] reduced power by 30% for a single FU and 30 - 40% for the overall pipelined system. *Pipelining* increases performance significantly by creating shorter critical paths and provides higher throughput. Pipelining, which is implemented by hand, has a disadvantage that power increases linearly when increasing the frequency unless clock gating and operand isolation is used. These optimizations are most efficient with multi-cycle architectures and very suitable for pipelined architectures.

Table 5. Comparing base (100MHz) with final instance (312MHz)

	Total		MIPS	MIPS/mW	mW/MHz
	Power (mW)	Energy (uJ)			
FFT					
Base	73.28	0.619	759	10.35	0.7328
Final	67.29	0.307	1190	17.68	0.2153
Improve	8.17%	50.4%	56.78%	70.82%	70.62%
IDCT					
Base	80.45	37.72	1409	17.51	0.8045
Final	81.99	19.14	2318	28.27	0.2624
Improve	-1.91%	49.25%	64.51%	61.45%	67.38%

5.1 Putting It All Together

Combining the *arch_8* architecture with the aforementioned optimizations results in a low power, high performance ADRES instance: *4x4_arch_8_4L_final*. A comparison between the proposed architecture with the base architecture (shown in Figure 1) is provided in Table 5. The results indicate a moderate improvement in power of 8%, but with a higher performance of 56 - 65% due to the pipelining and routings features. This results in lower energy dissipation of the architecture by 50%. The area of the proposed architecture was improved from 1.59mm^2 (544k gates) to 1.08mm^2 (370k gates), which is equivalent to a 32% improvement.

5.2 Final Architecture Power Decomposition

The final *4x4_arch_8_4L_final* architecture is placed and routed using Cadence SOC Encounter v4.2. The power and area of the proposed architecture layout are decomposed in Figures 12(a) and 12(b), respectively. These figures are of the ADRES core architecture excluding data and instruction memories. Due to the fact that the final architecture is pipelined the clock tree contribution (4.67mW) is included in these figures. The data memory and the instruction cache were not included in the synthesis for which no power estimations are made. The multiplexors in the CGA datapath were removed during synthesis by the synthesis tool as this was beneficial for performance.

Comparing Figure 3 with Figure 12(a) we notice that the shared local DRFs combined with clock gating results in lower power consumption. The configuration memories still require a vast amount of power and area, but have decreased in size as well. Further optimizations of the configuration memories require advance power management e.g. power gating, which was not applied in the final architecture. Interesting to note is the relatively higher power consumption of the CGA FUs compared to Figure 3. This is caused by the higher utilization of the array compared to the base architecture consuming more power, but providing higher performance. This increases power efficiency as noticeable in Table 3. The 16 CGA FUs and the CMs require 68.66% of all the area as depicted in Figure 12(b). The largest single component is the global DRF (noted as drf_vliw) with 8 read and 4 write ports.

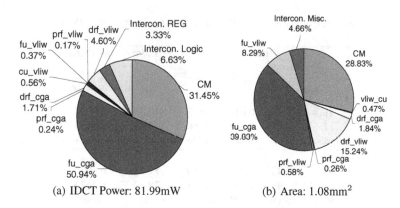

(a) IDCT Power: 81.99mW   (b) Area: 1.08mm^2

Fig. 12. Results of 4x4_arch_8_4L_final @ 312MHz

5.3   Energy-Delay Architectures Analysis of Different Array Sizes

The proposed architecture was created as a 4x4 array, however, different array sizes e.g. 2x2 and 8x8 are of interest to determine the most efficient architecture dimensions using the same interconnection network. The same sizes for the global (64 registers) and local RFs (4 registers) are maintained and the FUs are pipelined. Changing the array dimension implies different routing capabilities. For example, a 2x2 array has less routing overhead and requires reduces the possibilities for the compiler to map loops efficiently on the array. This requires deeper and larger configuration memories to map a loop on the array and increases power consumption. An 8x8 array improves the possibilities for the compiler to map loops on the array and reduces the sizes of the CMs.

We compare the pipelined architectures with non-pipelined key architectures mentioned in this paper. All key architectures in this paper are noted in Table 6 including their frequencies of which the energy-delays are depicted in Figures 13 and 14. The first three architectures are non-pipelined as the last three are pipelined. The *4x4_arch_8_16L* architecture has 16 register words in the local DRFs and PRFs. The architectures with *4L* in their name have 4 register words in the local DRFs and PRFs as explained in Section 4.3.

Table 6 shows that modifying the size of an ADRES instance creates different critical paths by increasing frequency of a 2x2 and decreasing for an 8x8 instance. The energy-delay charts in Figure 13 and 14 show that the proposed pipelined 4x4 architecture is superior to all other architectures. The 8x8 instance has the same performance as the 4x4 architecture for the IDCT code, however, due to its larger size and power consumption the energy consumption is also higher. For the FFT code the 8x8 architecture is

Table 6. Key Architectures

Non-pipelined Architecture	Freq (MHz)	Pipelined Architecture	Freq (MHz)
base	100	4x4_arch_8_4L_final	312
4x4_arch_8_16L (16L DRFs)	100	2x2_arch_8_4L_final	322
4x4_arch_8_4L (4L DRFs)	100	8x8_arch_8_4L_final	294

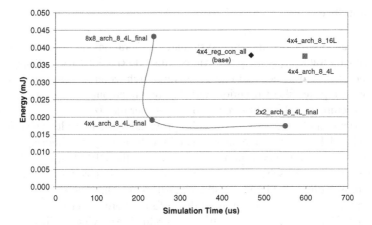

Fig. 13. Energy-Delay IDCT Results of Key Architectures

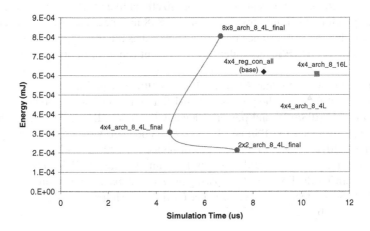

Fig. 14. Energy-Delay FFT Results of Key Architectures

minimally faster than the 2x2. This is because the scheduler failed to map one key loop of the FFT code on the array that is reducing performance considerably.

The key conclusions that can be drawn from our study are:

- The CGA is highly dependent on the local DRFs. Sharing DRFs among FUs improves routing for the DRESC compiler increasing scheduling density of the array;
- Replacing PRFs with busses is only beneficial if there are sufficient local DRFs;
- The optimal local DRF and PRF sizes of the proposed architecture is 4 words without influencing performance. The DRESC compiler can be enhanced for the array by improving the local DRF utilizations for loops;
- An array dimension of 4x4 balances energy vs. performance best for the FFT and IDCT kernels.

6 Conclusions

This paper delivers for the first time systematic explorations on the ADRES coarse-grained reconfigurable array template. An existing ADRES instance was optimized in terms of power, performance and energy. Several architectures were explored by focussing on the register file distributions and different interconnect topologies. The proposed architecture is evaluated for reduction of register file sizes.

The distribution of local data register files provided optimal results when the DRFs with 2 read and 1 write port are shared among 4 diagonally, neighboring functional units. This created additional routing capabilities for the DRESC scheduler and improved data sharing and scheduling density of the array. Replacing predicate register files with busses diminished power and energy-delay results. The results of the interconnection topology exploration showed that a fully interconnected array of the FUs and RFs in both row and column direction was optimal. Applying predicate busses improved power and energy consumption when there were sufficient local DRFs available. The final proposed ADRES instance consists of local PRFS and shared local DRFs, the Morphosys interconnection scheme and optimizations like clock gating, operand isolation and pipelining. Comparing 2x2, 4x4 and 8x8 instances based on the energy vs. delay shows that the 4x4 instance performed optimal as the instruction scheduling density is highest. The DRESC compiler has significant room for improvement for larger arrays.

In conclusion we show that ADRES offers an attractive path for low power scaling of e.g. VLIW DSP cores. The proposed ADRES architecture shows good performance efficiency of 25MIPS/mW and power efficiency 0.24mW/MHz at 312MHz. This improves the performance (MIPS/mW) by 60 - 70% and energy by 50% The energy consumption is 0.307uJ - 19.14uJ and the performance is 1190 - 2318 MIPS for FFT and IDCT, respectively. The area utilization is 1.08mm^2 for the ADRES core studied here targeting 90nm TSMC libraries. Comparing the ADRES base architecture with the proposed ADRES architecture the performance (MIPS/mW) improved by 60 - 70%, energy by 50% and area by 32%.

References

1. Mei, B., Vernalde, S., Verkest, D., Man, H.D., Lauwereins, R.: ADRES: An Architecture with Tightly Coupled VLIW Processor and Coarse-Grained Reconfigurable Matrix. In: IMEC 2003, Kapeldreef 75, B-3001, Leuven, Belgium (DATE 2004)
2. KressArray, http://kressarray.de
3. SiliconHive, http://www.silicon-hive.com
4. PACT XPP Technologies, http://www.pactxpp.com
5. Singh, H., Lee, M.-H., Lu, G., Kurdahi, F.J., Bagherzadeh, N.: MorphoSys: an integrated reconfigurable system for data-parallel and computation-intensive applications. In: University of California (US) and Federal University of Rio de Janeiro (Brazil), pp. 465–481. IEEE Transactions on Computers, Los Alamitos (2000)
6. Hartenstein, R.: A Decade of Reconfigurable Computing: A Visionary Retrospective, CS Dept (Informatik), University of Kaiserlautern, Germany, March 2001, Design, Automation and Test in Europe, 2001. Conference and Exhibition pp. 642–649 (2001)

7. Lambrechts, A., Raghavan, P., Jayapala, M.: Energy-Aware Interconnect-Exploration of Coarse Grained Reconfigurable Processors. In: WASP. 4th Workshop on Application Specific Processors (September 2005)
8. Bouwens, F., Berekovic, M., Kanstein, A., Gaydadjiev, G.: Architectural Exploration of the ADRES Coarse-Grained Reconfigurable Array. In: Diniz, P.C., Marques, E., Bertels, K., Fernandes, M.M., Cardoso, J.M.P. (eds.) ARC 2007. LNCS, vol. 4419, pp. 1–13. Springer, Heidelberg (2007)
9. Kwok, Z., Wilton, S.J.E.: Register File Architecture Optimization in a Coarse-Grained Reconfigurable Architecture. In: FCCM 2005. Proceedings of the 13th Annual IEEE Symposium on Field-Programmable Custom Computing Machines, vol. 00, University of British Columbia (2005)
10. http://www-sop.inria.fr/esterel.org/
11. Mei, B., Lambrechts, A., Mignolet, J.-Y., Verkerst, D., Lauwereins, R.: Architecture Exploration for a Reconfigurable Architecture Template. In: IEEE Design & Test of Computers, pp. 90–101. IMEC and Katholieke Universiteit Leuven (March 2005)
12. Münch, M., Wurth, B., Mehra, R., Sproch, J., Wehn, N.: Automating RT-Level Operand Isolation to Minimize Power Consumption in Datapaths. In: Proceedings Design, Automation and Test in Europe Conference and Exhibition 2000, pp. 624–631 (2000)

Implementation of an UWB Impulse-Radio Acquisition and Despreading Algorithm on a Low Power ASIP

Jochem Govers[1], Jos Huisken[2], Mladen Berekovic[3], Olivier Rousseaux[3],
Frank Bouwens[3], Michael de Nil[3], and Jef Van Meerbergen[1,4]

[1] Eindhoven University of Technology Den Dolech 2 5612 AZ Eindhoven, Netherlands
jgovers@gmx.net
[2] Silicon Hive High Tech Campus 45 5656 AA Eindhoven, Netherlands
jos.huisken@siliconhive.com
[3] Holst-centre High Tech Campus 42 5656 AA Eindhoven, Netherlands
mladen.berekovic@imec-nl.nl,
frank.bouwens@imec-nl.nl,
olivier.rousseaux@imec-nl.nl,
michael.denil@imec-nl.nl
[4] Philips Research Eindhoven High Tech Campus 5 5656 AA Eindhoven, Netherlands
jef.van.meerbergen@philips.com

Abstract. Impulse Radio-based Ultra-Wideband (UWB) technology is a strong candidate for the implementation of ultra low power air interfaces in low data rate sensor networks. A major challenge in UWB receiver design is the low-power implementation of the relatively complex digital baseband algorithms that are required for timing acquisition and data demodulation. Silicon Hive offers low-power application specific instruction set processor (ASIP) solutions. In this paper we target the low-power implementation of an UWB receiver's digital baseband algorithm on an ASIP, based on Silicon Hive's solutions.

We approach the problem as follows. First we implement the algorithm on an existing ASIP and analyze the power consumption. Next we apply optimizations such as algorithmic simplification, adding a loopcache and adding custom operations to lower the dissipation of the ASIP. The resulting ASIP consumes 0.98 nJ (*with a spreading factor of 16*) per actual data bit, which is lower than an existing application specific integrated circuit (ASIC).

1 Introduction

First-generation UWB Impulsed-Radio [1] (UWB-IR) transceivers have been developed at the Holst Centre with the goal of reducing the power consumption of wireless sensor nodes. In the current radio, an ASIC implementation of the digital baseband algorithm is used [2]. It is designed for worst case conditions and does not exploit the fact that the computational requirements can vary dependent on the input data. The goal of this paper is to show how the computation intensive part of the digital baseband algorithm can be implemented on a processor based solution. This leads to major challenges: designing a high speed processor to handle the algorithm and to compete with the low power consumption of the ASIC implementation.

P. Stenström et al. (Eds.): HiPEAC 2008, LNCS 4917, pp. 82–96, 2008.

Section 2 gives an introduction to UWB Impulse-Radio. The reference application code and processor are described in Sect. 3, also the performance numbers are given. Section 4 shows steps that can be taken to reduce the power. Section 5 shows how the optimized application and processor were constructed, also the corresponding performance numbers are given. In Sect. 6 we compare the performance of the ASIP with the ASIC. Finally the conclusions in this paper are stated in Sect. 7.

2 UWB Impulse-Radio

2.1 Introduction

The energy in a single UWB pulse compared to the energy in the noise is very small. The Federal Communications Commission (FCC) limits the UWB emission to -41.3 dBm/MHz. To still be able to retrieve the information from the channel a single data bit is transmitted over multiple pulses. A spreading code is used to map a single bit on multiple pulses. The length of this spreading code is called the spreading factor or N_{cpb}. This spreading code is usually a pseudo-random cyclic code consisting of N_{cpb} chips. In the developed prototype [2], N_{cpb} is 2^p, with a minimum length of 4 and a maximum length of 32 chips, thus p can vary between 2 and 5. The UWB-IR setup uses a fixed pulse repetition frequency (R_{pulse}) of 20 MHz, the bit transmission rate (R_{bit}) can be computed with Form. 1.

$$R_{bit} = \frac{R_{pulse}}{N_{cpb}} . \tag{1}$$

The number of pulses used to represent a single bit influences the SNR ratio (Form. 2). N_{cpb} is increased with decreasing SNR_{pulse} to maintain a constant bit-error-rate. The bit-error-rate is dependent of the SNR_{bit}.

$$SNR_{bit} = SNR_{pulse} + 10 \log N_{cpb} . \tag{2}$$

UWB-IR uses packets to transmit data (Fig. 1). The head and end of preamble sequence together are used to synchronize the receiver on the transmitter.

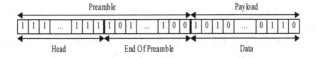

Fig. 1. Layout of a UWB packet

2.2 Transmitter

The transmitter is responsible for creating the pulse sequence from the incoming data stream. This is done in the following steps: first spreading of the incoming data stream with the spreading code, then modulation of the spread sequence into UWB pulses and finally generation of the pulse sequence. First the incoming data stream is spread by substituting each data bit with the spreading code or the inverted spreading code depending on the original value of the data bit (one/zero). For pulse position modulation (PPM) the spread sequence is converted to a sequence of unit pulses with or without time shift depending on the value of each chip (plus or minus one) in the spread sequence. This time shift is smaller than the inter-pulse period of each pulse being 50 ns and determined by R_{pulse}. For binary phase shift keying (BPSK) modulation the spread sequence is also converted to a sequence of unit pulses, however the phase of each unit pulse is inverted or not depending on the value of each chip in the spread sequence. The sequence of unit pulses is then fed to the antenna by means of a pulse shaper that complies with the FCC spectrum requirements.

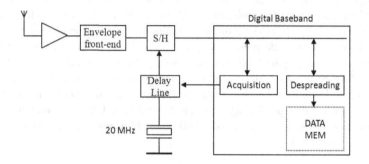

Fig. 2. Analog front-end receiver

2.3   Receiver

The UWB receiver consists of two major parts, an analog front-end (AFE) and a digital baseband (DBB).

The AFE architecture is outlined in Fig. 2. This architecture has been introduced in [3,4]. The received signal is amplified and down-converted in quadrature before analog matched filtering. The analog matched filter is implemented in the form of an integrator with integration time equal to the pulse duration (2 ns), which is equivalent to correlation with a rectangular pulse template. The output of the matched filter is sampled with one sample per pulse and fed to the DBB for demodulation.

The DBB must synchronize the AFE on the clock of the transmitter in order to successfully receive the payload. The clock frequency of the transmitter is assumed to be equal to that of the system clock ($f_{Tx} = f_{system}$). However the difference between the clock phase of f_{system} and f_{Tx} can not be ignored. A programmable delay line, called clock delay, is used to delay this f_{system} (minimizing the phase difference) and align the timing of the front-end with the timing of the incoming pulses.

The quadrature receiver can be used for both non-coherent PPM and coherent BPSK modulation. In the case of PPM modulation the information is in position of the received pulse. For BPSK the information is in the phase of the received pulse.

The DBB is responsible for the following tasks, which are described in further detail in Sect. 3:

- Demodulation of the payload data bits,
- Control of the timing circuit (programming the delay of the delay line),
- Synchronization of the spreading code with the received pulses.

3   Reference Application and Processor

First the algorithm, or application code, of the digital baseband is described. Then the architecture of the reference processor is given and finally the results of the application code running on the processor are given.

3.1   Application Code

The process of demodulating an UWB burst is done by the DBB. The most important modes of the DBB are called: ACQ1, ACQ2, EOP and DATA for respectively the first part of acquisition, the second part of acquisition, end of preamble and data mode.

ACQ1 Mode. In ACQ1 mode the DBB tests whether a signal is present on the channel for a given clock delay. If the DBB finds a signal it will switch to ACQ2 mode, otherwise it will remain in ACQ1 mode.

The test starts by retrieving N_{cpb} DVs. These DVs are correlated with N_{cpb} different rotations of the spreading code. A higher correlation result means that the DVs are more similar to the spreading code. The process of retrieving N_{cpb} DVs and correlating N_{cpb} times is repeated N_b times. N_b is the number of tries on each clock delay, in this paper we use $N_b = 3$. The N_{cpb} correlations are accumulated over N_b tries, resulting in N_{cpb} accumulated correlations. If one of these accumulated correlations is above a threshold there is signal on the channel for this clock delay. If not the AFE is switched to a different clock delay and the DBB tests for a signal on the channel again. The threshold is SNR_{pulse} dependent and is used to segregate noise from useful signal.

ACQ2 Mode. ACQ2 mode is quite similar to ACQ1 mode, however in this mode the DBB searches the optimal clock delay and spreading code phase. The process of retrieving N_{cpb} DVs and correlating N_{cpb} times is repeated for N_b times. Again the results are accumulated, but now the highest accumulated correlation, the corresponding spreading code phase and clock delay are stored. The spreading code phase can be easily computed from the spreading code used in the correlation. This process is repeated for every possible clock delay. When every clock delay is processed, the DBB determines whether the highest stored correlation is above a threshold. If not there was a false positive in ACQ1 mode and the DBB will go back to ACQ1 mode. If it is above the threshold the DBB switches the AFE to the stored clock delay corresponding to the highest stored correlation, depending on the corresponding spreading code phase the DBB will ignore a number of DVs and the DBB switches to EOP mode.

EOP Mode. When the DBB enters the EOP mode it is synchronized on the clock delay and spreading code phase, therefore it does not have to try all rotations of the spreading code. In this mode the DBB searches for the End-of-Preamble (EOP) sequence to know where the preamble ends and the payload begins. First N_{cpb} DVs are retrieved and correlated on the spreading code. The sign of the correlation result (1 or -1) is stored in memory, which also contains signs from EOP length previous correlations. To determine whether the EOP sequence is found a correlation is performed on the signs inside the memory and the EOP sequence. If the correlation is above a threshold, which is directly determined by the EOP length, the DBB switches to DATA mode. Also the number of signs, which are stored during EOP mode, are counted. If this number is too high the DBB switches back to ACQ1 mode, because this means that there was a false positive during ACQ1 mode.

DATA Mode. DATA mode is the final mode of the receiver and is also the one with the least complexity. At this point the DBB is also synchronized at bit level and each new bit is part of the payload. First N_{cpb} DVs are retrieved and despread. Despreading is the process of correlating N_{cpb} DVs with the spreading code. Depending on the sign of the correlation value the data bit value is 1 or 0, positive or negative respectively. Each data bit is stored in memory. Furthermore the number of received data bits is counted and once it is equal to the length of the payload, the DBB has finished demodulating an UWB burst. At this point the DBB will clear all the synchronization settings and switches to ACQ1 mode: ready to demodulate a new UWB burst.

3.2 Processor

The reference processor is a Moustique IC2 VLIW offered by Silicon Hive, based on the work in [5] . This processor has the following properties:

- Combination of very long instruction word (VLIW) and SIMD results in 128 GOPS at 200 MHz,
- 5-issue slot VLIW processor,
- 24-way SIMD processing,
- Scalar data path for standard C programs,
- Supports code compaction,
- Distributed register file architecture for scalability and silicon area reduction,
- Fine-grain clock gating for low power operation,
- Instruction set optimized for imaging applications,
- Extensive I/O support including AHB slave and master interfaces,
- Built using NXP 65 nm libraries,
- Synthesized with RTLCompiler for a clock frequency of 200 MHz.

This particular processor was selected because it also contains single instruction multiple data (SIMD) operations. These SIMD operations perform one operation onto multiple data and can be used to increase the data level parallelism. The algorithm strongly depends on correlations. Correlations are multiplications and additions that can be done in parallel, therefore SIMD operations are very useful to speed-up the algorithm.

3.3   Reference Results

The application can be simulated on the processor at different stages:

- sched: compilation of code with HiveCC and scheduled for the processor, simulated on a C model of the processor.
- netlist: compilation of code with HiveCC and scheduled for the processor, simulated on the netlist model of the processor (after layout, with back-annotated capacitances).

The power numbers of the Moustique IC2 processor were extracted with gate-level simulation. This processor was generated in RTL and synthesized with Cadence RTL-Compiler v06.10-s024_1 using NXP 65 nm libraries. This library allows eight metal layers, has a default supply voltage of 1.2 V and a standard threshold voltage. The chip layout was made using Cadence First Encounter v06.10-s086_1.

Using the output of the netlist simulation and the processor netlist after layout, power numbers were extracted using Synopsys PrimePower X-2005.12-SP1. The extracted power numbers can be divided into three domains:

- Active Power: The power that is consumed while executing operations.
- Idle Power: The power that is consumed while the processor is clocked, but not executing operations.
- Leakage Power: The current that is constantly leaking away when the processor is powered on. This current is only influenced by environmental parameters such as temperature.

Table 1 shows the average load and power consumption of the reference processor. The clock frequency (f_{clk}) of the processor was dynamically changed during each mode, to minimize the number of $Idle$ cycles. The reference processor has a maximum f_{clk} of 200 MHz.

Because each block of N_{cpb} DVs arrive at a certain time and we know how many cycles are needed to process this block we can calculate the average power consumption using the following formula:

$$P_{total} = \frac{E_{active} * N_{active} + E_{idle} * N_{idle}}{T} + P_{leakage} . \tag{3}$$

E denotes the average energy dissipation per cycle, N denotes the number of cycles and T denotes the time over which this energy is consumed. The processor runs one instruction each clock cycle.

From Table 1 we conclude that:

1. The Moustique IC2 can not meet the timing requirements (required f_{clk} too high).
2. The power consumption during EOP and DATA mode scales down with increasing N_{cpb}, due to a constant number of $Active$ cycles.
3. The power consumption during ACQ1 and ACQ2 mode increases slightly with increasing N_{cpb}, due to an increasing number of $Active$ cycles and SIMD operations.

Table 1. Average Load and Power Consumption of Reference Processor

N_{cpb}	ACQ1				
	Active	Idle	f_{clk}	Power	Energy
	[Cycles/bit]	[Cycles/bit]	[MHz]	[mW]	[nJ/bit]
4	51.7	0.3	260	53	10.5
8	83.7	0.3	210	55	22.0
16	145.0	3.0	185	64	50.9
N_{cpb}	ACQ2				
4	53.3	0.7	270	54	10.7
8	86.0	2.0	220	56	22.3
16	148.0	4.0	190	64	50.8
N_{cpb}	EOP				
4	22	1	115	21	4.2
8	22	2	60	13	5.2
16	22	2	30	7	5.7
N_{cpb}	DATA				
4	15	1	80	15.9	3.2
8	15	1	40	8.4	3.4
16	15	1	20	5.3	4.2
Leakage	0.94mW				

Furthermore we see in Fig. 3 that 37% of the total power is consumed by the program memory and 49% of the total power is consumed by SIMD operations. Therefore it is of interest to reduce these two components. Note that different modes show a similar partitioning of the power consumption. Before we improve the processor we first state a number of possible optimization steps in Sect. 4 and then apply these in Sect. 5.

4   Optimizing for Power Reduction

This section contains a number of options to reduce the power.

4.1   Reduction of the Instruction Word Size

It is possible to reduce the instruction word (IW) size by:

1. Reduction of the number of words in register files (RF). Each RF is controlled directly from the IW, therefore smaller RFs require a smaller IW. The reduction in IW size is only logarithmic with respect to the reduction in RF words.
2. Removing unnecessary operations, functional units or issue slots (IS). The reduction in IW size is only logarithmic with respect to the number of removed operations. This also has the advantage that the total hardware size is reduced.
3. Reduction of immediate size. Immediates require many bits in the IW, which are not efficiently used [6]. The reduction in immediate bits is directly reflected in the reduction of IW bits.

4. Reduction of connectivity and ports of RFs. Connectivity is the way each RF is connected to the ISs. Connections are made with switches and are controlled in the IW. Ports are used to read/write from/into RFs. The number of ports determines the number of possible concurrent reads/writes. Each port is directly controlled in the IW.

The draw-back of these optimizations is the loss in flexibility: smaller RFs or less operations mean that the processor can handle a smaller variety of applications. Smaller immediates can result in an increased cycle count to execute the same application.

4.2 Loopcache

Fetching instructions from program memory is an important power consumer in a processor. It is possible to reduce the program memory activity, and therefore power consumption, by adding a loopcache.

A loopcache of size n is a buffer that contains a fixed number of n IWs. With each IW fetch the loopcache tests whether the IW is stored in the buffer. If it is the IW is fetched from the buffer. If not the IW is fetched from program memory. Only if the loopcache is turned on the fetched IW is also stored in the buffer. The loopcache uses a direct mapping algorithm [6]. The user has full control over the loopcache to enable optimal usage of the loopcache and to minimize power usage.

4.3 Input Operand Isolation

The same input operand is often shared between multiple FUs. A FU that is not in use can still consume power, because the input transitions can propagate from the inputs to the rest of the circuit. This can be solved by isolation of the FU operands. Isolation is the process of holding the value of each input not used in the FU, see also [7].

4.4 Clock Gating

Clock gating means that the clock is decoupled from those parts of the circuit that are not active [8,9,10]. Fine grained clock gating is used in the reference processor. Coarse grained clock gating enables/disables the top-level clock. A consequence of top-level clock gating is that an external circuitry must enable the top-level clock when required. This is however not a problem when data arrives periodically.

4.5 Power Gating

Power gating is the process of cutting of the power from blocks that are not used [11,12]. Cutting of the power has the advantage that the block will consume no power at all. Power gating can be applied to both standard cells and memories and is typically easier to implement than adaptive voltage control.

4.6 Custom Operations

Custom operations can be used to meet specific goals, such as performance requirements or power reduction. Interesting custom operations can be found using detection of patterns of operations in the data flow graph of the application [13,14].

5 Constructing the Optimized Application and Processor

In this section the optimization steps are selected and the impact is quantified. This does not only include the architecture optimizations discussed in the previous section but also the application.

5.1 Application Code Modifications

The following modifications where applied to construct the optimized application:

1. The operations have been rewritten and rearranged to give the compiler more freedom. This resulted in smaller code loop bodies, compared to the loop bodies in the reference application and processor, where the cycle reductions ranged from 1 to 5 cycles.
2. The algorithm has been simplified. During ACQ1 and ACQ2 mode N_{cpb} correlations are accumulated N_b times. Resulting in $N_{cpb} * N_b$ correlations. By first accumulating the input of the correlation and then correlating, the number of correlations was decreased to N_{cpb} correlations. This reduced the number of correlations during ACQ1 and ACQ2 mode with a factor N_b.
3. Four custom operations have been added. 1 for ACQ1 and ACQ2 mode, 2 for EOP mode and 1 for DATA mode. They contain a combination of the following operations: correlation, quantization or shifting/rotation of bits or elements in a vector.

The resulting cycle reductions, to process one bit, are shown in Table 2. Also the number of IWs has been reduced from 180 to 110 IWs, leading to over 35% code size reduction.

Table 2. Cycle Reductions per bit: Optimized Application and Processor vs. Reference Application and Processor

N_{cpb}	ACQ1 [%]	ACQ2 [%]	EOP [%]	DATA [%]
4	80	84	62	63
8	88	88	62	63
16	91	91	62	63

Table 3. Maximum Reduction of Power dissipation of the Instruction fetch by means of a Loopcache

Loopcache [IWs]	ACQ1 [%]	ACQ2 [%]	EOP [%]	DATA [%]
2	24	25	24	37
4	35	37	46	71
8	62	64	87	87
16	74	76	76	76

5.2 Processor Modifications

The maximum power reductions gained by implementing a loopcache with different buffer sizes and $N_{cpb} = 8$ are shown in Table 3 (Form. 4). We assume that the direct mapping algorithm of the loopcache causes no collision of addresses to the same slot and that the operations needed to turn the loopcache on/off do not require additional cycles. Note on Form. 4: $P_{programmemory}$ and $P_{loopcache}$ in the numerator are consumed by a processor with a loopcache and $P_{programmemory}$ in the denominator is consumed by a processor without a loopcache.

$$reduction = 1 - \frac{P_{programmemory} + P_{loopcache}}{P_{programmemory}}. \qquad (4)$$

From Table 3 we conclude that a loopcache with size 16 gives the best overall reduction in power dissipation of the instruction fetch, assuming that the execution time is evenly distributed over each mode. This results in a power dissipation reduction, to fetch the IW, of a factor 4. Normally we expect an increasing power reduction with increasing size of the loopcache buffer, because more and more instructions words can be fetched from loopcache. This is however not the case with EOP and DATA mode. These two functions can be entirely stored in a loopcache buffer of 8 instruction words. Therefore increasing the size of buffer does not result in an increased number of instruction words fetched from the loopcache buffer. But the power consumption is increased due to a larger buffer.

The number of words in the scalar RFs was be reduced with a factor 4 and the program memory size was reduced from 64 to 12 kbits. Two ISs and six RFs were removed. Also 11 immediate bits were removed. This resulted in a reduced IW size from 224 to 91 bit.

To determine whether power gating of elements in SIMD operations is interesting we constructed 3 processors, 16-way, 32-way and 64-way. N-way is the number of elements in the SIMD operations. On these processors we executed the same application with $N_{cpb} = 8$. Only N_{cpb} elements of the SIMD operations are used during simulation, independent of N-way, therefore the percentage of elements actually used changes. Table 4 shows how the total power consumption of SIMD operations scales with different values of N-way. The column marked with $*$ is extrapolated using the other columns.

Table 4. Power Consumption of SIMD Operations with Scaling N-way running the same Application and Parameters

N-way	16	32	64	128*
P_{active} [mW]	1.8	2.4	4.0	7.2
$P_{leakage}$ [mW]	0.04	0.09	0.17	0.35
Elements Used	50%	25%	12.5%	6.25%

Table 4 shows that both active and leakage power almost double when N-way doubles. Therefore we conclude that the power consumption increases significantly with increasing N-way, even if the number of used elements in the SIMD operations is constant. Furthermore the number of elements used in the SIMD operations during an entire UWB burst is constant. Therefore it is of interest to cut-off power to elements that are not used, which is possible with power gating. We did not implement power gating but simulate it, since the automated design flow does not support this yet.

In the optimized processor we simulated a top-level clock gate, therefore the processor only consumes leakage power during *Idle* cycles. This resulted in a maximum power reduction of 1.2 mW.

5.3 Optimized Results

To construct the optimized processor the following modifications where combined:

- Removed unused FUs, ISs and RFs,
- Added four SIMD custom operations,
- Reduced and/or optimized RFs and memories,
- Reduced IW size from 224 to 91 bit,
- Introduced top-level clock gate,
- Introduced power gating of elements in SIMD operations,
- Introduced loopcache with a buffer for 16 instruction words.

To estimate (first order) the power consumption with power gating of elements in the SIMD operations we constructed three processors with N-way: 8, 16 and 32. We assume that there is no power consumption penalty with power gating. We use the $N_{cpb} - way$ processor to simulate in the case of N_{cpb} 8, 16 and 32. The 8-way processor is also used to simulate in the case $N_{cpb} = 4$.

Each processor was synthesized for f_{clk} of 100 MHz using Cadence RTLCompiler and 65 nm libraries. If the processor would be synthesized for higher frequencies the design area and power consumption would increase significantly [15]. The layout of the resulting 32-way processor is shown in Fig. 4.

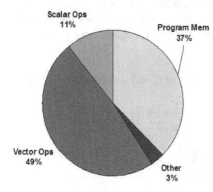

Fig. 3. Power partitioning of the reference processor running in ACQ1 mode with $N_{cpb}=8$

Fig. 4. Layout of 32-way Optimized Processor (0.23mm^2)

The average number of cycles needed to process one bit (N_{cpb} pulses), provided by the application schedule, and the average power consumption of the optimized processor running at 100 MHz are shown in Table 5.

From Table 5 we conclude that we have improved the energy dissipation, reducing the dissipation with a factor between 12 and 68, compared to the reference processor. Also conclusions 2 and 3 (found in Sect. 3.3) are also applicable to the optimized processor. Finally, if $N_{cpb} = 4$ the power consumption is much higher than expected from

Table 5. Average Load and Consumption of Optimized Processor

N_{cpb}	ACQ1			EOP		
	Active	Power	Energy	Active	Power	Energy
	[Cycles/bit]	[mW]	ref. → opt. [nJ/bit]	[Cycles/bit]	[mW]	ref. → opt. [nJ/bit]
4	9.0	1.43	10.5 → 0.29	8	1.30	4.2 → 0.26
8	10.3	0.92	22.0 → 0.37	8	0.74	5.2 → 0.30
16	13.0	0.94	50.9 → 0.75	8	0.59	5.7 → 0.48
32	18.3	1.07	1.71	8	0.52	0.83
N_{cpb}	ACQ2			DATA		
4	8.7	1.44	10.7 → 0.29	4.2	0.85	3.2 → 0.17
8	10.0	0.94	22.3 → 0.37	4.2	0.53	3.4 → 0.21
16	12.7	0.94	50.8 → 0.75	4.2	0.44	4.2 → 0.35
32	18.0	1.08	1.73	4.2	0.41	0.66

the results in the other cases. This is because the 8-way processor has been used during simulations and that the number of cycles to process a single pulse is significantly higher than in the other cases.

With the numbers shown in Table 5 we can calculate the energy dissipation to receive a net data bit (Table 6) during Use Case 1. Use Case 1 has the following properties:

- DBB is switched on 100 μs before the actual UWB burst,
- Header of 1024 bits,
- Payload of 1024 bits.

Table 6. Distribution of Execution Time and Overall Energy Consumption During Use Case 1

N_{cpb}	ACQ1	ACQ2	EOP	DATA	Energy
	[%]	[%]	[%]	[%]	[nJ/net-data-bit]
4	22.6	5.9	31.4	40.1	0.58
8	14.2	6.5	34.8	44.5	0.61
16	9.2	6.9	36.8	47.1	0.98
32	6.5	7.1	37.8	48.6	1.79

Table 7. Power Consumption: ASIP vs. ASIC

N_{cpb}	ACQ1	ACQ2	EOP	DATA
	[%]	[%]	[%]	[%]
4	151	151	137	90
8	97	98	78	55
16	99	99	63	47
32	113	114	54	43

6 Performance Comparison ASIP vs. ASIC Implementation

In this section we compare the performance of the ASIP implementation developed in this paper with the ASIC implementation [2].

The ASIC was build using 180 nm libraries, however the processor was build using NXP 65 nm libraries. To make a good comparison we scale the power numbers of the ASIC implementation as if it were build using 65 nm libraries [2]. The original power consumption was 10 mW, independent of any parameter, according to oral communications with the Holst Centre. The resulting power consumption after scaling was 0.95 mW.

Table 7 shows the power comparison between the ASIP and the ASIC implementation. Each number was calculated with the following formula:

$$comparison = \frac{P_{asip\ mode}(N_{cpb})}{P_{asic}}. \tag{5}$$

Using Use Case 1 of Sect. 5 we can compare the energy needed to receive one net data bit between the ASIP and ASIC (Fig. 5).

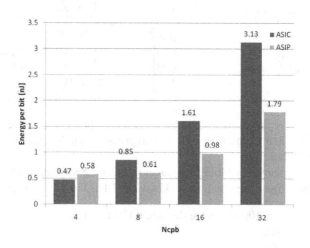

Fig. 5. Energy dissipation per net data bit during Use Case 1: ASIP vs. ASIC

In Fig. 5 we see that the ASIP solution proposed in this paper has a lower energy consumption with most settings ($N_{cpb} \geq 8$) than the ASIC. This is counter intuitive, because an well designed ASIC is specifically tuned to the application using minimal hardware. An ASIP solution is also tuned to the application, however the ASIP has a large control overhead, resulting in more hardware. The reason for this result is that the ASIC is designed for worst-case conditions and not much effort has been put in optimizing the design. Furthermore the ASIP adapts to the requirements of the algorithm, dependent of the situation. This flexible and dynamic behavior is possible, because the ASIP is programmable.

7   Conclusions

The programmable solution proposed in this paper is more flexible than the ASIC implementation [2]. This paper shows that an ASIP can be more power efficient than an ASIC. We can not generalize this, because we were able to exploit advantages with the ASIP and exploit disadvantages of the ASIC. These advantages or disadvantage are dependent of the application.

The energy per net data bit is reduced if the spreading factor is greater than or equal to 8, with a maximum reduction of 43%.

Large reductions have been accomplished by:

- Optimization and simplification of the algorithm,
- Adding custom operations,
- Removing unused register files, issue slots and functional units,
- Introducing a loopcache,
- Introducing top-level clock gating,
- Introducing power gating of elements in SIMD operations.

The algorithmic optimization and simplification combined with custom operations resulted in a reduced cycle count with a factor between 2 and 11, also the number of words was reduced from 180 to 110 instruction words. Custom operations resulted in a speed-up of a factor 5.

Customizing the architecture of the processor resulted in a reduced instruction word size from 224 to 91 bit.

Top-level clock gating reduced the *Idle* power consumption with a maximum of 1.2 mW. A loopcache reduced the power consumption to fetch an instruction word with a factor 4.

When the processor is combined with features such as adaptive voltage control, leakage power reduction and is tuned further to the application we believe that the energy dissipation for each net data bit, compared to the ASIC, can be reduced with a maximum of 70%.

Acknowledgement

This work is part of an innovation project at the High Tech Campus Eindhoven where Silicon Hive and the Holst Centre cooperate. This paper is written in partial fulfillment of obtaining a master's degree in Electrical Engineering at the Eindhoven University of Technology.

Thanks go out to M. Berekovic from IMEC-NL, J. Huisken from Silicon Hive, J. van Meerbergen from Philips Research and O. Rousseaux from IMEC-NL for their guidance and feedback.

References

1. IEEE Std P802.15.4a/d6, PART 15.4: Wireless medium access control (MAC) and physical layer (PHY) specifications for low-rate wireless personal area networks (LR-WPANs): Amendment to add alternate PHY (2006)
2. Badaroglu, M., Desset, C., Ryckaert, J., et al.: Analog-digital partitioning for low-power UWB impulse radios under CMOS scaling. EURASIP Journal on Wireless Communications and Networking 2006, Article ID 72430 8 (2006)
3. Ryckaert, J., Badaroglu, M., Desset, C., et al.: Carrier-based UWB impulse radio: simplicity, flexibility, and pulser implementation in 180 nm CMOS. In: CU 2005. Proceedings of the IEEE International Conference on Ultra-Wideband, Zurich, Switzerland, pp. 432–437 (2005)
4. Ryckaert, J., Badaroglu, M., DeHeyn, V., et al.: A 16mA UWB 3-to-5GHz 20MPulses/s quadrature analog correlation receiver in 180 nm CMOS. In: Proceedings of IEEE International Solid-State Circuits Conference, Digest of Technical Papers, San Francisco Marriott, California, USA (2006)

5. Kastrup, B., van Wel, A.: Moustique: Smaller than an ASIC and fully programmable. In: International Symposium on System-on-Chip 2003, Silicon Hive, Philips Technology Incubator, The Netherlands, vol. 2003 (2003)
6. Patterson, D.A., Hennessy, J.L.: Computer organization and design, 2nd edn. The hardware/software interface. Morgan Kaufmann Publishers Inc, San Francisco (1998)
7. Munch, M., Wurth, B., Mehra, R., Sproch, J., Wehn, N.: Automating RT-level operand isolation to minimize power consumption in datapaths. In: DATE 2000. Proceedings of the conference on Design, automation and test in Europe, pp. 624–633. ACM Press, New York (2000)
8. Li, H., Bhunia, S., Chen, Y., Vijaykumar, T.N., Roy, K.: Deterministic clock gating for microprocessor power reduction. In: HPCA 2003. Proceedings of the 9th International Symposium on High-Performance Computer Architecture, p. 113. IEEE Computer Society Press, Washington, DC, USA (2003)
9. Garrett, D., Stan, M., Dean, A.: Challenges in clockgating for a low power ASIC methodology. In: ISLPED 1999. Proceedings of the 1999 international symposium on Low power electronics and design, pp. 176–181. ACM Press, New York (1999)
10. Heo, S.: A low-power 32-bit datapath design. Master's thesis, Massachusetts Institute of Technology (2000)
11. Jiang, H., Marek-Sadowska, M., Nassif, S.R.: Benefits and costs of power-gating technique. In: ICCD 2005. Proceedings of the 2005 International Conference on Computer Design, pp. 559–566. IEEE Computer Society, Washington, DC, USA (2005)
12. Agarwal, K., Deogun, H.S., Sylvester, D., Nowka, K.: Power gating with multiple sleep modes. In: ACM/IEEE International Symposium on Quality Electronic Design (2006)
13. Arnold, M., Corporaal, H.: Automatic detection of recurring operation patterns. In: CODES 1999, pp. 22–26. ACM Press, New York (1999)
14. Athanas, P.M., Silverman, H.F.: Processor reconfiguration through instruction-set metamorphosis. Computer 26(3), 11–18 (1993)
15. Ysebodt, L., Nil, M.D., Huisken, J., Berekovic, M., Zhao, Q., Bouwens, F.J., van Meerbergen, J.: Design of low power wireless sensor nodes on energy scanvengers for biomedical monitoring. In: Vassiliadis, S., Bereković, M., Hämäläinen, T.D. (eds.) SAMOS 2007. LNCS, vol. 4599, Springer, Heidelberg (2007)

Part IIb

Compiler Optimizations

Fast Bounds Checking Using Debug Register

Tzi-cker Chiueh

Computer Science Department
Stony Brook University
chiueh@cs.sunysb.edu

Abstract. The ability to check memory references against their associated array/buffer bounds helps programmers to detect programming
errors involving address overruns early on and thus avoid many difficult bugs down the line. This paper proposes a novel approach called
Boud to the array bounds checking problem that exploits the debug
register hardware in modern CPUs. *Boud* allocates a debug register to
monitor accesses to an array or buffer within a loop so that accesses
stepping outside the array's or buffer's bound will trigger a breakpoint
exeption. Because the number of debug registers is typically small, in
cases when hardware bounds checking is not possible, *Boud* falls back to
software bounds checking. Although *Boud* can effectively eliminate per-
array-reference software checking overhead in most cases, it still incurs a
fixed set-up overhead for each *use* of an array within a loop. This paper
presents the detailed design and implementation of the *Boud* compiler,
and a comprehensive evaluation of various performance tradeoffs associated with the proposed array bounds checking technique. For the set of
real-world network applications we tested, including Apache, Sendmail,
Bind, etc., the latency penalty of *Boud*'s bounds checking mechanism
is between 2.2% to 8.8%, respectively, when compared with the vanilla
GCC compiler, which does not perform any bounds checking.

1 Introduction

Checking memory references against the bounds of the data structures they belong to at run time provides a valuable tool for early detection of programming
errors that could have otherwise resulted in subtle bugs or total application
failures. In some cases, these software errors might lead to security holes that
attackers exploit to break into computer systems and cause substantial finan-
cial losses. For example, the buffer overflow attack, which accounts for more
than 50% of the vulnerabilities reported in the CERT advisory over the last
decade [4, 20, 15], exploits the lack of array bounds checking in the compiler
and in the applications themselves, and subverts the victim programs to transfer control to a dynamically injected code segment. Although various solutions
have been proposed to subjugate the buffer overflow attack, inoculating application programs with strict array bounds checking is considered the best defense
against this attack. Despite these benefits, in practice most applications developers still choose to shy away from array bounds checking because its performance

P. Stenström et al. (Eds.): HiPEAC 2008, LNCS 4917, pp. 99–113, 2008.

overhead is considered too high to be acceptable [14]. This paper describes a novel approach to the array bounds checking problem that can reduce the array bounds checking overhead to a fraction of the input program's original execution time, and thus make it practical to apply array bounds checking to real-world programs.

The general problem of bounds checking requires comparing the target address of each memory reference against the bound of its associated data structure, which could be a statically allocated array, or a dynamically allocated array or heap region. Accordingly, bounds checking involves two subproblems: (1) identifying a given memory reference's associated data structure and thus its bound, and (2) comparing the reference's address with the bound and raising an exception if the bound is violated. The first subproblem is complicated by the existence of pointer variables. As pointers are used in generating target memory addresses, it is necessary to carry with pointers the ID of the objects they point to, so that the associated bounds could be used to perform bounds checking. There are two general approaches to this subproblem. The first approach, used in BCC [5], tags each pointer with additional fields to store information about its associated object or data structure. These fields could be a physical extension of a pointer, or a shadow variable. The second approach [13] maintains an index structure that keeps track of the mapping between high-level objects and their address ranges, and dynamically searches this index structure with a memory reference's target address to identify the reference's associated object. The first approach performs much faster than the second, but at the expense of compatibility of legacy binary code that does not support bounds checking. The second subproblem accounts for most of the bounds checking overhead, and indeed most of the research efforts in the literature were focused on how to cut down the performance cost of address-bound comparison, through techniques such as redundancy elimination or parallel execution. At the highest compiler optimization level, the minimum number of instructions required in BCC [5], a GCC-derived array bounds checking compiler, to check a reference in a C-like program against its lower and upper bounds is 6, two to load the bounds, two comparisons, and two conditional branches. For programs that involve many array/buffer references, software-based bounds checking still incurs a substantial performance penalty despite many proposed optimizations. In this paper, we propose a new approach, called *Boud*[1], which exploits the debug register hardware support available in mainstream CPUs to perform array bounds checking *for free*. The basic idea is to use debug registers to watch the end of each array being accessed, and raise an alarm when its bound is exceeded. Because debug registers perform address monitoring transparently in hardware, *Boud*'s approach to checking array bounds violation incurs no *per-array-reference overhead*. In some cases, hardware bounds checking is not possible, for example, when all debug registers are used up, and *Boud* falls back to traditional software bounds checking. Therefore, the overhead of *Boud* mainly comes from debug register set-up required for hardware bounds checking, and occasional software-based bounds checking.

---

[1] BOunds checking Using Debug register.

The general bounds checking problem requires checking for each memory reference, including references to a field within a C-like structure. Because *Boud* incurs a per-array-use set-up overhead, the debug register approach only makes sense for array-like references inside a loop, i.e., those of the form `A[i]`, `A++`, `++A`, `A--`, or `--A`, where `A` could be a pointer to a static array or a dynamically allocated buffer. For example, if a dynamic buffer is allocated through a `malloc()` call of the following form

```
X = (* TYPE) malloc(N * sizeof(TYPE))
```

where N is larger than 1, then *Boud* takes X as a pointer into an array of N elements, and *Boud* will check the references based on X if these references are used inside a loop. For array-like references outside loops, *Boud* applies conventional software-based bounds checking.

The rest of this paper is organized as follows. Section 2 reviews previous work on array bound checking and contrasts *Boud* with these efforts. Section 3 describes the detailed design decisions of the *Boud* compiler and their rationale. Section 4 presents a performance evaluation of the *Boud* compiler based on a set of array-intensive programs, and a discussion of various performance overheads associated with the *Boud* approach. Section 5 concludes this paper with a summary of the main research ideas and a brief outline of the on-going improvements to the *Boud* prototype.

2   Related Work

Most previous array bounds checking research focused on the minimization of run-time performance overhead. One notable exception is the work from the Imperial College group [13], which chose to attack the reference/objection association problem in the presence of legacy library routines. The general approach towards optimizing array bounds checking overhead is to eliminate unnecessary checks, so that the number of checks is reduced. Gupta [17, 18] proposed a flow analysis technique that avoids redundant bounds checks in such a way that it still guaranteed to identify any array bound violation in the input programs, although it does not necessarily detect these violations immediately after they occur at run time. By trading detection immediacy for reduced overhead, this approach is able to hoist some of the bounds checking code outside the loop and thus reduce the performance cost of array bounds checking significantly. Asuru [12] and Kolte and Wolfe [14] extended this work with more detailed analysis to further reduce the range check overhead.

Concurrent array bounds checking [7] first derives from a given program a reduce version that contains all the array references and their associated bounds checking code, and then runs the derived version and the original version on separate processors in parallel. With the aid of a separate processor, this approach is able to achieve the lowest array bounds checking overhead reported until the arrival of *Boud*.

Unlike most other array bounds checking compiler projects, the Bounds Checking GCC compiler (BCC) checks the bounds for both array references and general pointers. Among the systems that perform both types of bounds checks, BCC shows the best software-only bounds checking performance. However, BCC only checks the upper bound of an array when the array is accessed directly through the array variable (not pointer variable) while *Boud* automatically checks both the upper and lower bounds. Since the *Boud* compiler is based on BCC, it can also check the bounds for general pointers.

The array bounds checking problem for Java presents new design constraints. Because bounds checking code cannot be directly expressed at bytecode level, elimination of bounds checks can only be performed at run time, after the bytecode program is loaded. Directly applying existing array bounds checking optimizers at run time is not feasible, however, because they are too expensive for dynamic compilation. ABCD [19] is a light-weight algorithm for elimination of Array Bounds Checks on Demand, which adds a few edges to the SSA data flow graph and performs a simple traversal of the resulting graph. Despite its simplicity, ABCD has been proven quite effective.

Intel X86 architecture includes a **bound** instruction [10] for array bounds checking. However, the bound instruction is not widely used because on 80486 and Pentium processors, the **bound** instruction is slower than the six normal equivalent instructions. The **bound** instruction requires 7 cycles on a 1.1 GHz P3 machine while the 6 equivalent instructions require 6 cycles.

Previously, we developed an array bounds checking compiler called CASH [?] that exploits the segment limit checking hardware in Intel's X86 architecture [11] and successfully reduces the performance penalty of array bounds checking of large network applications such as Apache, Bind and Sendmail under 9%. The basic idea of CASH is to allocate a segment for each statically allocated array or dynamically allocated buffer, and then generate array/buffer reference instructions in such a way that the segment limit check hardware performs array bounds checking for free. Because CASH does not require software checks for individual buffer/array references, it is the world's fastest array bounds checking compiler for C programs on Intel X86 machines. Unfortunately, the segment limit check hardware exists only on the Intel IA32 architecture. It is not supported even on AMD64, EMT64 or Itanium, let alone in other RISC processors such as Sparc, MIPS, ARM, Xscale or PowerPC.

Qin et al. [16] proposed to exploit the fine-grained memory address monitoring capability of physical memory error correction hardware to detect array bound violations and memory leaks. Although the conceptual idea of this ECC-based scheme is similar to *Boud*, there are several important differences. First, the minimal granularity of the ECC-based scheme is a cache line rather than an individual work as in the case of *Boud*. Second, the ECC-based scheme did not seem to be able to handle array references with arbitrary strides. Third, setting up a honeypot-like cache line in the ECC-based scheme requires not only making a system call, but also enabling/disabling multiple hardware components, and is thus considered very expensive. Finally, implementation of the ECC-based scheme may be device-specific and is thus not generally portable across different hardware platforms.

3   The Boud Approach

3.1   Association Between References and Referents

To check whether a memory reference violates its referent's bound, one needs to identify its referent first. To solve this reference-object association problem, *Boud* allocates a metadata structure for each high-level object, for example, an array or a buffer, that maintains such information as its lower and upper bounds. Then *Boud* augments each *stand-alone* pointer variable P with a shadow pointer P_A that points to the metadata structure of P's referent. P and P_A then form a new fat pointer structure that is still pointed to by P. Both P and its P_A are copied in all pointer assignment/arithmetic operations, including binding of formal and actual pointer arguments in function calls. Because P and P_A are guaranteed to be adjacent to each other, it is relatively straightforward to identify the bounds of a pointer's referent by following its associated shadow pointer. For array bounds checking purpose, each array or buffer's metadata structure contains its 4-byte lower and upper bounds. For example, when a 100-byte array is statically allocated, *Boud* allocates 108 bytes, with the first two words dedicated to this array's information structure. The same thing happens when an array is allocated through malloc().

For pointer variables that are embedded into a C structure or an array of pointers, the fat pointer scheme is problematic because it may break programs that make assumptions about the memory layout or size of these aggregate structures. For these *embedded* pointer variables, *Boud* uses an index tree [13] scheme to identify their referents. That is, when a memory object is created, *Boud* inserts a new entry into the index tree based on the object's address range, and the new entry contains a pointer pointing to the memory object's metadata structure. When an embedded pointer variable is dereferenced or copied to a stand-alone pointer variable, *Boud* inserts code to look up the index tree with the pointer variable's value to locate its referent's bound. Although index tree look-up is slower than direct access using shadow pointer, the performance cost is small in practice as most pointer variables are stand-alone rather than embedded.

Fat pointers could raise compatibility problems when a *Boud* function interacts with a legacy function, because legacy functions do not expect the additional shadow pointers. To solve this problem, *Boud* allocates a shadow stack, one per thread, to pass the shadow pointers of pointer arguments. Specifically, before calling a function, the caller places in the shadow stack the entry point of the callee and the shadow pointers of all input arguments that are pointers. If a *Boud* callee is called, it first checks if the first argument in the shadow stack matches its entry point, if so composes its fat pointer variables using the shadow pointers on the shadow stack, and finally removes these shadow stack entries. When a *Boud* callee returns a pointer, it uses the same shadow stack mechanism to record the associated return address and the shadow pointer of the returned pointer. If the caller is also compiled by *Boud*, it compares the return address on the shadow stack with the call site, and if matched composes a fat pointer representation for the returned pointer based on the shadow pointer on the shadow stack.

When a legacy function calls a *Boud* callee, the callee's comparison between its entry point and the first argument on the shadow stack fails, and the callee simply assigns the shadow pointers of all its pointer arguments to NULL. When a *Boud* callee returns, the shadow pointer that it puts on the shadow stack is ignored by the legacy caller. When a *Boud* function calls a legacy function, the information that the caller puts on the shadow stack is ignored by the callee. When the legacy callee returns, the caller's comparison of its return address and the return address on the shadow stack fails, and the caller then sets the shadow pointer of the returned pointer to NULL and continues. *Boud*'s shadow stack mechanism effectively solves the pointer argument passing problem associated with fat pointers when a legacy function calls a *Boud* function and when a *Boud* function calls a legacy function.

3.2 Debug Register in Intel X86 Architecture

A key innovation in *Boud* is its use of debug register in detecting array bounds violation. Debug register hardware is universally supported by most if not all mainstream CPUs such as Intel's 32-bit and 64-bit X86, Itanium, ARM, SPARC, MIPS, PowerPC, etc. In addition, the interfaces these CPUs expose to the software are largely the same. In this paper, we will focus only on the Intel X86 processor [11]. However, the technique described below is equally applicable to other CPUs without much modification.

Debug register is designed to support instruction and data breakpointing functions required by software debuggers. In the X86 architecture, there are totally eight debug registers (DB0 through DB7) and two model-specific registers (MSRs). Among them, DB0 to DB3 are used to hold memory addresses or I/O locations that the debugger wants to monitor. Whenever a memory or instruction address matches the contents of one of these four registers, the processor raises a debug exception. With this support, the debugger does not need to perform expensive intercept-and-check in software. DB4 and DB5 are reserved. DB6 keeps the debugger status while DB7 is for control/configuration. The detailed layout of these DR registers is shown in Figure 1.

The primary function of the four *debug address registers* (DR0 to DR3) is for holding 32-bit linear breakpoint addresses. The hardware compares every instruction/data memory address with these breakpoint addresses in parallel with the normal virtual to physical address translation, and thus incurs no additional performance overhead. The *debug status register* (DR6) reports the status of the debugging conditions when a debugging exception is generated. For example, B_n bit signifies that the nth breakpoint was reached. BS and BT bits indicate the exception is due to single stepping and task switching, respectively. The *debug control register* (DR7) allows fine-grained control over each breakpoint condition. The nth

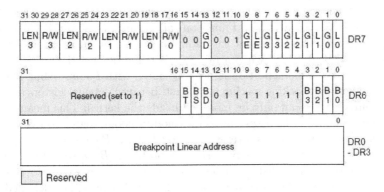

Fig. 1. Debug registers in Intel X86 processor [11]. DR4 and DR5 are reserved and thus not shown. The semantics of individual fields are explained in the text.

breakpoint could be enabled or disabled through setting the corresponding L_n or G_n bit in DR7. L_n bit enables the nth breakpoint for the current task while G_n bit is for all tasks. When both bits are cleared, the corresponding breakpoint is essentially disabled. R/W_n field controls the access mode of the nth breakpoint. For example, value 11 means breaking on either data read or write but not instruction fetch. LEN_n field specifies the size of the memory location associated with the nth breakpoint. Value 00, 01 and 11 indicate length of 1-byte, 2-byte and 4-byte respectively. For other fields that are not directly related to this project, please refer to the IA32 architectural manual [11] for their interpretation.

3.3   Detecting Bounds Violations Using Debug Registers

Fundamentally, debug register hardware provides an efficient way to detect situations when the CPU accesses certain memory addresses. *Boud* exploits this capability to detect array bounds violations by monitoring the boundary words of the arrays accessed within a loop. Almost all known buffer overflow vulnerabilities occur in the context of a loop. The attacker's input steps through an array/buffer from one end to the other and eventually outside of the upper or lower bound. To apply debug register to array bounds checking, *Boud* allocates an extra memory word above and below each array/buffer as a *honeypot word*, and puts the addresses of an array's honeypot words in debug registers before the array is accessed. Because honeypot words are introduced by the compiler and thus transparent to the program, they should never be accessed at run time. Therefore, when a honeypot word in a program is read or written, a breakpoint exception is raised and the program is terminated immediately as it signifies an attempt to overflow an array/buffer. As in the case of Cash, this approach does not require any software-based bounds check for each array/buffer reference.

For an array/buffer reference statement within a loop, *Boud* allocates a debug register and determines the address of the honeypot word that should be put into the debug register. Because debug registers are used in bounds checking, they become part of a process's context, and therefore need to be saved and restored across context switch and function call/return. Moreover, because some debuggers also use debug registers, the debug register set-up instructions inserted by *Boud* should be disabled when a program is being debugged.

There are three implementation issues associated with *Boud*'s debug register-based array bounds checking mechanism. First, because debug registers are privileged resources, they can only be modified inside the kernel. This means a user application needs to make a system call to modify debug registers, even within a small function that accesses a temporary local array. *Boud* uses two following two techniques to mitigate this performance problem. *Boud* sets up *all* debug registers required in a called function using a single system call, so that the fixed system call invocation overhead (about 200 CPU cycles) is amortized over multiple debug register set-ups. In addition, *Boud* implements a user-level debug register cache that contains the current contents of debug registers. When a user application needs a debug register for bounds checking, *Boud*'s run-time library first checks the user-level cache to see if the corresponding honeypot word address is already in some debug registers, and returns the matched debug register if there it is. If the target honeypot word address is not in any debug register, *Boud*'s run-time library allocates a debug register and makes a system call to put the target honeypot word in the chosen debug register. Empirically this debug register cache saves many unnecessary system calls, and is particularly useful for programs that repeatedly call a function with local arrays within a loop.

Second, most CPUs, including the Intel IA32/X86 architecture, support only 4 debug registers. If the *Boud* compiler requires two debug registers to check each array's upper/lower bound, it can guard at most two arrays or buffers at a time using this mechanism, and has to resort to software bounds checks for other arrays/buffers that are being accessed simultaneously. Fortunately, for most programs, when an array/buffer is accessed within a loop, one only needs to monitor its upper or lower bound but not both; therefore only one debug register is needed. To reduce the number of debug registers per array to one, the *Boud* compiler statically analyzes a program to determine the direction in which each array is accessed (increment or decrement), and sets up a debug register to protect its lower or upper bound accordingly.

Finally, debug register hardware is less powerful than Cash's segment limit check hardware because the former performs *point* check whereas the latter performs *range* check. As a result, it is possible that debug register may fail to detect certain bound violations that segment limit check hardware can catch. We have identified two corner cases in which debug register-basec check alone may be ineffective. The first case is exemplified in the following code:

```
int a[10];
int i;
int *p;
p = &a[10]+5;
for(i = 0; i < 10; i++)
  *p++ = i;
```

Because the first array reference is already outside the loop, no accesses within the loop will touch the associated honeypot word and the debug register hardware cannot catch this overflow. In contrast, a normal buffer overflow attack typically starts from a legitimate element within the buffer and eventually progresses beyond its bound. To solve this problem, the *Boud* compiler checks the first array reference separately in software to ensure that it is within the array's bound, and then checks the remaining array references within the loop using debug register.

The second case in which debug register hardware is ineffective is when the array references within a loop happen to skip the honeypot word. For example, when an array reference progresses in steps of 2 words and the honeypot word is one word beyond the last array element, even if the references step outside the array's bound, the debug register cannot help much because the honeypot word is never accessed. For example,

```
int a[10];
for(i = 0; i < 10; i++)
    a[2*i+1] = i;
```

Boud solves this problem by statically determining the index gap of each within-loop array reference and allocating the honeypot words accordingly. This means that *Boud* may need to allocate multiple honeypot words for an array's lower and upper bound: If the maximum index gap used in a program to traverse through an array A is K, then the *Boud* compiler allocates K honeypot words for both A's lower and upper bounds. However, at run time, only one of these K honeypot words is monitored.

For some within-loop array references, their direction of traversal or index gap cannot be determined statically, but they are fixed throughout the loop at run time. For these array references, *Boud* generates code to extract their direction of traversal or index gap and use the extracted values to set up honeypot words and debug registers accordingly at run time. Consequently, even for this type of array references, *Boud* still needs only one debug register per array reference.

3.4   Optimizations

Setting up a debug register requires making a system call. One way to reduce the performance cost of debug register set-up is to cache the contents of recently de-allocated debug registers and reuse them whenever possible. More concretely, *Boud* maintains a `free_dr_entry` list in user space to keep track of the contents of recently de-allocated debug resgiters. Whenever a debug register is de-allocated, *Boud* does not go into the kernel to modify the debug register; instead it puts the debug register's ID and content to the `free_dr_entry` list. Whenever a debug register is to be allocated, *Boud* checks the memory address to be monitored against the contents of the debug registers in the `free_dr_entry` list. If there is a match, *Boud* uses the debug register whose content matches the monitored address, and chooses any available debug register otherwise.

When a new monitored memory address matches the previous contents of a currently available debug register, *Boud* does not need to make a system call to modify the matched debug register, because it already contains the desired value. This optimization dramatically reduces the frequency of debug register set-up system calls for functions that contain local arrays and are called many times inside a loop.

There are only four debug registers in the X86 architecture. *Boud* allocates debug registers on a first-come-first-serve basis. The first three arrays the *Boud* compiler encounters during the parsing phase inside a (possibly nested) loop are assigned one of the three segment registers. If more than three arrays are involved within a loop, *Boud* falls back to software array bounds checking for references associated with those arrays beyond the first three.

4   Performance Evaluation

4.1   Methodology

The current *Boud* compiler prototype is derived from the Bounds Checking GCC [5], which is derived from GCC 2.96 version, and runs on Red Hat Linux 7.2. We chose BCC as the base case for the two reasons. BCC is one of the most advanced array bounds checking compilers available to us, boasting a consistent performance penalty of around 100%. It has been heavily optimized. The more recent bounds checking performance study from University of Georgia [2] also reported that the average performance overhead of BCC for a set of numerical kernels is around 117% on Pentium III. Moreover, all previous published research on software-based array bounds checking for C programs *always* did far worse than BCC. Finally, the fact that BCC and *Boud* are based on the same GCC code basis makes the comparison more meaningful. Existing commercial products such as Purify are not very competitive. Purify is a factor of 5-7 slower than the unchecked version because it needs to perform check on every read and write. The VMS compiler and Alpha compiler also supported array bounds checking, but both are at least twice as slow compared with the unchecked case on the average. In all the following measurements, the compiler optimization level of both BCC and *Boud* is set to the highest level. All test programs are statically linked with all required libraries, which are also recompiled with *Boud*.

To understand the quantitatively results of the experiments run on the *Boud* prototype presented in the next subsection, let's first analyze qualitatively the performance savings and overheads associated with the *Boud* approach. Compared with BCC, *Boud*'s bounds checking mechanism does not incur any per-array-reference overhead, because it exploits debug register hardware to detect array bound violations. However, there are other overheads that exist only in *Boud* but not in BCC. First, there is a *per-program overhead*, which results from the initial set-up of the debug register cache. Then there is a *per-array overhead*, which is related to debug register setting and resetting. On a Pentium-III 1.1-GHz machine running Red Hat Linux 7.2, the measured *per-program overhead* is 98 cycles and the *per-array overhead* is 253 cycles.

Table 1. Characteristics of a set of batch programs used in the macro-benchmarking study. The source code line count includes all the libraries used in the programs, excluding `libc`.

Program Name	Lines of Code	Brief Description Brief Description	Array-Using Loops	> 3 Arrays
Toast	7372	GSM audio compression utility	51	6 (0.6%)
Cjpeg	33717	JPEG compression utility	236	38 (1.5%)
Quat	15093	3D fractal generator	117	19 (3.4%)
RayLab	9275	Raytracer-based 3D renderer	69	4 (0.2%)
Speex	16267	Voice coder/decoder	220	23 (2.8%)
Gif2png	47057	Gif to PNG converter	277	9 (1.3%)

Table 2. The performance comparison among GCC, BCC, and based on a set of batch programs. GCC numbers are in thousands of CPU cycles, whereas the performance penalty numbers of and BCC are in terms of execution time percentage increases with respect to GCC.

Program Name	GCC	*Boud*	BCC
Toast	4,727,612K	4.6%	47.1%
Cjpeg	229,186K	8.5%	84.5%
Quat	9,990,571K	15.8%	238.3%
RayLab	3,304,059K	4.5%	40.6%
Speex	35,885,117K	13.3%	156.4%
Gif2png	706,949K	7.7%	130.4%

4.2 Batch Programs

We first compare the performance of GCC, BCC, and *Boud* using a set of batch programs, whose characteristics are listed in Table 1, and the results are shown in Table 2. In general, the performance difference between *Boud* and BCC is pretty substantial. In call cases, the performance overhead of *Boud* is below 16%, whereas the worst-case performance penalty for BCC is up to 238%.

A major concern early in the *Boud* project is that the number of debug registers is so small that *Boud* may be forced to frequently fall back to the software-based bounds check. Because *Boud* only checks array references within loops, a small number of debug registers is a problem only when the body of a loop uses more than 3 arrays/buffers. That is, the limit on the number of simultaneous array uses is per loop, not per function, or even per program. To isolate the performance cost associated with this problem, we measure the number of loops that involve array references, and the number of loops that involve more than 3 distinct arrays (called *spilled loops*) during the execution of the test batch programs (assuming one debug register is reserved for the debugger). The results are shown in Table 1, where the percentage numbers within the parenthesis indicate the percentage of loop iterations that are executed in the experiments and that belong to spilled loops. In general, the majority of array-referencing loops in these programs use fewer than

Table 3. Characteristics of a set of popular network applications that are known to have buffer overflow vulnerability. The source code line count includes all the libraries used in the programs, excluding `libc`.

Program Name	Lines of Code	Array-Using Loops	> 3 Arrays
Qpopper-4.0	32104	67	1 (0.9%)
Apache-1.3.20	51974	355	12 (0.5%)
Sendmail-8.11.3	73612	217	24 (1.4%)
Wu-ftpd-2.6.1	28055	138	1 (0.4%)
Pure-ftpd-1.0.16b	22693	45	1 (0.5%)
Bind-8.3.4	46844	734	22 (0.6%)

Table 4. The latency/throughput penalty and space overhead of each network application compiled under *Boud* when compared with the baseline case without bounds checking

Program Name	Latency Penalty	Throughput Penalty	Space Overhead
Qpopper	5.4%	5.1%	58.1%
Apache	3.1%	2.9%	51.3%
Sendmail	8.8%	7.7%	39.8%
Wu-ftpd	2.2%	2.0%	62.3%
Pure-ftpd	3.2%	2.8%	55.4%
Bind	4.1%	3.9%	48.7%

5 arrays. Furthermore, the percentage of spilled loop iterations seems to correlate well with the overall performance penalty. For example, the two programs that exhibit the highest spilled loop iteration percentage, Quat and Speex, also incur the highest performance penalty under *Boud*.

4.3   Network Applications

Because a major advantage of array bounds checking is to stop remote attacks that that exploit buffer overflow vulnerability, we apply *Boud* to a set of popular network applications that are known to have such a vulnerability. The list of applications and their characteristics are shown in Table 3. At the time of writing this paper, BCC still cannot correctly compile these network applications. because of a BCC bug [5] in the nss (name-service switch) library, which is needed by all network applications. Because of this bug, the bounds-checking code BCC generates will cause spurious bounds violations in nss_parse_service_list, which is used internally by the GNU C library's name-service switch. Therefore, for network applications, we only compare the results from *Boud* and GCC.

To evaluate the performance of network applications, we used two client machines (one 700-MHz Pentium-3 with 256MB memory and the other 1.5-GHz

Pentium-4 with 512 MB memory), that continuously send 2000 requests to a server machine (2.1-GHZ Pentium-4 with 2 GB memory) over a 100Mbps Ethernet link. The server machine's kernel was modified to record the creation and termination time of each forked process. The throughput of a network application running on the server machine is calculated by dividing 2000 with the time interval between creation of the first forked process and termination of the last forked process. The latency is calculated by taking the average of the CPU time used by the 2000 forked processes. The Apache web server program is handled separately in this study. We configured Apache to handle each incoming request with a single child process so that we could accurately measure the latency of each Web request.

We measured the latency of the most common operation for each of these network applications when the bounds checking mechanism in *Boud* is turned on and turned off. The operation measured is sending a mail for Sendmail, retrieving a web page for Apache, getting a file for Wu-ftpd, answering a DNS query for Bind, and retrieving mails for Qpopper. For network applications that can potentially involve disk access, such as Apache, we warmed up the applications with a few runs before taking the 10 measurements used in computing the average. The throughput penalty for these applications ranges from 2.0% (Wu-ftpd) to 7.7% (Sendmail), and the latency penalty ranges from 2.2% (Wu-ftpd) to 8.8% (Sendmail), as shown in Table ??. In general, these numbers are consistent with the results for batch programs, and demonstrate that *Boud* is indeed a highly efficient bounds checking mechanism that is applicable to a wide variety of applications. Table ?? also shows the increase in binary size due to *Boud*, most of which arises from tracking of the reference-object association.

Table 3 also shows the percentage of spilled loop iterations for each tested network applications, which is below 3.5% for all applications except Sendmail, which is at 11%. Not surprisingly, Sendmail also incurs the highest latency and throughput penalty among all tested network applications.

One major concern is the perfromance cost associated with debug register setting and resetting, which require making system calls. Among all tested applications, Toast makes the most requests (415,659 calls) to allocate debug registers. 223,781 of them (or 53.8% hit ratio) can find a match in the 3-entry debug register cache and 191,878 requests actually need to go into the kernel to set up the allocated debug register. Each call gate invocation takes about 253 cycles, which means that it takes 50,464K cycles for the 191,878 calls, and this is relatively insignificant as compared with Toast's total run time (4,727,612K cycles). Therefore, the overhead of the Toast application compiled under *Boud* is still very small (4.6%) though it makes a large number of debug register requests.

5   Conclusion

Although array bounds checking is an old problem, it has seen revived interest recently out of concerns on security breaches exploiting array bound violation.

Despite its robustness advantage, most real-world programs do not incorporate array bounds checking, because its performance penalty is too high to be considered practical. Whereas almost all previous research in this area focused on static analysis techniques to reduce redundant bounds checks and thus minimize the checking overhead, this work took a completely different approach that relies on the debug register hardware feature available in most mainstream CPUs. By leveraging debug registers' address monitoring capability, *Boud* can accurately detect array bound violations almost for free, i.e., without incurring any per-array-reference overhead most of the time. We have successfully built a *Boud* prototype based on the bound-checking GCC compiler under Red Hat Linux 7.2. The current *Boud* prototype can check bound violations for array references both within and outside loops, although it applies debug register-based bounds checking only to within-loop array references. Performance measurements collected from running a set network applications on the *Boud* prototype demonstrate that the throughput and latency penalty of *Boud*'s array bounds checking mechanism is below 7.7% and 8.8%, respectively, when compared with the vanilla GCC compiler, which does not perform any bounds checking. This puts *Boud* as one of the fastest array bounds checking compilers ever reported in the literature for C programs on the X86 architecture.

References

1. Perens, B.: Electric fence: a malloc() debugger for linux and unix. http://perens.com/FreeSoftware/
2. Bentley, C., Watterson, S.A., Lowenthal, D.K.: A comparison of array bounds checking on superscalar and vliw architectures. In: The annual IEEE Workshop on Workload Characterization (submitted)
3. Lam, L.-C., Chiueh, T.-C.: Checking array bound violation using segmentation hardware. In: DSN 2005. Proceedings of 2005 International Conference on Dependable Systems and Networks (June 2005)
4. Cowan, C., et al.: Stackguard: Automatic adaptive detection and prevention of buffer-overflow attacks. In: Proc. 7th USENIX Security Conference, San Antonio, Texas, pp. 63–78 (January 1998)
5. GCC. Bounds-checking gcc, http://www.gnu.org/software/gcc/projects /bp/ main.html
6. Pearson, G.: Array bounds checking with turbo c. Dr. Dobb's Journal of Software Tools 16(5) 72, 74, 78–79, 81–82, 104–107 (1991)
7. Patil, H., Fischer, C.N.: Efficient run-time monitoring using shadow processing. In: Proceedings of Automated and Algorithmic Debugging Workshop, pp. 119–132 (1995)
8. Xi, H., Pfenning, F.: Eliminating array bound checking through dependent types. In: SIGPLAN Conference on Programming Language Design and Implementation, pp. 249–257 (1998)
9. Xi, H., Xia, S.: Towards array bound check elimination in java virtual machine language. In: Proceedings of CASCON 1999, Mississauga, Ontario, pp. 110–125 (November 1999)
10. Intel. IA-32 Intel Architecture Software Developer's Manual vol. 2 Instruction Set Reference, http://www.intel.com/design/Pentium4/manuals/

11. Intel. Ia-32 intel architecture software developer's manual. volume 3: System programming guide,
    http://developer.intel.com/design/pentium4/manuals/245472.htm
12. Asuru, J.M.: Optimization of array subscript range checks. ACM letters on Programming Languages and Systems 1(2), 109–118 (1992)
13. Jones, R.W.M., Kelly, P.H.J.: Backwards-compatible bounds checking for arrays and pointers in c programs. In: Proceedings of Automated and Algorithmic Debugging Workshop, pp. 13–26 (1997)
14. Kolte, P., Wolfe, M.: Elimination of redundant array subscript range checks. In: SIGPLAN Conference on Programming Language Design and Implementation, pp. 270–278 (1995)
15. Prasad, M., Chiueh, T.-C.: A binary rewriting approach to stack-based buffer overflow attacks. In: Proceedings of 2003 USENIX Conference (June 2003)
16. Qin, F., Lu, S., Zhou, Y.: Safemem: Exploiting ecc-memory for detecting memory leaks and memory corruption during production runs. In: HPCA 2005. Proceedings of the 11th International Symposium on High-Performance Computer Architecture (February 2005)
17. Gupta, R.: A fresh look at optimizing array bound checking. In: SIGPLAN Conference on Programming Language Design and Implementation, pp. 272–282 (1990)
18. Gupta, R.: Optimizing array bound checks using flow analysis. ACM Letters on Programming Languages and Systems 2(1-4), 135–150 (1993)
19. Bodik, R., Gupta, R., Sarkar, V.: Abcd: eliminating array bounds checks on demand. In: SIGPLAN Conference on Programming Language Design and Implementation, pp. 321–333 (2000)
20. Chiueh, T.-C., Hsu, F.-H.: Rad: A compiler time solution to buffer overflow attacks. In: ICDCS. Proceedings of International Conference on Distributed Computing Systems, Phoenix, Arizona (April 2001)
21. Chiueh, T.-C., Venkitachalam, G., Pradhan, P.: Integrating segmentation and paging protection for safe, efficient and transparent software extensions. In: Proceedings of 17th ACM Symposium on Operating Systems Principles, Charleston, SC (December 1999)

Studying Compiler Optimizations on Superscalar Processors Through Interval Analysis

Stijn Eyerman[1], Lieven Eeckhout[1], and James E. Smith[2]

[1] ELIS Department, Ghent University, Belgium
[2] ECE Department, University of Wisconsin – Madison
{seyerman,leeckhou}@elis.UGent.be, jes@ece.wisc.edu

Abstract. Understanding the performance impact of compiler optimizations on superscalar processors is complicated because compiler optimizations interact with the microarchitecture in complex ways. This paper analyzes this interaction using interval analysis, an analytical processor model that allows for breaking total execution time into cycle components. By studying the impact of compiler optimizations on the various cycle components, one can gain insight into how compiler optimizations affect out-of-order processor performance. The analysis provided in this paper reveals various interesting insights and suggestions for future work on compiler optimizations for out-of-order processors. In addition, we contrast the effect compiler optimizations have on out-of-order versus in-order processors.

1 Introduction

In modern processors, both the hardware implementation and optimizing compilers are very complex, and they often interact in unpredictable ways. A high performance microarchitecture typically issues instructions out-of-order and must deal with a number of disruptive *miss events* such as branch mispredictions and cache misses. An optimizing compiler implements a large number of individual optimizations which not only interact with the microarchitecture, but also interact with each other. These interactions can be constructive (improved performance), destructive (lost performance), or neutral. Furthermore, whether there is performance gain or loss often depends on the particular program being optimized and executed.

In practice, the only way that the performance gain (or loss) for a given compiler optimization can be determined is by running optimized programs on the hardware and timing them. This method, while useful, does not provide insight regarding the underlying causes for performance gain/loss. By using the recently proposed method of *interval analysis* [1,2,3,4], one can decompose total execution time into intuitively meaningful cycle components. These components include a base cycle count, which is a measure of the time required to execute the program in the absence of all disruptive miss events, along with additional cycle counts for each type of miss event. Performance gain (or loss) resulting from a compiler optimization can then be attributed to either the base cycle count or to specific miss event(s).

By analyzing the various cycle count components for a wide range of compiler optimizations one can gain insight into the underlying mechanisms by which compiler

P. Stenström et al. (Eds.): HiPEAC 2008, LNCS 4917, pp. 114–129, 2008.

optimizations affect out-of-order processor performance. To the best of our knowledge, this paper is the first to analyze compiler optimizations on out-of-order processors using an analytical-based superscalar processor model. The work reported here provides and supports a number of key insights. Some of these insights provide quantitative support for conventional wisdom, while others provide a fresh view of how compiler optimizations interact with superscalar processor performance. To be more specific:

- We demonstrate the use of interval analysis for studying the impact of compiler optimizations on superscalar processor performance; this is done by breaking up the total execution time into cycle components and by analyzing the effect of compiler optimizations on the various cycle components. Compiler builders can use this methodology to better understand the impact of compiler optimizations.
- Our analysis provides a number of interesting insights with respect to how compiler optimizations affect out-of-order processor performance. For one, the critical path leading to mispredicted branches is the only place during program execution where optimizations reducing the length of the chain of dependent operations affect overall performance on a balanced out-of-order processor — inter-operation dependencies not residing on the critical path leading to a mispredicted branch are typically hidden by out-of-order execution. Second, reducing the dynamic instruction count (an important optimization objective dating back to sequential processors) still is an important compiler optimization criterion for today's out-of-order processors. Third, some compiler optimizations (unintentionally) bring long-latency loads closer to each other in the dynamic instruction stream, thereby exposing more memory-level parallelism (MLP) and improving performance.
- We show that compiler optimizations have a different performance impact on in-order versus out-of-order processors. In fact, the biggest fraction of the total performance gain on in-order processors is achieved by reducing the dynamic instruction count and critical path length. For out-of-order processors on the other hand, only about half the performance gain comes from reducing the dynamic instruction count and critical path length; the other half of the performance gain comes from optimizations related to the I-cache, L2 D-cache and branch predictor behavior.

2 Decomposing Execution Time into Cycle Components

In order to gain insight into how compiler optimizations affect out-of-order processor performance, we use a previously developed analytical model called interval analysis. This section briefly summarizes interval analysis; for a more elaborate discussion the reader can refer to a number of prior references [1,2,3,4].

2.1 Interval Analysis

Interval behavior observed on superscalar processors is illustrated in Figure 1. The number of (useful) instructions issued per cycle (IPC) is shown on the vertical axis, and time (in clock cycles) is shown on the horizontal axis. As illustrated in the figure, an interval begins at the time new instructions start to fill the issue and reorder buffers following

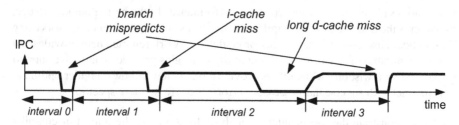

Fig. 1. Performance can be analyzed by dividing time into intervals between miss events

the preceding miss event (regardless of which type). Initially, only a small number of instructions are in the issue buffer, so relatively few can be found to issue in parallel. However, as instructions continue to fill the window, the scope for finding parallel instructions increases, as does the issue rate. In the limit, the window becomes full (or nearly so) and a steady state issue rate is achieved. At some point, the next miss event occurs and the stream of useful instructions entering the window ceases. The window begins draining of useful instructions as they commit, but no new instructions take their place. Finally, there are no more instructions to issue until the interval ends. In the meantime, the miss event is being handled by the hardware, for example, an instruction cache miss is serviced. After the time during which no instructions issue or commit, the next interval begins with a ramp-up transient as the window re-fills, and instructions once again begin issuing. The exact mechanisms which cause instructions to stop filling the window and the timing of the window drain with respect to the occurrence of the miss event are dependent on the type of miss event, so each type of miss event should be analyzed separately.

When we use interval analysis to decompose performance into cycle count components, there are three main aspects: base cycle counts, miss event cycle counts, and overlap of miss events.

Base Cycle Counts. If there are N instructions in a given interval and the dispatch width is D, then it will take $\lceil N/D \rceil$ cycles to dispatch them into the window. In the absence of all miss events, a balanced superscalar processor can then issue and retire the instructions at (nearly) the dispatch rate. Consequently, the base cycle count is computed as $\lceil N/D \rceil$ for an interval containing N instructions.

This stems from the observation that for practical pipeline widths, say up to eight, one can, in most cases, make the window size big enough that an issue rate matching the pipeline width can be achieved (under ideal, no miss event, conditions) [5,6,7]. Note that we equate the dispatch width D with the processor's 'pipeline width', because it typically defines the maximum sustainable instruction fetch/decode/execution rate. We call a superscalar processor design *balanced* when the ROB and other resources such as the issue buffer, load/store buffers, rename registers, MSHRs, functional units, *etc.*, are sufficiently large to support the processor width in the absence of all miss events.

Miss Event Cycle Counts. The cycle counts (penalties) for miss events depend on the type of miss event.

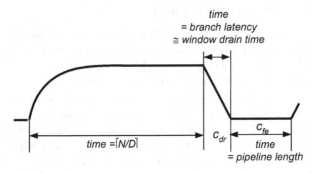

Fig. 2. Interval behavior for a branch misprediction

- For a front-end miss event such as an L1 I-cache miss, L2 I-cache miss or an I-TLB miss, the penalty equals the access time to the next cache level [3]. For example, the cycle count penalty for an L1 I-cache miss event is the L2 cache access latency.
- The penalty for a branch misprediction equals the branch resolution time plus the number of pipeline stages in the front-end pipeline c_{fe}, see Figure 2. Previous work [2] has shown that the branch resolution time can be approximated by the window drain time c_{dr}; *i.e.*, the mispredicted branch is very often the last instruction being executed before the window drains. Also, this previous work has shown that, in many cases, the branch resolution time is the main contributor to the overall branch misprediction penalty.
- Short back-end misses, *i.e.*, L1 D-cache misses, are modeled as if they are instructions that are serviced by long latency functional units, not miss events. In other words, it is assumed that the latencies can be hidden by out-of-order execution, which is the case in a balanced processor design.
- The penalty for isolated long back-end misses, such as L2 D-cache misses and D-TLB misses, equals the main memory access latency.

Overlapping Miss Events. The above discussion of miss event cycle counts essentially assumes that the miss events occur in isolation. In practice, of course, they may overlap. We deal with overlapping miss events in the following manner.

- For long back-end misses that occur within an interval of W instructions (the ROB size), the penalties overlap completely [8,3]. We refer to the latter case as *overlapping* long back-end misses; in other words, memory-level parallelism (MLP) is present.
- Simulation results in prior work [1,3] show that the number of front-end misses interacting with long back-end misses is relatively infrequent. Our simulation results confirm that for all except three of the SPEC CPU2000 benchmarks, less than 1% of the cycles are spent servicing front-end and long back-end misses in parallel; only gap (5.4%), twolf (4.9%), vortex (3.1%) spend more than 1% of their cycles servicing front-end and long data cache misses in parallel.

2.2 Evaluating Cycle Count Components

To evaluate the cycle count components in this paper, we use detailed simulation. We compute the following cycle components: base (no miss events), L1 I-cache miss, L2 I-cache miss, I-TLB miss, L1 D-cache miss, L2 D-cache miss, D-TLB miss, branch misprediction and resource stall (called 'other' throughout the paper). The cycle counts are determined in the following way: (i) cycles caused by a branch misprediction as the branch resolution time plus the number of pipeline stages in the front-end pipeline, (ii) the cycles for an I-cache miss event as the time to access the next level in the memory hierarchy, (iii) the cycles for overlapping long back-end misses are computed as a single penalty, and (iv) the L1 D-cache and resource stall cycle components account for the cycles in which no instructions can be committed because of an L1 D-cache miss or long latency instruction (such as a multiply or floating-point operation) blocking the head of the ROB. Furthermore, we do not count miss events along mispredicted control flow paths. The infrequent case of front-end miss events overlapping with long back-end miss events is handled by assigning a cycle count to the front-end miss event unless a full ROB triggers the long back-end miss penalty. Given the fact that front-end miss events only rarely overlap with long back-end miss events, virtually any mechanism for dealing with overlaps would suffice. The base cycle component then is the total cycle count minus all the individual cycle components.

Note that although we are using simulation in this paper, this is consistent with what could be done in real hardware. In particular, Eyerman *et al.* [1] proposed an architected hardware counter mechanism that computes CPI components using exactly the same counting mechanism as we do in this paper. The hardware performance counter architecture proposed in [1] was shown to compute CPI components that are accurate to within a few percent of components computed by detailed simulations. Note that in this paper we are counting cycle components (C alone) and not CPI components as done in [1] because the number of instructions is subject to compiler optimization. However, the mechanisms for computing cycle components and CPI components are essentially the same.

3   Experimental Setup

This paper uses all the C benchmarks from the SPEC CPU2000 benchmark suite. Because we want to run all the benchmarks to completion for all the compiler optimizations, we use the `lgred` inputs provided by MinneSPEC [9]. The dynamic instruction count of the `lgred` input varies between several hundreds of millions of instructions and a number of billions of instructions.

The simulated superscalar processor is detailed in Table 1. It is a 4-wide out-of-order microarchitecture with a 128-entry reorder buffer (ROB). This processor was simulated using SimpleScalar/Alpha v3.0 [10].

All the benchmarks were compiled using `gcc` v4.1.1 (dated May 2006) on an Alpha 21264 processor machine. We chose the `gcc` compiler because, in contrast to the native Compaq `cc` compiler, it comes with a rich set of compiler flags that can be set individually. This enables us to consider a wide range of optimization levels. The 22 optimization levels considered in this paper are given in Table 2. This ordering of optimization settings is inspired by `gcc`'s `-O1`, `-O2` and `-O3` optimization levels; the

Table 1. Processor model assumed in our experimental setup

ROB	128 entries
processor width	4 wide
fetch width	8 wide
latencies	load 2 cycles, mul 3 cycles, div 20 cycles, arith/log 1 cycle
L1 I-cache	16KB 4-way set-associative, 32-byte cache lines
L1 D-cache	16KB 4-way set-associative, 32-byte cache lines
L2 cache	unified, 1MB 8-way set-associative, 128-byte cache lines
	10 cycle access time
main memory	250 cycle access time
branch predictor	hybrid predictor consisting of 4K-entry meta, bimodal and
	gshare predictors
front-end pipeline	5 stages

compiler optimizations are applied on top of each other to progressively evolve from the base optimization level to the most advanced optimization level. The reason for working with these optimization levels is to keep the number of optimization combinations at a tractable number while exploring a wide enough range of optimization levels — the number of possible optimization settings by setting individual flags is obviously huge and impractical to do. We believe the particular ordering of optimization levels does not affect the overall conclusions from this paper.

4   The Impact of Compiler Optimizations

This section first analyzes the impact various compiler optimizations have on the various cycle components in an out-of-order processor. We subsequently analyze how compiler optimizations affect out-of-order processor performance as compared to in-order processor performance.

4.1   Out-of-Order Processor Performance

Before discussing the impact of compiler optimizations on out-of-order processor performance in great detail on a number of case studies, we first present and discuss some general findings.

Figure 3 shows the average normalized execution time for the sequence of optimizations used in this study. The horizontal axis shows the various optimization levels; the vertical axis shows the normalized execution time (averaged across all benchmarks) compared to the base optimization setting. On average, over the set of benchmarks and the set of optimization settings considered in this paper, performance improves by 15.2% compared to the base optimization level. (Note that our base optimization setting already includes a number of optimizations, and results in 40% better performance than the -O0 compiler setting.) Some benchmarks, such as **ammp** and **mesa** observe no or almost no performance improvement. Other benchmarks benefit substantially, such as mcf (19%), **equake** (23%) and **art** (over 40%).

Table 2. Compiler optimization levels considered in this paper

Abbreviation	Description

base	base optimization level: `-O1 -fnotree-ccp -fno-tree-dce`
	`-fno-tree-dominator-opts -fno-tree-dse -fno-tree-ter -fno-tree-lrs`
	`-fno-tree-sra -fno-tree-copyrename -fno-tree-fre -fno-tree-ch`
	`-fno-cprop-registers -fno-merge-constants -fno-loop-optimize`
	`-fno-if-conversion -fno-if-conversion2 -fno-unit-at-a-time`

basic tree opt	basic optimizations on intermediate SSA code tree
const prop/elim	merge identical constants across compilation units constant propagation and copy elimination
loop opt	loop optimizations: move constant expressions out of loop and simplify exit test conditions
if-conversion	if-conversion: convert control dependencies to data dependencies using predicated execution through conditional move (`cmov`) instructions
O1	optimization flag `-O1`
O2 -fnoO2	optimization flag `-O2` with all individual `-O2` optimization flags disabled
CSE	apply common subexpression elimination
BB reorder	reorder basic blocks in order to reduce the number of taken branches and improve code locality
strength red	strength reduction optimization and elimination of iteration variables
recursion opt	optimize sibling and tail recursive function calls
insn scheduling	reorder instructions to eliminate stalls due to required data being unavailable includes scheduling instructions across basic blocks is specific for target platform on which the compiler runs
strict aliasing	assumes that an object of one type never reside at the same address as an object of a different type, unless the types are almost the same
alignment	align the start of branch targets, loops and functions to a power-of-two boundary
adv tree opt	advanced intermediate code tree optimizations
O2	optimization flag `-O2`
aggr loop opt	perform more aggressive loop optimizations
inlining	integrate simple functions (determined based on heuristics) into their callers
O3	optimization flag `-O3`
loop unroll	unroll loops whose number of iterations can be determined at compile time or upon entry to the loop
software pipelining	modulo scheduling
FDO	feedback-directed optimization using edge counts

Figure 4 summarizes the total performance improvement for the individual cycle components. This graph divides the total 15.2% performance improvement by the contributions in each of the cycle components. There are a number of interesting insights to be gained from the above analysis concerning the impact of compiler optimizations on out-of-order processor performance.

First, compiler optimizations reduce the dynamic instruction count and improve the base cycle component. Figure 4 shows that an absolute 6.6% performance improvement (or 43.9% of the total improvement) comes from reducing the base cycle component. As such, we conclude that reducing the dynamic instruction count, which has been a traditional objective for optimization dating back to sequential (non-pipelined) processors, is still an important optimization criterion for today's out-of-order processors.

Compiler optimizations that aim at improving the critical path of inter-operation dependencies only improve the branch misprediction penalty. This is a key new insight from this paper: the critical path of inter-operation dependencies is only visible through the branch misprediction penalty and by consequence, optimizations targetted at reducing chains of dependent instructions only affect the branch resolution time; on a balanced processor, inter-operation dependencies not residing on the critical path leading to a mispredicted branch can be effectively hidden by out-of-order execution. Note that optimizations targeting the inter-operation critical path may also improve the base and resource stall cycle components in case of unbalanced execution, *i.e.*, when the

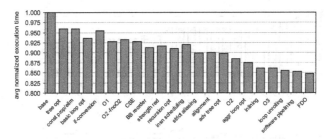

Fig. 3. Averaged normalized cycle counts on a superscalar out-of-order processor

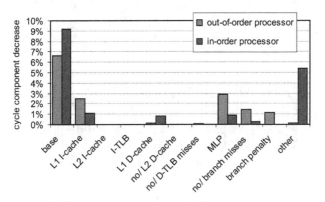

Fig. 4. Overall performance improvement on an out-of-order processor and an in-order processor across the various compiler settings partitioned by cycle component

reorder buffer is too small to sustain a given issue rate of instructions; in practice though, this is an infrequent case. Figure 4 shows the improvement in the branch resolution time across the optimization settings; this is a 1.2% absolute improvement or a 7.8% relative improvement.

Finally, compiler optimizations significantly affect the number of miss events and their overlap behavior. According to Figure 4, 9.6% of the total performance improvement comes from a reduced number of branch mispredictions, and 16.7% and 19.5% of the total performance improvement comes from improved L1 I-cache and the L2 D-cache cycle components, respectively. The key observation here is that the reduced L2 D-cache cycle component is almost entirely due to improved memory-level parallelism (MLP). In other words, compiler optimizations that bring L2 cache miss loads closer to each other in the dynamic instruction stream improve performance substantially by increasing the amount of MLP.

4.2   Compiler Optimization Analysis Case Studies

We now present some case studies illustrating the power of interval analysis for gaining insight into how compiler optimizations affect out-of-order processor performance. Figure 5 shows normalized cycle distributions for individual benchmarks — we selected the benchmarks that are affected most by the compiler optimizations. These bars are

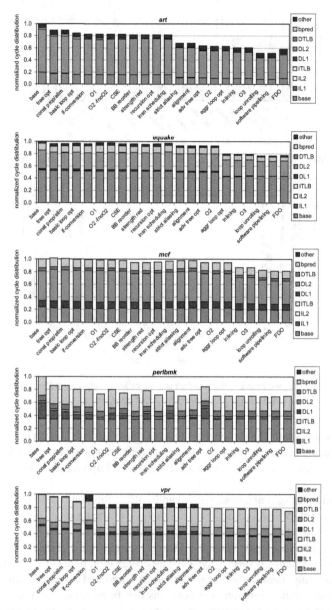

Fig. 5. Normalized cycle distributions for the out-of-order processor for art, equake, mcf, perlbmk and vpr

computed as follows. For all compiler optimization settings, we compute the cycle counts for each of the nine cycle components: base, L1 I-cache, L2 I-cache, I-TLB, L1 D-cache, L2 D-cache, D-TLB, branch misprediction and other resource stalls. Once these cycle counts are computed we then normalize the cycle components for all optimization settings to the total cycle count for the base optimization setting.

Table 3. The number of benchmarks (out of 15) for which a given compiler optimization has an positive (more than 0.1%) effect on the various cycle components, the number of retired instructions, the number long back-end misses and their MLP, and the number of branch mispredictions and their penalties. Numbers larger than or equal to 9 are shown in bold.

optimization	cycle components										#insns	DL2 and DTLB misses			br mispredicts	
	total	base	IL1	IL2	ITLB	DL1	DL2	DTLB	bpred	other		#DL2	#DTLB	MLP	#bmp	pen
basic tree opt	**11**	**14**	5	0	0	2	6	2	**11**	0	**14**	3	0	5	**11**	3
cst prop/elim	6	2	1	0	0	1	0	0	8	0	7	0	0	1	4	4
loop opt	**12**	**12**	3	0	0	3	3	0	8	8	**13**	3	0	3	3	**9**
if-conversion	7	1	3	0	0	1	6	1	**10**	1	1	2	0	6	8	5
jump opt (O1)	**9**	**10**	4	0	0	2	2	0	3	1	**11**	1	0	2	3	5
O2 -fnoO2	5	0	3	0	0	2	2	1	8	1	0	1	0	1	5	6
CSE	6	5	3	0	0	2	1	1	8	2	**9**	1	1	1	6	6
BB reordering	**10**	**10**	6	0	0	2	2	0	4	1	**11**	2	1	0	6	1
strength red	4	3	1	0	0	0	1	1	3	0	2	1	0	1	2	1
recursion opt	7	4	4	0	0	0	3	0	4	0	6	3	0	0	4	3
insn scheduling	5	1	2	0	0	4	3	1	**10**	4	0	1	0	3	5	**10**
strict aliasing	8	**11**	2	0	0	5	3	1	6	3	**11**	1	1	5	0	**10**
alignment	5	3	2	0	0	0	3	1	5	0	4	2	0	2	4	2
adv tree opt	6	3	3	0	0	2	4	2	4	3	5	1	2	3	3	5
O2	**9**	7	4	0	0	0	2	0	6	0	7	3	0	2	4	4
aggr loop opt	7	2	3	0	0	1	2	0	4	1	3	1	0	1	4	0
inlining	**12**	**10**	3	0	0	0	7	1	**9**	1	**12**	4	1	4	7	4
O3	5	2	2	0	0	0	1	0	3	0	2	0	0	1	3	1
loop unrolling	**9**	**11**	1	0	0	3	4	0	7	2	**12**	0	0	5	3	6
software pipelining	3	1	2	0	0	1	1	0	1	1	0	1	1	0	4	0
FDO	8	7	3	1	0	2	3	1	6	1	**10**	5	2	1	7	5

Table 4. The number of benchmarks (out of 15) for which a given compiler optimization has a negative (more than 0.1%) effect on the various cycle components, the number of retired instructions, the number of long back-end misses and their MLP, and the number of branch mispredictions and their penalties. Numbers larger than or equal to 9 are shown in bold.

optimization	cycle components										#insns	DL2 and DTLB misses			br mispredicts	
	total	base	IL1	IL2	ITLB	DL1	DL2	DTLB	bpred	other		#DL2	#DTLB	MLP	#bmp	pen
basic tree opt	4	0	1	0	0	2	3	0	3	5	1	2	1	4	1	**10**
cst prop/elim	6	1	4	0	0	0	2	1	2	0	0	2	0	2	3	2
loop opt	1	1	2	0	0	1	3	1	4	0	0	2	1	2	6	3
if-conversion	6	7	3	0	0	2	1	1	1	1	**11**	1	0	2	2	4
jump opt (O1)	4	1	1	0	0	1	3	2	7	2	0	3	1	3	5	4
O2 -fnoO2	8	**11**	3	0	0	0	3	0	3	0	**13**	1	0	2	4	1
CSE	6	6	3	0	0	1	0	1	3	1	4	1	0	1	5	4
BB reordering	2	1	0	0	0	1	3	2	8	2	2	1	1	4	5	**11**
strength red	3	1	1	0	0	0	1	0	1	0	1	0	0	1	0	0
recursion opt	2	1	1	0	0	0	2	1	4	0	0	1	0	2	4	3
insn scheduling	8	**10**	4	0	0	1	5	0	1	1	**11**	3	1	1	3	1
strict aliasing	4	0	2	0	0	0	3	1	2	1	0	3	0	1	6	2
alignment	4	1	4	0	0	2	2	0	3	1	0	2	0	2	3	2
adv tree opt	7	3	3	0	0	0	2	1	7	0	4	2	0	2	6	2
O2	3	1	2	0	0	1	3	1	1	0	2	3	0	1	3	3
aggr loop opt	2	0	1	0	0	1	1	0	1	0	0	1	0	0	1	2
inlining	1	2	2	2	0	3	0	1	4	1	1	1	1	0	3	5
O3	4	1	3	0	0	0	2	0	1	1	1	2	0	0	1	2
loop unrolling	5	1	6	2	0	1	1	0	3	1	1	3	0	1	5	2
software pipelining	3	1	2	0	0	0	1	1	2	0	1	1	0	2	3	4
FDO	6	4	2	0	0	2	3	0	5	2	3	0	0	6	5	7

During the analysis presented in the next discussion we will also refer to Tables 3 and 4 which show the number of benchmarks for which a given compiler optimization results in a positive or negative effect, respectively, on the various cycle components. These tables also show the number of benchmarks for which the dynamic instruction count is significantly affected by the various compiler optimizations; likewise for the number of long back-end misses and their amount of MLP as well as for the number of branch mispredictions and their penalty. We do not show average performance improvement numbers in these tables because outliers make the interpretation difficult; instead, we treat outliers in the following discussion.

Basic Loop Optimizations. Basic loop optimizations move constant expressions out of the loop and simplify loop exit conditions. Most benchmarks benefit from these loop optimizations; the reasons for improved performance include a smaller dynamic instruction count which reduces the base cycle component. A second reason is that the simplified loop exit conditions result in a reduced branch misprediction penalty. Two benchmarks that benefit significantly from loop optimizations are perlbmk (6.7% improvement) and art (5.9% improvement). The reason for these improvements is different for the two benchmarks. For perlbmk, the reason is a reduced L1 I-cache component and a reduced branch misprediction component. The reduced L1 I-cache component is due to fewer L1 I-cache misses. The branch misprediction cycle component is reduced mainly because of a reduced branch misprediction penalty — the number of branch mispredictions is not affected very much. In other words, the loop optimizations reduce the critical path leading to the mispredicted branch so that the branch gets resolved earlier. For art on the other hand, the major cycle reduction is observed in the L2 D-cache cycle component. The reason being an increased number of overlapping L2 D-cache misses: the number of L2 D-cache misses remains the same, but the reduced code footprint brings the L2 D-cache misses closer to each other in the dynamic instruction stream which results in more memory-level parallelism.

If-conversion. The goal of if-conversion is to eliminate hard-to-predict branches through predicated execution. The potential drawback of if-conversion is that more instructions need to be executed because instructions along multiple control flow paths need to be executed and part of these will be useless. Executing more instructions reflects itself in a larger base cycle component. In addition, more instructions need to be fetched; we observe that this also increases the number of L1 I-cache misses for several benchmarks. Approximately half the benchmarks benefit from if-conversion; for these benchmarks, the reduction in the number of branch mispredictions outweights the increased number of instructions that need to be executed. For the other half of the benchmarks, the main reason for the decreased performance is the increased number of dynamically executed instructions.

An interesting benchmark to consider more closely is vpr: its base, resource stall and L1 D-cache cycle components increase by 4.5%, 9.6% and 3.9%, respectively. This analysis shows that if-conversion adds to the already very long critical path in vpr — vpr executes a tight loop with loop-carried dependencies which results in very long dependence chains. If-conversion adds to the critical path because registers may need to be copied using conditional move instructions at the reconvergence point. Because of this very long critical path in vpr, issue is unable to keep up with dispatch which causes the reorder buffer to fill up. In other words, the reorder buffer is unable to hide the instruction latencies and dependencies through out-of-order execution, which results in increased base, L1 D-cache and resource stall cycle components.

Instruction Scheduling. Instruction scheduling tends to increase the dynamic instruction count which, in its turn, increases the base cycle component. This observation was also made by Valluri and Govindarajan [11]. The reason for the increased dynamic instruction count is that spill code is added during the scheduling process by the compiler. Note also that instruction scheduling reduces the branch misprediction penalty for 10 out of 15 benchmarks, see Table 3, *i.e.*, the critical path leading to the mispredicted branch is shortened through the improved instruction scheduling. Unfortunately, this does not compensate for the increased dynamic instruction count resulting in a net performance decrease for most of the benchmarks.

Strict Aliasing. The assumption that references to different object types never access the same address allows for more aggressive scheduling of memory operations — this is a safe optimization as long as the C program complies with the ISO C99 standard[1]. This results in significant performance improvements for a number of benchmarks, see for example art (16.2%). Strict aliasing reduces the number of non-overlapping L2 D-cache misses by 11.5% for art while keeping the total number of L2 D-cache misses almost unchanged; in other words, memory-level parallelism is increased.

4.3   Comparison with In-Order Processors

Having discussed the impact of compiler optimizations on out-of-order processor performance, it is interesting to compare against the impact these compiler optimizations have on in-order processor performance. Figure 6 shows the average normalized cycle counts on a superscalar in-order processor. Performance improves by 17.5% on average compared to the base optimization level. The most striking observation to be made when comparing the in-order graph (Figure 6) against the out-of-order graph (Figure 3) is that instruction scheduling improves performance on the in-order processor whereas on the out-of-order processor, it degrades performance. The reason is that on in-order architectures, the improved instruction schedule outweights the additional spill code that may be generated for accommodating the improved instruction schedule. On an out-of-order processor, the additional spill code only adds overhead through an increased base cycle component.

To better understand the impact of compiler optimizations on out-of-order versus in-order processor performance we now compare in-order processor cycle components against out-of-order processor cycle components. In order to do so, we use the following cycle counting mechanism for computing the cycle components on the in-order processor. For a cycle when no instruction can be issued in a particular cycle, the mechanism increments the count of the appropriate cycle component. For example, when the next instruction to issue stalls for a register to be produced by an L2 miss, the cycle is assigned to the L2 D-cache miss cycle component. Similarly, if no instructions are

---

[1] The current standard for Programming Language C is ISO/IEC 9899:1999, published 1999-12-01.

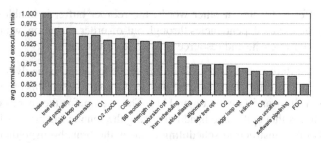

Fig. 6. Average normalized cycle counts on a superscalar in-order processor

available in the pipeline to issue because of a branch misprediction, the cycle is assigned to the branch misprediction cycle component.

The result of comparing the in-order processor cycle components against the out-of-order processor cycle components is presented in Figure 4. To facilitate the discussion, we make the following distinction in cycle components. The first group of cycle components is affected by the dynamic instruction count and the critical path of inter-operation dependencies; these are the base, resource stall, and branch misprediction penalty cycle components. We observe from Figure 4 that these cycle components are affected more by the compiler optimizations for the in-order processor than for the out-of-order processor: 14.6% versus 8.0%. The second group of cycle components are related to the L1 and L2 cache and TLB miss events and the number of branch misprediction events. This second group of miss events is affected more for the out-of-order processor: this is only 2.3% for the in-order processor versus 7% for the out-of-order processor. In other words, most of the performance gain through compiler optimizations on an in-order processor comes from reducing the dynamic instruction count and shortening the critical path of inter-operation dependencies. On an out-of-order processor, the dynamic instruction count and the critical path are also important factors affecting overall performance, however, about one half of the total performance speedup comes from secondary effects related to I-cache, long-latency D-cache and branch misprediction behavior.

There are three reasons that support these observations. First, out-of-order execution hides part of the inter-operation dependencies and latencies which reduces the impact of critical path optimizations. In particular, in a balanced out-of-order processor, the critical path of inter-operation dependencies is only visible on a branch misprediction. Second, the base and resource stall cycle components are more significant for an in-order processor than for an out-of-order processor; this makes the miss event cycle components *relatively* less significant for an in-order processor than for an out-of-order processor. As such, an improvement to these miss event cycle components results in a smaller impact on overall performance for in-order processors. Third, scheduling instructions can have a bigger impact on memory-level parallelism on an out-of-order processor than on an in-order processor. A good static instruction schedule will place independent long-latency D-cache and D-TLB misses closer to each other in the dynamic instruction stream. An out-of-order processor will be able to exploit the available MLP at run time in case the independent long-latency loads appear within a ROB size from each other in the dynamic instruction stream. An in-order processor on the other hand, may not be able to get to the independent long-latency loads because of the processor stalling on instructions that are dependent on the first long-latency load.

5 Related Work

A small number of research papers exist on compiler optimizations for out-of-order processors, however, none of this prior work analyzes the impact of compiler optimizations in terms of their impact on the various cycle components.

Valluri and Govindarajan [11] evaluate the effectiveness of postpass and prepass instruction scheduling techniques on out-of-order processor performance. In postpass scheduling, register allocation precedes instruction scheduling. The potential drawback is that false dependencies introduced by the register allocator may limit the scheduler's ability to efficiently schedule instructions. A prepass scheduling on the other hand only allocates registers after completing instruction scheduling. The potential drawback is that register lifetimes may increase which possibly leads to more spill code. Silvera *et al.* [12] also emphasize the importance of reducing register spill code in out-of-order issue processors. This is also what we observe in this paper. Instruction scheduling increases the dynamic instruction count which degrades the base cycle component and, for most benchmarks, also degrades overall performance. This paper is different from the study conducted by Valluri and Govindarajan [11] in two main ways. First, Valluri and Govindarajan limit their study to instruction scheduling; our paper studies a wide range of compiler optimizations. Second, the study done by Valluri and Govindarajan is an empirical study and does not provide the insight that we provide using an analytical processor model.

Pai and Adve [13] propose read miss clustering, a code transformation technique suitable for compiler implementation that improves memory-level parallelism on out-of-order processors. Read miss clustering strives at scheduling likely long-latency independent memory accesses as close to each other as possible. At execution time, these long-latency loads will then overlap improving overall performance.

Holler [14] discusses various compiler optimizations for the out-of-order HP PA-8000 processor. The paper enumerates various heuristics for driving various compiler optimizations such as loop unrolling, if-conversion, superblock formation, instruction scheduling, *etc.* However, Holler does not quantify the impact of each of these compiler optimizations on out-of-order processor performance.

Cohn and Lowney [15] study feedback-directed compiler optimizations on the out-of-order Alpha 21264 processor. Again, Cohn and Lowney do not provide insight into how compiler optimizations affect cycle components.

Vaswani *et al.* [16] build empirical models that predict the effect of compiler optimizations and microarchitecture configurations on superscalar processor performance. Those models do not provide the insights in terms of cycle components obtained from interval analysis as presented in this paper.

6 Conclusion and Impact on Future Work

The interaction between compiler optimizations and superscalar processors is difficult to understand, especially because of overlap effects in superscalar out-of-order processors. This paper analyzed the impact compiler optimizations have on out-of-order processor performance using interval analysis by dividing total execution time into cycle components.

This paper provides a number of key insights that can help drive future work in compiler optimizations for out-of-order processors. First, the critical path leading to mispredicted branches is the only place during program execution where the impact of the critical path of inter-operation dependencies is visible on overall performance. As such, limiting the focus of instruction scheduling to paths leading to mispredicted branches could yield improved performance and/or limit compilation time; the latter is an important consideration for dynamic compilation systems. Second, the analysis in this paper showed that reducing the dynamic instruction count improves performance by reducing the base cycle component. As such, compiler builders can use this insight for gearing towards optimizations for out-of-order processors that minimize the dynamic instruction count, rather than to increase the amount of ILP — ILP can be extracted dynamically by the hardware. The results presented in this paper shows that reducing the dynamic instruction count remains an important optimization criterion for today's high-performance microprocessors. Third, since miss events have a large impact on overall performance, more so on out-of-order processors than on in-order processors, it is important to make compiler optimizations conscious of their potential impact on miss events. In particular, across the optimization settings considered in this paper, 47.3% of the total performance improvement comes from reduced miss event cycle components for the an out-of-order processor versus only 17.3% for the in-order processor. Fourth, compiler optimizations can improve the amount of memory-level parallelism by scheduling long-latency back-end loads closer to each other in the binary. Independent long-latency loads that occur within ROB size instructions from each other in the dynamic instruction stream overlap at run time which results in memory-level parallelism and thus improved performance. In fact, most of the L2 D-cache miss cycle component reduction observed in our experiments comes from improved MLP, not from reducing the number of L2 D-cache misses. We believe more research can be conducted in exploring compiler optimizations that expose memory-level parallelism.

Acknowledgements

The authors would like to thank the reviewers for their insightful comments. Stijn Eyerman and Lieven Eeckhout are supported by the Fund for Scientific Research in Flanders (Belgium (FWO-Vlaanderen). Additional support was provided by the European HiPEAC Network of Excellence.

References

1. Eyerman, S., Eeckhout, L., Karkhanis, T., Smith, J.E.: A performance counter architecture for computing accurate CPI components. In: ASPLOS, pp. 175–184 (2006)
2. Eyerman, S., Smith, J.E., Eeckhout, L.: Characterizing the branch misprediction penalty. In: ISPASS, pp. 48–58 (2006)
3. Karkhanis, T.S., Smith, J.E.: A first-order superscalar processor model. In: ISCA, pp. 338–349 (2004)

4. Taha, T.M., Wills, D.S.: An instruction throughput model of superscalar processors. In: RSP, pp. 156–163 (2003)
5. Michaud, P., Seznec, A., Jourdan, S.: Exploring instruction-fetch bandwidth requirement in wide-issue superscalar processors. In: Malyshkin, V. (ed.) Parallel Computing Technologies. LNCS, vol. 1662, pp. 2–10. Springer, Heidelberg (1999)
6. Riseman, E.M., Foster, C.C.: The inhibition of potential parallelism by conditional jumps. IEEE Transactions on Computers C-21, 1405–1411 (1972)
7. Wall, D.W.: Limits of instruction-level parallelism. In: ASPLOS, pp. 176–188 (1991)
8. Chou, Y., Fahs, B., Abraham, S.: Microarchitecture optimizations for exploiting memory-level parallelism. In: ISCA, pp. 76–87 (2004)
9. KleinOsowski, A.J., Lilja, D.J.: MinneSPEC: A new SPEC benchmark workload for simulation-based computer architecture research. Computer Architecture Letters 1, 10–13 (2002)
10. Burger, D.C., Austin, T.M.: The SimpleScalar Tool Set. Computer Architecture News (1997), See also http://www.simplescalar.com
11. Valluri, M.G., Govindarajan, R.: Evaluating register allocation and instruction scheduling techniques in out-of-order issue processors. In: Malyshkin, V. (ed.) Parallel Computing Technologies. LNCS, vol. 1662, pp. 78–83. Springer, Heidelberg (1999)
12. Silvera, R., Wang, J., Gao, G.R., Govindarajan, R.: A register pressure sensitive instruction scheduler for dynamic issue processors. In: Malyshkin, V. (ed.) Parallel Computing Technologies. LNCS, vol. 1277, pp. 78–89. Springer, Heidelberg (1997)
13. Pai, V.S., Adve, S.V.: Code transformations to improve memory parallelism. In: MICRO, pp. 147–155 (1999)
14. Holler, A.M.: Optimization for a superscalar out-of-order machine. In: MICRO, pp. 336–348 (1996)
15. Cohn, R., Lowney, P.G.: Design and analysis of profile-based optimization in Compaq's compilation tools for Alpha. Journal of Instruction-Level Paralellism 3, 1–25 (2000)
16. Vaswani, K., Thazhuthaveetil, M.J., Srikant, Y.N., Joseph, P.J.: Microarchitecture sensitive empirical models for compiler optimizations. In: CGO, pp. 131–143 (2007)

An Experimental Environment Validating the Suitability of CLI as an Effective Deployment Format for Embedded Systems*

Marco Cornero, Roberto Costa, Ricardo Fernández Pascual**,
Andrea C. Ornstein, and Erven Rohou

STMicroelectronics
Advanced System Technology
Via Cantonale 16E
6928 Manno (Switzerland)

Abstract. Software productivity for embedded systems is greatly limited by the fragmentation of platforms and associated development tools. Platform virtualization environments, like Java and Microsoft .NET, help alleviate the problem, but they are limited to host functionalities running on the system microcontroller. Due to the ever increasing demand for processing power, it is desirable to extend their benefits to the rest of the system. We present an experimental framework based on GCC that validates the choice of *CLI* as a suitable processor-independent deployment format. In particular, we illustrate our GCC port to *CLI* and we evaluate the generated bytecode in terms of code size and performance. We inject it back into GCC through a *CLI* front-end that we also illustrate, and we complete the compilation down to native code. We show that using *CLI* does not degrade performance. Compared to other *CLI* solutions, we offer a full development flow for the C language, generating a subset of pure *CLI* that does not require any virtual machine support other than a JIT compiler. It is therefore well suited for deeply embedded media processors running high performance media applications.

Keywords: Common Language Infrastructure, embedded systems, deployment, GCC.

1 Introduction

The productivity of embedded software development is heavily limited by several factors, the most important being the high fragmentation of the hardware platforms combined with the multiple target operating systems and associated tools. Indeed, in order to reach a wide customer base, software developers need to port, test and maintain their applications to tens of different configurations, wasting a great deal of effort in the process. Platform virtualization technologies have been very successful in alleviating this problem, as it is evident by the

---

* This work was partially funded by the HiPEAC Network of Excellence.
** This author performed this work as a HiPEAC PhD student at STMicroelectronics.

P. Stenström et al. (Eds.): HiPEAC 2008, LNCS 4917, pp. 130–144, 2008.

widespread distribution of Java solutions on multiple platforms and operating systems, as well as .NET on Microsoft-supported platforms. However, because of their high-level language support, complemented by sophisticated runtimes and libraries, Java and .NET are well suited only for host functionalities on the system microcontroller. With the growing demand for new and computational intensive applications, such as multimedia, gaming and increasingly sophisticated man-machine interfaces, there is a clear need to extend the computing resources available to software programmers of embedded systems, well beyond the reach of the system microcontrollers. Historically performance scaling has been achieved through increased clock frequency, a path which is not available anymore, especially for portable embedded system, where power consumption is a primary concern. The alternative is multiprocessing, that by the way has been adopted in embedded systems well before its more recent introduction in the PC domain. Multiprocessing comes in many different flavors though, and for efficiency reasons embedded systems have clearly favored highly heterogeneous architectures, typically resulting into two well defined and separated subsystems: the host processing side, composed of one microcontroller (possibly several ones in the future), and the deeply embedded side composed of multiple dedicated processors. Because of the difficulty in programming the resulting systems, the embedded side is mostly programmed by the silicon vendors and sometimes by the platform providers, while only the host part is open to independent software vendors (ISV). In order to respond to the increasing demand for computational power, while keeping the required efficiency, it is highly desirable to grant access to at least part of the deeply embedded resources to the ISV.

Two main issues must be addressed in order to achieve this goal: 1) the programming model and 2) the associated development tools. Indeed, heterogeneous multiprocessor systems are equivalent to small-scale distributed systems, for which a suitable programming model is required. We privilege component-based software engineering practices to tackle this point, but this is not the subject of this paper. For the second point, it is unconceivable to worsen the fragmentation problem by introducing new tools for each variant of the embedded processors. We propose to extend the platform virtualization approaches already adopted in environments such as Java and .NET, to offer a homogeneous software development framework targeting both the host and the embedded subsystems.

Specifically, we need a processor-independent format, well suited for software deployment on a wide variety of embedded systems, which can be efficiently compiled just-in-time (JIT), and which can interact at no additional cost with existing native environments, such as native optimized libraries, as well as with existing managed frameworks like Java and .NET. We have selected a subset of the *CLI* standard [7,13], better known as Microsoft .NET, and the goal of this paper is to illustrate the experimental setup that we have used to validate this choice. Note that one could just serialize the internal representation of a compiler, but we believe that *CLI* provides a number of significant advantages:

- it has been standardized, which means that its definition is clear and public, and it is not subject to changes without notice;

- this format is directly executable on various platforms;
- there is a lot of interest around this format, for example Microsoft .NET, Mono [3] or DotGNU [1], just to name a few.

Given our primary target of performance scalability, our most important requirement is the quality of the final code generated by the JIT, and the code size as a second priority. Besides, given the target domain, *i.e.* compute intensive code on deeply embedded processors, we also constrain ourselves to the traditional programming language used in this context, which is C (we will certainly consider C++ as well later). Finally, given the real-time nature of our applications, we avoid for the time being dynamic configurations where the JIT can be invoked while the application is already running. Instead we pre-compile the input *CLI* code on the target embedded device in one of the following configurations:

1. at application install-time, *i.e.* the user downloads an application in *CLI* format and during the installation procedure the JIT is invoked to translate the *CLI* into native code, which is then stored into the device persistent memory once and for all; or
2. at load time, *i.e.* the device keeps the application in its permanent memory in *CLI* format; each time the application is executed it gets translated by the JIT into native code to the main memory.

Like in any platform virtualization environment, the compilation process is split in two phases: the generation of the processor-independent format, occurring in the development platform, and the JIT compilation which occurs on the device after the deployment of the applications in a processor-independent format. For the first compilation phase we have chosen the GCC compiler because of its wide adoption and because of the relatively recent introduction of the *GIMPLE* middle-level internal representation, which we prove in this paper to be well suited for the purpose of generating very efficient *CLI* bytecode. For the JIT part, we are developing our JIT infrastructure targeting our embedded processor family, as well as the ARM microcontroller, with very encouraging results. However the JIT is still work in progress, so we do not illustrate it in this paper. Instead, in order to validate our choice of *CLI*, we have developed an experimental GCC *CLI* front-end, so that we can re-inject the generated *CLI* bytecode back into GCC, and complete the compilation process down to native code, whose quality is compared to the code obtained by the normal GCC flow (see Figure 1). In so doing we prove that using *CLI* as an intermediate processor-independent deployment format does not degrade performance. We also report the *CLI* code size obtained with our GCC *CLI* generator, which proves to be competitive with respect to native code.

Finally, *CLI* provides the right primitives for interoperability (*pinvoke*): once the bytecode is JIT-ted, it can be either statically or dynamically linked with native libraries without any specific restriction or penalty with respect to native code compiled with a normal static flow.

The following section describes our implementation. Section 3 presents our experimental results and analyses. We review some related works in Section 4 before concluding.

Application

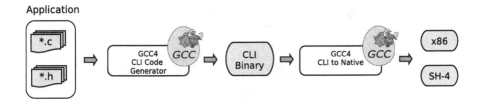

Fig. 1. Experimental setup

2   Implementation

We implemented our experiments inside the GCC compiler [8] for several reasons: the source code is freely available, it is quite robust, being the outcome of hundreds of developers over fifteen years; it already supports many input languages and target processors; and there is a large community of volunteers and industrials that follow the developments. Its tree-based middle end is also particularly well suited both to produce optimized *CIL* bytecode and to be regenerated starting from *CIL* bytecode.

In the first step, GCC is configured as a *CLI* back-end [4]: it compiles C source code to *CLI*. A differently configured GCC then reads the *CLI* binary and acts as a traditional back-end for the target processor. The *CLI* front-end necessary for this purpose has been developed from scratch for this research [19].

2.1   GCC Structure

The structure of GCC is similar to most portable compilers. A *front-end*, different for each input language, reads the program and translates it into an abstract syntax tree (AST). The representation used by GCC is called *GIMPLE* [18]. Many high-level, target independent, optimizations are applied to the AST (dead code elimination, copy propagation, dead store elimination, vectorization, and many others). The AST is then *lowered* to another representation called register transfer language (*RTL*), a target dependent representation. *RTL* is run through low-level optimizations (if-conversion, combining, scheduling, register allocation, etc.) before the assembly code is emitted. Figure 2 depicts this high-level view of the compiler. Note that some languages first produce a representation called *GENERIC*, which is then lowered to *GIMPLE* [18,23].

2.2   *CLI* Code Generator

GCC gets the information about the target from a target machine model. It consists of a machine description which gives an algebraic formula for each of the machine's instructions, in a file of instruction patterns used to map *GIMPLE* to *RTL* and to generate the assembly and in a set of C macro definitions that specify the characteristic of the target, like the endianness, how registers are used, the definition of the ABI, the usage of the stack, etc.

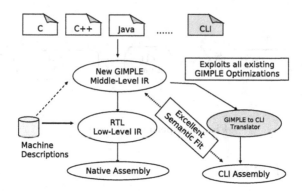

Fig. 2. Structure of the GCC compiler

This is a very clean way to describe the target, but when the compiler needs information that is difficult to express in this fashion, GCC developers have not hesitated to define an ad-hoc parameter to the machine description. The machine description is used throughout *RTL* passes.

RTL is the lowest level GCC intermediate representation; in *RTL*

- each instruction is target-specific and it describes its overall effects in terms of register and memory usage;
- registers may be physical as well as virtual registers, freely inter-mixed (until register allocation pass is run, which leaves no virtual registers);
- memory is represented through an address expression and the size of the accessed memory cell;
- finally, *RTL* has a very low-level representation of types, which are called *machine modes*. They correspond to the typical machine language representation of types, which only includes the size of the data object and the representation used for it.

CIL bytecode is much more high-level than a processor machine code. *CIL* is guaranteed by design to be independent from the target machine and to allow effective just-in-time compilation through the execution environment provided by the *Common Language Runtime*. It is a stack-based machine, it is strongly typed and there is no such a concept as registers or frame stack; instructions operate on an unbound set of locals (which closely match the concept of local variables) and on elements on top of an evaluation stack.

We initially considered writing a standard GCC back-end. However. much of the high-level information needed to dump *CLI* is lost at *RTL* level, whereas there is a good semantic fit between *GIMPLE* and *CLI*. It seemed awkward to augment a lowered representation with high-level information.

Thus, we decided to stop the compilation flow at the end of the middle-end passes without going through any *RTL* pass, and to emit CIL bytecode from *GIMPLE* representation (see Figure 2).

We wrote three specific *CLI* passes:

- CLI *simplification*: most *GIMPLE* tree codes closely match what is representable in *CIL*, this pass expands the ones that do not follow this rule. The output of the pass is still *GIMPLE* but it does not contain tree codes that the emission pass do not handle. The pass can be executed multiple times to avoid putting constraints on other passes. It is idempotent by construction.
- *Removal of temporary variables*: In *GIMPLE*, expressions are broken down into a 3-address form, using temporary variables to hold intermediate values. This pass merges *GIMPLE* expressions to eliminate such temporary variables. Intermediate results are simply left on the evaluation stack. This results in cleaner code and a lower number of locals.
- CLI *emission*: this pass receives a *CIL*-simplified *GIMPLE* form as input and it produces a *CLI* assembly file as output.

With these three passes and a minimal target machine description we are able to support most of C99 [1] [14]. More details of the implementation can be found in [5], and the code is freely available [4].

2.3   *CLI* to Native Translation

We have implemented a GCC front-end only for a subset of the *CLI* language, pragmatically dictated by the need to compile the code produced by our back-end. However, nothing in the design of the front-end forbids us to extend it to a more complete implementation in the future. The supported features include most base *CIL* instructions, direct and indirect calls to static methods, most *CIL* types, structures with explicit layout and size (very frequently used by our back-end), constant initializers, limited access to native platform libraries (*pInvoke*) support and other less frequently used features required by our back-end. On the other hand, unsupported features include object model related functionality, exceptions, garbage collection, reflection and support for *generics*.

Our front-end is analogous to the GNU Compiler for Java (GCJ) [9] which compiles JVM bytecodes to native code (GCJ can also directly compile from Java to native code without using bytecodes). Both front-ends perform the work that is usually done by a JIT compiler in traditional virtual machines. But unlike JIT compilers, these front-ends are executed *ahead of time*. Hence, they can use much more time-consuming optimizations to generate better code, and the startup overhead of the JIT compilation is eliminated. In particular, our front-end compiles *CIL* using the full set of optimizations available in GCC.

The front-end can compile one or more *CLI* assemblies into an object file. The assembly is loaded and its metadata and code streams are parsed. Instead of writing our own metadata parser, we rely on Mono [3] shared library. Mono provides a comprehensive API to handle the *CLI* metadata and it has been easy to extend where it was lacking some functionality. Hence, the front-end only has to parse the code stream of the methods to compile.

---

[1] In the interest of time, we skipped a few features that were uninteresting for our immediate purposes, for example complex numbers.

Once the assembly has been loaded, the front-end builds GCC types for all the *CLI* types declared or referenced in the assembly. To do this, some referenced assemblies may need to be loaded too.

After building GCC types, the front-end parses the *CIL* code stream of each method defined in the assembly in order to build GCC *GENERIC* trees for them. Most *CIL* operations are simple and map naturally to *GENERIC* expressions or to GCC built-in functions. *GENERIC* trees are then translated to the more strict *GIMPLE* representation (*gimplified*) and passed to the next GCC passes to be optimized and translated to native code.

Finally, the front-end creates a main function for the program which performs any required initialization and calls the assembly entry point.

Currently, the main source of limitations in the implementation of a full *CIL* front-end is the lack of a run-time library which is necessary to implement virtual machine services like garbage collection, dynamic class loading and reflection. These services are not required in order to use *CIL* as an intermediate language for compiling C or other traditional languages. Also, *CIL* programs usually require a standard class library which would need to be ported to this environment. The effort to build this infrastructure was outside the scope of our experiment.

2.4   Tools

From the user's point of view, the toolchain is identical to a native toolchain. We essentially use an assembler and a linker. As expected, the assembler takes the *CLI* in textual form and generates an object representation. The linker takes several of those object files and produces the final *CLI* executable.

At this point we rely on tools provided by the projects Mono [3] and Portable.-NET [1]. We plan to switch to a Mono only solution, to limit the number of dependences we have on other projects, and to avoid using the non-standard file format used by Portable.NET for object files.

3   Experiments and Results

3.1   Setup

This section describes the experimental setup we used to compare the code generated through a traditional compilation flow with the one generated using *CLI* as intermediate representation. GCC 4.1 is the common compilation technology for all the experiments; of course, different compilation flows use different combinations of GCC front-ends and back-ends. The compilation flows under examination are:

- *configuration a*: C to native, -O2 optimization level. In other words, this is the traditional compilation flow, it is used as a reference to compare against.
- *configuration b*: C to *CLI* at -O2 optimization level, followed by *CLI* to native, also at -O2. This gives us an upper bound of the achievable performance when going through *CLI*.

– *configuration c*: C to *CLI*, -O2 optimization level, followed by *CLI* to native, -O0 optimization level for *GIMPLE* passes and -O2 for *RTL* ones. This is still a *CLI*-based compilation flow, in which optimizations at *GIMPLE* level are skipped in the final compilation step. Even though it seems a bit contorted, this setup is important to evaluate up to which degree high-level optimizations can be performed only in the first step. As a matter of fact, in dynamic environments the second compilation step may be replaced by just-in-time compilation, which is typically more time constrained and is likely to apply only target-specific optimizations.

The benchmarks come from several sources: MediaBench [16] and MiBench [11], others are internally developed. We focused on applications or computational kernels that are relevant to our field (audio, video, cryptography, etc.) We also had to eliminate some benchmarks that had execution times close to the resolution of the timer and thus were not reliable. Table 1 gives the list of benchmarks along with a short description.

Table 1. Benchmarks used in our experiments

benchmark	description	benchmark	description
ac3	AC3 audio decoder	mp4dec	MPEG4 decoder
adpcm	ADPCM decoder	mpeg1l2	MPEG1 audio layer 2 decoder
adpcmc	ADPCM encoder	mpeg2enc	MPEG2 encoder
render	image rendering pipeline	divx	DivX decoder
compress	Unix compress utility	sha	Secure Hash Algorithm
crypto	DES, RSA and MD5	video	video player
dijkstra	shortest path in network	yacr2	channel routing
ft	minimum spanning tree	bitcount	count bits in integers
g721c	G721 encoder	cjpeg	JPEG encoder
g721d	G721 decoder	tjpeg	optimized for embedded
ks	graph partitioning	crc32	32-bit CRC polynomial
mp2avswitch	MPEG2 intra loop encoder + MPEG1 layer 2 audio encoder		

We ran our experiments on two targets. The first one is an PC Intel Pentium III clocked at 800 MHz, with 256 Mbytes of RAM, running Linux 2.6. The second one is a board developed by STMicroelectronics named STb7100 [24]. The host processor is a *SH-4* clocked at 266 MHz. It features a 64-Mbits flash memory and 64-Mbytes of DDR RAM. The board itself is actually a complete solution single-chip, low-cost HD set-top box decoder for digital TV, digital set-top box or cable box. However, in these experiments we only take advantage of the host processor.

3.2 Experiments

To evaluate the relevance of the *CLI* as a deployment format, we ran two experiments. The first one evaluates the size of the code that needs to be shipped on a device: on one hand the *CLI* file, on the other hand the respective native

Table 2. Code size results for *CLI*, *x86* and *SH-4* (in bytes)

benchmark	CLI size	x86 size	%	SH-4 size	%
ac3	86016	63381	-26.3%	66407	-22.8%
adpcm	8704	11160	28.2%	13974	60.5%
adpcmc	8704	10943	25.7%	13621	56.5%
render	144384	114988	-20.4%	122232	-15.3%
compress	16384	18555	13.3%	23567	43.8%
crypto	73216	80796	10.4%	87040	18.9%
dijkstra	7680	11208	45.9%	13990	82.2%
ft	18944	21359	12.7%	23868	26.0%
g721c	19456	18226	-6.3%	21392	10.0%
g721d	19456	18159	-6.7%	21321	9.6%
ks	16896	16196	-4.1%	22034	30.4%
mp2avswitch	272384	202446	-25.7%	198486	-27.1%
mp4dec	67584	53824	-20.4%	57636	-14.7%
mpeg1l2	104960	86279	-17.8%	84863	-19.1%
mpeg2enc	88576	85415	-3.6%	185632	109.6%
divx	67584	49134	-27.3%	55869	-17.3%
sha	7680	10960	42.7%	13858	80.4%
video	1036288	275819	-73.4%	264067	-74.5%
yacr2	37376	34441	-7.9%	39653	6.1%
bitcount	9728	12678	30.3%	15912	63.6%
cjpeg	226304	153161	-32.3%	158330	-30.0%
tjpeg	54272	52826	-2.7%	56682	4.4%
crc32	8704	10794	24.0%	13428	54.3%
average			-1.8%		18.9%

binaries. In Table 2, the second column gives the size of the *CLI* executable. The following two columns give the size of the *x86* binary, in absolute value, and as a percentage of the *CLI*. The respective numbers for *SH-4* are given in the last two columns. Those numbers are graphically represented on Figure 3, left bar for *x86* and right bar for *SH-4*.

The second experiment is about performance. Since we break the compilation flow, one might expect that the compiler loses information in the back-end, and thus performance. Table 3 shows the execution times (in seconds, averaged over five runs) of our set of benchmarks compiled with the three compilation flows for *x86* and *SH-4*.

3.3   Analysis

The first comment we make on code size is that, even though *x86* and *SH-4* have quite dense instruction sets, the *CLI* binary is often smaller. The case of *mpeg2enc* on *SH-4* is extreme and comes from the fact that the native compiler decided to statically link part of the math library to take advantage of specialized trigonometric routines. Several benchmarks see their code size increased by the

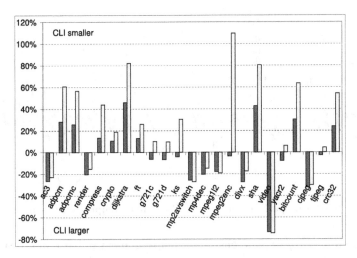

Fig. 3. Native code size (config. a) wrt. *CLI*. Left bar is *x86*, right bar is *SH-4*.

Table 3. Performance results on *x86* and *SH-4* (in seconds)

benchmark	x86			SH-4		
	a	b	c	a	b	c
ac3	0.17	0.18	0.19	0.68	0.71	0.71
adpcm	0.04	0.04	0.04	0.16	0.17	0.17
adpcmc	0.07	0.07	0.06	0.27	0.27	0.27
render	2.15	1.97	2.08	9.87	8.85	8.86
compress	0.03	0.03	0.03	0.50	0.48	0.47
crypto	0.12	0.14	0.15	0.52	0.51	0.53
dijkstra	0.20	0.22	0.22	1.32	1.34	1.34
ft	0.35	0.35	0.29	2.64	2.44	2.62
g721c	0.47	0.46	0.48	1.86	1.66	1.69
g721d	0.43	0.46	0.42	1.54	1.73	1.64
ks	28.00	29.27	30.32	123.44	144.04	140.27
mp2avswitch	2.55	2.55	2.67	12.09	11.55	11.78
mp4dec	0.05	0.06	0.06	0.33	0.35	0.34
mpeg1l2	0.67	0.64	0.63	1.77	1.96	1.95
mpeg2enc	0.76	0.50	0.79	3.37	3.50	4.19
divx	0.39	0.41	0.41	1.27	1.25	1.25
sha	0.30	0.30	0.37	1.98	2.17	2.17
video	0.10	0.10	0.10	0.36	0.37	0.37
yacr2	0.67	0.65	0.70	3.16	3.18	3.08
bitcount	0.03	0.03	0.03	0.13	0.11	0.11
cjpeg	1.72	1.72	1.70	7.73	7.53	7.80
tjpeg	0.48	0.44	0.45	3.05	2.90	3.02
crc32	0.57	0.58	0.55	1.53	1.48	1.52

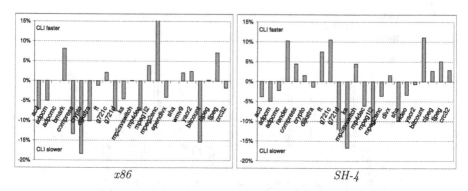

Fig. 4. Impact on performance of the *CLI* based compilation (config a vs. b)

introduction of *SH-4* nops to ensure proper alignment of basic blocks and functions, required to achieve high performance of this architecture.

The worst case comes from the benchmark *video*, where *CLI* is roughly 74% larger than *x86* or *SH-4*: two thirds of the *CLI* code is made of initializers of arrays of bitfields, for which we emit very naive code, one bitfield at a time. A smarter code emission (which we have planned, but not yet implemented) will combine bitfields to generate the values in-place, getting rid of most initializers.

Excluding the pathological cases, *video* for both architectures and *mpeg2enc* for *SH-4*, the *SH-4* (resp. *x86*) is 19% (resp. 2%) larger than *CLI*.

There are other opportunities for improvements: in some cases, we have to generate data segments for both little-endian and big-endian architectures. It is likely that, at deployment-time, the endianness is known[2]. In this case, the useless data definition could be dropped. Another reduction can come from the fact that *CLI* retains all the source code function and type names in the metadata. In the absence of reflection, which is true for the C language, those names can be changed to much shorter ones. Using only lower case and upper case letters, digits and underscore, one can encode $(2 \times 26 + 10 + 1)^2 = 5329$ names on two characters, drastically reducing the size of the string pool.

Our experiments confirm a previous result [6] that *CLI* is quite compact, similar to *x86* and roughly 20% smaller (taking into account the preceding remarks) than *SH-4*, both notoriously known for having dense instruction sets.

On the performance side, consider the Figure 4 which represents the performance of the binaries generated by the configuration *b* (through *CLI*, at -O2) with respect to *a* (classical flow also at -O2). It measures the impact on performance of using the intermediate representation. The code generated through *CLI* in configuration *b* is, on average, barely slower than *a*. In other words, using -O2 optimization level in all cases causes a 1.5% performance degradation on *x86* and 0.6% on *SH-4*. The worst degradation is also contained, with -18% for *crypto* on *x86* and -17% for *ks* on *SH-4*.

---

[2] Some platforms are made of processors of both endiannesses. It could be advantageous to migrate the code from one to another and thus to keep both definitions.

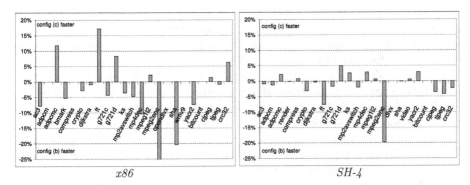

Fig. 5. Impact of high-level optimizations on performance (config b vs. c)

Understanding the reasons of variations is quite difficult. Even though the compiler infractucture is the same, each target triggers the heuristics in different ways. For example, in the case of *bitcount*, a inner loop has been unrolled by the *SH-4* compiler and not by the *x86* compiler, even though the input file is identical. This leads to the difference in performance seen on Figure 4.

Figure 5 compares the two configurations that use *CLI*, evaluating the need to rerun high-level optimizations in the *CLI* to native translation. The average slowdown is 1.3% on *SH-4* and 4% on *x86*. Excluding the extreme case *mpeg2enc*, they are respectively 0.4% and 1.3%. Most performance degradations are within 5% on the *SH-4* and within 10% on the *x86*. This is a good news because it means that there is little need to run high-level optimizations on the *CLI* executable, it is enough to run the back-end (target specific) optimizer. Some poor results are explained by inefficient *CLI* patterns. Array accesses are expressed in *GIMPLE* by a single node, *e.g.* a[i]. There is no such abstraction in *CLI* (at least for non managed data). We are forced to emit the code sequence corresponding to *(@a+sizeof_elem*i). When a loop contains several array accesses, we repeat the address computation, but there is no later code cleanup. In configuration *b*, the high level loop optimizer moves loop invariants and rewrites induction variables. In configuration *c*, this does not happen, leaving the back-end with poor quality code. This is obviously an inefficiency we will fix.

Keep also in mind that those experiments rely on a prototype implementation of the *CLI* to native code generator. Emphasis has been put on correctness, not yet on quality. Even though the *CLI* generator is in a much better state, we have identified a number of areas where it could be improved. This lack of tuning also contributes to the deviation observed in the results.

4   Related Work

4.1   Not *CLI*-Based

In many aspects, the Java framework [17] is the precursor of *CLI*. Similarly to *CLI*, Java defines a bytecode based virtual machine, a standard library and it offers services like garbage collection, multi-threading, etc. Java is widely used in embedded systems in order to provide complementary capabilities, like games for cellphones or TV guides for set-top-boxes. However, it is not adapted for the core software for several reasons.

Java typically incurs a significant performance overhead, not acceptable for performance critical applications; this is mostly because it does not offer install-time compilation, and also because it does not provide the lower-level abstraction the way C does: pointer arithmetic, no garbage collection, no array bound checks, etc. The Java language [10] is high-level and object-oriented language. Porting source code from C to Java typically involves significant changes that may even lead to a full redesign of the application.

AppForge used to be a company selling Crossfire, a plugin for Microsoft Visual Studio .NET that converted the *CLI* bytecode to their own proprietary bytecode. Developers could use VB.NET or C# to develop applications for various mobile devices. The bytecode is interpreted and is not meant to run the performance critical parts of the application, which are still executed natively.

4.2   *CLI*-Based

The *CIL* bytecode was first introduced by Microsoft .NET. It has also been standardized by ECMA [7] and ISO [13]. *CIL* has been designed for a large variety of languages, and Microsoft provides compilers for several of them: C++, C#, J#, VB.NET. The C language, though, cannot be compiled to *CIL*.

Mono [3] is an open source project sponsored by Novell. It provides the necessary software to develop and run .NET applications on Linux, Solaris, Mac OS X, Windows, and Unix. It is compatible with compilers for many languages [2].

DotGNU Portable.NET [1] is another implementation of the *CLI*, that includes everything you need to compile and run C# and C applications that use the base class libraries. It supports various processors and operating systems.

Lcc is a simple retargetable compiler for Standard C. In [12], Hanson describes how he targeted lcc to *CLI*. He covered most of the language and explains the reasons for his choices, and the limitations. The port was meant more as an experiment to stress lcc itself than to produce a robust compiler.

Singer [22] describes another approach to generate *CLI* from C, using GCC. While based on the same compiler, it differs in the implementation: he starts from the *RTL* representation and suffers from the loss of high level information. As the title suggests, this is a feasibility study that can handle only toy benchmarks.

Löwis and Möller [26] developed a *CLI* front-end for GCC with a different goal: while we focus on very optimized C code, they aim at running all the features of *CLI* on the Lego Mindstorm platform [25]. However, they currently support a fraction of the *CLI* features and they can run only small programs.

Very similar to our work is another *CLI* port of GCC done by a student as part of the Google Summer of Code and sponsored by the Mono project [15]. This work is still very preliminary and stopped at the end of the internship.

Some applications may have a long startup time because they are linked against large libraries. Even if the application requires only few symbols, the runtime system might scan a large portion of the library. This also increases the memory footprint off the application. Rabe [20] introduces the concept of *self-contained assembly* to address these problems. He builds a new *CLI* assembly that merges all previous references and does not depend on any other library.

While we priviledged programming embedded systems in C, using *CLI* as an intermediate format, Richter *et al.* [21] proposed to extend *CLI* with attributes to be able to express low-level concepts in C#. They encapsulate in *CLI* classes the notions of direct hardware access, interrupt handler and concurrency.

5 Conclusion

We have illustrated the motivations of our platform virtualization work and the experimental framework that we have used for validating the choice of *CLI* as an effective processor-independent deployment format for embedded systems, in terms of code size and performance. In addition we have described the implementation of our open source *CLI* generator based on GCC4. The presented results show that using *CLI* as an intermediate deployment format does not penalize performance, and that code size is competitive with respect to native code.

We are currently working on optimized JIT compilers for our target embedded processors as well as for the ARM microcontroller. We are also investigating how to optimally balance the static generation of highly effective *CLI* byte-code, complemented with additional information resulting from advanced static analyses, with the dynamic exploitation of that information by our JIT compilers in order to generate highly optimized native code as quickly as possible in the target embedded devices.

References

1. DotGNU project, http://dotgnu.org
2. Mono-compatible compilers, http://www.mono-project.com/Languages
3. The Mono Project, http://www.mono-project.com
4. Bona, A., Costa, R., Ornstein, A., Rohou, E.: GCC CLI back-end project, http://gcc.gnu.org/projects/cli.html
5. Costa, R., Ornstein, A., Rohou, E.: CLI Back-End in GCC. In: GCC Developers' Summit, pp. 111–116, Ottawa, Canada (July 2007)
6. Costa, R., Rohou, E.: Comparing the Size of .NET Applications with Native Code. In: Proceedings of the 3rd IEEE/ACM/IFIP International Conference on Hardware/Software Codesign and System Synthesis, Jersey City, NJ, USA, pp. 99–104. ACM Press, New York (2005)
7. ECMA International, Rue du Rhône 114, 1204 Geneva, Switzerland. Common Language Infrastructure (CLI) Partitions I to IV, 4th edn. (June 2006)
8. Free Software Foundation. The GNU Compiler Collection, http://gcc.gnu.org
9. The GNU Compiler for the Java Programming Language. http://gcc.\discretionary{-}{}{}gnu.\discretionary{-}{}{}org/java
10. Gosling, J., Joy, B., Steele, G., Bracha, G.: The Java Language Specification, 2nd edn. Addison-Wesley, Reading (2000)

11. Guthaus, M.R., Ringenberg, J.S., Ernst, D., Austin, T.M., Mudge, T., Brown, R.B.: MiBench: A free, commercially representative embedded benchmark suite. In: IEEE 4th Annual Workshop on Workload Characterization, Austin, TX, USA (December 2001)
12. Hanson, D.R.: Lcc.NET: Targeting the .NET Common Intermediate Language from Standard C. Software: Practice and Experience 34(3), 265–286 (2003)
13. International Organization for Standardization and International Electrotechnical Commission. International Standard ISO/IEC 23271:2006 - Common Language Infrastructure (CLI), Partitions I to VI, 2nd edn.
14. International Organization for Standardization and International Electrotechnical Commission. International Standard ISO/IEC 9899:TC2 - Programming languages - C (1999)
15. Kottalam, J.: Blog of Jeyasankar Kottalam (2005), http://gcc-cil.blogspot. com , http://forge.novell.com/modules/xfmod/project/?gcc-cil
16. Lee, C., Potkonjak, M., Mangione-Smith, W.H.: MediaBench: A Tool for Evaluating and Synthesizing Multimedia and Communications Systems. In: Proceedings of the 30th Annual IEEE/ACM International Symposium on Microarchitecture, pp. 330–335 (1997)
17. Lindholm, T., Yellin, F.: The Java Virtual Machine Specification, 2nd edn. Addison-Wesley, Reading (1999)
18. Merill, J.: GENERIC and GIMPLE: A New Tree Representation for Entire Functions. In: GCC Developers' Summit (2003)
19. Fernández Pascual, R.: HiPEAC PhD Internship – GCC CIL Frontend (2006), http://www.hipeac.net/node/823
20. Rabe, B.: Towards a CLI Assembly Format for Embedded Systems. In: International Conference on Embedded Systems and Applications, Las Vegas, NE, USA (June 2006)
21. Richter, S., Rasche, A., Polze, A.: Hardware-near Programming in the Common Language Infrastructure. In: Proceedings of the 10th IEEE International Symposium on Object and Component-oriented Real-time Distributed Computing, Santorini Island, Greece (May 2007)
22. Singer, J.: GCC .NET – a Feasibility Study. In: 1st International Workshop on C# and .NET Technologies on Algorithms, Computer Graphics, Visualization, Distributed and WEB Computing, Plzen, Czech Republic (2003)
23. Stallman, R.M., and the GCC Developer Community. GNU Compiler Collection Internals. Free Software Foundation
24. STMicroelectronics. STb7100-MBoard Datasheet – Single-chip, low-cost HD set-top box decoder for digital TV, digital set-top box or cable box (December 2005)
25. Operating Systems and Middleware Group. Lego.NET website, http://www.dcl. hpi.uni-potsdam.de/research/lego.NET
26. Löwis, M.v., Möller, J.: A Microsoft .NET Front-End for GCC. In: Proceedings of .NET Technologies 2006, Plzen, Czech Republic (June 2006) ISBN 80-86943-11-9

Part III

Industrial Processors and Application Parallelization

Compilation Strategies for Reducing Code Size on a VLIW Processor with Variable Length Instructions

Todd T. Hahn, Eric Stotzer, Dineel Sule, and Mike Asal

Texas Instruments Incorporated
12203 Southwest Freeway, Stafford, TX 77477
{tthahn,estotzer,dineel,m-asal}@ti.com

Abstract. This paper describes the development and compiler utilization of variable length instruction set extensions to an existing high-performance, 32-bit VLIW DSP processor. We describe how the instruction set extensions (1) reduce code size significantly, (2) are binary compatibile with older object code, (3) do not require the processor to switch "modes", and (4) are exploited by a compiler. We describe the compiler strategies that utilize the new instruction set extensions to reduced code size. When compiling our benchmark suite for best performance, we show that our compiler uses the variable length instructions to decreases code size by 11.5 percent, with no reduction in performance. We also show that our implementation allows a wider code size and performance tradeoff range than earlier versions of the architecture.

1 Introduction

VLIW (very long instruction word) processors are well-suited for embedded signal and video processing applications, which are characterized by mathematically oriented loop kernels and abundant ILP (instruction level parallelism). Because they do not have hardware to dynamically find implicit ILP at run-time, VLIW architectures rely on the compiler to statically encode the ILP in the program before its execution [1]. Since ILP must be explicitly expressed in the program code, VLIW program optimizations often replicate instructions, increasing code size. While code size is a secondary concern in the computing community overall, it can be significant in the embedded community. In this paper we present an approach for reducing code size on an embedded VLIW processor using a combination of compiler and instruction encoding techniques.

VLIW processors combine multiple instructions into an execute packet. All instructions in an execute packet are issued in parallel. Code compiled for a VLIW will often include many NOP instructions, which occur because there is not enough ILP to completely fill an execute packet with useful instructions. Since code size is a concern, instruction encoding techniques have been developed to implicitly encode VLIW NOP instructions [2]. Another approach to reduce code size is to store a compressed image of the VLIW program code in external

P. Stenström et al. (Eds.): HiPEAC 2008, LNCS 4917, pp. 147–160, 2008.

memory, and use run-time software or hardware to decompress the code as it is executed or loaded into a program cache [3,4]. Other approaches have used variable length instruction encoding techniques to reduce the size of execute packets [5]. Finally, recognizing that code size is often the priority in embedded systems, other approaches use processor modes with smaller opcode encodings for a subset of frequently occurring instructions. Examples of mode-based architectures are the ARM Limited ARM architecture's Thumb mode [6,7] and the MIPS Technologies MIPS32 architecture's MIPS16 mode [8].

In this paper, we discuss a hybrid approach for reducing code size on a VLIW, using a combination of compilation techniques and compact instruction encodings. We provide an overview of the TMS320C6000 (C6x) family of VLIW processors and how instructions are encoded to reduce the code size. We then describe a unique modeless binary compatible encoding for variable length instructions that has been implemented on the TMS320C64+ (C64+) processor, which is the latest member of the C6x processor family. We describe how, consistent with the VLIW architecture philosophy, the compact instruction encoding is directed by the compiler. We discuss how the different compiler code size strategies leverage the compact instructions to reduce program code size and balance program performance. Finally, we conclude with results showing how program code size is reduced on a set of typical DSP applications. We also show that our implementation allows a significantly wider range of size and performance tradeoffs versus earlier versions of the architecture.

2   The TMS320C6000 VLIW DSP Core

The TMS320C62x (C62) is a fully pipelined VLIW processor, which allows eight new instructions to be issued per cycle. All instructions can be optionally guarded by a static predicate. The C62 is the base member of the Texas Instruments' C6x family (Fig. 1), providing a foundation of integer instructions. It has 32 static general-purpose registers, partitioned into two register files. A small subset of the registers may be used for predication. The TMS320C64x (C64) builds on the C62 by removing scheduling restrictions on existing instructions and providing additional instructions for packed-data/SIMD (single instruction multiple data) processing. It also extends the register file by providing an additional 16 static general-purpose registers in each register file [9].

The C6x is targeted toward embedded DSP (digital signal processing) applications, such as telecom and image processing. These applications spend the bulk of their time in computationally intensive loop nests which exhibit high degrees of ILP. Software pipelining, a powerful loop-based transformation, is key to extracting this parallelism and exploiting the many functional units on the C6x [10].

Each instruction on the C6x is 32-bit. Instructions are fetched eight at a time from program memory in bundles called *fetch packets*. Fetch packets are aligned on 256-bit (8-word) boundaries. The C6x architecture can execute from one to eight instructions in parallel. Parallel instructions are bundled together

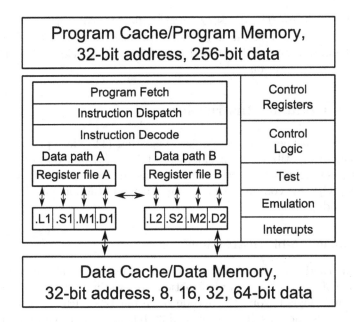

Fig. 1. TMS320C6000 architecture block diagram

31	29	28	27	23	22	18	17	13	12	11	2	1	0
creg		z	dst		src2		src1		x	op		s	p

Fig. 2. Typical 32-bit instruction encoding format

into an *execute packet*. As fetch packets are read from program memory, the instruction dispatch logic extracts execute packets from the fetch packets. All of the instructions in an execute packet execute in parallel. Each instruction in an execute packet must use a different functional unit.

The execute packet boundary is determined by a bit in each instruction called the *parallel-bit* (or *p-bit*). The p-bit (bit 0) controls whether the next instruction executes in parallel.

On the C62, execute packets cannot span a fetch packet boundary. Therefore, the last p-bit in a fetch packet is always set to 0, and each fetch packet starts a new execute packet. Execute packets are padded with parallel NOP instructions by the assembler to align spanning execute packets to a fetch packet boundary. The C64 allows execute packets to span fetch packet boundaries with some minimal restrictions, thus reducing code size by eliminating the need for parallel padding NOP instructions.

Except for a few special case instructions such as the NOP, each instruction has a predicate encoded in the first four bits. Figure 2 is a generalization of the C6x 32-bit three operand instruction encoding format. The predicate register is encoded in the condition (creg) field, and the z-bit encodes the true or not-true sense of the predicate. The dst, src2, and src1 fields encode operands. The x-bit encodes whether src2 is read from the opposite cluster's register file. The op field encodes the operation and functional unit. The s-bit specifies the cluster that the instruction executes on.

3   C64+ Compact Instructions

The C64+ core has new instruction encodings that (1) reduce program size, (2) allow binary compatibility with older object files, (3) and do not require the processor to switch modes to access the new instructions encodings. In addition, the existing C/C++ compiler exploits these new instruction encodings without extensive modification.

3.1   Compact 16-bit Instructions

A 16-bit instruction set was developed in which each 16-bit instruction is a compact version of an existing 32-bit instruction. All existing control, data path, and functional unit logic beyond the decode stage remains unchanged with respect to the 16-bit instructions. The 16-bit and 32-bit instructions can be mixed.

The ability to mix 32- and 16-bit instructions has several advantages. First, an explicit instruction to switch between instruction sets is unnecessary, eliminating the associated performance and code size penalty. Second, algorithms that need more complex and expressive 32-bit instructions can still realize code size savings since many of the instructions can be 16-bit. Finally, the ability to mix 32- and 16-bit instructions in the C64+ architecture frees the compiler from the complexities associated with a processsor mode.

The 16-bit instructions selected are frequently occurring 32-bit instructions that perform operations such as addition, subtraction, multiplication, shift, load, and store. By necessity, the 16-bit instructions have reduced functionality. For example, immediate fields are smaller, there is a reduced set of available registers, the instructions may only operate on one functional unit per cluster, and some standard arithmetic and logic instructions may only have two operands instead of three (one source register is the same as the destination register). All 16-bit instructions do not have a condition operand and execute unconditionally except for certain branch instructions.

The selection and makeup of 16-bit instructions was developed by rapidly prototyping the existing compiler, compiling many different DSP applications, and examining the subsequent performance and code size. In this way, we were able to compare and refine many different versions of the 16-bit instruction set. Due to design requirements of a high performance VLIW architecture, the C6x 32-bit instructions must be kept on a 32-bit boundary. Therefore, the 16-bit instructions occur in pairs in order to honor the 32-bit instruction alignment.

Standard Fetch Packet

32-bit opcode
32-bit opcode
32-bit opcode
32-bit opcode
32-bit opcode
32-bit opcode
32-bit opcode
32-bit opcode

Header-Based Fetch Packet

32-bit opcode	
16-bit opcode	16-bit opcode
32-bit opcode	
16-bit opcode	16-bit opcode
16-bit opcode	16-bit opcode
32-bit opcode	
32-bit opcode	
Header	

Fig. 3. C64+ fetch packet formats

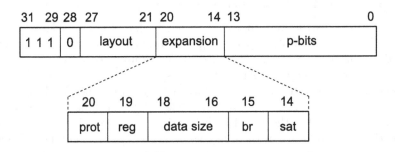

Fig. 4. Compact instruction header format

3.2 The Fetch Packet Header

The C64+ has a new type of fetch packet that encodes a mixture of 16-bit and 32-bit instructions. Thus, there are two kinds of fetch packets: A standard fetch packet that contains only 32-bit instructions and a header-based fetch packet that contains a mixture of 32- and 16-bit instructions. Figure 3 shows a standard fetch packet and an example of a header-based fetch packet. Fetch packet headers are detected by looking at the first four bits of the last word in a fetch packet. A previously unused creg/z value indicates that the fetch packet is header-based. The header-based fetch packet encodes how to interpret the bits in the rest of the fetch packet. On C64+, execute packets may span standard and header-based fetch packets.

Figure 4 shows the layout of the fetch packet header. The predicate field used to signify a fetch packet header occupies four bits (bits 28-31). There are seven *layout bits* (bits 21-27) that designate if the corresponding word in the fetch packet is a 32-bit instruction or a pair of 16-bit instructions. Bits 0-13 are p-bits for 16-bit instructions. For a 32-bit instruction, the corresponding two p-bits in the header are not used (set to zero). The remaining seven *expansion bits* (bits 14-20) are used to specify different variations of the 16-bit instruction set.

The expansion bits and p-bits are effectively extra opcode bits that are attached to each instruction in the fetch packet. The compressor software (discussed in section 4) encodes the expansion bits to maximize the number of instructions in a fetch packet.

The protected load instruction bit (bit 20) indicates if all load instructions in the fetch packet are protected. This eliminates the NOP that occurs after a load instruction in code with limited ILP, which is common in control oriented code. The register set bit (bit 19) indicates which set of eight registers is used for three operand 16-bit instructions. The data size field (bits 16-18) encodes the access size (byte, half-word, word, double-word) of all 16-bit load and store instructions. The branch bit (bit 15) controls if branch instructions or certain S-unit arithmetic and shift instructions are available. Finally, the saturation bit (bit 14) indicates if many of the basic arithmetic operations saturate on overflow.

3.3   Branch and Call Instructions

Certain branch instructions appearing in header-based fetch packets can reach half-word program addresses. Ensuring that branch instructions can reach intended destination addresses is handled by the compressor software.

A new 32-bit instruction, CALLP, can be used to take the place of a B (branch) instruction and an ADDKPC (set up return address) instruction. However, unlike branch instructions, where the five delay slots must be filled with other instructions or NOPs, the CALLP instruction is "protected," meaning other instructions cannot start in the delay slots of the CALLP. The use of this instruction can reduce code size up to six percent on some applications with a small degradation in performance.

4   The Compressor

When compiling code for C64+, an instruction's size is determined at assembly-time. (This is possible because each 16-bit instruction has a 32-bit counterpart.) The *compressor* runs after the assembly phase and is responsible for converting as many 32-bit instructions as possible to equivalent 16-bit instructions. The compressor takes a specially instrumented object file (where all instructions are 32-bit), and produces an object file where some instructions have been converted to 16-bit instructions. Figure 5 depicts this arrangement. Code compression could also be performed in the linker since the final addresses and immediate fields of instructions with relocation entries are known and may allow more 16-bit instructions to be used.

The compressor also has the responsibility of handling certain tasks that cannot be performed in the assembler because the addresses of instructions will change during compression. In addition, the compressor must fulfill certain architecture requirements that cannot be easily handled by the compiler. These

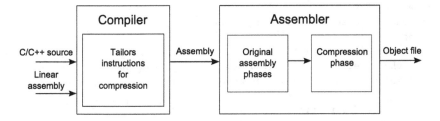

Fig. 5. Back-end compiler and assembler flow depicting the compression of instructions

requirements involve pairing 16-bit instructions, adding occasional padding to prevent a stall situation, and encoding the fetch packet header when 16-bit instructions are present.

Compression is an iterative process consisting of one or more *compression iterations*. In each compression iteration the compressor starts at the beginning of the section's instruction list and generates new fetch packets until all instructions are consumed. Each new fetch packet may contain eight 32-bit instructions (a regular fetch packet), or contain a mixture of 16- and 32-bit instructions (a header-based fetch packet).

The compressor must select an *overlay* which is an expansion bit combination used for a fetch packet that contains 16-bit instructions. There are several expansion bits in the fetch packet header that indicate how the 16-bit instructions in the fetch packet are to be interpreted. For each new fetch packet, the compressor selects a window of instructions and records for each overlay which instructions may be converted to 16-bit. It then selects the overlay that packs the most instructions in the new fetch packet. Figure 6 outlines the high-level compressor algorithm.

The compressor looks for several conditions at the end of a compression iteration that might force another iteration. When the compressor finds none of these conditions, no further compression iterations are required for that section. Next, we describe one of the conditions that forces another compression iteration.

Initially, the compressor optimistically uses 16-bit branches for all forward branches whose target is in the same file and in the same code section. These 16-bit branches have smaller displacement fields than their 32-bit counterparts and so may not be capable of reaching their intended destination. At the end of a compression iteration, the compressor determines if any of these branches will not reach their target. If so, another compression iteration is required and the branch is marked indicating that a 32-bit branch must be used.

During a compression iteration, there is often a potential 16-bit instruction with no other potential 16-bit instruction immediately before or after to complete the 16-bit pair. In this case, the compressor can swap instructions *within* an execute packet to try to make a pair. Since the C6x C/C++ compiler often produces execute packets with multiple instructions, the swapping of instructions within an execute packet increases the conversion rate of potential 16-bit instructions. The compressor does not swap or move instructions outside of

```
compressor(){
  for each code section in object file {
    do {
      compress_section()
      check legality of section and note any problems
    } while (section has one or more problems)

    finalize instructions
    adjust debug, symbol, and relocation info
    write compressed section
  }
  finalize and emit the object file
}


compress_section(){

  idx = 0; // idx denotes start of "window"

  while (idx < number_of_instructions) {
    window_sz = set_window_size();

    for (each instruction in window)
      for (each overlay)
        // 128 possible combinations of expansion bits
        record if instruction can be 16-bit

    for (each overlay) {
      record how a fetch packet encodes
      // Note that the best packing may be a regular fetch packet
      <best_mode, best_insts_packed> = determine_best_overlay();
    }

    idx += best_insts_packed;
  }
}
```

Fig. 6. High-level compressor algorithm

execute packets, nor change registers of instructions in order to improve compression. The compressor will always converge on a solution, typically after five or fewer compression iterations.

5   Compiler Strategies

The C64+ architecture's novel implementation of variable length instructions provides unique opportunities for compiler-architecture collaboration. The primary benefit is that it provides flexibility to users for selecting and managing code-size and performance tradeoffs while maintaining full backward compatibility for established code bases.

In our implementation, the compressor has the responsibility for packing instructions into fetch packets. The compiler does not make the final decision whether an instruction will become a 16-bit instruction. It does, however, play the most critical role in specializing instructions so that they are likely to become 16-bit instructions. We call such instruction specialization *tailoring*.

Because instructions tailored to be 16-bit are restricted to use a subset of the register file and functional units, they can potentially degrade performance. Therefore, the compiler implements a set of command line options that allow users to control the aggressiveness of the tailoring optimizations.

In this section, we describe the various compilation strategies developed to help exploit the new instruction set features of the C64+ core.

5.1 Instruction Selection

The first strategy involves biasing the compiler to select instructions that have a high probability of becoming 16-bit instructions. This is done aggressively in regions of code that have obvious and repetitive patterns. One instance involves the construction and destruction of local stack frames. Here the compiler prefers using memory instructions with smaller or zero offsets, increasing their chance of becoming 16-bit instructions. Another instance is the usage of the CALLP instruction which handles the common code sequences around function calls.

The compiler will replace a single 32-bit instruction with two instructions that will likely compress to two 16-bit instructions. Since 16-bit instructions must be paired in the compressor, replacing a 32-bit instruction with two potential 16-bit instructions reduces the impact of 32-bit alignment restrictions, which improves the compression of the surrounding instructions. These transformations are more aggressively performed when the user is compiling for smaller code size.

During instruction selection, the compiler chooses different sequences of instructions based on the user's goal of either maximum speed or minimum code size. When compiling for minimum code size, the compiler attempts to generate instructions that have only 16-bit formats.

The compiler assumes that any potential 16-bit instruction will ultimately become 16-bit in the compressor. That is, the compiler assumes another 16-bit instruction will be available to complete the required 16-bit instruction pair.

5.2 Register Allocation

The 16-bit instructions can access only a subset of the register file. The compiler implements register allocation using graph-coloring [11]. When compiling for minimum code size, one of the strategies employed by the compiler is to tailor the register allocation to maximize the usage of the 16-bit instructions' register file subset. This improves the likelihood that the compressor will be able to convert these instructions into their 16-bit forms.

We call this register allocation strategy *tiered register allocation*. Internally, the compiler keeps all instructions in their 32-bit format. An oracle is available that determines whether an instruction can become a 16-bit instruction given its current state.

Using tiered register allocation, the compiler limits the available registers for operands in potential 16-bit instructions to the 16-bit instructions' register file subset. If the register allocation attempt succeeds, the operands in potential 16-bit instructions are allocated registers from the 16-bit instructions' register file subset. If the register allocation attempt fails, the compiler incrementally releases registers for allocation from the rest of the register file for the operands of potential 16-bit instructions. The release of registers is done gradually, initially for operands with the longest live ranges. Should register allocation attempts continue failing, the whole register set is made available for all instruction operands thereby falling back on the compiler's traditional register allocation mechanism.

There can be a performance penalty when using tiered register allocation. When the user has directed the compiler to balance performance and code size, the compiler limits tiered register allocation to the operands of potential 16-bit instructions outside of critical loops.

When compiling to maximize performance, the compiler disables tiered register allocation and instead relies on register preferencing. Preferencing involves adding a bias to register operands of potential 16-bit instructions. Potential 16-bit instruction operands are biased to the 16-bit instructions' register file subset. During register allocation, when the cost among a set of legal registers is the same for a particular register operand, the register allocater assigns the register with the highest preference.

5.3   Instruction Scheduling

When performing instruction scheduling, the compiler is free to place instructions in the delay slot of a load instruction. After instruction scheduling, if there are no instructions in the delay slot of a load, the compressor removes the NOP instruction used to fill the delay slot and marks the load as protected. An improvement would be to restrict the scheduler to place instructions in the delay slot of a load only when it is necessary for performance, and not simply when it is convenient. This helps maximize the number of protected loads and thus reduces code size.

When compiling to minimize code size, the compiler prevents instructions from being placed in the delay slots of call instructions, which allows the compiler to use the CALLP instruction and eliminates any potential NOP instructions required to fill delay slots.

5.4   Calling Convention Customization

The calling convention defines how registers are managed across a function call. The set of registers that must be saved by the caller function are the SOC (save on call) registers. The set of registers that are saved by the callee function are the SOE (save on entry) registers. Since SOE registers are saved and restored by the called function, the compiler attempts to allocate SOE registers to operands that have live ranges across a call. For backward compatibility, new versions of the compiler must honor the existing calling convention.

Because the 16-bit instructions' register file subset does not include SOE registers, the compiler implements *calling convention customization*. This concept is similar to veneer functions outlined by Davis et. al. [12]. The compiler identifies call sites with potential 16-bit instruction operands that have live ranges across a call. The call is then rewritten as an indirect call to a run-time support routine, which takes the address of the original call site function as an operand. The run-time support routine saves the 16-bit instructions' register file subset on the stack. Control is then transferred to the actual function that was being called at that call site. The called function returns to the run-time support routine, which restores the 16-bit instructions' register file subset and then returns to the original call site.

This technique effectively simulates changing the calling convention to include the 16-bit instructions' register file subset in the SOE registers. This greatly improves the usage of 16-bit instructions in non-leaf functions. However, there is a significant performance penalty at call sites where the calling convention has been customized. Calling convention customization is used only when compiling to aggressively minimize code size.

6   Results

A set of audio, video, voice, encryption, and control application benchmarks that are typical to the C6x were chosen to evaluate performance and code size. We ran the C6x C/C++ v6.0 compiler [13] on the applications at full optimization with each code size option. The applications were compiled with (C64+) and without (C64) instruction set extensions enabled. They were run on a cycle accurate simulator. In order to focus only on the effect of the instruction set extensions, memory sub-system delays were not modeled.

Figure 7 shows the relative code size on each application when compiling for maximum performance (no -ms option) between C64 and C64+. At maximum performance, the compact instructions allow the compiler to reduce code size by an average 11.5 percent, while maintaining equivalent performance. Figure 8 shows the relative code size on each application when compiling with the -ms2 option which tells the compiler to favor lower code size. When compiled with the -ms2 option for C64+, the applications are 23.3 percent smaller than with -ms2 for C64.

In general, software pipelining increases code size. The C64+ processor implements a specialized hardware loop buffer, which, among other things, reduces the code size of software pipelined loops. The details of the loop buffer are beyond the scope of this paper, but a similar loop buffer is described by Merten and Hwu [14]. (Results shown in figures 7 and 8 do not include the effects of the loop buffer.)

Figure 9 shows the relative code size and performance differences between C64 and C64+ at all code size levels, averaged across the applications. The x-axis represents normalized bytes and the y-axis represents normalized cycles. All results are normalized to a C64 compiled for maximum performance. As

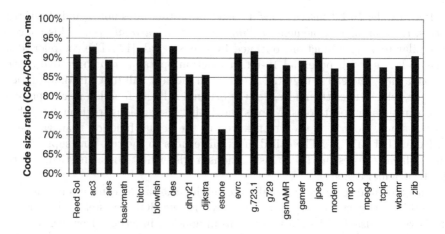

Fig. 7. Comparison of code size between C64x and C64+ at maximum performance

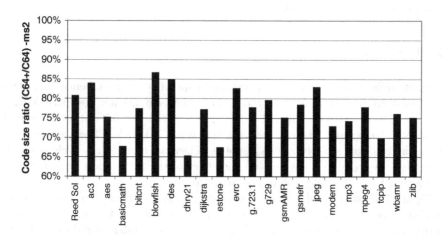

Fig. 8. Comparison of code size between C64x and C64+ at "-ms2"

the figure shows, when compiling for maximum performance, the instruction set extensions yield an average 11.5 percent code size savings with no reduction in performance (points on the middle line). The points on the leftmost line indicate the performance and code size with the addition of the software pipelined loop buffer (SPLOOP). When compiling for maximum performance, the use of the instruction set extensions and the software pipelined loop buffer result in an average 17.4 percent code size reduction with no change in performance.

As shown in fig. 9, the instruction set extensions create a larger code size and performance tradeoff range. When a developer's primary desire is to control code size, this additional range can be useful in balancing performance and code size in a memory-constrained application common in embedded systems.

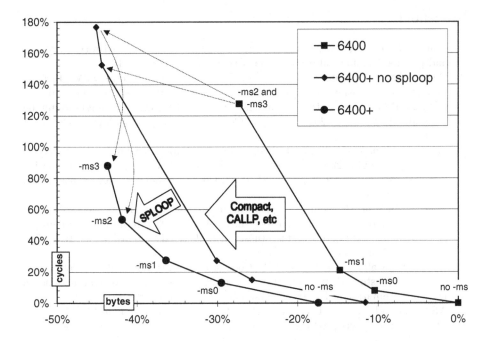

Fig. 9. Comparison of performance and code size between C64x and C64+ at various performance and code size tradeoff levels

7   Conclusions

We have presented a hybrid approach for compressing VLIW programs using a combination of compact instruction encoding and compilation techniques. The C64+ implements a unique method for encoding variable length instructions using a fetch packet header. A post-code generation tool, the compressor, ultimately selects the size of the instructions. This approach relieves the code generator of unnecessary complexity in our constrained VLIW implementation, where 32-bit instructions cannot span a 32-bit boundary and 16-bit instructions must occur in pairs. The compiler tailors a 32-bit instruction with the potential to become 16-bit depending on the code size priority selected by the user and the location and nature of the instruction. The compiler uses various techniques, including tiered register allocation and calling convention customization to tradeoff code size and performance.

For a set of representative benchmarks, we presented results that showed an 11.5 percent to 23.3 percent code size reduction. Finally, the approach presented here is implemented in the C64+ processor and its production compiler. Future work includes improvements to the compiler to more effectively tailor code size optimizations for non-performance critical regions of a function.

References

1. Rau, B.R., Fisher, J.A.: Instruction-level parallel processing: History, overview, and perspective. Journal of Supercomputing 7(1-2), 9–50 (1993)
2. Conte, T.M., Banerjia, S., Larin, S.Y., Menezes, K.N., Sathaye, S.W.: Instruction fetch mechanisms for VLIW architectures with compressed encodings. In: MICRO 29: Proceedings of the 29th annual ACM/IEEE International Symposium on Microarchitecture, pp. 201–211. IEEE Computer Society, Washington, DC, USA (1996)
3. Lin, C.H., Xie, Y., Wolf, W.: LZW-based code compression for VLIW embedded systems. In: DATE 2004. Proceedings of the Conference on Design, Automation and Test in Europe, vol. 3, pp. 76–81. IEEE Computer Society Press, Washington, DC, USA (2004)
4. Ros, M., Sutton, P.: Compiler optimization and ordering effects on VLIW code compression. In: CASES 2003. Proceedings of the 2003 International Conference on Compilers, Architecture and Synthesis for Embedded Systems, pp. 95–103. ACM Press, New York (2003)
5. Aditya, S., Mahlke, S.A., Rau, B.R.: Code size minimization and retargetable assembly for custom EPIC and VLIW instruction formats. ACM Transactions on Design Automation of Electronic Systems 5(4), 752–773 (2000)
6. ARM Limited: ARM7TDMI (Rev. 4) Technical Reference Manual (2001)
7. Phelan, R.: Improving ARM code density and performance. Technical report, ARM Limited (2003)
8. MIPS Technologies: MIPS32 Architecture for Programmers, Vol. IV-a: The MIPS16 Application Specific Extension to the MIPS32 Architecture (2001)
9. Texas Instruments: TMS320C64x/C64x+ DSP CPU and Instruction Set Reference Guide, Literature number spru732c (2006)
10. Stotzer, E., Leiss, E.: Modulo scheduling for the TMS320C6x VLIW DSP architecture. In: LCTES 1999. Proceedings of the ACM SIGPLAN 1999 Workshop on Languages, Compilers, and Tools for Embedded Systems, pp. 28–34. ACM Press, New York (1999)
11. Briggs, P., Cooper, K.D., Torczon, L.: Improvements to graph coloring register allocation. ACM Transactions on Programming Languages and Systems 16(3), 428–455 (1994)
12. Davis, A.L., Humphreys, J.F., Tatge, R.E.: Maintaining code consistency among plural instruction sets via function naming convention, U.S. Patent 6,002,876 (1999)
13. Texas Instruments: TMS320C6000 Optimizing Compiler User's Guide, Literature number spru187 (2000)
14. Merten, M.C., Hwu, W.W.: Modulo schedule buffers. In: MICRO 34: Proceedings of the 34th annual ACM/IEEE international symposium on Microarchitecture, pp. 138–149. IEEE Computer Society, Washington, DC, USA (2001)

Experiences with Parallelizing a Bio-informatics Program on the Cell BE

Hans Vandierendonck, Sean Rul, Michiel Questier, and Koen De Bosschere

Ghent University, Department of Electronics and Information Systems/HiPEAC,
B-9000 Gent, Belgium
{hvdieren,srul,mquestie,kdb}@elis.ugent.be

Abstract. The Cell Broadband Engine Architecture is a new heterogeneous multi-core architecture targeted at compute-intensive workloads. The architecture of the Cell BE has several features that are unique in high-performance general-purpose processors, such as static instruction scheduling, extensive support for vectorization, scratch pad memories, explicit programming of DMAs, mailbox communication, multiple processor cores, etc. It is necessary to make explicit use of these features to obtain high performance. Yet, little work reports on how to apply them and how much each of them contributes to performance.

This paper presents our experiences with programming the Cell BE architecture. Our test application is Clustal W, a bio-informatics program for multiple sequence alignment. We report on how we apply the unique features of the Cell BE to Clustal W and how important each is to obtain high performance. By making extensive use of vectorization and by parallelizing the application across all cores, we speedup the pairwise alignment phase of Clustal W with a factor of 51.2 over PPU (superscalar) execution. The progressive alignment phase is sped up by a factor of 5.7 over PPU execution, resulting in an overall speedup by 9.1.

1 Introduction

Computer architectures are changing: while previous generations of processors gained performance by increasing clock frequency and instruction-level parallelism, future processor generations are likely to sustain performance improvements by increasing the number of cores on a chip. These performance improvements can, however, only be tapped when applications are parallel. This requires a large additional effort on the side of the programmer. Furthermore, it is likely that future multi-core architectures will be heterogeneous multi-cores, i.e., the chip's cores have significantly different architectures. This further increases the programming challenge.

The Cell Broadband Engine Architecture [1] is such a new heterogeneous multi-core architecture targeted at compute-intensive workloads. The Cell BE has one superscalar processor (Power processing element) and 8 SIMD *synergistic* processing elements (SPE). The SPEs have a unique architecture, with features that are uncommon in high-performance general-purpose processors:

P. Stenström et al. (Eds.): HiPEAC 2008, LNCS 4917, pp. 161–175, 2008.
© Springer-Verlag Berlin Heidelberg 2008

static instruction scheduling, scratch pad memories, explicit programming of DMAs, mailbox communication, a heterogeneous multi-core architecture, etc. While these features hold promise for high performance, achieving high performance is difficult as these features are exposed to the programmer.

In this paper, we implement Clustal W [2], a bio-informatics program, on the Cell Broadband Engine and report on the optimizations that were necessary to achieve high performance. Apart from overlapping memory accesses with computation and apart from avoiding branches, we spend a lot of effort to vectorize code, modify data structures, and to remove unaligned vector memory accesses. These optimizations increase performance on an SPE. Furthermore, we extract thread-level parallelism to utilize all 8 SPEs. We report on the impact of each of these optimizations on program speed.

In the remainder of this paper, we first explain the Cell Broadband Engine Architecture (Section 2) and the Clustal W application (Section 3). We analyze Clustal W to find the most time-consuming phases (Section 4). Then, we explain our optimizations on Clustal W (Section 5) and evaluate the performance improvements from each (Section 6). Finally, Section 7 discusses related work and Section 8 concludes the paper.

2   The Cell BE Architecture

The Cell Broadband Engine [1] is a heterogeneous multi-core that is developed by Sony, Toshiba and IBM. The Cell consists of nine cores: one PowerPC processor element (PPE) and eight SIMD synergistic processor elements (SPE).[1]

The PPE serves as a controller for the SPEs and works with a conventional operating system. It is derived from a 64-bit PowerPC RISC-processor and is an in-order two-way superscalar core with simultaneous multi-threading. The instruction set is an extended PowerPC instruction set with SIMD Multimedia instructions. It uses a cache coherent memory hierarchy with a 32 KB L1 data and instruction cache and a unified L2 cache of 512 KB.

The eight SPEs [3,4] deliver the compute power of the Cell processor. These 128-bit in-order vector processors distinguish themselves by the use of explicit memory management. The SPEs each have a *local store* of 256 KB dedicated for both data and instructions. The SPE only operates on data in registers which are read from or written to the local store. Accessing data from the local store requires a constant latency of 6 cycles as opposed to processors with caches who have various memory access times due to the underlying memory hierarchy. This property allows the compiler to statically schedule the instructions for the SPE. To access data that resides in the main memory or other local stores, the SPE issues a DMA command. The register file itself has 128 registers each 128-bit wide allowing SIMD instructions with varying element width (e.g. ranging from

---

[1] The processing units are referred to as the power processing unit (PPU) and synergistic processing unit (SPU) for the PPE and SPE, respectively. We will use the terms PPE and PPU, and SPE and SPU, interchangeably.

2x64-bit up to 16x8-bit). There is no hardware branch predictor in order to keep the design of the SPE simple. To compensate for this, the programmer or compiler can add branch hints which notifies the hardware and allows prefetching the upcoming 32 instructions so that a correctly hinted taken branch incurs no penalty. Since there is a high branch misprediction penalty of about 18 cycles it is better to eliminate as much branches as possible. The SIMD select instruction can avoid branches by turning control flow into data flow.

All nine cores, memory controller and I/O controller are connected through the Element Interconnect Bus (EIB). The EIB consists of 4 data rings of 16 bytes wide. The EIB runs at half the frequency of the processor cores and it supports a peak bandwidth of 204.8 GBytes/s for on chip communication. The bandwidth between the DMA engine and the EIB bus is 8 bytes per core per cycle in each direction. Because of the explicit memory management that is required in the local store one has to carefully schedule DMA operations and strive for total overlap of memory latency with useful computations.

3   Clustal W

In molecular biology Clustal W [2] is an essential program for the simultaneous alignment of nucleotide or amino acid sequences. It is also part of Bioperf [5], an open benchmark suite for evaluating computer architecture on bioinformatics and life science applications.

The algorithm computes the most likely mutation of one sequence into the other by iteratively substituting amino acids in the sequences and by introducing gaps in the sequences. Each modification of the sequences impacts the score of the sequences, which measures the degree of similarity.

The alignment of two sequences is done by dynamic programming, using the Smith-Waterman algorithm [6]. This technique, however, does not scale to aligning multiple sequences, where finding a global optimum becomes NP-hard [7]. Therefore, a series of pairwise alignments is compared to each other, followed by a progressive alignment which adds the sequence most closely related to the already aligned sequences.

The algorithm consists of three stages. In the first stage, all pairs of sequences are aligned. The second stage forms a phylogenetic tree for the underlying sequences. This is achieved by using the Neighbor-Joining algorithm [8] in which the most closely related sequences, as given by the first stage, are located on the same branch of the guide tree. The third step progressively aligns the sequences according to the branching order in the guide tree obtained in the second step, starting from the leaves of the tree proceeding towards the root.

4   Analysis of Clustal W

Both the space and time complexity of the different stages of the Clustal W algorithm are influenced by the number of aligned sequences N and the typical sequence length L. Edgar [9] has computed the space and time complexity of

Table 1. Complexity of Clustal W in time and space, with N the number of sequences and L the typical sequence length

Stage	$\mathcal{O}$(Space)	$\mathcal{O}$(Time)
PW: Pairwise calculation	$N^2 + L^2$	N^2L^2
GT: Guide tree	N^2	N^4
PA: Progressive alignment	$NL + L^2$	$N^3 + NL^2$
Total	$N^2 + L^2$	$N^4 + L^2$

each phase in terms of N and L (see Table 1). This theoretical analysis indicates that the second stage of Clustal W will become more important as the number of sequences increases, but it is indifferent to the length of these sequences. In the other stages both the number of sequences and the length are of importance.

The time and space complexity indicate how each phase scales with increasing problem size, but they does not tell us the absolute amount of time spent in each phase. In order to understand this, we analyze the program by randomly creating input sets with preset number of sequences N and sequence length L. Statistical data of protein databases [10] indicates that the average length of sequences is 366 amino acids, while sequences with more than 2000 amino acids are very rare. So we randomly created input sets with a sequence length ranging from 10 to 1000 amino acids and with a number of sequences in the same range.

Figure 1 shows the percentage of execution time spent in each stage. Each bar indicates a certain configuration of the number of sequences (bottom X-value) and the sequence length (top X-value). The pairwise alignment becomes the dominant stage when the number of sequences is high, taking responsibility for more than 50% of execution time when there are at least 50 sequences. In contrast, when the number of sequences is small, then progressive alignment takes the larger share of the execution time.

The guide tree only plays an important role when the input set contains a large number of short sequences. In other cases this stage is only responsible for less than 5% of the execution time. In a previous study, G-protein coupled receptor

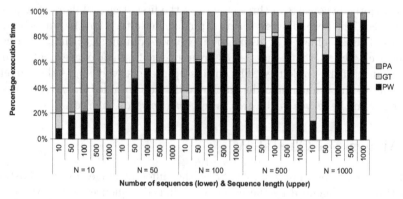

Fig. 1. Percentage of execution time of the three major stages in Clustal W

(GPCR) proteins are used as input sets [11]. These proteins are relatively short, so the guide tree plays a prominent role. A profile analysis of ClustalW-SMP [12] shows a more important role for the guide tree, but this is the effect of the SMP version of Clustal W in which both the pairwise and progressive alignment are parallelized.

The analysis above shows that the pairwise alignment and progressive alignment phases are responsible for the largest part of the execution time. In the remainder of this paper, we focus on optimizing these two phases and pay no attention to the guide tree phase (which is parallelized in [12]).

5   Optimization of Clustal W

The inner loops of the pairwise alignment and progressive alignment phases have very similar structure, so most optimizations apply to both phases. We discuss first how to optimize these phases for the SPUs. Then we turn our attention to parallelizing these phases to utilize multiple SPUs.

5.1   Optimizing for the SPU

Loop Structure. The majority of work in the PW and the PA phases is performed by 3 consecutive loop nests. Together, these loop nests compute a metric of similarity (score) for two sequences. The first loop nest iterates over the sequences in a forward fashion, i.e., it uses increasing indices for the sequence arrays. We call this loop the forward loop. The second loop nest iterates over the sequences in a backward fashion (using decreasing indices for the sequence arrays), so we call it the backward loop. From a computational point of view, a single iteration of the forward and the backward loops perform comparable computations. The third loop nest computes the desired score using intermediate values from the forward and backward loops (note that in PA the third loop nest also uses recursion besides iteration).

In both the PW and PA phases, the third loop performs an order of magnitude less work than the forward and the backward loops, so we do not bother to optimize the third loop.

In PW, the forward loop is by far more important than the backward loop, as the forward loop computes reduced limits on the iteration space of the backward loop. In PA, the forward and the backward loop have the same size of iteration space. Hence, they take a comparable share in the total execution time.

The forward and backward loop bodies contain a non-vectorizable part. In the PW loops, these are scattered accesses to a substitution matrix, while in the PA loops, these involve calls to a function called prfscore(). This structure limits the speedup achievable by vectorization of the surrounding loops.

We optimize the forward and backward loops using vectorization (SIMD) and loop unrolling. These optimizations are known to be very effective on the Cell BE. Before applying them, we must understand the control flow inside the inner loop bodies as well as the data dependencies between successive loop iterations.

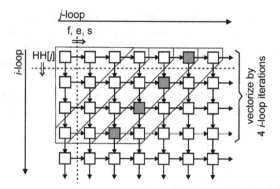

Fig. 2. Data dependencies between distinct iterations of the inner loop body of two nested loops

Vectorization of prfscore(). The prfscore() function called from the PA loops computes a vector dot product. The vector length is input-dependent but it cannot exceed 32 elements by definition of the data structures. Furthermore, the vector length remains constant during the whole PA phase.

We completely unroll the loop assuming 32 iterations of the loop and we perform a 4-way vectorization. This removes all control flow at the cost of code size increase. To take the loop iteration limit into account, we use the spu_sel() primitive together with a pre-computed mask array. The spu_sel() primitive selects only those words for which the mask contains ones, so it allows us to sum over only those values that are required.

Control Flow Optimization. The inner loop body of the backward and forward loops contains a significant amount of control flow, related to finding the maximum of a variable over all loop iterations. In the PW phase, the code also remembers the *i*-loop and *j*-loop iteration numbers where that maximum occurs. It is important to avoid this control flow, since mispredicted branch instructions have a high penalty on the SPUs. Updating the running maximum value (if(b > a) a=b;) can be simply avoided by using the SPUs compare and select assembly instructions to turn control flow into data flow (a=spu_sel(a,b,spu_cmpgt(b,a));). In the same vein, it is also possible to remember the *i*-loop and *j*-loop iteration numbers of the maximum (imax=spu_sel(imax,i,spu_cmpgt(b,a));).

Vectorization. The forward and backward loops in the PW and PA phases have the same data dependencies, which are depicted in Figure 2. There are two nested loops, with the *j*-loop nested inside the *i*-loop. Every box in the figure depicts one execution of the inner loop body corresponding to one pair of *i* and *j* loop indices. The execution of the inner loop body has data dependencies with previous executions of the inner loop body, as indicated by edges between the boxes. Data dependencies carry across iterations of the *j*-loop, in which case the dependencies are carried through scalar variables. Also, data dependencies carry across iterations of the *i*-loop, in which case the dependences are carried through arrays indexed by j. Thus, the execution of the inner loop body has data dependencies with two prior executions of the loop body.

To vectorize the forward and backward loops, we need to identify V data-independent loop iterations, where V is the vectorization factor. In these loops, the vectorization factor is 4, since scalar variables are 32-bit integers and the vector length is 128 bits. Data-independent loop iterations occur for skewed iteration counts for the i-loop and the j-loop. In particular, loop iterations (i_0, j_0) and (i_1, j_1) are independent when $i_0 + j_0 = i_1 + j_1$. Consequently, vectorization requires the construction of loop pre-ambles and post-ambles to deal with non-vectorizable portions of the loop body.

The PW forward loop computes the position of the maximum score. The original code records the "first" loop iteration where the maximum value occurs (`if(b > a){a=b; imax=i; jmax=j;}`). Here, the "first" loop iteration is the one that occurs first in the lexicographic ordering

$$(i, j) < (i', j') \quad \text{if} \quad (i < i') \vee ((i = i') \wedge (j < j')).$$

Since vectorization changes the execution order of the loop iterations, we need to take care that the *same* loop iteration is recorded in order to obtain the same output of the algorithm. In the vectorized code, we simultaneously remember 4 positions where the maximum value occurs, each one corresponding to one of the 4 vector lanes. When the vectorized loop has finished, we need to select the maximum value among the per-lane maxima and, if that maximum occurs in multiple lanes, we need to select the appropriate loop iterations corresponding to the lexicographic ordering in the original code.

Loop Unrolling to Avoid Unaligned Memory Accesses. Loop unrolling can increase performance by increasing the range across which instructions can be scheduled and by reducing control flow overhead. Loop unrolling is particularly important for statically scheduled architectures like the SPU. In the case of Clustal W, however, loop unrolling did not allow the compiler to create a better instruction schedule as the loop body already contains sufficient instruction-level parallelism. Thus, performance remains the same.

In this paper, we show that loop unrolling is also useful to enable other optimizations, in this case the removal of unaligned memory accesses. Unaligned memory accesses should be avoided as the hardware supports only aligned memory accesses. Consequently, unaligned vector loads and stores translate into a sequence of several instructions.

The interaction of loop unrolling and alignment is illustrated on the $HH[\cdot]$ array, which is used in the inner loop body (Figure 3). We assume that the vector covering elements 1 to 4 of the $HH[\cdot]$ array is aligned. This is the optimal situation since the j-loop starts at index 1.

In the vectorized loops, each loop iteration loads a 4-element vector from the $HH[\cdot]$ array. Depending on the iteration count, this vector may or may not be aligned on a natural boundary. Every iteration, the vector moves one scalar position in the $HH[\cdot]$ array, so the loaded vector is aligned exactly once every fourth iteration of the loop and it is unaligned in the other iterations.

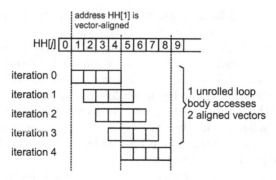

Fig. 3. Elements of the intermediary $HH[\cdot]$ array accessed by successive iterations of the vectorized loop

Four consecutive iterations of the vectorized loop access 7 distinct scalars from the $HH[\cdot]$ array (Figure 3). These 7 scalars are located in two consecutive aligned vectors, so it is possible to load them all at once into vector registers using two aligned loads, and to store them back using two aligned stores. All further references to the $HH[\cdot]$ array are now redirected to the vector registers holding the two words. This optimization removes all unaligned memory accesses to the arrays that carry dependences between iterations of the i-loop. We apply a similar optimization to the character arrays holding the sequences in the pairwise alignment phase.

5.2   Modifications to Data Structures

As the local store is not large enough to hold all data structures, we stream all large data structures in and out of the SPUs. This is true in particular for the sequence arrays (PW phase) and for the profiles (PA phase). We also carefully align all datastructures in the local store to improve vectorization.

In the PA phase, we also modify the second profile, which streams through the SPU most quickly. Each element of the profile is a 64-element vector of 32-bit integers. This vector is accessed sparsely: the first 32 elements are accessed sequentially, the next 2 elements are accessed at other locations in the code and the remainder is unused. To improve memory behavior, we create two new arrays to store the 32nd and 33rd elements. Accesses to these arrays are optimized in the same way as to the $HH[\cdot]$ array of the previous paragraph. When streaming the second profile, only the first 32 elements are fetched.

5.3   Parallelization of Pairwise Alignment

Pairwise alignment computes a score for every pair of sequences. The scores can be computed independently for all pairs, which makes parallelization trivial. We dynamically balance the work across the SPUs by dividing the work in $N - 1$ work packages where N is the number of sequences. The i-th work package

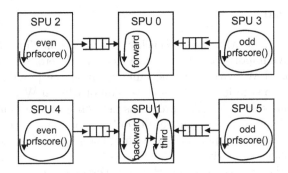

Fig. 4. Parallelization of `pdiff()` on 6 SPUs

corresponds to comparing the i-th sequence to all other sequences j where $j > i$. Work packages are sent to SPUs in order of decreasing size to maximize load balancing.

5.4   Parallelization of Progressive Alignment

Progressive alignment is more difficult to parallelize. Although the forward, backward and third loop nests are executed multiple times, there is little parallelism between executions of this set of loops. A parallelization scheme similar to the PW phase is thus not possible. Instead, we note that the first two loop nests are control- and data-independent. The third loop nests has data-dependencies with the first two loop nests, but its execution time is several orders of magnitude smaller. So a first parallelization is to execute the first two loop nests in parallel, an optimization that is also performed in the SMP version of Clustal W.

A higher degree of parallelization is obtained by observing that most of the execution time is spent in the `prfscore()` function. As the control flow through the loops is entirely independent of the data, we propose to extract DO-ACROSS parallelism from the loop. Indeed, the `prfscore()` function can be evaluated ahead of time as it is independent of the remainder of the computation. As the `prfscore()` function takes a significant amount of time, we reserve two threads to evaluate this function, each handling different values.

Thus, we instantiate three copies of the loop (Figure 4). Two copies compute each a subset of the `prfscore()`s and send these values to the third copy through a queue. The third copy of the loop performs the remaining computations and reads the results of the `prfscore()`s from the queue. As control flow is highly predictable, it is easy to divise a static distribution of work, such that each copy of the loop can proceed with minimum communication. The only communication is concerned with reading and writing the queue.

In total, a single call to `pdiff()` is executed by 6 SPU threads: one for the forward loop, one for the backward and third loop, two threads to deal with the `prfscore()`s for the forward loop and two more threads to deal with the `prfscore()`s for the backward loop.

6 Evaluation

We separately evaluate the effect of each optimization on Clustal W to understand the relative importance of each optimization. Hereto, we created distinct
versions of Clustal W, with each one building upon the previous version and
adding optimizations to it. The baseline version of Clustal W is taken from the
BioPerf benchmark suite [5]. The programs are run with the B input from the
same benchmark suite. We present results only for one input set, as distinct input sets assign different importance to each of the phases, but the performance
of each phase scales similarly across input sets.

We evaluate the performance of each of our versions of Clustal W by running
it on a Dual Cell BE-based blade, with two Cell Broadband Engine processors at
3.2 GHz with SMT enabled. The compiler is gcc 4.0.2 and the operating system
is linux (Fedora Core 5). We added code to measure the overall wall clock time
that elapses during the execution of each phase of Clustal W. Each version of
Clustal W is run 5 times and the highest and lowest execution times are dropped.
We report the average execution time over the 3 remaining measurements.

We first discuss the effect of SPU-specific optimizations on performance. Here,
only a single SPU thread is used. Then, we discuss how performance scales with
multiple SPUs.

6.1 Pairwise Alignment

Figure 5(a) shows the effects of the individual optimizations on the performance
of pairwise alignment. The first bar (labeled "PPU") shows the execution time
of the original code running on the PPU. The second bar ("SPU-base") shows
the execution time when the pairwise alignment is performed on a single SPU.
The code running on the SPU is basically the code from the original program,
extended with the necessary control, DMA transfers and mailbox operations.
Although this overhead adds little to nothing to the overall execution time, we
observe an important slowdown of execution. Inspection of the code shows a
high density of control transfers inside the inner loop body of the important
loop nests. Removing this control flow makes a single SPU already faster than
the PPU ("SPU-control").

The next bar ("SPU-SIMD") shows the performance when vectorizing the
forward loop. Vectorization yields a 3.6 times speedup. The next step is to unroll
the vectorized loop with the goals of removing unaligned memory accesses. This
shortens the operation count in a loop iteration and improves performance by
another factor 1.7. The overall speedup over PPU-only execution is a factor 6.7.
At this point, the backward loop requires an order of magnitude less computation
time than the forward loop, so we do not optimize it.

6.2 Progressive Alignment

We perform a similar analysis of progressive alignment (Figure 5(b)). Again we
use a single SPU, so the forward and backward loops are executed sequentially on
the same SPU and the `prfscore()` functions are executed by the same thread.

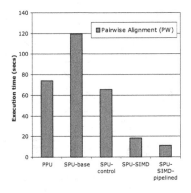

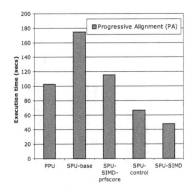

(a) Effect of optimizations on PW   (b) Effect of optimizations on PA

Fig. 5. The effect of each of the optimizations on the execution time of pairwise alignement and progressive alignment

Again, executing the original code on the SPU is slower than running on the PPU (bar "SPU-base" vs. "PPU"). Again, we attribute this to excessive control flow. In PA, we identify two possible causes: the loop inside the `prfscore()` function and the remaining control flow inside the loop bodies of the forward and backward loops. First, we remove all control flow in the `prfscore()` function by unrolling the loop, vectorizing and by using pre-computed masks to deal with the loop iteration count (see Section 5.1). This brings performance close to the PPU execution time (bar "SPU-SIMD-prfscore"). Second, we remove the remaining control flow in the same way as in the PW loop nests. This gives an overall speedup of 1.6 over PPU execution (bar "SPU-control").

Vectorizing the forward and backward loops improves performance, but the effect is relatively small (bar "SPU-SIMD"). The reason is that the inner loop contains calls to `prfscore`. The execution of these calls remains sequential, which significantly reduces the benefit of vectorization. Since these calls are also responsible for most of the execution time, there is no benefit from unrolling the vectorized loops as the unaligned memory accesses are relatively unimportant compared to `prfscore()`. Furthermore, removing unaligned memory accesses requires many registers but the vectorized loop nest is already close to using all registers.

6.3   Scaling with Multiple SPUs

The final part of our analysis concerns the scaling of performance when using multiple SPUs. In the following, we use the best version of each phase. Figure 6(b) shows the speedup over PPU-only execution when using an increasing number of SPUs.

As expected, the PW phase scales very well with multiple SPUs. With 8 SPUs, the parallelized and optimized PW phase runs 51.2 times faster than the original code on the PPU.

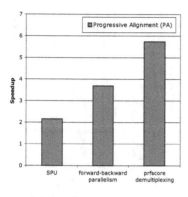
(a) Parallelization of PA

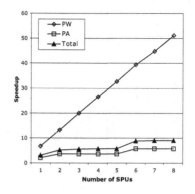
(b) Speedup against number of SPUs

Fig. 6. Speedup of a multi-threaded Clustal W over PPU-only execution

The PA phase has less parallelism than the PW phase. We present results for three versions (Figure 6(a)): a single-SPU version, a 2-SPU version where the forward and backward loops execute in parallel, and a 6-SPU version where the prfscore() function is evaluated by separate threads.

Executing the forward and backward loops in parallel yields a 1.7 speedup over single-SPU execution. The 6-SPU version improves the 2-SPU version by 1.6. This latter speedup is not very high, as we replace the straight-line code of prfscore() by control-intensive code to send the values to a different SPU. Although this communication is buffered, it is necessary to perform additional checks on buffer limits and to poll the incoming mailbox.

Figure 6(b) also shows the overall speedup for the B input of Clustal W. For this input, the guide tree phase requires virtually no execution time. The total execution time is represented by the PW and PA phases. With a single SPU, our Cell BE implementation is 3 times faster than the original PPU-only version. With 8 SPUs, our parallel version is 9.1 times faster.

6.4 Discussion

Optimizing the Clustal W program for the Cell BE has given us valuable insight into this processor. There are a few things that deserve pointing out.

First, although the SPE's local store can be perceived of as small (256 KB), there is little point in having larger local stores. Clearly, there isn't a local store that will be large enough to hold all of the application's data, regardless of input set size. So it will always be necessary to prepare a version of the SPU code that streams all major data structures in and out of the local store. Given this assumption, our experience is that 256 KB is enough to hold the compute-intensive kernels, some small data structures as well as buffers to stream the major data structures.

Second, the DMA interface is rich and easy to use, although it is necessary to carefully plan when each DMA is launched. An interesting trick is the use of barriers, which force the execution of DMAs in launch order. We use this feature when copying a buffer from one SPU to another, followed by sending a mailbox message[2] to notify the destination SPU that the buffer has arrived. By using a barrier, we can launch the message without waiting for completion of the buffer DMA. Furthermore, tag queues can be specified such that the barrier applies only to the DMAs in the specified tag queue. Thus, other DMAs (e.g., to stream data structures) are not affected by the barrier.

We experienced some properties of the Cell BE as limitations. E.g., 32-bit integer multiplies are not supported in hardware. Instead, the compiler generates multiple 16-bit multiplies. This is an important limitation in the `prfscore()` function, which extensively uses 32-bit multiplies. Also, the DMA scatter/gather functionality was not useful to us as we needed 8 byte scatter/gather operations but the cell requires that the data elements are at least 128 byte large.

Finally, although mailbox communication is easy to understand, it is a very raw device to implement parallel primitives. We find that mailboxes provide not enough programmer abstraction and are, in the end, hard to use. One problem results from sending all communication through a single mailbox. This makes it impossible to separately develop functionality to communicate with a single SPU, as this functionality can receive unexpected messages from a different SPU and it must know how to deal with these messages. An interesting solution could be the use of tag queues in the incoming mailbox, such that one can select only a particular type or source of message.

7   Related Work

The Cell BE Architecture promises high performance at low power consumption. Consequently, several researchers have investigated the utility of the Cell BE for particular application domains.

Williams et al. [13] measure performance and power consumption of the Cell BE when executing scientific computing kernels. They compare these numbers to other architectures and find potential speedups in the 10-20x range. However, the low double-precision floating-point performance of the Cell is a major down-side for scientific applications. A high-performance FFT is described in [14].

Héman et al. [15] port a relational database to the Cell BE. Only some database operations (such as projection, selection, etc.) are executed on the SPUs. The authors point out the importance of avoiding branches and of properly preparing the layout of data structures to enable vectorization.

Bader et al. [16] develop a list ranking algorithm for the Cell BE. List ranking is a combinatorial application with highly irregular memory accesses. As memory accesses are hard to predict in this application, it is proposed to use software-managed threads on the SPUs. At any one time, only one thread is running. When it initiates a DMA request, the thread blocks and control switches to another thread. This results in a kind of software fine-grain multi-threading and yields speedups up to 8.4 for this application.

---

[2] SPU-to-SPU mailbox communication is implemented using DMA commands.

Bagojevic et al. [17] port a randomized axelerated maximum likelihood kernel for phylogenetic tree construction to the Cell BE. They use multiple levels of parallelism and implement a scheduler that selects at runtime between loop-level parallelism and task-level parallelism.

Also, the Cell BE has been tested using bio-informatics applications. Sachdeva et al. [18] port the FASTA and Clustal W applications to the Cell BE. For Clustal W, they have only adapted the forward loop in the pairwise alignment phase for the SPU. Their implementation of the PW phase takes 3.76 seconds on 8 SPUs, whereas our implementation takes 1.44 seconds. Our implementation is faster due to the removal of unaligned memory accesses, due to the vectorization of address computations when accessing the substitution matrix and also due to optimizing control flow in the backward pass. Furthermore, Sachdeva et al. apply static load balancing while our experiments (not discussed) reveal that dynamic load balancing works better since the comparison of two sequences has variable execution time.

8   Conclusion

The Cell Broadband Engine Architecture is a recent heterogeneous multi-core architecture targeted at compute-intensive workloads. The SPUs, which are the workhorse processors, have rare architectural features that help them to sustain high performance, but they also require specific code optimizations. In this paper, we have investigated what optimizations are necessary and we measured how much they improve performance. We performed our experiments on Clustal W, a well-known bio-informatics application for multiple sequence alignment where we found that (i) executing unmodified code on an SPU is slower than execution on the PPU, (ii) removing control flow from inner loops makes the SPU code already faster than the PPU, (iii) 4-way vectorization improves performance up to 3.6x and (iv) removing unaligned memory accesses gives an important additional speedup in one loop nest. Using these optimizations, we demonstrated a speedup of 51.2 over PPU-only execution for the pairwise alignment phase, 5.7 for the progressive alignment phase and an overall 9.1 speedup.

We found the lack of support for 32-bit integer multiplies most limiting to performance and we found mailbox communication to be the most programmer-unfriendly feature of the SPUs.

Acknowledgements

Hans Vandierendonck is Postdoctoral Research Fellow with the Fund for Scientific Research - Flanders (FWO). Sean Rul is supported by the Institute for the Advancement of Science and Technology in the Industry (IWT). This research was also sponsored by Ghent University and by the European Network of Excellence on High-Performance Embedded Architectures and Compilation (HiPEAC). The authors are gratefull to the Barcelona Supercomputing Center - Centro Nacional de Supercomputacion for access to a Cell Blade.

References

1. Pham, D., et al.: The design and implementation of a first-generation Cell processor. In: IEEE International Solid-State Circuits Conference, pp. 184–592 (2005)
2. Thompson, J.D., Higgins, D.G., Gibson, T.J.: CLUSTAL W: improving the sensitivity of progressive multiple sequence alignment through sequence weighting, position-specific gap penalties and weight matrix choice. Nucleic Acids Res. 22(22), 4673–4680 (1994)
3. Flachs, B., et al.: The microarchitecture of the synergistic processor for a Cell processor. Solid-State Circuits, IEEE Journal of 41(1), 63–70 (2006)
4. Gschwind, M., Hofstee, P.H., Flachs, B., Hopkins, M., Watanabe, Y., Yamazaki, T.: Synergistic processing in cell's multicore architecture. IEEE Micro 26(2), 10–24 (2006)
5. Bader, D., Li, Y., Li, T., Sachdeva, V.: BioPerf: A Benchmark Suite to Evaluate High-Performance Computer Architecture on Bioinformatics Applications. In: The IEEE International Symposium on Workload Characterization, pp. 163–173 (October 2005)
6. Smith, T.F., Waterman, M.S.: Identification of common molecular subsequences. Journal of Molecular Biology 147(1), 195–197 (1981)
7. Just, W.: Computational complexity of multiple sequence alignment with SP-score. Journal of Computational Biology 8(6), 615–623 (2001)
8. Saitou, N., Nei, M.: The neighbor-joining method: a new method for reconstructing phylogenetic trees. Mol. Biol. Evol. 4(4), 406–425 (1987)
9. Edgar, R.C.: Muscle: a multiple sequence alignment method with reduced time and space complexity. BMC Bioinformatics 5(1) (2004)
10. Uniprotkb/swiss-prot protein knowledgebase 52.5 statistics, http://www.expasy.ch/sprot/relnotes/relstat.html
11. Mikhailov, D., Cofer, H., Gomperts, R.: Performance Optimization of ClustalW: Parallel ClustalW, HT Clustal, and MULTICLUSTAL. White Paper, CA Silicon Graphics (2001)
12. Chaichoompu, K., Kittitornkun, S., Tongsima, S.: MT-ClustalW: multithreading multiple sequence alignment. In: Sixth IEEE International Workshop on High Performance Computational Biology, p. 8 (2006)
13. Williams, S., Shalf, J., Oliker, L., Kamil, S., Husbands, P., Yelick, K.: The potential of the Cell processor for scientific computing. In: Proceedings of the 3rd conference on Computing frontiers, pp. 9–20 (May 2006)
14. Greene, J., Cooper, R.: A parallel 64K complex FFT algorithm for the IBM/Sony/Toshiba Cell broadband engine processor. White Paper (November 2006)
15. Heman, S., Nes, N., Zukowski, M., Boncz, P.A.: Vectorized Data Processing on the Cell Broadband Engine. In: Proceedings of the International Workshop on Data Management on New Hardware (June 2007)
16. Bader, D.A., Agarwal, V., Madduri, K.: On the design and analysis of irregular algorithms on the cell processor: A case study on list ranking. In: 21st IEEE International Parallel and Distributed Processing Symposium (March 2007)
17. Blagojevic, F., Stamatakis, A., Antonopoulos, C.D., Nikolopoulos, D.E.: RAxML-Cell: Parallel phylogenetic tree inference on the cell broadband engine. In: International Symposiumon Parallel and Distributed Processing Systems (2007)
18. Sachdeva, V., Kistler, M., Speight, E., Tzeng, T.H.K.: Exploring the viability of the Cell Broadband Engine for bioinformatics applications. In: Proceedings of the 6th Workshop on High Performance Computational Biology, p. 8 (March 2007)

Drug Design Issues on the Cell BE

Harald Servat[1], Cecilia González-Alvarez[2], Xavier Aguilar[1],
Daniel Cabrera-Benitez[2], and Daniel Jiménez-González[2]

[1] Barcelona Supercomputing Center
[2] Universitat Politècnica de Catalunya
Jordi Girona 1-3, Campus Nord-UPC, Modul C6, E-08034 Barcelona
harald.servat@bsc.es xavier.aguilar@bsc.es,
cecilia,dcabrera,djimenez@ac.upc.es

Abstract. Structure alignment prediction between proteins (protein docking) is crucial for drug design, and a challenging problem for bioinformatics, pharmaceutics, and current and future processors due to it is a very time consuming process. Here, we analyze a well known protein docking application in the Bioinformatic field, Fourier Transform Docking (FTDock), on a 3.2GHz Cell Broadband Engine (BE) processor. FTDock is a geometry complementary approximation of the protein docking problem, and baseline of several protein docking algorithms currently used. In particular, we measure the performance impact of reducing, tuning and overlapping memory accesses, and the efficiency of different parallelization strategies (SIMD, MPI, OpenMP, etc.) on porting that biomedical application to the Cell BE. Results show the potential of the Cell BE processor for drug design applications, but also that there are important memory and computer architecture aspects that should be considered.

1 Introduction

Protein-protein docking algorithms predict the structure alignment between two or more proteins to form a complex, without the need of experimental measurements at the laboratory. The computational cost of those algorithms is high due to the large number of aspects to consider. There are three main types of docking: flexible docking, rigid-body docking, and their combination. In this paper we focus on the rigid-body docking, that consideres that the geometries of the proteins are not modified when forming the complex. Rigid-body docking is inadequate when there are several conformational changes during the complex formation, but it is a very good baseline for flexible protein docking algorithms.

In particular, we focus on the fine- and coarse-grain parallelization of the Fourier Transform Docking (FTDock) application [14,20] on a Cell processor. We present experiment results using MPI, OpenMP, function offloading, and vectorization. Note however that we do not intend to propose the fastest version of the FTDock on a Cell BE blade. Our main objective is to show the performance impact of different implementation and parallelization decisions that one can take when porting code to a Cell BE blade.

P. Stenström et al. (Eds.): HiPEAC 2008, LNCS 4917, pp. 176–190, 2008.

The Cell processor is a joint initiative of Sony, Toshiba and IBM. The first version of the Cell is the Cell Broadband Engine (CBE) [19]. Cell processor is composed by a Power-Architecture-compliant Power Processor Element (PPE), and eight Synergistic Processor Elements (SPE) [13,17], each with a small Local Store (LS) memory. PPE and SPEs are connected each other and to main memory through the Element Interconnect Bus (EIB). Different performance analysis have been done on the Cell BE [7,18,22]. We have followed their results in order to implement serveral versions of the FTDock. The performance analysis of those versions shows memory bandwidth limitations on the Cell BE and how different strategies may improve overall performance. To our knowledge, there is not any other work that analyzes the performance of the FTDock using High Performance Computers, specially on a Cell BE.

Finally, we compare the coarse and fine-grain parallelization of the Cell-BE FTDock implementation analyzed to a coarse-grain parallelization of FTDock, running on a POWER5 multicore. Cell-BE FTDock outperforms by more than 2.4x that coarse-grain parallelization.

2   Related Work

This paper presents the evaluation of a drug design application, FTDock, on a Cell BE blade. FTDock is baseline of several other rigid-body and flexible docking algorithms as [6,12]. Authors in [6] develop the *pyDockRST* software, based on the FTDock application, by defining distance restraints that help to score rigid-body docking solutions obtained with FTDock.

Here, we present the porting (following the indications done by CellPerformance.com [1]) and the analysis of FTDock in order to reflect the computer architecture bottlenecks of Cell BE pointed out by [7,18,22].

FTDock uses 3D FFTs to reduce computation time. In this paper, as part of the analysis, we evaluate two generic implementations of a power-of-2 single-precision complex-data 3D FFTs, based on the 1D FFT library function of the IBM SDK 1.1 for Cell, by following the ideas of the 3D FFT on Blue Gene [11]. To our knowledge, authors in [9,16] evaluate and propose fast 1D FFT on Cell BE. Also, the recent version of FFTW 3.2alpha2, with support for Cell BE, implements fast 3D FFTs. Furthermore, there are other works on GPGPU that use graphic processing to accelerate FFT computation, for instance [23,15], where GPU cache-conscious 1D FFT are proposed. For a Cell BE, double buffering processing combined with function offloading will help to exploit memory and interconnection bus bandwidth. Here, we use different implementations of the 3D FFT as a way to evaluate memory and EIB bandwidth of the Cell BE blade.

One important part of the 3D FFT is the matrix transpositions to be done. In this paper we implement a SIMD version of the Eklundh's matrix transposition [10]. Authors in [8] show how to implement an efficient parallel matrix transposition on a distributed memory machine. Nevertheless, unlike [8,11], we are dealing with a small number of processors, Local Store in each SPE is very small (256 Kbytes) and memory accesses are done by DMA memory transfers.

Other biomedical applications have been ported and analyzed on Cell BE machines, for instance, the RAxML Phylogenetic Tree Inference application [4,5]. In those works authors show some hints for porting RAxML to SPE, and propose a dynamic parallelization technique in order to get maximum benefit from the processing units of the Cell BE.

3 Experimental Setup

Our experiments have been run on a dual processor Cell BE based blade. It contains two SMT-enabled Cell BE processors at 3.2 GHz with 1GB DD2.0 XDR RAM (512 MB per processor). The system runs Linux Fedora Core 6, kernel 2.6.20 (NUMA enabled) with 64 KB Local Store page mapping.

All codes have been developed in C and use the SPE Management Library 1.1 (libspe). Codes running in the SPE components are compiled using spu-gcc 4.1.1 with "-O3" optimization option. Codes running on the PPE are compiled using gcc 4.1.1 20061011 (Red Hat 4.1.1-30) and "-O3 -maltivec" optimization options. The OpenMP implementation used is the one supported by our version of gcc, whereas OpenMPI 1.2 is the MPI implementation library we worked with. Performance has been analyzed using gprof profiler, *gettimeofday*, and time-based *decrementers*.

In order to analyze the FTDock application we use only one of the enzyme/inhibitor tests of the benchmark used in [14] since all the tests have similar sizes. The size of the problem is given by the sizes of the grids used to discretize the enzyme and the inhibitor. The execution time of the FTDock mostly depends on thoses grid sizes. We evaluate the application for the only two power-of-two dimension grid sizes that make sense under a point of view of structure alignment, 128^3 and 256^3 grid sizes. For those sizes, the data structures used in FTDock fit in main memory of the blade we use for the evaluation.

Finally, we stop the FTDock run after a certain number of iterations of its main loop, enough to characterize the complete application.

4 FTDock Algorithm

Fourier Transform Protein Docking (FTDock) uses the shape recognition algorithm of [20], measuring shape complementarity by Fourier correlation [14]. The algorithm uses Fast Fourier transforms (FFT) to scan all the possible translations of the two rotating rigid molecules. In this way, the algorithm reduces the cost of scanning all translational space from $O(N^6)$ to $O(N^3 \log N^3)$.

4.1 Algorithm Description

First, FTDock discretizes molecule A. This molecule is the largest one and will not be rotated, discretized, or translated any more during the complementary shape search. Then, FTDock rotates molecule B (the smallest one) and, for each rotation, discretizes and performs a translational scan of this molecule relative to molecule A. For each rotation and translation of molecule B, the surface complemetarity of the two molecules is evaluated with the correlation of the two discretized molecules. Molecules are discretized on two N^3 grids. For more details about the algorithm see [14]. In [14], the grid size used is $128 \times 128 \times 128$ nodes. We evaluate FTDock for 128^3 and 256^3 grid sizes.

For each rotation, the correlation cost of the translational scan of molecule B is $O(N^6)$. However, it can be solved in $O(N^3 \log N^3)$ using FFTs to compute the correlation of all the possible translations as follows:

$$F_A = FFT(f_A)$$
$$F_B = FFT(f_B)$$
$$F_C = (F_A^*)(F_B)$$
$$f_C = iFFT(F_C)$$

where FFT and $iFFT$ denote forward and inverse 3D FFT respectively. f_A and f_B functions define the value of a grid node for discretized molecules A and B respectively. (F_A^*) denotes complex conjugate and $(F_A^*)(F_B)$ denotes complex multiplication. For each rotation, FTDock scans f_C to find the three best correlation scores using the scoring filter function. The number of partial results depends on the number of possible orientations (rotations) scanned, that is $360 \times 360 \times 180/\alpha$, where α is the angular deviation. α is 15 as in [14].

5   Cell BE Implementation of FTDock

We have implemented a Cell-BE FTDock version based on profiling information, code analysis and using the existing parallelism levels on a Cell BE Blade. The profiling information obtained running FTDock on the PPE of a Cell BE shows that the most time consuming functions are: 3D FFT/iFFTs (54% of total execution time), complex multiplication $((F_A^*)(F_B))$ (12%), the scoring filter function (21%), and the discretize function (12%). Code analysis indicates that rotations are data independent. Finally, the different levels of parallelization that a programmer can exploit on a Cell BE Blade are:

1. Two Cell BEs on a Blade (i.e. using MPI).
2. Dual-threaded PPE (i.e. using OpenMP).
3. 8 SPEs per Cell BE (i.e. using Function-Offloading).
4. SIMD at each SPE, and at the PPE.

So, we have parallelized rotations with MPI. For each rotation, functions 3D FFT, complex multiplication, 3D iFFT and scoring filter have been offloaded to the SPEs. Discretize function has been parallelized using OpenMP. Finally, we have vectorized the scoring filter and the complex multiplication functions.

Below, we detail the 3D FFT/iFFT implementation and its algorithm parameters. Also, we briefly explain the offloaded complex multiplication and the new version of the scoring filter.

5.1   3D FFT/iFFT

We implement a 3D FFT/iFFT (from this point, only FFT) using sequential 1-stride 1D FFT as a building block [11]. The sizes of the 1D FFTs we use are relatively small (128 and 256 single-precision complex-data elements), and can be done within a SPE using the IBM SDK 1-stride *fft_1d_r2* routine for SPEs.

Figure 1 shows our understanding of a grid of size $N_x \times N_y \times N_z$.

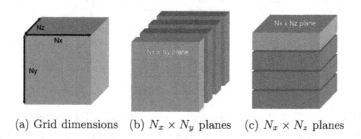

(a) Grid dimensions   (b) $N_x \times N_y$ planes   (c) $N_x \times N_z$ planes

Fig. 1. Grid Example with $N_x = N_y = N_z = 4$

The algorithm we have implemented computes the following steps:

- **Step 1:** For each $N_x \times N_y$ plane, N_y 1D FFTs along x dimension.
- **Step 2:** Matrix transposition of each $N_x \times N_y$ plane.
- **Step 3:** For each $N_x \times N_y$ plane, N_y 1D FFTs along current x dimension.
- **Step 4:** Matrix transposition of each current $N_x \times N_z$ plane.
- **Step 5:** For each current $N_x \times N_y$ plane, N_y 1D FFTs along x dimension.
- **Step 6:** Optional: Matrix Transposition of each current $N_x \times N_z$ plane.
- **Step 7:** Optional: Matrix Transposition of each current $N_x \times N_y$ plane.

In Steps 1, 3 and 5, each SPE performs DMA get transfers of a set of rows of N_x complex-data elements, performs the 1D FFT of those rows, and DMA put transfers them back to main memory[1]. Note that 1D FFTs are always done along 1-stride x dimension thanks to Steps 2 and 4. Otherwise, DMA transfers of elements that are discontinuous in memory and non-1-stride 1D FFTs would be much more expensive [18]. Steps 2 and 4 perform matrix transpostions of all planes along one dimension. We have implemented an in-place $B \times B$ SIMD version of the Eklundh Matrix transposition algorithm [10] as the blocking unit for plane transpositions. B is the blocksize algorithm parameter. Figure 2 shows an example of the Eklundh matrix transposition of a 4×4 matrix.

The Eklundh matrix transpostion idea can be used to perform a blocking version of the plane transposition. In this case, each element of Figure 2 can be considered a $B \times B$ submatrix block, where each submatrix should be transposed as well.

In Cell BE, swapping and matrix transposition of two $B \times B$ submatrices during plane transposition can be done by one or two SPEs. In the case of using

---

[1] We do not detail the double buffering code for simplicity.

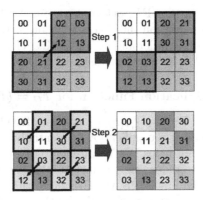

Fig. 2. Eklundh matrix transposition idea for a 4×4 matrix

one SPE, no synchronization is needed in order to DMA transfer (swap) the submatrices to main memory after being transposed in the SPE. Indeed, double buffering can be implemented overlapping the DMA transfers (put or get) of one submatrix and the transposition of the other submatrix. In this case, blocksize B can be up to 64 since one SPE has to keep two $B \times B$ submatrices in its LS. In the case of using two SPEs, those have to be synchronized to DMA transfer (swap) the submatrices transposed to main memory. The synchronization is done by using the _atomic_read intrinsic of the IBM SDK. In this case, blocksize B can be up to 128 since each SPE has to keep one $B \times B$ submatrix in the LS.

In any case, for 128×128 planes, one SPE can locally transpose a complete plane since a plane fits in the LS of the SPE. Moreover, in this case, Steps 1, 2, and 3, and Steps 4 and 5 of the 3D FFT can be performed together in the same SPE before transfering the data back to main memory.

Sumarizing, our 3D FFT may follow different execution paths depending on the plane transposition strategy (one or two SPEs swapping submatrices) and the B blocksize algorithm parameter:

1. Case $B \times B$ submatrix is not the complete plane and/or does not fit in the LS of a SPE. Plane transposition is done by blocking. We evaluate two different strategies:
   (a) One SPE transposes two $B \times B$ submatrices in its LS and DMA transfers (swaps) them to main memory. B blocksize can be up to 64.
   (b) Two SPEs transpose two $B \times B$ submatrices, and synchronize each other to DMA transfer them to main memory. B blocksize can be up to 128.
2. Case 128×128 planes and B blocksize is 128. One SPE can locally transpose a complete plane. Steps 1, 2 and 3 of the 3D FFT are done together in a SPE. Steps 4 and 5 are also done together.

Finally, Steps 6 and 7 of the 3D FFT are optional in the context of FTDock because the complex multiplication $((F_A^*)(F_B))$ can be done using the element orientation obtained on the matrix transposition of Step 4 of the 3D FFT. Therefore, we do not have to perform Steps 6 and 7 for each 3D FFT in our FTDock implementation. Then, in that FTDock context, our iFFT implementation has to take that element orientation into account in order to perform the matrix transpositions in the correct order and obtain original element orientation. With that, we save a total of $2N_y N_x$ matrix transpositions per rotation in the FTDock.

5.2   Complex Multiplication Function for $F_C = (F_A^*)(F_B)$

Complex multiplication $F_C = (F_A^*)(F_B)$ has been offloaded to SPEs and vectorized. Note that complex multiplication sequentially accesses grid elements continuous in memory, that helps DMA transfers to take profit of memory bandwidth. Indeed, in order to reduce the number of DMA transfers to be done, and maximize the re-use of data in a SPE, we have joined the complex multiplication with previous and next computation on the FTDock application. That is, the 1D FFTs (Step 5 of the 3D FFT) of a set of rows of the mobile grid, the complex multiplication of those rows with the corresponding rows on the static grid, and the 1D iFFTs (Step 1 of the 3D FFT) of the complex multiplication result are computed together in a SPE. All that process is done using double buffering.

5.3   Scoring Filter Function

For each rotation of the mobile molecule, the scoring filter function scans each element of the F_C grid looking for the three best scorings.

For each grid element, scoring filter function uses Straightinsertion sorting algorithm [21] to insert the grid element into a three-element sorted vector. We have implemented a SIMD version of the three-element vector Straightinsertion algorithm using few SIMD instructions, and removing the three iteration loop.

Also, we have offloaded the SIMD scoring filter to the SPEs. In our implementation, each SPE looks for the best three local scorings and performs a DMA put transfer its local scorings to main memory. Finally, PPE sorts all those local scorings with quicksort. That sorting process does not have a significant cost since the total number scorings to sort is small.

5.4   Discretize Function

We have parallelized Discretize Function using OpenMP in order to show the performance impact on the FTDock application when using the dual-thread feature of the PPU of the Cell BE.

6   Performance Evaluation

In this section, first we analyze the performance of the 3D FFTs (alone) based on the blocksize B parameter, used for the plane transposition. We present results for the different strategies followed in the implementation of the 3D FFT in order to show how the memory and EIB bandwidth may affect the overall performance. For FTDock analysis, we evaluate the performance contribution of offloading and vectorizing complex multiplication and scoring filter functions to the total execution time of FTDock. That analysis may help a programmer to decide if the development effort needed to offload and vectorize a code is worth or not. Finally, we analyze the MPI parallelization of the FTDock using two tasks, and the parallelization of Discretize function using OpenMP. With that, one can decide which is the best way of exploiting the different levels of parallelism of the Cell BE blade.

6.1   Memory Bandwidth Issues and 3D FFT

Figures 3 and 4 show the execution time in seconds of the 3D FFT implementation presented in Section 5.1 using 1, 2, 4 and 8 SPEs. Each bar is labeled in the x-axis as *blocksize*-A or *blocksize*-B. Blocksize determines the size of the submatrix basic unit in the plane transposition. *A* and *B* stand for using one or two SPEs, respectively, in order to transpose and swap two submatrices.

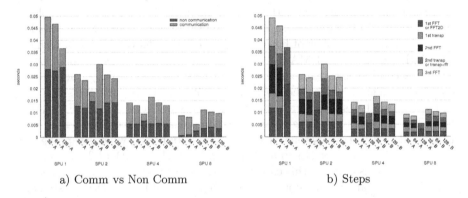

a) Comm vs Non Comm   b) Steps

Fig. 3. Communication and non-communication elapsed time of the total execution time for 128^3 FFTs (left). Total execution time divided by steps (right). Legends in reverse order.

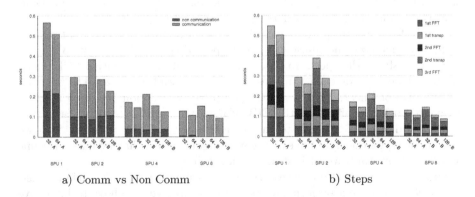

a) Comm vs Non Comm   b) Steps

Fig. 4. Communication and non-communication elapsed time of the total execution time for 256^3 FFTs (left). Total execution time divided by steps (right).

Figures 3.a and 4.a show the total execution time divided on communication and non communication time of the 3D FFT. We have measured the communication time done in the executions with no computation into the SPEs. Non communication time in the Figures is the total execution time minus the communication time. That is, non communication time is the computation that is not overlapped with communication. Figures 3.b and 4.b show the total execution time divided on the five mandatory steps of the 3D FFT, but the 128-A and 128^3 grid size case (Figure 3.b). For 128-A and 128^3 grid size case, the 128×128 plane fits in the LS of the SPE and Steps 1, 2, and 3 are joined together in one Step called FFT2D in the Figure, and Steps 4, 5 are joined into another Step called transf+fft in the Figure.

First, independently of using one or two SPEs to swap submatrices on the transpositions, communication time increases when reducing the blocksize because this reduction affects the memory bandwidth that we obtain. In particular, one row DMA transfers, which happens on the second matrix transpostion (for $N_x \times N_z$ planes), misuse the EIB memory bandwidth, specially for 32 blocksize. For rows of 32 elements, there are only 256 bytes to transfer, which is less than the minimum number of bytes (1024 bytes) to achieve near peak memory bandwidth [18]. Besides, DMA list transfers can help to improve memory bandwidth on second matrix transposition. A DMA list transfer allows gather/scatter operations, which increases the size of those 256-byte DMA transfers.

Figures 3 and 4 show performance differences between A 3D FFT and B 3D FFT transposition strategies on the communication part. That is because, in the A 3D FFT strategy, one SPE uses double buffering when swapping and transposing the two $B \times B$ submatrices, while, in the B 3D FFT strategy no double buffering is done; in this case one SPE performs the matrix transposition of only one submatrix. Therefore, the execution time of the A 3D-FFT strategy, for the same blocksize, is less than for B 3D-FFT strategy. However, for 256^3 grid size, B 3D FFT strategy shows better performance when using 128 blocksizes (Figure 4). That is because we increase the usage of the memory bandwidth of the EIB and the computation to be done in a SPE. The minimum DMA transfer size is 1024 bytes, that is a row of 128 elements, two 4-byte floats per element. That is the minimum size to achieve peak memory bandwidth [18].

Finally, for 128-A and 128^3 grid size case, we have reduced the DMA transfers to do, and increased the re-use of the data per DMA transfer (Figure 3).

Figure 5 shows the speed-up based on the execution time with 1 SPE, using the best blocksize for each transposition strategy and grid size. The speedup achieved is not linear. That is mostly due to the contention accessing to main memory and the conflicts on the EIB. However, one SPE strategy scales very well for grid size 128^3 thanks to the reduction of the DMA transfers. For two SPE strategy, we estimate the execution time considering that we have the same speedup for one and two SPE strategies for 2 SPEs.

Finally, synchronization, necessary on accessing to the work scheduler list, does not seem to be a performance bottleneck. However, we have to interleave wait loops to read an atomic counter to reduce the contention.

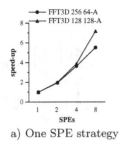

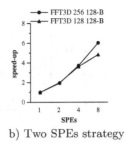

a) One SPE strategy   b) Two SPEs strategy

Fig. 5. Speed-up obtained for each block swapping strategy

6.2   Function Offloading and SIMDization

Figure 6 shows the total execution time of FTDock application (certain number of iterations) for 128^3 and 256^3 grid sizes, left and right respectively. Figure 6 shows results for FTDock running on 1 PPU and 1 SPU. For each grid size the Figure represents nine different versions of the FTDock application:

1. Total execution time without doing the complex multiplication, and running the scalar version of scoring filter function in the PPU.
2. Total execution time when we only access data (no computation is done) in the complex multiplication using prefetch directives. Scalar version of scoring filter function runs in the PPU.
3. Total execution time when running the scalar versions of the complex multiplication and scoring filter functions in the PPU.
4. Total execution time when running the Altivec version of the complex multiplication and the scalar version of the scoring filter functions, both in PPU.
5. Total execution time when running the offloaded complex multiplication in 1 SPU. However, in this version data is only accessed (GET and PUT DMA transfers) and no computation is done. Scalar scoring filter runs in the PPU.
6. Total execution time when using the offloaded complex multiplication in 1 SPU. Scalar scoring filter function runs in the PPU.
7. Total execution time when running the offloaded SIMD version of the complex multiplication in 1 SPU. Scalar scoring filter function runs in the PPU.
8. Total execution time when running the offloaded SIMD version of the complex multiplication and the scalar scoring filter functions in 1 SPU.
9. Total execution time when running the offloaded SIMD versions of the complex multiplication and the scoring filter functions in 1 SPU.

Table 1 shows versions 4 and $6-9$ for 128^3 and 256^3 grid sizes, for 1, 2, 4 and 8 SPEs. Table also shows the speed-up achieved when offloading and vectorization are done compared to the SIMD PPU version (Spup in the Table). Offloading and vectorization performance impact is slightly better for 128^3 grid size than for 256^3 grid size since 3D-FFT execution time is less significant.

Several conclusions can be obtained. First, offloading to SPEs and vectorizing those two functions improve significantly the performance of the drug design

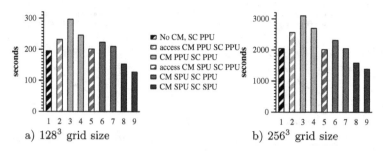

a) 128^3 grid size   b) 256^3 grid size

Fig. 6. Total execution time of FTDock. CM stands for complex multiplication. SC stands for Scoring Filter. PPU or SPU indicates where the function is running. Number labels explained in text.

Table 1. Total execution times in seconds for 128^3 and 256^3 grid sizes using different levels of optimizations. We also show the speed-up compared to the vectorial PPU version. Each level is identified by a number that is explained in the text.

SPEs	128^3					Spup	256^3					Spup
	4	6	7	8	9	4/9	4	6	7	8	9	4/9
1	246	223	210	153	127	1.9	2703	2316	2046	1585	1390	1.9
2	216	167	151	82	70	3.1	2132	1564	1466	842	745	2.9
4	207	139	131	47	41	5.0	1746	1207	1135	469	422	4.2
8	196	131	131	30	27	7.3	1632	1025	1020	301	273	6.0

application. In particular, compared to their vectorial versions on the PPU, using only 1 SPE, the speed-up achieved is nearly 2. Indeed, offloading helps scalability as we can see in Table 1.

Second, Figure 6 shows that memory hierarchy seem to be a bottleneck when accessing data from PPU. Bars 1, 2 and 5 can help to understand that. Bar 1 represents the execution time without doing the complex multiplicaction. In bars 2 and 5, data is only accessed (loads/stores in bar 2, DMA transfers in bar 5) on the complex multiplication function but no computation is done. So, the execution time difference with bar 1 is the memory access time. Bars show a significant performance difference. The reason of that is that load/store pending queue of cache miss accesses (MSHR) seems to limit the PPU version performance, making the PPU pipeline stall. DMA transfers do not have that limit. Therefore, it is worth to offload a function to one SPE if it has to do several memory accesses and temporal locality is not exploited. Indeed, in our case, we can see that a SPE scalar version of the function complex multiplication (bar 6) is faster than a PPE Altivec version (bar 4) due to the data memory access difference. Moreover, vectorization is important in both PPE and SPE, achieving around 20% of improvement for the code we have analyzed.

By offloading and vectorizing Scoring filter function we obtain the same kind of improvements as with complex multiplications.

6.3   Parallelization Using the Two Cell BE of the Blade

So far, we have presented FTDock execution time results using several SPEs on the same Cell BE processor of a Cell BE Blade. In this section we present results for the MPI FTDock parallelization using the two Cell BE of a Blade.

Figure 7 shows the total execution time using 1 or 2 MPI tasks (1 task on 1 PPE), and 1, 2, 4 and 8 SPEs per task, for 128^3 (left) and 256^3 (right) grid sizes. Using 1 task with n SPEs is slower (less efficient) than using 2 tasks with $n/2$ SPEs. The main reason is that we distribute the contention of the EIB and the main memory between the two Cell BEs of a Blade. Actually, that can be seen comparing the execution time of 1 task and 2 tasks for the same number of SPEs; execution time is not divided by two.

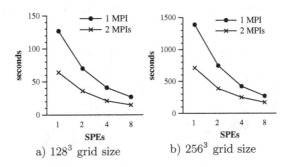

Fig. 7. Total execution time of the parallel implementation of FTDock using 1 or 2 MPI tasks and 1, 2, 4 and 8 SPEs/task, for 128^3 (left), and 256^3 (right) grid sizes

6.4   Parallelization Using Dual-Thread PPU Feature

The PPE hardware supports two simultaneous threads of execution [2], duplicating architecture and special purpose registers, except for some system-level resources such as memory.

Discretize function accesses a working data set that perfectly fits in second level of cache. Indeed, the discretize function has a lot of branches that may not be predicted by the PPE branch-prediction hardware. Hence, a second thread may make forward progress and increase PPE pipeline use and system throughput. We achieve 1.5x of the Discretize function when parallelizing it using OpenMP, and a $1.1 - 1.2$x overall improvement of the FTDock application.

In any case, function offloading and vectorization of that function would get better performance improvements and scalability.

7   Comparison with a POWER5 Multicore Platform

In this section we compare our Cell BE implementation of the FTDock with a parallel version of the FTDock, running on a POWER5 multicore with two

1.5GHz POWER5 chips with 16GBytes of RAM. Each POWER5 chip is dual-core and dual-thread (giving a total of 8 threads on the system). The parallel version of the FTDock for that multicore uses the FFTW3.2alpha2 library in order to do the 3D FFT, and consists on dividing the rotations among different tasks using OpenMPI. Therefore, we are comparing a coarse-grain parallelization on that multicore against a fine-grain parallelization on a Cell BE.

Figure 8 shows the total execution times of FTDock for 1, 2, 4 and 8 tasks or SPEs on a POWER5 multicore and on a Cell BE respectively, for 128^3 and 256^3 grid sizes. We can see that Cell BE FTDock outperforms that multicore parallel implementation of the FTDock. The reasons seems to be the same that we commented when comparing PPU and SPU on Section 6.2. Memory hierarchy becomes a bottleneck for the POWER5 tasks, meanwhile SPEs of the Cell BE avoid the MSHR limitation accessing to main memory. Moreover, Cell is more cost-effective and more power-efficient than the POWER5 multicore [24].

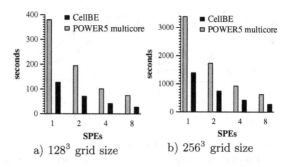

Fig. 8. Total execution time of the parallel implementation of FTDock for a multicore POWER5 and a CellBE for 128^3 grid size(left), and 256^3 grid size (right)

8   Conclusions

In this paper we have evaluated and analyzed an implementation of a protein docking application, FTDock, on a Cell BE Blade using different algorithm parameters and levels of parallelization.

We have achieved a significant speedup of FTDock when we have offloaded the most time consuming functions to the SPEs. However, improving the PPU processor and its memory hierarchy would improve the potential of Cell BE for applications that can not be completely offloaded to the SPEs. Indeed, increasing the number of SPEs per task (one thread running on one PPE) improves the performance of the application. However, linear speedup is not achieved because main memory and EIB contention increases when several SPEs access to main memory in the same Cell BE. Therefore, one should parallelize the application in such a way the main memory and EIB contention is distributed between the two Cell BE of the blade [18].

The relatively small Local Store of the SPE increases the main memory accesses in order to keep partial results. With FTDock, we have seen that increasing the re-use of data within of the SPE, and so, reducing the amount of DMA transfers to main memory, significantly improves the performance of the application. In any case, double buffering is necessary to achieve good performance.

Vectorization is important when porting code to the SPEs. Large performance degradation may happen in the case of using scalar code. However, offloading functions, vectorized or not, that access large amounts of data without exploiting temporal locality, is crucial for scalability and for avoiding current memory hierarchy access bottlenecks. We have shown significant performance improvements when accessing data from a SPE, compared to accessing the same data from the PPE.

Finally, the 3x speedup achieved compared to a Power5 multicore shows the potential of this heterogeneous multiprocessor, and makes worth enough the porting effort. However, automatic mechanisms [3], as a first approximation, would help to accelerate application porting to Cell.

Acknowledgements

We would like to acknowledge Alex Ramirez and Xavi Martorell for their insightful comments while analyzing the data collected in the experiments. Also, to Sergi More for their technical assistance, and reviewers for their contributions to this paper. This work has been performed in the Cell BE-based blades in the Barcelona Supercomputing Center, obtained through the IBM SUR Program. The work has been supported by the European Comission in the context of the SARC project (contract no. 27648), the HiPEAC fellowship grants for Cecilia Gonzalez and Daniel Cabrera, and the Spanish Ministry of Education (contract no. TIN2004-07739-C02-01, TIN2007-60625).

References

1. http://CellPerformance.com
2. Cell broadband engine programming handbook v1.0
3. Bellens, P., Perez, J.M., Badia, R.M., Labarta, J.: CellSs: A programming model for the cell be architecture. In: Conference on Supercomputing (2006)
4. Blagojevic, F., et al.: Dynamic multigrain parallelization on the cell broadband engine. In: PPoPP (2007)
5. Blagojevic, F., et al.: RAxML-Cell: Parallel phylogenetic tree inference on the cell broadband engine. In: Proceedings of the 21st IEEE/ACM International Parallel and Distributed Processing Symposium (2007)
6. Chelliah, V., et al.: Efficient restraints for protein-protein docking by comparison of observed amino acid substitution patterns with those predicted from local environment. In: JMB 357 (2006)
7. Chen, T., et al.: Cell broadband engine architecture and its first implementation
8. Choi, J., et al.: Parallel matrix transpose algorithms on distributed memory concurrent computers. Parallel Computing 21(9), 1387–1405 (1995)
9. Chow, A.C., et al.: A programming example: Large FFT on the cell broadband engine. White Paper IBM (2005)

10. Eklundh, J.: A fast computer method for matrix transposing. IEEE transactions on computers 21, 801–803 (1972)
11. Eleftheriou, M., et al.: Scalable framework for 3D FFTs on the blue gene/l supercomputer: Implementation and early performance measurements. IBM J. RES. & DEV 49(2/3) (2005)
12. Fernández-Recio, J., Totrov, M., Abagyan, R.: Soft protein-protein docking in internal coordinates. Protein Science 11V, 280–291 (2002)
13. Flachs, B., et al.: The Microarchitecture of the Synergistic Processor for a Cell Processor. IEEE Journal of Solid-State Circuits 41(1)V (2006)
14. Gabb, H.A., et al.: Modelling protein docking usign shape complementary, electrostatics and biochemical information. J. Mol. Biol. 272 (1997)
15. Govindaraju, N.K., et al.: A memory model for scientific algorithms on graphics processors. In: Proceedings of the 2006 ACM/IEEE conference on Supercomputing, p. 89. ACM Press, New York (2006)
16. Greene, J., Cooper, R.: A parallel 64k complex FFT algorithm for the ibm/sony/toshiba cell broadband engine processor. In: Tech. Conf. Proc. of the Global Signal Processing Expo (GSPx) (2005)
17. Gschwind, M., et al.: Synergistic Processing in Cell's Multicore Architecture. IEEE Micro 26(2) (March 2006)
18. Jimenez-Gonzalez, D., et al.: Performance analysis of cell broadband engine for high memory bandwidth applications. In: ISPASS (2007)
19. Kahle, J.A., et al.: Introduction to the Cell multiprocessor. IBM Journal of Research and Development 49(4/5) (2005)
20. Katchalski-Katzir, E., et al.: Molecular sufrace recognition: Determination of geometric fit between proteins and their ligands by correlation techniques. Proc. Natl. Acad. Sci. USA, Biohphysics 89, 2195–2199 (1992)
21. Knuth, D.: The art of computer programming: Sorting and searching. Addison-Wesley Publishing Company 3 (1973)
22. Krolak, D.: Unleashing the cell broadband engine processor. MPR Fall Processor Forum (November 2005)
23. Naga, K., Govindaraju, D.M.: Cache-Efficient Numerical Algorithms using Graphics Hardware. Tech. rep., UNC (2007)
24. Wang, D.: Cell mircroprocessor iii. Real World Technologies (2005)

Part IV

Power-Aware Techniques

COFFEE: COmpiler Framework for Energy-Aware Exploration

Praveen Raghavan[1,2], Andy Lambrechts[1,2], Javed Absar[1,2,3], Murali Jayapala[1],
Francky Catthoor[1,2], and Diederik Verkest[1,2,4]

[1] IMEC vzw, Heverlee, Belgium
{ragha,lambreca,absar,jayapala,catthoor,verkest}@imec.be
[2] ESAT, KULeuven, Leuven, Belgium
[3] ST Microelectronics, Singapore
[4] Dept. of Electrical Engineering, VUB, Brussels, Belgium

Abstract. Modern mobile devices need to be extremely energy efficient. Due to the growing complexity of these devices, energy aware design exploration has become increasingly important. Current exploration tools often do not support energy estimation, or require the design to be very detailed before the estimate is possible. It is important to get early feedback on both performance and energy consumption during all phases of the design and at higher abstraction levels. This paper presents a unified optimization and exploration framework, from source level transformation to processor architecture design. The proposed retargetable compiler and simulator framework can map applications to a range of processors and memory configurations, simulate and report detailed performance and energy estimates. An accurate energy modeling approach is introduced, which can estimate the energy consumption of processor and memories at a component level, which can help to guide the design process. Fast energy-aware architecture exploration is illustrated using an example processor. The flow is demonstrated using a representative wireless benchmark on two state of the art processors and on a processor with advanced low power extensions for memories. The framework also supports exploration of various novel low power extensions and their combinations. We show that a unified framework enables fast feedback on the effect of source level transformations of the application code on the final cycle count and energy consumption.

1 Introduction and Motivation

Modern consumers demand portable devices that provide functionality comparable to that of their non-mobile counterparts, but still having a long battery life. In order to achieve these ambitious goals, designers need to optimize all parts of these systems. At the same time an efficient mapping of the application code onto the platform is key to achieve a high energy efficiency. A mapping can be considered to be efficient if it is using the available hardware to its full potential.

Currently energy estimation is often only performed at the final stage of the design, when the hardware is completely fixed and gate level simulations are possible. This approach restricts extensive energy driven architecture exploration, taking into account the impact of the compiler and possible transformations on the source code. When

P. Stenström et al. (Eds.): HiPEAC 2008, LNCS 4917, pp. 193–208, 2008.

optimizing applications for a given architecture, designers try to minimize the energy consumption by improving other metrics like a reduction in the number of memory accesses. This indirect way is however inconclusive for more complex trade-offs, like introducing extra operations, and therefore accesses to the instruction memory, in order to minimize accesses to the data memory. To correctly perform this type of optimizations, an integrated energy-aware estimation flow is needed.

Decisions at different levels of abstraction have an impact on the efficiency of the final implementation, from algorithmic level choices to source level transformations and all the way down to micro-architectural changes. In this paper, we present an integrated compilation and architecture exploration framework with fast performance and energy estimation. This work enables designers to evaluate the impact of various optimizations in terms of energy and performance. The optimizations explored can be either in the source code, in the compiler or in the architecture.

Current embedded platforms consist of a number of processors, custom hardware and memories. Because of increasing production costs, flexibility is getting more important and platforms have to be used for many different and evolving products. In this work we focus on one of the programmable processors, potentially including special purpose Functional Units (FUs), that improve the energy efficiency for a certain application domain. The data and instructions memory hierarchy of this processor are taken into account.

In this context designers are facing multiple problems. Firstly, given a set of target applications, the Instruction Set Architecture (ISA, decides on number and type of FUs), the processor style (correct mix of instruction (ILP) and data level parallelism (DLP)), the usage of application specific accelerator units, sizes of memories and register files and the connectivity between these components have to be fixed. In order to reach the required performance and energy efficiency, the retargetable tool-flow presented here will enable a fast architecture exploration and lead to better processor designs, taking into account all parts of the system. Our framework will correctly identify the energy and performance bottlenecks and prevent designers from improving one part at the cost of other parts. Since our framework allows the use of novel low power extensions for different components of the processor, combinations of these extensions can be explored. Secondly, after the processor has been fixed, architecture dependent software optimizations using code transformations can dramatically improve the performance and energy efficiency. An example of such a transformation is loop merging. This technique can improve data locality, but can have the adverse effect of increasing register pressure, thereby causing register spilling. Our framework will guide the designer to choose these transformations. It directly shows the effect of software-optimizations on the final platform metrics: cycles and Joules. Thirdly, compiler optimizations like improved scheduling and allocation techniques can be evaluated for a range of relevant state of the art architectures. Their effect on different parts of the system (e.g. register files, memories and datapath components) can be tracked correctly.

Optimizing this hardware-software co-design problem is complicated by the large size of the design space. In order to be of practical use, estimation tools should be sufficiently fast to handle realistic application sizes. Currently, energy estimation during processor design is done using time consuming gate level simulations. This approach is accurate, but requires the hardware design to be completed, which restricts thorough exploration. Energy estimation at ISA level, enables such a fast estimation, by trading off some accuracy for speed. The energy estimation of the proposed framework has been validated against a real design.

The novel contributions of this paper include the following:

1. an accurate ISA level and profiling level energy estimation, early in the design flow
2. a framework that enables simulation and compilation for a wide range of state of the art processors and advanced low power architectural extensions
3. an integrated framework, which is automated to a large extent, to perform code transformations, compilation, simulation and energy estimation

The rest of the paper is organized as follows. Section 2 gives an overview of frameworks that support co-design exploration. Section 3 introduces the proposed framework, describes the modeled components and the exploration space. Section 4 illustrates the energy estimation process for different components of the processor and estimation of the energy consumption of the complete platform. Section 5 describes the results and analysis for representative optimizations in the embedded context for a WCDMA application using the proposed flow. Finally Section 6 gives a summary and outlines the future work.

2   Related Work

Various attempts to make retargetable compiler and architectural level exploration tools have been made: e.g. Trimaran [1], Simplescalar [2] and Epic Explorer [3]. All these frameworks are capable of exploring a restricted design space and do not support important architectural features like software controlled memories, data parallelism or SIMD (Single Instruction Multiple Data), clustered register files, loop buffers etc. These features have become extremely important for embedded handheld devices as energy efficiency is a crucial design criterion. Although these frameworks (except Epic Explorer) do not directly provide energy estimation, several extensions have been built for this purpose. Wattch [4] and SimplePower, for example, are based on Simplescalar, but their power models are not geared towards newer technologies and their parameter range is still too restricted. Other industrial tools like Target's Chess/Checkers, Tensilica's XPRES and Coware's Processor Designer provide architectural and compiler retargetability, but the supported design space is limited to a restricted template and they do not provide fast, high-level energy estimates. Detailed energy estimates can be obtained by synthesizing the generated RTL and using the traditional hardware design flow. Generating such detailed estimates are too time consuming for wide exploration and for evaluating compiler and architectural optimizations. Energy estimates based on a library of architectural components, as proposed in this paper, do not suffer from these drawbacks, as they are fast and sufficiently accurate for these purposes.

In the code transformation space SUIF [5] pioneered enabling loop transformations and analysis. Wrap-IT [6] from INRIA uses the polyhedral model for analysis and to perform transformations. These tools alone are not sufficient as transformations can have an impact (positive, negative or neutral) on various parts of the processors. This is because these transformations are not platform independent and therefore essential to have one integrated flow. In our flow, we directly couple the Wrap-IT loop transformation framework to the retargetable compiler, simulator and energy estimation engine.

ACE's CoSy framework and GCC are retargetable compiler frameworks which support a wide range of high-level compiler optimizations and code generation for a range of processors. However, these frameworks do not support instruction set simulation and energy aware exploration. GCC is mainly targeting code generation for general purpose oriented processors (like x86, Alpha, PowerPC etc.) rather than for low power embedded processors, which is our focus. The roadmap of GCC extensions indicates this is slowly changing, e.g. providing support for loop transformations and vectorization. In our future work we will be investigating the possibility of integrating our energy aware exploration framework and our backend compilation framework with GCC. Although the CoSy framework targets low power embedded processors, the scope of retargetability is limited.

The proposed framework combines the benefits of all the above frameworks, while giving fast estimates of energy and performance early in the design. It also provides a framework which can analyze the impact of high level code transformations on the architecture's performance and power consumption. This framework can be used to explore hw/sw co-design, architectural optimizations or software optimizations.

3   Compiler and Simulator Flow

Figure 1 shows the retargetable compiler and simulator framework. For a given application and a machine configuration, the flow is automated to a large extent, requiring minimal designer intervention. Manual steps are only needed for inserting specific *intrinsics* from the intrinsic library or in the case of specifiying a particular loop transformation. Since the framework is retargetable, it facilitates exploring different machine configurations for a given application.

The loop transformation engine is part of the Wrap-IT/Uruk framework [6], which is integrated into the tool chain (shown in Figure 1) and forms the first part of the proposed flow. Essentially, this engine creates a polyhedral model of the application, which enables automating the loop transformations. The compiler and the simulation framework are built on top of Trimaran [1], but are heavily extended in order to support a wider range of target architectures and to perform energy estimation. The integrated and extended flow forms the COFFEE framework, as described in the following subsections.

The application code is presented to the flow as ANSI-C code. A user-friendly XML schema is used to describe the target architecture (machine description). It is read in by processor aware parts of the flow, e.g. the compiler (Coffee-Impact, Coffee-Elcor), simulator (Coffee-Simulator) and power estimator. The application code can be transformed by the Uruk front-end, before it is passed on to the rest of the compiler and eventually used for simulation. The simulator generates detailed trace files to track the activation of the components of the processor. These are finally processed by power and performance estimation.

The compiler and simulator have been extended to support exploration of the following architectural features:

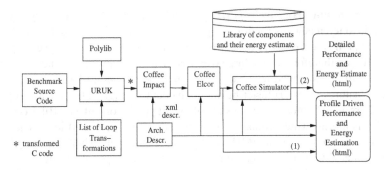

Fig. 1. COFFEE Compiler and Simulator Framework for transformations, simulation and performance/energy estimation

3.1 Memory Architecture Subsystem

The simulator supports both Harvard and Von-Neumann based memory architectures. The supported features for the data and instruction memory are described below:

Data Memory Hierarchy. The extended simulator supports complete data memory hierarchy simulations, both for software controlled caches (scratchpad memories or SPMs) and hardware caches. The presented toolflow assists the designer when selecting a cache or a scratchpad, by reporting energy and performance results. In this way application characteristics can be taken into consideration during this choice.

For scratchpads, the data transfers to and from the higher level memories are handled by the DMA. When using scratchpads, the DMA has to be programmed to perform the correct data transfers and the correct timing is accounted for. The compiler will schedule these DMA operations on the DMA, and correctly handle dependencies. If the data transfer, e.g. for a large chunk of data to be transfered, can not be finished in parallel to the computation, the processor will stall. We have added an intrinsic library to provide an interface to the designer to program the transfers to and from the higher level data memory, e.g. *DMA_TRANSFER (source_addr, spm_dest_addr, transfer_size)*. This is similar to how state of the art scratchpads and DMAs are controlled. The DMA can also support more complex functionality, like changing the data layout during the transfer, interleaving or tiling data. This type of advanced DMA can help to reduce the power consumption further. For caches, hardware cache controllers manage these memory transfers. The choice for either cache or scratchpad depends on the dynamic or static nature of the application, and should be made by the designer based on analysis and simulation. In both cases, the energy and performance is appropriately accounted for by the simulator.

Another important design decision to be explored is the size and the number of ports of memories and the usage of multi-level memory hierarchies. These decisions heavily affect the overall power consumption of the system and hence it is crucial to be able to explore the entire design space. The COFFEE simulator has been extended from the original Trimaran 2.0, in order to accurately simulate multi-level cache and scratchpad based hierarchies. Connectivity, sizes, number of ports etc. are specified in the XML machine description and can be easily modified for exploration.

Instruction Memory Hierarchy (IMH). A traditional instruction memory is activated every cycle to fetch new instructions. Especially in wide architectures, like VLIWs, this can be one of the most energy consuming parts of the system. Design space exploration of the IMH can therefore have a large overall effect on the processor energy efficiency. The IMH can be simulated as a cache, a scratchpad or a multi-level hierarchy. Other advanced features, like L0 clustering and loop counters (e.g. [7,8]), are also supported. Loop buffers are commonly used in state of the art processors, like [9,10]. Loop buffers are small memories which contains the instructions for one nested loop. They reduce the energy consumption of the IMH by exploiting the locality when executing loops. A loop controller (LC) iterates over the instructions of the loop in the buffer.

Figure 2 shows different supported configurations of the instruction memory. Figure 2(a) is a conventional L1 configuration where the Program Counter (PC) fetches instructions from the L1 instruction cache and executes them on the FUs. Figure 2(b) shows a centralized loop buffer, where the loops are loaded from the L1 instruction memory to the loop buffer when the loop starts. During the loop execution, the LC (Loop Controller) fetches the instructions from the loop buffer instead of the L1 memory. Figure 2(c) shows a distributed loop buffers that can been customized to the application loop size for every slot to minimize energy consumption, but are still controlled by a single LC. The COFFEE framework supports automatic identification and loading of loops into the loop buffers. Compilation and design space exploration for distributed loop buffers is described in detail in [8,11]. More complex loop buffer organizations, where every loop buffer is controlled by a separate LC [12], are also supported, but a description of this concept is outside the scope of this paper. For all these cases, compilation, simulation and energy estimation are supported.

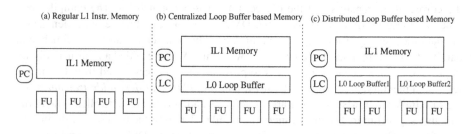

Fig. 2. Variants of Instruction Memory Configuration are supported in Coffee

3.2 Processor Core Subsystem

The processor core subsystem consists of the datapath units and register file. These components are described below:

Processor Datapath. Our flow supports a large datapath design space. Different styles of embedded processors can be modeled, from small RISC processors with a single slot, to wide VLIW processors with many heterogeneous execution slots. Multiple slots can execute instructions in parallel, and can internally consist of multiple functional units that execute mutually exclusively. The number of slots and the instructions that can be executed by each slot (this depends on the functional units in that particular slot) can be specified in the XML machine description. New functional units can be added to the architecture, compiler and simulator easily by modifying the machine description and adding the behavior of the new instruction (in C) to the *intrinsic* library. The framework provides a user-friendly XML schema to add new functional units and specify its properties. The operation's latency, operand specification, pipelining, association of the functional unit to a certain slot, are specified in the XML machine description and correctly taken into account during simulation. Different datapath widths can be supported: 16-bit, 32-bit, 64-bit, 128-bit. By varying the width and number of slots, the trade off between ILP and DLP can be explored. The width can be specified for each FU separately, allowing the usage of SIMD and scalar units in one architecture. An example of this approach is shown for ARM's Cortex A8 in Section 5. SIMD units can be exploited by using *intrinsics*, similar to those available in Intel's SSE2, Freescale's Altivec. We have also used the proposed tools so simulate other novel architectures like SyncPro [13].

The pipeline depth of the processor can be specified in the machine description and the compiler correctly schedules operations onto pipelined functional units. Based on the activity, the energy consumption of the pipeline registers is automatically estimated. This is crucial for architectures with deep pipelines (high clock frequency), and for wide SIMD architectures. In both cases the number of pipeline registers is large and accounts for a large amount of the energy cost and performance.

Register File. Register Files are known to be one of the most power consuming parts of the processor. Hence it is important to ensure that the register file design space is explored properly. The COFFEE flow can handle centralized register files, clustered register files, with or without a bypass network between the functional units and the register files. The size, number of ports and connectivity of the register files are specified in the machine description file.

Figure 3 shows different register file configurations that are supported by our framework. Combinations of the configurations shown in Figure 3 are supported, both in the simulator and the register allocation phase of the compiler. Separate register files for scalar and vector slots can be used together with heterogeneous datapath widths. An example of such a scalar and vector register file is shown in section 5 using ARM's Cortex-A8 core [14]. Communication of data between clusters is supported for various ways, as shown in Figure 3, ranging from extra copy units to a number of point to point connections between the clusters. The performance vs. power trade-off (as inter cluster copy operations take an extra cycle, while increasing the fan-out of register file ports costs energy in interconnections) can be explored using our framework.

A detailed study of register file configurations and the impact on power and performance has been done in [15,16], but these studies are limited to the register file and do not provide a framework for exploring other parts of the processor.

3.3 Loop Transformations

Having an automated transformation framework integrated to the backend compiler is crucial for efficient optimization. The URUK framework [6] performs designer directed

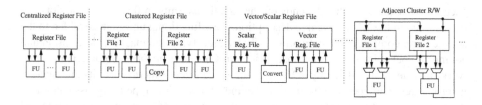

Fig. 3. Variants of Register File architectures that are supported in Coffee

source level transformations to optimize locality in the data memory, improve the number of Instructions Per Cycle (IPC) and to enable vectorization. Automated transformations provided by the framework include: loop split, loop fusion, loop interchange, loop tiling etc. The designer needs to specify the required transformation in a predefined format and the URUK tool performs the transformations automatically, which is less error prone. In Section 5 we use URUK for transformations which optimize locality and enable vectorization. Since the designer gets early feedback on the effect on energy consumption and performance of code transformations for state of the art and experimental architectures. The designer can judiciously iterate over different (combinations of) transformations, like proposed in [17], to optimize e.g. the energy for the final platform.

4 Energy Estimation Flow

In order to get fast and fairly accurate energy estimates, to guide code transformations or architecture exploration, we propose energy estimates coupled to the instruction set simulator. At this abstraction level, the full hardware description is not yet needed and therefore exploration can be fast. To enable early estimates with sufficient accuracy, we propose the following methodology.

The components of the processor (Register File, ALU, pipeline registers, Multipliers, Instruction Decoders etc.) are up-front designed at RTL level (optimized VHDL description). This is done for various instances of each component, e.g. various register file configurations, in terms of ports, number of words and width.

Once the VHDL for a component with a particular parameter set is available, the description is used as input to the flow shown in Figure 4. The target clock frequency of the system is imposed as a fixed timing constraint on the design. We use the UMC90nm general purpose standard cell library from Faraday [18] for all experiments shown in this paper. Each component is passed through logic synthesis (using Synopsys Design Compiler [19]), Vdd/Ground Routing, Place and Route, Clock Tree Synthesis (if needed), DRC, LVS checks (using Cadence SoC Encounter [20]). The extracted netlists (with parasitics) is backannotated to the gate level netlist in Prime Power [21]. A testbench is generated for (each instance of) all the components, using input data with realistic toggle behavior. The energy per activation and leakage power for the different components are estimated from the activity information from gate level simulation and the parasitic information. This results in a library of parameterized energy models.

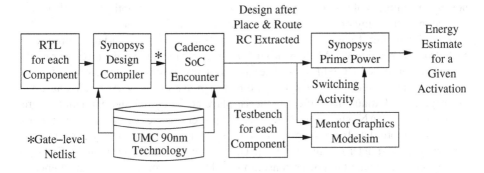

Fig. 4. Flow used for Power Estimation for different components of the processor

Because memories are highly optimized custom hardware blocks, the standard cell flow cannot be used. Therefore we created a library of energy consumptions (dynamic and leakage) using a commercial memory compiler (from Artisan). Finally, our pre-computed library contains the energy consumption (dynamic and leakage) for various components of the processor using the standard cell flow, and for memories, using a commercial memory compiler.

The energy estimation can be done at two possible levels: after profiling or after instruction set simulation.

After compilation, the code is profiled on the host for the given input stimuli. Each of the individual basic/super/hyperblock is annotated with a weight. The weight of the block corresponds to the number of times the block was executed for the given input stimuli at profile time. Based on the weight of each block, the compiled code and the energy/access of the individual components, the COFFEE tool is capable of estimating the energy consumption of the processor. This is the flow marked as (1) in Figure 1. A profiling based estimation is extremely fast as no instruction set simulation is performed. In this case accuracy is traded off for estimation speed with respect to an instruction set simulation flow (described below), because the profiling based estimation is not capable of keeping track of the dynamic effects, like e.g. cache behavior. Profiling based estimation can be used for quick and early exploration.

The instruction set simulation based estimation flow, described in Section 3, counts the number of activations for each of the components. Based on this activation and the components' energy/access from the pre-computed library described above, the energy consumption of the complete system is computed (marked as (2) in Figure 1). This approach correctly keeps track of dynamic effects and is slower than the profiling based approach, but it is still orders of magnitude faster than a detailed gate level simulation for the complete processor, and therefore fast exploration is possible. Given such a fast exploration a wide range of architecture exploration can be perfomed quickly.

Leakage energy consumption can also be obtained as the individual leakage energy for the different components is present[1]. The total energy consumption and average

---

[1] In our 90nm library, leakage in logic is less than 5% and is ignored in the rest of this paper, but it can be estimated using the proposed flow.

power consumption of the complete system can be analyzed and optimized (either by a change in architecture or a compiler optimization or transformation).

To validate our framework, the energy consumption of an in-house processor SyncPro[13][2] running WLAN Synchronization was compared to same processor modeled in the proposed COFFEE flow. The processor was designed separately and there was no sharing of tools/sources between this design and our flow. As a reference, detailed gate-level simulation (after synthesis, placement+routing and extraction) were performed on WLAN synchronization code. The power was then estimated using Prime-Power. For more details on the precise flow used for estimating energy consumption for SyncPro, the reader is refered to [13]. The same code was then run on the COFFEE framework to estimate the power consumption. The net error in the estimated energy using the COFFEE estimation and the energy estimate from PrimePower and gate level simulation is less than **13%** for the complete platform (including the memories). More validation points against other processors are currently being added.

5   Experimental Setup and Results

In this section we demonstrate the COFFEE framework on a representative benchmark for two state of the art processors (TI's C64 and ARM's Cortex-A8). We further illustrate the potential of architectural design space exploration on a standard embedded VLIW.

5.1   Benchmark Driver: WCDMA

WCDMA is a Wideband Direct-Sequence Code Division Multiple Access (DS-CDMA) system, i.e. user information bits are spread over a wide bandwidth by multiplying the user data with quasi-random bits derived from CDMA spreading codes. WCDMA [22] is one of the dominant 3G cellular protocols for multimedia services, including video telephony on a wireless link.

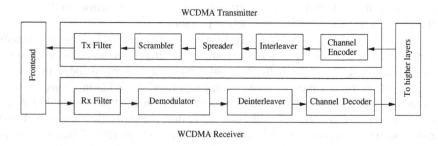

Fig. 5. Wideband CDMA as in Signal Processing On Demand (SODA, [23])

---

[2] [13] is a 5 issue SIMD VLIW and heterogenous distributed register file and a novel interconnection network.

We have used the proposed compiler and simulator flow to optimize the WCDMA receiver code from [23] for a baseline VLIW processor. Starting from the detailed performance estimate on the complete code, the receiver filter (Rx Filter in Figure 5) was identified to be the single most important part of the application in terms of computational requirements and energy consumption (85% percent of the WCDMA's Receiver cycles). Optimizing code transformations using the URUK flow will be illustrated on this part.

It should be emphasized here that the presented COFFEE framework can be used for any ANSI-C compliant application. WCDMA is shown as a relevant example from our target application domain, being multimedia and wireless communication algorithms for portable devices.

5.2 Processor Architectures

The wide range of architectural parameters supported by the presented framework allows designers to explore many different architectural styles and variants quickly. It enables experiments with combinations of parameters or components not commonly found in current processors. In the experimental results shown here, we have optimized the WCDMA receiver filter for two architectures described in this subsection, as an example of the range and complexity of architectures that can be supported.

TI C64-like VLIW processor. The TI C64 [10] is a clustered VLIW processor with two clusters of 4 Functional Units (FUs) each. This processor is chosen as a typical example of an Instruction Level Parallel (ILP) processor. In this heterogeneous VLIW each FU can perform a subset of all supported operations. The Instruction Set Architecture (ISA) and the sizes of memory hierarchy are modeled as described in [10]. The TIC64 also supports a number of hardware accelerators (e.g. Viterbi decoder). These blocks can be correctly modeled by our flow by using intrinsics, but since are not needed for the WCDMA benchmark, they are not modeled in this case study.

ARM Cortex A8-like processor. The Cortex A8 processor [14] is an enhanced ARMv7 architecture with support for SIMD, and is used here as a typical example of a Data Level Parallel (DLP) architecture. The processor consists of separate scalar and vector datapaths. Each datapath has a register file and specialized FUs. The vector units in the vector datapath support up to 128-bit wide data in various subword modes. The FUs have a different number of execute stages, which result in different latencies. The details of the modeled architecture including its memory hierarchy can be found in [14].

Novel Design Space architectures. To illustrate the wide design space that is supported by our tools, we start with a standard processor and modify the most power consuming parts of it. Both architectures are shown in shown in Figure 6. *Architecture A* is a 4 issue homogeneous VLIW with a 4kB L1 data cache, 4kB L1 instruction memory and a centralized register file of 32 deep, 12 ports. *Architecture B* optimizes some important parts of the architecture: the cache is replaced with a data scratchpad memory and a DMA, the L1 instruction memory is enhanced with a distributed loop buffer

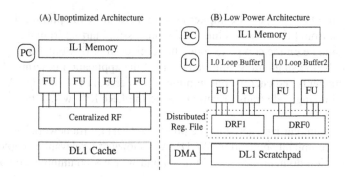

Fig. 6. Low Power Architecture Design Space

(16 instructions deep). The register file is clustered (16 deep, 6 ports each). Both these architectures have a standard 5 stage pipeline.

5.3 Loop Transformations

Figure 7 shows the transformations performed on the benchmark code. The first three, loop split-loop merge-loop merge, improve data locality in memory and IPC. For the Cortex A8 processor loop tiling is performed as an enabling transformation, vectorization is performed manually using intrinsics. The decision on which transformations to do is up to the designer, and defining an optimal set of transformations for a certain platform and application domain is outside the scope of this paper.

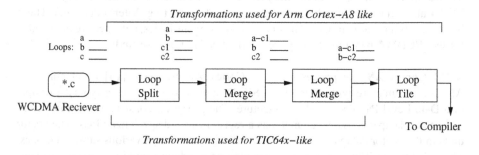

Fig. 7. Transformations Used in Uruk for Optimizations

5.4 Results and Analysis

Figure 8 shows the normalized performance in cycles for the TI C64-like processor and the ARM Cortex A8-like processor, both before and after the transformations. The numbers have been normalized to each processor's initial cycle count. For the ARM, *loop-tiling* was performed on the initial and transformed code to enable SIMD. Therefore the gains are the result of an improvement in locality in the data memory. For the TI, the performance gains are due to improved data locality and improved ILP. The *loop-merge*

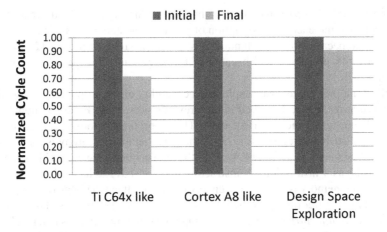

Fig. 8. Performance results for WCDMA running on the two processors

transformations in Figure 7 bring more instructions together inside the same loop and hence the compiler can schedule more instructions in parallel. Resulting performance gains are higher for the ILP-targeted TI C64x-like processor than for the ARM Cortex A8-like processor.

Figure 9 shows resulting gains in terms of energy consumption. The graphs have been normalized to each processor's initial energy consumption. In both cases the gains are about 15% on the complete processor (L1 Data memory, L1 Instruction memory, processor core included). Figure 9 shows the relative contribution of the different parts of the processor. As both processors (TI C64x and ARM Cortex A8) target high clock

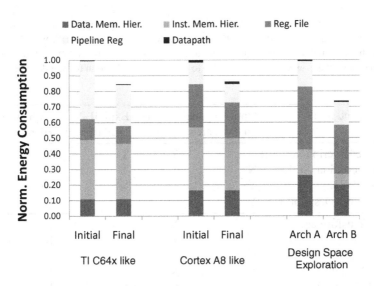

Fig. 9. Energy results for WCDMA running on the two processors

frequencies (600 MHz to 1GHz) the number of pipeline stages in the datapath is quite large and hence the energy consumption of pipeline registers is high. The register file costs are high because of the high number of ports (two register files of 12-ports each) for the TI C64x processor, and because of the large width for the ARM Cortex A8 (128-bits).

To illustrate the design space exploration capability of the proposed framework, we optimize *Architecture A*, described in the previous subsection. Figure 9 show that the register file consumes most of the energy. Therefore, the 12-ported register file is replaced by a distributed register file. Next, the data memory hierarchy is replaced by a cache with a scratchpad and a DMA, as all the data accessed have affine index expressions. Finally, as 4 instructions (1 instruction per slot) have to be fetched every cycle, the instruction memory is also a large energy consumer. It can be improved by adding a distributed loop buffer on top of the L1 instruction cache. The proposed modifications are shown in *Architecture B*. The processor pipeline is not modified, as it depends on the target frequency. Optimizing different parts of the processor can be done fast using the integrated framework presented in this paper. Performance and energy gains for *Architecture B* are shown in the right-most columns of Figure 8 and 9. Further optimizations can be performed on *Architecture B* in following design iterations.

5.5   Use Cases

Table 1 provides an overview of the complete range of which the proposed COFFEE flow can be used for. The table also shows which parts are completely automated. Individual columns show different use cases of the flow. Each entry in the table denotes if a modification is needed (marked as *Y*) or not (marked as *N*). The table shows various

Table 1. Use cases for the tools under different exploration and mapping cases: Y denotes a modification is needed and N denotes the process is fully automated. (1): Provided the added instruction fits within the wide set of power models available in the library. (2): In case a software controlled scratchpad is used, then it is needed to change the application to include explicit DMA transfers.

Component/Tool	Opti. mapping on fixed arch	Add new Instr.	Expl. ILP-DLP trade-off	Expl. Mem. Hierarchy
Machine Description (xml)	N	Y	Y	Y
ISA Description (xml+c)	N	Y	Y	N
Application (c)	Y	N	N	N(2)
Loop Transf Description	Y	N	N	N
Loop Transformer	N	N	N	N
Compiler	N	N	N	N
Simulator	N	N	N	N
Power Model	N	N(1)	N	N
Prof. Energy Est	N	N	N	N
Sim. Energy Est	N	N	N	N

different interesting explorations which the designer may want to perform during the early phase of the design process. It can be clearly seen that for various architecture-compiler co-exploration, the proposed tools are quite user friendly. Even for a large exploration task like finding an optimal architecture by balancing ILP-DLP for a given application, only the machine description and the ISA description needs to be modified and the rest of the flow is fully automatic.

6 Conclusion and Future Work

In this paper we presented a framework to perform energy-aware architecture exploration. The proposed framework provides all the necessary low power architecture features to optimize processors for handheld embedded systems. We illustrated this by modeling and compiling a representative wireless communication application (WCDMA) on two state of the art processors (including the instruction memory and data memory). We validated the accuracy of our energy estimation compared to detailed gate level simulations, using an in-house processor design. We have also shown that the proposed framework is capable of compiling, simulating, and estimating energy for a wide range of architectures and advanced low power architectural features. In the future we plan perform architecture exploration for Software Defined Radio using the COFFEE framework.

References

1. Trimaran: An Infrastructure for Research in Instruction-Level Parallelism (1999), http://www.trimaran.org
2. Austin, T., Larson, E., Ernst, D.: Simplescalar: an infrastructure for computer system modeling. IEE Computer Magazine 35(2), 59–67 (2002)
3. Ascia, G., Catania, V., Palesi, M., Patti, D.: Epic-explorer: A parameterized VLIW-based platform framework for design space exploration. In: Proc of ESTIMedia, pp. 3–4 (2003)
4. Brooks, D., Tiwari, V., Martonosi, M.: Wattch: A framework for architectural-level power analysis and optimizations. In: Proc of ISCA, pp. 83–94 (June 2000)
5. SUIF2 Compiler System (2001), http://suif.stanford.edu
6. Cohen, A., Sigler, M., Girbal, S., Temam, O., Parello, D., Vasilache, N.: Facilitating the search for compositions of program transformations. In: Proc of ICS, pp. 151–160 (2005)
7. Gordon-Ross, A., Cotterell, S., Vahid, F.: Exploiting fixed programs in embedded systems: A loop cache example. In: Proc of IEEE Computer Architecture Letters (January 2002)
8. Jayapala, M., Barat, F., Vander Aa, T., Catthoor, F., Corporaal, H., Deconinck, G.: Clustered loop buffer organization for low energy VLIW embedded processors. IEEE Transactions on Computers 54(6), 672–683 (2005)
9. Starcore DSP Techology, SC140 DSP Core Reference Manual (June 2000), http://www.starcore-dsp.com
10. Texas Instruments, Inc. TMS320C64x/C64x+ DSP CPU and Instruction Set Reference Guide (May 2006), http://focus.ti.com/docs/apps/catalog/resources/appnoteabstract.jhtml?abstractName=spru732b
11. Vander Aa, T., Jayapala, M., Barat, F., Deconinck, G., Lauwereins, R., Catthoor, F., Corporaal, H.: Instruction buffering exploration for low energy VLIWs with instruction clusters. In: Proc. of ASPDAC 2004, Yokohama, Japan (January 2004)

12. Raghavan, P., Lambrechts, A., Jayapala, M., Catthoor, F., Verkest, D.: Distributed loop controller architecture for multi-threading in uni-threaded VLIW processors. In: Proc of DATE (2006)
13. Schuster, T., Bougard, B., Raghavan, P., Priewasser, R., Novo, D., Vanderperre, L., Catthoor, F.: Design of a low power pre-synchronization asip for multimode sdr terminals. In: Proc. of SAMOS (2007)
14. Baron, M.: Cortex a8:high speed, low power. In Microprocessor Report (October 2005)
15. Rixner, S., Dally, W.J., Khailany, B., Mattson, P.R., Kapasi, U.J., Owens, J.D.: Register organization for media processing. In: HPCA, pp. 375–386 (January 2000)
16. Gangawar, A., Balakrishnan, M., Kumar, A.: Impact of intercluster communication mechanisms on ilp in clustered VLIW architectures. In: ACM TODAES, pp. 1–29 (2007)
17. Girbal, S., Vasilache, N., Bastoul, C., Cohen, A., Parello, D., Sigler, M., Temam, O.: Semi-automatic composition of loop transformations for deep parallelism and memory hierarchies. International Journal of Parallel Programming, 261–317 (October 2006)
18. Faraday Technology, Corporation Faraday UMC 90nm RVT Standard Cell Library (2007), http://www.faraday-tech.com
19. Synopsys, Inc. Design Compiler User Guide (2006)
20. Cadence, Inc. Cadence SoC Encounter User Guide (2006)
21. Synopsys, Inc. Prime Power User Guide (2006)
22. Holma, H., Toskala, A.: WCDMA for UMTS: Radio Access for Third Generation Mobile Communications. John Wiley, Chichester (2001)
23. Lin, Y., Lee, H., Woh, M., Harel, Y., Mahlke, S., Mudge, T., Chakrabarti, C., Flautner, K.: SODA: A low-power architecture for software radio. In: Proc of ISCA (2006)

Integrated CPU Cache Power Management in Multiple Clock Domain Processors

Nevine AbouGhazaleh, Bruce Childers, Daniel Mossé, and Rami Melhem

Department of Computer Science, University of Pittsburgh
{nevine,childers,mosse,melhem}@cs.pitt.edu

Abstract. Multiple clock domain (MCD) chip design addresses the problem of increasing clock skew in different chip units. Importantly, MCD design offers an opportunity for fine grain power/energy management of the components in each clock domain with dynamic voltage scaling (DVS). In this paper, we propose and evaluate a novel integrated DVS approach to synergistically manage the energy of chip components in different clock domains. We focus on embedded processors where core and L2 cache domains are the major energy consumers. We propose a policy that adapts clock speed and voltage in both domains based on each domain's workload and the workload experienced by the other domain. In our approach, the DVS policy detects and accounts for the effect of inter-domain interactions. Based on the interaction between the two domains, we select an appropriate clock speed and voltage that optimizes the energy of the entire chip. For the Mibench benchmarks, our policy achieves an average improvement over no-power-management of 15.5% in energy-delay product and 19% in energy savings. In comparison to a traditional DVS policy for MCD design that manages domains independently, our policy achieves an 3.5% average improvement in energy-delay and 4% less energy, with a negligible 1% decrease in performance. We also show that an integrated DVS policy for MCD design with two domains is more energy efficient for simple embedded processors than high-end ones.

1 Introduction

With the increase in number of transistors and reduced feature size, higher chip densities create a problem for clock synchronization among chip computational units. With a single master clock for the entire chip, it has become difficult to design a clock distribution network that limits clock skew among the chip components. Several solutions have been proposed to this problem using globally-asynchronous locally synchronous (GALS) design. In GALS design, a chip is divided into multiple clock domains (MCD), where individual chip units are associated with a particular domain. Each domain operates synchronously with its own clock and communicates with other domains asynchronously through queues.

In addition to addressing clock skew, MCD design offers important benefits to reducing power consumption with dynamic voltage scaling (DVS) at the domain level. Such fine-grain power management is important for embedded systems, which often have especially tight constraints on power/energy requirements. Indeed, National Semiconductor has recently developed a technology, called PowerWise, that uses multiple domains

P. Stenström et al. (Eds.): HiPEAC 2008, LNCS 4917, pp. 209–223, 2008.

to manage the power consumption of ARM-based system-on-a-chip designs [1]. Since each domain maintains its own clock and voltage independently of other domains, DVS can be applied at the domain level, rather than at the chip level. Power and energy consumption can be reduced by dynamically adjusting an individual domain's clock and voltage according to domain activity. Throughout this paper we use the term *speed* to collectively refer to voltage and frequency.

Several power management policies have been proposed to incorporate DVS into MCD chips. For example, Magklis et al.'s seminal online power management policy [2] monitors queue occupancy of a domain and computes the change in the average queue length in consecutive intervals. When queue length increases, the domain speed is increased; when queue length decreases, the speed is decreased. In general, policies in the literature [3][4][5][6] focus on each domain in *isolation* without considering possible inter-domain effects when varying speed.

In this paper, we propose an **integrated** power management policy for embedded processors with multiple clock domains. Unlike other techniques, our policy takes into account activity and workload in all domains to decide the best set of speed settings. Our policy stems from our observation that current online DVS policies for MCD chips have a localized view and control of the DVS in each domain and do not account for domain interactions. For the Mibench and the SPEC2000 benchmarks, our policy improves the energy-delay product by 15.5% and 18.5% on average (up to 26%) while energy savings are 19% and 23.5% on average (up to 32%). The performance penalty is less than 5% and 6.5%, respectively. Compared to a well-known online MCD DVS policy [3], we show an additional improvement in the energy-delay product of 3.5% and 7%, on average (up to 13%), with minimal performance degradation. Our policy requires no additional hardware beyond what is already available in MCD design.

The contribution of this paper is threefold. First, we identify a significant inefficiency in current online DVS policies, and show the sources and implications of this inefficiency. Second, we propose a new DVS policy that adapts the core and L2 cache speeds in a way that avoids these inefficiencies, taking into account domain interactions. Third, we show positive gains of our policy against a well-known online DVS policy [3].

The remaining portion of this paper is organized as follows. As background, we first describe application characteristics and MCD hardware design in Section 2. Section 3 compares independent and integrated DVS policies for MCD in terms of design and implementation. Section 4 presents our integrated DVS policy and identifies scenarios where it performs better than an independent DVS policy. Evaluation and sensitivity analysis of our policy against a well-known DVS policy is presented in Section 5. Other related work is presented in Section 6 and concluding remarks are in Section 7.

2 Application and MCD Chip Models

In this paper, because of the focus on embedded systems, we first consider a simple MCD processor with two domains (see Figure 1), namely the *core* and the *L2 cache*, and later expand it to include processors with more domains. We consider the core and the L2 cache domains due to their high influence on the overall performance and energy consumption. The core domain includes all computational units such as the register

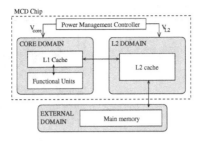

Fig. 1. MCD processor with two domains

file, functional units, issue unit, decode unit and L1 cache. In the core domain, each individual unit consumes a small fraction of the total power, but when grouped, that domain consumes a large fraction of the total chip power. On the other hand, caches consume a large fraction of the total chip power. For example, caches consume 50% power for ARM10TDMI running at 400MHz [7] . Moreover, it is predicted that the L2 cache will continue to be one of the major consumers of energy (due to increasing on-chip L2 cache sizes) [8].

A typical application goes through phases during its execution. An application has varying cache/memory access patterns and CPU stall patterns. In general, application phases correspond to loops, and a new phase is entered when control branches to a different code section. Since we are interested in the performance and energy of the CPU core and L2 cache, we characterize each code segment in a program using performance monitors that relate to the activity in each of these domains [3]. Figure 2 shows the variations in two performance counters (cycle-per-instruction and number of L2 accesses) as examples of monitors that can be used to represent a program behavior. We obtain these traces from running the shown benchmarks on Simplescalar with a StrongArm-like processor configuration (see Section 5). From these graphs, applications go through varying phases, which cause varying activity in different chip domains.

3   DVS in Multiple Clock Domains

As briefly mentioned above, there are two categories of DVS policies for MCD processors that can be implemented in hardware. We discuss them in the context of a two-domain MCD design shown in Figure 1.

The first is called *Independent DVS policy*. This policy periodically sets the speed of each domain independently based on the activity of the domain, which is measured through performance counters in that domain. For example, we may use the number of instructions-per-cycle (IPC) and the number of L2 cache accesses as an indication of the activity in the core and L2 cache domains. IPC encompasses the effects of several factors affecting performance that occur within the core such as number and type (INT/FP) of issued instructions, branch mispredictions, L1 and TLB accesses. Higher (lower) IPC indicates that more (less) instructions finished execution and the presence of fewer (more) stall cycles in the different core units. Similarly, in the L2 cache domain higher (lower) L2 requests indicate higher (lower) activity in the cache's different

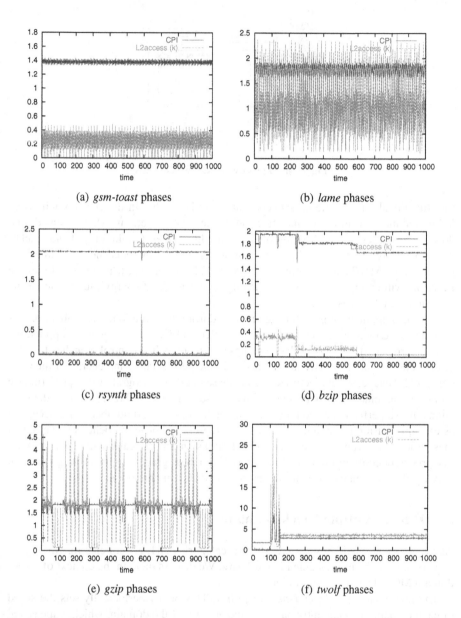

Fig. 2. Variations in Cycle-per-Instruction (CPI) and L2 accesses (L2access) of six Mibench and SPEC2000 benchmarks

sections. The policy periodically monitors the variations in IPC and L2 accesses across interval periods. The IPC and number of L2 accesses can be monitored through commonly available event counters in most modern architectures. Based on the trend in a counter, the policy decides to change the speed of the corresponding domain. This scheme is efficient because it can be done locally and with very little overhead.

The second is the *Integrated DVS policy*, which takes into account the effect of speed changes of one domain on the other domain. For example, reducing speed in a non-critical domain may result in an indirect slow-down in the performance-critical domain. This slowdown is not necessarily due to a change in application behavior, but rather a reaction to the other domain's slowdown. Detailed discussion of different domain interactions is described in Section 4.1. Domain interaction is the driving force behind our approach.

Our goal is to design an integrated core- L2 cache DVS policy that (1) selects appropriate speeds for each domain, adapting to application's run-time behavior (phases) and (2) minimizes the overall energy-delay product[1].

The general idea of our integrated MCD DVS approach is the use of a power management controller that collects information about the workload of *all* domains, and sets the speed of each appropriately. The power management controller uses the combined behavior in all domains in a given interval to decide the speed of each domain in the following interval. Details of our proposed policy are presented in Section 4.2.

4   Domain Interaction-Aware DVS

In this section, we discuss the inefficiency of independent online DVS policies (Section 4.1), and propose an interaction-aware DVS policy to overcome this inefficiency (Section 4.2).

4.1   MCD Inter-domain 3Interactions

Applying DVS independently in an MCD processor creates domain interactions that may negatively affect the performance and/or energy of other domains. We present an example to illustrate the cause of these effects and their undesired implications; the reader is encouraged to follow the numbered steps in Figure 3. (1) Assume an MCD processor is running an application that experiences some pipeline stalls (e.g., due to branch misprediction). The increased number of stalls results in reduced IPC. (2) The independent DVS policy triggers a lower speed setting in the core domain. Slowing down the core will reduce the rate of issuing instructions, including L2 accesses. (3) Fewer L2 accesses per interval causes the independent policy to lower the speed in the L2 cache domain. (4) This, in turn, increases the cache access latency, which (5) causes more stalls in the core-domain. Hence, this interaction starts a vicious cycle, which spirals downward.

The duration of this positive feedback[2] depends on the application behavior. For benchmarks with low activity/load variations per domain, this feedback scenario results in low speeds for both domains. While these low speeds reduce power, they clearly hurt performance and do not necessarily reduce total energy-delay product. Analogously, positive feedback may cause increased speeds in both domains, which potentially improves delay

---

[1] The metric to optimize can vary; we have experimented with the usual metrics, namely energy, delay, and the most used, the energy-delay product.

[2] A positive feedback control is where the response of a system is to change a variable in the same direction of its original change.

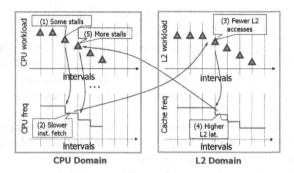

Fig. 3. Example of positive feedback in independent power management in each domain

at the expense of increasing energy consumption. These two scenarios illustrate that the independent policy may not properly react to a domain's true workload.

These undesired positive feedback scenarios arise from the fact that the independent policy monitors only the local performance of a given domain to set its speed. This local information does not identify whether the source of the load variability is local to a domain or induced by other domains. As a result, the policy cannot take the correct action. In our example, the variation in IPC can be induced by local effects such as executing a large number of floating point instructions or suffering many branch mispredictions. Alternatively, effects from other domains such as higher memory and L2 access latency can induce variations in IPC. Although the effect on IPC is similar, the DVS policy should behave differently in these two cases.

Table 1. Percentage of time intervals that experience positive feedback scenarios in some Mibench and SPEC2000 benchmarks

adpcm_dec	adpcm_enc	basicmath	crc32	gsm_toast	gsm_untoast	lame	rsynth
0.28%	1.73%	0.24 %	0.18%	27.7%	20.09%	22.56%	47.56%
bzip	equake	gcc	gzip	parser	twolf	vortex	vpr
26.22%	13.98%	23.35 %	21.07%	26.44%	23.69%	12.38%	23.73%

To find out how often applications experience such undesired positive feedback, we analyzed applications under Semeraro et al.'s independent DVS policy [3]. Table 1 illustrates the percentage of time intervals where positive feedback occurs in some Mibench and SPEC2000 benchmarks. The data is collected over a window of 500M instructions (after fast-forwarding simulations for 500M instructions). We divide the execution into 100K instruction intervals then count the percentage of consecutive intervals that experience positive feedback in both the CPU and L2 domains simultaneously. The table shows that some applications experience high rates of positive feedback, while others are largely unaffected. In the former (e.g., *gsm, lame, rsynth, bzip, parser,* and *vpr*), we expect that the independent policy will result in relatively high delays or high energy because it reacts with inappropriate speed setting for more than 20% of the time.

To have a better indication of the core and L2 cache workloads, the policy has to be aware of the status of both domains, because each domain may indirectly influence the workload in the other domain. This motivates the need for run-time policies that take into account the core and the L2 cache interactions to appropriately set the speeds for both domains in a way that minimizes total energy, delay or energy-delay product.

4.2   Integrated Core and L2 Cache DVS Policy

In our integrated policy, we monitor the IPC and the number of L2 accesses with performance counters. The speeds are driven by the change in the *combined* status of IPC and number of L2 accesses in a given execution interval. The rate of increase or decrease in speed is based on the rate of increase or decrease in the monitored counter subject to exceeding a threshold as proposed by Zhu et al. [9]. We introduce a new set of rules (listed in Table 2) to be executed by the DVS policy for controlling the speeds. The symbols ⇑, ⇓, and − depict an increase, decrease, and no-change in the corresponding metric. Columns 2 and 3 in the table show the change in the monitored counters while columns 4 and 5 (columns 6 and 7) show the action taken by independent (our) policy on the corresponding domain speeds.

Table 2. Rules for adjusting core and L2 cache speeds in independent and proposed policies

rule #	Event to monitor		Action by independent policy		Action by our integrated policy	
	IPC	L2access	V_c	$V_\$$	V_c	$V_\$$
1	⇑	⇑	⇑	⇑	⇓	⇑
2	⇑	⇓	⇑	⇓	⇑	⇓
3	⇑	−	⇑	−	⇑	−
4	⇓	⇑	⇓	⇑	⇓	⇑
5	⇓	⇓	⇓	⇓	−	⇓
6	⇓	−	⇓	−	⇓	−
7	−	⇑	−	⇑	−	⇑
8	−	⇓	−	⇓	−	⇓
9	−	−	−	−	−	−

Given the evidence from Table 1, we decided to focus on the positive feedback cases described in Section 4.1. These cases only cause a change in rules 1 and 5 in Table 2, and maintain the other rules exactly the same. It only changes the rules when there is a simultaneous increase or decrease in IPC and L2 cache accesses. As a result, our policy requires minimal changes to existing policies (i.e., it can be readily supported without any additional cost), yet it achieves better energy savings. Contrary to the independent policy, which seems intuitive, our integrated policy does **not** increase (or decrease) the speed if both the counters show an increase/decrease during a given interval. Instead, the policy changes speeds as shown in the table.

Next, we describe both cases and the reasons behind the counter-intuitive actions of our policy.

Simultaneous increase in IPC and L2 cache access (rule 1): Our approach reacts to the first positive feedback case by reducing the core speed rather than increasing it, as in the independent policy. This decision is based on the observation that the increase in IPC was accompanied by an increase in the number of L2 cache accesses. This increase may indicate a start of a program phase with high memory traffic. Hence, we preemptively reduce the core speed to avoid overloading the L2 cache domain with excess traffic. In contrast, increasing the core speed would exacerbate the load in both domains. We choose to decrease the core speed rather than keeping it unchanged to save core energy, especially with the likelihood of longer core stalls due to the expected higher L2 cache traffic.

Simultaneous decrease in IPC and L2 cache access (rule 5): We target the second un-desired positive feedback scenario where the independent policy decreases both core and cache speeds. From observing the cache workload, we deduce that the decrease in IPC is not due to higher L2 traffic. Thus, longer core stalls are a result of local core activity such as branch misprediction. Hence, increasing or decreasing the core speed may not eliminate the source of these stalls. By doing so, we risk unnecessarily increasing in the application's execution time or energy consumption. Hence, we choose to maintain the core speed without any change in this case, to break the positive feedback scenario without hurting delay or energy.

5   Evaluation

In this section, we evaluate the efficacy of our integrated DVS policy, which considers domain interactions, on reducing a chip's energy and energy-delay product. We use the Simplescalar and Wattch architectural simulators with an MCD extension by Zhu et al. [9] that models inter-domain synchronization events and speed scaling overheads. To model the MCD design in Figure 1, we altered the simulator kindly provided by Zhu et al. by merging different core domains into a single domain and separating the L2 cache into its own domain. In the independent DVS policy, we monitor the instruction fetch queue to control the core domain, and the number of L2 accesses to control the L2 cache domain.

Since our goal is to devise a DVS policy for an embedded processor with MCD extensions, we use *Configuration A* from Table 3 as a representative of a simple embedded processor (Simplescalar's StrongArm configuration [10]). We use Mibench benchmarks with the *long* input datasets. Since Mibench applications are relatively short, we fast-forward only 500 million instructions and simulate the following 500 million instructions or until benchmark completion.

To extend our evaluation and check whether our policy can be extended to different arenas (in particular, higher performance processors), we also use the SPEC2000 benchmarks and a high-end embedded processor [9] (see *Configuration B* in Table 3). We run the SPEC2000 benchmarks using the *reference* data set. We use the same execution window and fastforward amount (500M) for uniformity.

Our goal is twofold. First, to show the benefit of accounting for domain interactions, we compare our integrated DVS policy with the independent policy described in Section 3. For a fair comparison, we use the same policy parameters and thresholds used by

Table 3. Simulation configurations

Parameter	Config. A (simple embedded)	Config. B (high-end embedded)
Dec./Iss. Width	1/1	4/6
dL1 cache	16KB, 32-way	64KB, 2-way
iL1 cache	16KB, 32-way	64KB, 2-way
L2 Cache	256KB 4-way	1MB DM
L1 lat.	1 cycles	2 cycles
L2 lat.	8 cycles	12 cycles
Int ALUs	2+1 mult/div	4+1 mult/div
FP ALUs	1+1 mult/div	2+1 mult/div
INT Issue Queue	4 entries	20 entries
FP Issue Queue	4 entries	15 entries
LS Queue	8	64
Reorder Buffer	40	80

Zhu et al. [9]. The power management controller is triggered every 100K instructions. Moreover, our policy implementation uses the same hardware used in [9], in addition to trivial (low overhead) addition in the monitoring and control hardware of an MCD chip. Second, to quantify the net savings in energy and delay, we compare our policy to a *no-DVS* policy, which runs all domains at highest speed. We show all results normalized to the no-DVS policy.

We first evaluate the policies using an embedded processor (Configuration A in Table 3). Figure 4-a shows that for the Mibench applications, the improvement in the energy-delay product is 15.5% on average (up to 21% in *rsynth*) over no-DVS policy. For the SPEC2000 benchmarks, the improvement in the energy-delay product is 18% on average (up to 26% in *twolf*) over no-DVS policy. Most of the improvement is a result of energy savings (an average of 21% across applications) as seen in Figure 4-b, with much less performance degradation as seen in Figure 4-c (note different Y-axis scale).

The integrated, interaction-aware policy achieves an extra 7% improvement in energy-delay product above the independent policy gains. These savings are beyond what the independent policy can achieve over the no-DVS policy[3]. The improvement over the independent policy comes from avoiding the undesired positive feedback scenarios by using coordinated DVS control in the core and L2 cache domains. However, the energy-delay product improvement beyond the gain achieved by the independent policy is highly dependent on the frequency of occurrence of the positive feedback scenarios, the duration of the positive feedback and the change in speed during these

---

[3] Reported results of the independent policy are not identical to the one reported in [3] due to few reasons: (a) The latest distribution of the MCD simulation tool set has a different implementation of the speed change mechanism. (b) We simulate two-domain processor versus five-domain processor in the original independent policy. (c) We execute applications with different simulation window, as well.

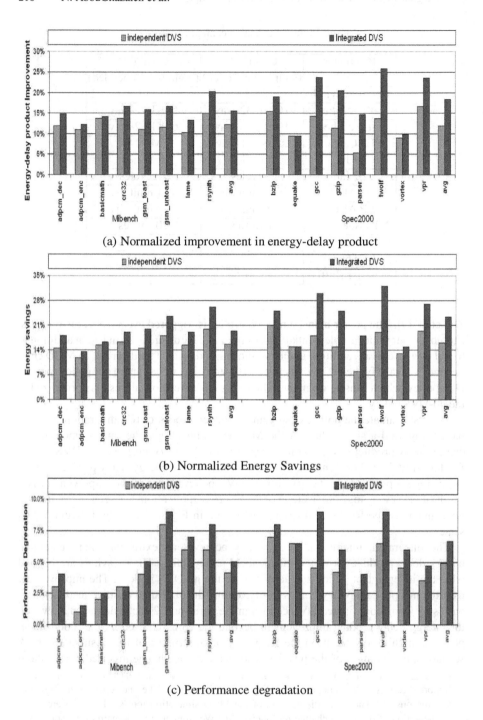

(a) Normalized improvement in energy-delay product

(b) Normalized Energy Savings

(c) Performance degradation

Fig. 4. Energy and delay of independent policy (Independent DVS) and our policy (Integrated DVS) relative to no-DVS policy in configuration A and two voltage domains processor

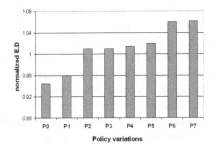

Fig. 5. Average degradation in energy-delay product relative to the independent policy

positive feedback cases throughout the application execution. From Table 1, we notice that the frequency of the positive feedback in *adpcm, basicmath,* and *crc32* is almost negligible; accordingly, there are significantly smaller benefits from our policy as shown in Figure 4. On the other hand, applications like *gsm, rsynth, gcc, parser,* and *twolf* show high energy savings due to repeated occurrence of positive feedback cases.

With respect to performance, we note that our proposed integrated policy has a slow-down of 5% on average for Mibench (7% on average for SPEC2000). This slowdown is only 1% more than the slowdown of the independent policy.

To test whether a different policy that avoids the undesired positive feedback scenarios using alternative actions (specifically, different actions for rules 1 and 5 in Table 2) would perform better, we experimented with different rules for these two cases. Table 4 shows the actions of our proposed policy and seven policy variants, in addition to our proposed integrated policy P0. Figure 5 shows the average degradation in energy-delay product relative to the independent policy. It is clear that other actions for dealing with positive feedback scenarios are not as effective in reducing the energy-delay product. The degradation in energy-delay product of the policy variants ranges from 2% to 12% over our proposed policy.

Table 4. Variants of our proposed policy: actions of setting the core voltage (V_c) and the cache speed ($V_\$$) in rules 1 & 5 from Table 2

rule	P0		P1		P2		P3		P4		P5		P6		P7	
#	V_c	$V_\$$	V_c	$V_\$$	V_c	$V_\$$	V_c	$V_\$$	V_c	$V_\$$	V_c	$V_\$$	V_c	$V_\$$	V_c	$V_\$$
1	⇓	⇑	⇓	—	⇓	—	⇓	—	—	⇑	—	—	—	⇑	—	⇑
5	—	⇓	—	⇓	—	—	⇑	—	—	⇓	⇑	—	⇑	—	—	—

Sensitivity Analysis

We study the benefit of using a domain interaction-aware DVS policy under different system configurations. We explore the state space by varying key processor configurations and the granularity of DVS control (that is, number of MCD domains). In addition to a simple embedded single-issue processor (configuration A in Table 3), we experiment with a more complex embedded processor (configuration B, the same processor configuration used in [9]). This test should identify the benefit of interaction-aware policy in a simple embedded processor versus a more powerful one. This more powerful processor, such as Intel's Xeon 5140 and Pentium M, are used in portable medical, military and aerospace applications [11]. Figure 6-a compares configuration A versus configuration B in terms of energy-delay product, energy saving, and performance degradation. The figure shows the average values over the Mibench and SPEC2000 benchmarks for 2 domains. One observation is that we achieve larger energy-delay improvement in embedded single-issue processor (Config A) than the more complex one (Config B). This larger improvement is mainly due to higher energy savings. In single-issue processors, cache misses cause more CPU stalls (due to lower ILP) than in higher-issue processors. This is a good opportunity for the DVS policy to save energy by slowing down domains with low workloads while having small impact on performance.

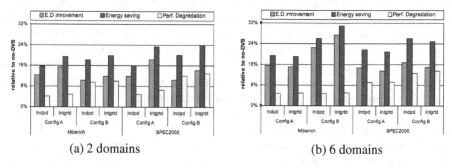

(a) 2 domains   (b) 6 domains

Fig. 6. Energy and delay for independent policy (Indpnd) and our integrated policy (Intgrtd) relative to no-DVS policy for processors with (a) two domains and (b) six domains

Comparing our results with the independent policy, we notice that the average benefit of considering domain interactions decreases with the increase in issue width. This is because processors with small issue width are more exposed to stalls from the memory hierarchy, which makes it important to consider the core and L2 cache domain interaction. In contrast, with wider issue width, these effects are masked by the core's higher ILP. This result shows that applying the integrated policy can benefit simple embedded processors. Whereas energy-delay savings in high-end embedded processor do not favor the use of the integrated policy over independent counterpart.

Because we are also interested in the effect of interactions across multiple domains on energy savings, we examined the effect of increasing the number of clock domains. To perform this test, we simulated the five domains used in [3], but added a separate domain for the L2 cache. The resultant domains are: reorder buffer domain, fetch unit, integer FUs, floating point FUs, load/store queue, and L2 cache domains. We use our policy to control the fetch unit and L2 domains, and set the speeds of the remaining domains using the independent policy [3] [9].

Figure 6-b shows the results for the two processor configurations when dividing the chip into 6-domains. Comparing Figures 6-a and 6-b, we find that DVS in processors with large number of domains enables finer-grain power management, leading to larger energy-delay improvements. However, for embedded systems, a two-domain processor is a more appropriate design choice when compared to a processor with a larger number of domains (due to its simplicity). Figure 6 shows that increasing the number of domains had little (positive or negative) impact on the difference in energy-delay product between our policy and the independent policy. This indicates that the core-L2 cache interaction is most critical in terms of its effect on energy and delay, which yielded higher savings in the two-domain case. We can conclude that a small number of domains is the most appropriate for embedded processors, not only from a design perspective but also for improving energy-delay.

6 Related Work

MCD design has the advantages of alleviating some clock synchronization bottlenecks and reducing the power consumed by the global clock network. Semeraro et al. explored the benefit of the voltage scaling in MCD versus globally synchronous designs [3]. They find a potential 20% average improvement in the energy-delay product. Similarly, Iyer at al. analyzed the power and performance benefit of MCD with DVS [4]. They find that DVS provides up to 20% power savings over an MCD core with single voltage.

In industrial semiconductor manufacturing, National Semiconductor in collaboration with ARM developed the PowerWise technology that uses Adaptive Voltage Scaling and threshold scaling to automatically control the voltage of multiple domains on chip [1]. The PowerWise technology can support up to 4 voltage domains [12]. Their current technology also provides power management interface for dual-core processors.

Another technique by Magklis et al. is a profile-based approach that identifies program regions that justify reconfiguration [5]. This approach involves extra overhead of profiling and analyzing phases for each application. Zhu et al presented architectural optimizations for improving power and reducing complexity [9]. However, these policies do not take into account the cascading effect of changing a domain voltage on the other domains.

Rusu et al. proposed a DVS policy that controls the domain's frequency using machine learning approach [13][14]. They characterize applications using performance counter values such as cycle-per-instruction and number of L2 accesses per instruction. In a training phase, the policy searches for the best frequency for each application phase. During runtime, based on the values of the monitors performance counters, the policy sets the frequency for all domains based on their offline analysis. The paper shows improvement in energy-delay product close to a near-optimal scheme. However, the technique requires an extra offline training step to find the best frequencies for each domain and application characterization.

Wu et al. present a formal solution by modeling each domain as a queuing system [6]. However, they study each domain in isolation and incorporating domain interactions increases the complexity of the queuing model. Varying the DVS power management interval is another way to save energy. Wu et al. adaptively vary the controlling interval to react to changes in workload in each domain was presented in [15]. They do not take into account the effect induced by voltage change in one domain on the other domains.

MCD design is applied for the multicore and simultaneous multithreading processors such as in [16][17][18]. In [16][17], each core has its own clock network, and the DVS policy independently controls each core's voltage. Lopez et al. studies the trade-off between adapting the L2 cache capacity and speed based on the number of active threads in the core domain [18].

7 Conclusion

In MCD processors, applying DVS in each domain can significantly reduce energy consumption. However, varying the voltage and clock independently in each domain indirectly affects the workload in other domains. This results in an inefficient DVS policy. In this paper, we identify these inefficiencies in online MCD-DVS policies, and propose a simple DVS policy that accounts for inter-domain interactions. Our policy separately assigns the voltage and clock of the core and L2 cache domains based on activity in **both** domains. We show that our policy achieves higher energy and energy-delay savings than an MCD DVS policy that is oblivious to domain interactions. Our policy achieves average savings in energy-delay product of 18.5% for the SPEC2000 and 15.5% for the Mibench suites. Moreover, our policy achieves higher savings in energy-delay product over past independent DVS approaches (7% for SPEC2000 and 3.5% for Mibench benchmarks) using the same hardware. We also show that processors with narrow issue widths have a larger improvement in the energy-delay product with our integrated DVS policy. Finally, our results show that a simple MCD design using two domains is more energy efficient for simple embedded processors than for high-end ones.

References

1. National Semiconductor, PowerWise Technology (2007),
   http://www.national.com/appinfo/power/powerwise.html
2. Magklis, G., Semeraro, G., Albonesi, D.H., Dropsho, S.G., Dwarkadas, S., Scott, M.L.: Dynamic Frequency and Voltage Scaling for a Multiple-Clock-Domain Microprocessor. IEEE Micro 23(6), 62–68 (2003)
3. Semeraro, G., Albonesi, D.H., Dropsho, S.G., Magklis, G., Dwarkadas, S., Scott, M.L.: Dynamic frequency and voltage control for a multiple clock domain microarchitecture. In: MICRO 1935. Proc Intl Symp on Microarchitecture, pp. 356–367 (2002)
4. Iyer, A., Marculescu, D.: Power and performance evaluation of globally asynchronous locally synchronous processors. In: ISCA 2002. Proc Intl Symp on Computer architecture, pp. 158–168 (2002)
5. Magklis, G., Scott, M.L., Semeraro, G., Albonesi, D.H., Dropsho, S.: Profile-based dynamic voltage and frequency scaling for a multiple clock domain microprocessor. In: ISCA 2003. Proc Intl Symp on Computer Architecture, pp. 14–27 (2003)
6. Wu, Q., Juang, P., Martonosi, M., Clark, D.W.: Formal online methods for voltage/frequency control in multiple clock domain microprocessors. In: ASPLOS-XI. Proc Intl Conf on Architectural support for programming languages and operating systems, pp. 248–259 (2004)
7. Ben Naser, M., Moritz, C.A.: A Step-by-Step Design and Analysis of Low Power Caches for Embedded Processors (2005), http://www.lems.brown.edu/iris/BARC2005/Webpage/BARCpresentations/ben-naser.pdf

8. Kaxiras, S., Hu, Z., Martonosi, M.: Cache decay: exploiting generational behavior to reduce cache leakage power. In: ISCA 2001. Proc Intl Symp on Computer Architecture, pp. 240–251 (2001)
9. Zhu, Y., Albonesi, D.H., Buyuktosunoglu, A.: A High Performance, Energy Efficient GALS Processor Microarchitecture with Reduced Implementation Complexity. In: ISPASS 2005. Proc Intl Symp on Performance Analysis of Systems and Software (2005)
10. SimpleScalar/ARM. SimpleScalar-Arm Version 4.0 Test Releases, http://www.simplescalar.com/v4test.html/
11. Intel Embedded products. High-Performance Energy-Efficient Processors for Embedded Market Segments (2006), http://www.intel.com/design/embedded/downloads/315336.pdf
12. Pennanen, J.: Optimizing the Power for Multiple Voltage Domains. Spring Processor Forum, Japan (2006)
13. Rusu, C., AbouGhazaleh, N., Ferreria, A., Xu, R., Childers, B., Melhem, R., Mossé, D.: Integrated CPU and L2 cache Frequency/Voltage Scaling using Supervised Learning. In: Workshop on Statistical and Machine learning approaches applied to ARchitectures and compilation (SMART) (2007)
14. AbouGhazaleh, N., Ferreria, A., Rusu, C., Xu, R., Childers, B., Melhem, R., Mossé, D.: Integrated CPU and L2 cache Voltage Scaling using Supervised Learning. In: LCTES 2007. Proc. of ACM SIGPLAN on Language, compiler, and tool for embedded systems (2007)
15. Wu, Q., Juang, P., Martonosi, M., Clark, D.W.: Voltage and Frequency Control With Adaptive Reaction Time in MCD Processors. In: HPCA 2005: Proc Intl Symp on High-Performance Computer Architecture, pp. 178–189 (2005)
16. Oliver, J., Rao, R., Sultana, P., Crandall, J., Czernikowski, E., Jones IV, L.W., Franklin, D., Akella, V., Chong, F.T.: Synchroscalar: A Multiple Clock Domain, Power-Aware, Tile-Based Embedded Processor. In: ISCA 2004. Proc Intl Symp on Computer Architecture (2004)
17. Juang, P., Wu, Q., Peh, L.S., Martonosi, M., Clark, D.W.: Coordinated, distributed, formal energy management of chip multiprocessors. In: ISLPED 2005: Proc Intl Symp on Low Power Electronics and Design, pp. 127–130 (2005)
18. Lopez, S., Dropsho, S., Albonesi, D., Garnica, O., Lanchares, J.: Dynamic Capacity-Speed Tradeoffs in SMT Processor Caches. In: High Performance Embedded Architecure and Compilation (HiPEAC) (2007)

Variation-Aware Software Techniques for Cache Leakage Reduction Using Value-Dependence of SRAM Leakage Due to Within-Die Process Variation

Maziar Goudarzi, Tohru Ishihara, and Hamid Noori

Kyushu Univesity, Fukuoka, Japan
{goudarzi,ishihara}@slrc.kyushu-u.ac.jp,
noori@c.csce.kyushu-u.ac.jp

Abstract. We observe that the same SRAM cell leaks differently, under within-die process variations, when storing 0 and 1; this difference can be up to 3 orders of magnitude (averaging 57%) at 60mv variation of threshold voltage (V_{th}). Thus, leakage can be reduced if most often the values with less leakage are stored in the cache SRAM cells. We show applicability of this proposal by presenting three binary-optimization and software-level techniques for reducing instruction cache leakage: we *(i)* reorder instructions within basic-blocks so as to match up the instructions with the less-leaky state of their corresponding cache cells, *(ii)* statically apply register-renaming with the same aim, and *(iii)* at boot time, initialize unused cache-lines to their corresponding less-leaky values. Experimental results show up to 54%, averaging 37%, leakage energy reduction at 60mv variation in V_{th}, and show that with technology scaling, this saving can reach up to 84% at 100mv V_{th} variation. Since our techniques are one-off and do not affect instruction cache hit ratio, this reduction is provided with only a negligible penalty, in rare cases, in the data cache.

Keywords: Leakage power, power reduction, cache memory, process variation.

1 Introduction

Cache memories, as the largest component of today's processor-based chips (e.g. 70% of StrongARM [1]) are among the main sources of power dissipation in such chips. In nanometer SRAM cells, most of the power is dissipated as leakage [2] due to lower threshold-voltage (V_{th}) of transistors and higher V_{th} variation caused by random dopant fluctuations (RDF) [3] when approaching atomic sizes. This inherent variation impacts stability, power and speed of the SRAM cells. Several techniques exist that reduce cache leakage power at various levels [4]-[11], but none of them takes advantage of a new opportunity offered by this increasing variation itself: *the subthreshold leakage current (I_{off}) of a SRAM cell depends on the value stored in it and this difference in leakage increases with technology scaling*. When transistor channel length approaches atomic sizes, process variation due to random placement of dopant atoms increases the variation in V_{th} of same-sized transistors even within the

P. Stenström et al. (Eds.): HiPEAC 2008, LNCS 4917, pp. 224–239, 2008.

same die [13]. This is an unavoidable physical effect which is even more pronounced in SRAM cells as area-constrained devices that are typically designed with minimum transistor sizes. Higher V_{th}-variation translates to much higher I_{off}-variation ($I_{off} \propto exp(-v_{th} / (s / \ln(10)))$) where s is the subthreshold swing [13]) even in the transistors of a single SRAM cell. Since some of these transistors leak when storing a 1 and others when storing a 0, cell leakage differs in the two states. Thus cache leakage can be reduced if the values stored in it can be better matched with the characteristics of their corresponding cache cells; i.e., if most of the time a 0 is stored in a cache cell that leaks less when storing a 0, and vice versa. To the best of our knowledge, no previous work has observed this saving opportunity. Monte Carlo simulations in Section 3 show that theoretically 70% leakage saving (comparing full match to the full mismatch) would be available in a technology node with 60mv standard deviation of within-die V_{th} variation.

In this paper, we *(i)* reschedule instructions inside each basic-block (BB) of a given application to let them better match their corresponding cache cells, *(ii)* at the same time, we use register-renaming to further improve the match between the instructions and their cache cells, and *(iii)* the least-leaky values are stored in the cache-lines that won't be used by the embedded application. In total, these techniques result in up to 54.18% leakage reduction (36.96% on average) on our set of benchmarks, with only a negligible penalty in the data-cache caused by the instruction-reordering since techniques *(i)* and *(ii)* are applied offline and *(iii)* is only applied once at the processor boot time. Furthermore, it is important to note that this technique reduces leakage in the active- as well as standby-mode of system operation (even when the memory cells are being accessed) and that it is orthogonal to current circuit/device-level techniques.

2 Related Works

Leakage in CMOS circuits can be reduced by power gating [4], source-biasing [2], reverse- and forward-body-biasing [5][6] and multiple or dynamic V_{th} control [7]. For cache memories, selective turn-off [8][9] and dual-supply drowsy caches [10] disable or put into low-power drowsy mode those parts of the cache that are not likely to be accessed again. All these techniques, however, need circuit/device-level modification of the SRAM design while our proposal is a software technique and uses the cache as is. Moreover, none of the above techniques specifically addresses the leakage variation issue (neither variation from cell to cell, nor the difference between storing 0 and 1) caused by within-die process variation. We do that and we work at system-level such that our technique is orthogonal to them. Furthermore, all previous works focus on leakage power reduction when the SRAM cell is not likely to be in use, but our above *(i)* and *(ii)* techniques save power even when the cell is actively in use.

The leakage-variation among various cache-ways in a set-associative cache is used in [11] to reduce cache leakage by disabling the most-leaky cache ways. Our techniques, in contrast, do not disable any part of the cache and use it at its full capacity, and hence, do not incur any performance penalty due to reduced cache size. Moreover, our techniques are applicable to direct-map caches as well.

In logic circuits, value-dependence of leakage power has been identified and used in [12] to set the input vector to its leakage-minimizing value when entering standby mode. We show this value-dependence exists, with increasing significance, in nano-scale SRAM cells and can benefit power saving even out of standby time.

Register-renaming is a well-known technique that is often used in high-performance computing to eliminate false dependence among instructions that otherwise could not have been executed in parallel. It is usually applied dynamically at runtime, but we apply it statically to avoid runtime overhead. To the best of our knowledge, register-renaming has not been used in the past for power reduction.

Cache-initialization, normally done at processor reset, is traditionally limited to resetting all *valid*-bites to indicate emptiness of the entire cache. We extend this initialization to store less-leaky values in all those cache-lines that won't be used by the embedded application. This is similar to cache-decay [9] in addressing leakage power dissipated by unused cache-lines, but our technique does not require circuit-level modification of the cache design that has prevented cache-decay from widespread adoption.

3 Motivation and Our Approach

Leakage is increasing in nanometer-scale technologies, especially in cache memories which comprise the largest part of processor-based embedded systems. Fig. 1 shows the breakdown of energy consumption of the 8KB instruction-cache of M32R embedded processor [13] running MPEG2 application. The figure clearly shows that although dynamic energy decreases with every technology node, the static (leakage) energy increases such that, unlike in micrometer technologies, total energy of the cache increases with the shrinking feature sizes. Thus it is increasingly more important to address leakage reduction in cache memories in nanometer technologies.

We focus on I_{off} as the primary contributor to leakage in nanometer caches [13]. Fig. 2 shows a 6-transistor SRAM cell storing a 1 logic value. Clearly, only M5, M2, and M1 transistors can leak in this state while the other three may leak only when the cell stores a 0 (note that bit-lines are precharged to supply voltage, V_{DD}). Process variation, especially

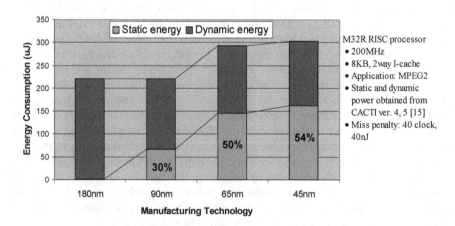

Fig. 1. Cache energy consumption in various technology nodes

in such minimum-geometry devices, causes each transistor to have a different V_{th} and consequently different I_{off} value, finally resulting in different subthreshold leakage currents when storing 1 and 0. Since the target V_{th} is in general reduced in finer technologies, in order to keep the circuit performance when scaling dimensions and V_{DD}, the I_{off} value is exponentially increased, and consequently, the above leakage difference is no longer negligible.

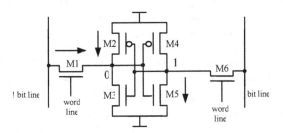

Fig. 2. A 6-transistor SRAM cell storing a logic 1. Arrows show leakage paths.

To quantify this effect, we used Monte Carlo simulation to model several similar caches and for each one computed maximum leakage difference once in each cell and once more in the entire cache. Notations and formulas are:

- **leak0 (leak1):** leakage power of the cell when storing 0 (1).
- **low** = min(leak0, leak1)
- **high** = max(leak0, leak1)

$$per-cell \quad saving = |leak0 - leak1| / high \tag{1}$$

$$Upper \quad bound \quad of \quad per-cache \quad saving = (\sum_{all \; cells} high - \sum_{all \; cells} low) / \sum_{all \; cells} high \tag{2}$$

Eq. 1 gives leakage difference between less-leaky and more-leaky states of a single cell, while Eq. 2 gives, in the entire cache, the difference between the worst case (all cells storing more-leaky values) and the best case (all cells storing less-leaky values).

Variation in transistors V_{th} results from die-to-die (inter-die) as well as within-die (intra-die) variation. We considered both in these experiments. Inter-die variation, which results in varying average V_{th} among different chips, is generally modeled by Gaussian distribution [16] while for intra-die variation, which results in different V_{th} values for different transistors even within the same chip and the same SRAM cell, independent Gaussian variables are used to define V_{th} of each transistor of the SRAM cell [17][18]. We used the same techniques to simulate manufacturing of 1000 16KB caches (direct-map, 512-set, 32-byte lines, 23 bits per tag) and obtained the maximum theoretical per-cell and per-chip savings given in Fig. 3 for $\sigma_{Vth\text{-}intra}$ (i.e. standard-deviation of intra-die V_{th} variations) varying from 10 to 100mv. We assumed each cache is within a separate die and used a single $\sigma_{Vth\text{-}inter}=20mv$ for all dies. The mean value of V_{th} was set to 320mv but our experiments with other values showed that the diagrams are independent of the V_{th} mean value; i.e., although the absolute value of the saving does certainly change with different V_{th} averages (and indeed increases with lower V_{th} in finer technologies), but the maximum *saving ratio* (Eq. 1 and 2) remains invariant for a given $\sigma_{\text{Vth-intra}}$, but the *absolute value* of the saved power increases with decreasing V_{th}. This makes sense since this saving opportunity is enabled by the V_{th} *variation*, not the V_{th} *average value*.

Since $\sigma_{\text{Vth-intra}} \propto 1/\sqrt{L \times W}$ [3], where L and W are effective channel length and width respectively, the V_{th} variation is only to increase with technology scaling, and as Fig. 3 shows, this increases the significance of value-to-cell matching. In 0.13μm process, empirical study [19] reports $\sigma_{\text{Vth-intra}}$=22.1mv for W/L=4 which by extrapolation gives $\sigma_{\text{vth-intra}}$>60mv in 90nm for minimum-geometry transistors; ITRS roadmap also shows similar prospects [20]. (We found no public empirical report on 90nm and 65nm processes, apparently due to sensitiveness and confidentiality.) Thus we present results at various $\sigma_{\text{vth-intra}}$ values, but consider 60mv as a typical case. Note that even if the extrapolation is not accurate for 90nm process, $\sigma_{\text{vth-intra}}$=60 finally happens at a finer technology node due to $\sigma_{\text{Vth-intra}} \propto 1/\sqrt{L \times W}$. Fig. 3 shows that maximum theoretical saving using this phenomenon at 60mv variation can be as high as 70%.

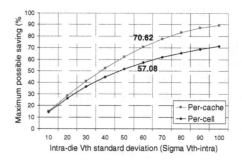

Fig. 3. Leakage saving opportunity increases with V_{th}-variation

3.1 Our Approach

We propose three techniques applicable to instruction-caches: rescheduling instructions within basic-blocks, static register-renaming, and initializing unused cache-lines. We first illustrate them by examples before formal formulation.

Illustrative Example 1: Intra-BB Instructions Rescheduling. Fig. 4 illustrates our approach applied to a small basic block (shown at left in Fig. 4) consisting of three 8-bit instructions against a 512-set direct-mapped cache with 8-bit line size. The arrow at the right of instruction-memory box represents dependence of instruction 2 to instruction 1. For simplicity, we assume *(i)* all the 3 instructions spend the same amount of time in the cache, and *(ii)* the leakage-saving (i.e., |leak0-leak1|) is the same for all bits of the 3 cache lines. An SRAM cell is called *1-friendly* (*0-friendly*) or equivalently *prefers 1* (*prefers 0*), if it leaks less power when storing a 1 (a 0). This *leakage-preference* of the cache lines are given in gray in the middle of Fig. 4; for example, the leftmost bit of cache line number 490 prefers 0 (is 0-friendly) while its rightmost bit prefers 1 (is 1-friendly). The *Matching table* in Fig. 4 shows the number of matched bits for each *(instruction, cache-line)* pair. Due to instruction dependencies, only three schedules are valid in this example: 1-2-3 (i.e., the original one), 1-3-2, and 3-1-2 with respectively

3+1+3, 3+3+7, and 1+7+7 number of matched bits (see the *Matching table* in Fig. 4). We propose to reschedule basic-blocks, subject to dependencies among the instructions, so as to match up the instructions with the leakage-preference of cache lines. Thus, the best schedule, shown at right in Fig. 4, is 3-1-2 which improves leakage of this basic-block by 47% (from 24-7 mismatches to 24-15 ones).

Obviously, the two simplifying assumptions in the above example do not hold in general. Potential leakage-saving differs from cell to cell, and also the amount of time spent in the cache differs from instruction to instruction even in the same BB. We consider and analyze these factors in our formulation and experiments.

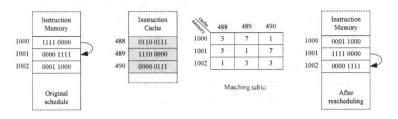

Fig. 4. An example illustrating instruction-rescheduling

Illustrative Example 2: Register-Renaming. Assume that the two right-most bits of each instruction in Fig. 5 represent a source register and the two left-most bits give the other source which is also the destination register. Fig. 5 depicts a simple example of register-renaming on the cache in the middle of the figure; for presentational purposes, we ignore instruction rescheduling here and merely apply register-renaming although our algorithm applies both at the same time. When applying merely register-renaming to these instructions, R0 can be renamed to R3 in the first two instructions (note that this implies similar renaming in all predecessor, and successor, instructions that in various control-flow scenarios produce, or consume, the value in R0; this is not shown in the figure). Similarly, original R3 in the same two instructions can be equally-well renamed to either R1 or R0; it is renamed to R1 in Fig. 5. For the third instruction, there is no better choice since source and destination registers are the same while their corresponding cache cells have opposite preferences (renaming to R1, which results in only the same leakage-preference-matching, is inappropriate since the instruction would then conflict with the now-renamed first instruction).

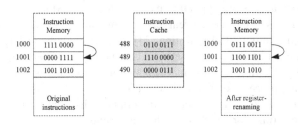

Fig. 5. An example illustrating register-renaming

Illustrative Example 3: Initializing Unused Cache-Lines. Depending on the cache size and the application, some parts of the instruction cache may never be used during application execution. Fig. 6 shows the histogram of *cache-fill* operations in the 8KB instruction cache of M32R processor [13] (a 32-bit RISC processor) when executing FFT application. 69 out of the 512 16-byte cache-lines are never used in this case. We propose to initialize such unused cache-lines with values that best match the leakage-preference of their SRAM cells. Many processors today are equipped with cache-management instructions (e.g. ARM10 family [21] and NEC V830R processor [22]) that can load arbitrary values to every cache location. Using these instructions, the unused cache-lines can be initialized at boot time to effectively reduce their leakage-power during the entire application execution. For instance, if in Fig. 5 cache-line number 490 were not to be used at all by the application, it would be initialized to 00000111 to fully match its leakage-preference. A minimum power-ON duration is required to break even the dynamic energy for cache initialization and the leakage energy saved. We consider this in our problem formulation and experiments.

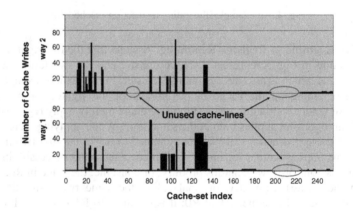

Fig. 6. Unused cache-lines for FFT application (8KB 2-way cache with 16-byte cache-lines)

Leakage-Preference Detection. This can be incorporated in the manufacturing test procedure that is applied to each chip after fabrication. Usually walking-1 and walking-0 test sequences are applied to memory devices [23] to test them for stuck-at and bridging faults. Leakage current can be measured at each step of this test procedure (similar to delta-IDDQ testing [24]) to determine the leakage-preference of cells. This can even be done in-house since commodity ammeters can easily measure down to 0.1fA [25] while the nominal leakage of a minimum geometry transistor is 345pA in 90nm process available to us. For some cells, this difference may be negligible, but one can detect more important cells that cause larger leakage differences. Test time for an 8KB cache, assuming 1MHz current measurements, would be 128ms (measuring *leak0* and *leak1* for each SRAM cell).

4 Problem Formulation

We formulate the problem using the following notation:

- N_s, N_w: The number of sets and ways of the cache.
- N_{BB}: The number of basic-blocks in the given application.
- $N_i(bb)$: The number of instructions in basic-block no. bb.
- $L(i, bb, w)$: Leakage power dissipated by the corresponding word of the cache line at way w of the cache when instruction number i of basic-block number bb is stored there. Note that the cache set corresponding to the instruction is fixed, but the cache way may differ over time.
- $T(i, bb, w)$ or *cache-residence time*: The amount of time that instruction number i of basic-block number bb remains in way w of the corresponding cache set.
- E_{BB}: Total leakage energy of instruction cache due to basic-block instructions:

$$E_{BB} = \sum_{bb=1}^{N_{BB}} \sum_{i=1}^{N_i(bb)} \sum_{w=1}^{N_w} L(i,bb,w) \times T(i,bb,w) \tag{3}$$

Each term in this summation gives the leakage energy dissipated by instruction i of basic-block bb at way w of cache.

- T_{viable}: The minimum amount of time that the embedded system should remain ON so that the cache-initialization technique would be *viable* (i.e., would save energy).

The problem is formally defined as *"For a given application and cache organization (i.e. for given N_s, N_w, N_{BB}, and $N_i(bb)$ vector), (i) minimize E_{BB}, and (ii) find T_{viable}."*

Algorithms. We use a list-scheduling algorithm for problem *(i)* above to achieve high efficiency; register-renaming is performed at each iteration of the algorithm:

```
Algorithm 1. ListScheduling(G)
Inputs:  (G: control-data-flow Graph of application)
Output:  (S: obtained Schedule for instructions of the application)
1   S = empty-list;
2   foreach basic-block do
3      BA = Base-Address of the basic-block;
4      L  = Length of the basic-block;
5      for addr=BA to BA + L do
6         lowestLeakage = +INFINITY;    bestChoice = 0
7         for each i in ready-list(G, BA) do
8            (ni, src, dst, flag) = applyRegRenaming(i, addr);
9            leak = get_instruction_leakage(ni, addr)
10           if leak < lowestLeakage then
11              lowestLeakage = leak;    bestChoice = ni;
12              bestRegs = (src, dst, flag);
13           endif
14        endfor
15        propagateRegRenamings( G, bestRegs );
16        S = S + {bestChoice};
17        Mark {bestChoice} as scheduled in G to update ready-list(G, BA);
18     endfor
19  endfor
20  return S
```

The algorithm sequentially processes each basic-block in the application binary and stores the new schedule with the new register-names in S as output. It needs the control-data-flow graph of the application for register-renaming so as to figure out live registers and the instructions that produce and consume them. For each basic-block, all *ready* instructions (i.e. those with all their predecessors already scheduled), represented by ready-list(G, BA) in line 7, are tried and the one with the least leakage is chosen (lines 9-13) and appended to the schedule (lines 16, 17); line 9 computes the leakage corresponding to the instruction by giving the innermost summation of Eq. 3. Register-renaming is also applied to each *ready*-instruction (line 8) and if chosen as the best, its corresponding new register-names are propagated to all predecessor and successor instructions (line 15); these procedures are given below:

Procedure: applyRegRenaming(i, addr)

Inputs: (i: the instruction binary to manipulate),
        (addr: the address of i in memory)
Outputs:(new_i: instruction after register-renaming),
        (src, dst: new source and destination regs),
        (flag: shows which regs were finally renamed)

```
1   src = first-source-register of i;
3   dst = destination-register of i;
3   flag = 0;
4   if src not affixed
5       src = get_best_src1_choice(i, addr); flag+=1;
6   if dst not affixed
7       dst = get_best_dest_choice(i, addr); flag+=2;
8   new_i = i with src, and dst;
9   return new_i, src, dst, flag;
```

This procedure checks the two source and destination registers (in M32R, the destination register and the second source register are the same) and if each of them is not *affixed*, tries to rename it to the best available choice. A source or destination register is *affixed* if due to an already-applied register-renaming it is previously determined and should be kept unchanged; the below procedure pseudo-code shows this. In some cases, it may be beneficial to reconsider renaming since the leakage reduction by the new register-renaming may outweigh the loss in previously renamed instructions; we did not consider this for simplicity and efficiency.

Procedure: propagateRegRenamings(G, i, src, dst, flag)

Inputs: (G: control data flow Graph of application),
        (i: instruction before register-renaming),
        (src, dst: new source and destination regs)
        (flag: shows which regs are renamed)

```
1 org_src = first-source-register of i;
2 org_dst = destination-register of i;
3 if (flag & 1)
4    rename org_src to src, and mark it affixed, in all predecessors and
     successors of i in G
5 if (flag & 2)
6    rename org_dst to dst, and mark it affixed, in all predecessors and
     successors of i in G
```

The algorithm has a time complexity of $O(m.n^2)$ and memory usage of $O(m.n)$ where m and n respectively represents the number of basic-blocks in the application and the number of instructions in the basic-block. Note that the algorithm correctly handles set-associative caches since the innermost summation in Eq. 3 considers individual leakages of each cache-way. The algorithm does not necessarily give the absolute best schedule neither the best register-names, but comparing its experimental results to that of exhaustive search in the feasible cases, which is still prohibitively time-consuming, shows the results are no more than 12% less optimal than the absolute best schedule.

5 Experimental Results

We used benchmarks from MiBench, MediaBench, and also Linux compress (Table 1) in our experiments. Monte Carlo simulation was used to model within-die process variation; independent Gaussian random values for V_{th} of each transistor of the cache were generated with 320mv as the mean and 60mv as the standard deviation.

Table 1. Benchmarks specifications

Benchmark	No of basic-blocks	Basic-block size (#instr.) Average	Largest
MPEG2 encoder ver. 1.2	16000	5.36	596
FFT	12858	4.83	75
JPEG encoder ver. 6b	11720	5.68	248
Compress ver. 4.1	9586	5.11	718
FIR	450	7.59	57
DCT	508	4.96	64

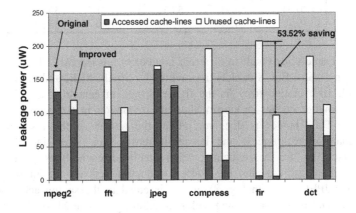

Fig. 7. Average leakage power on 1000 8KB direct-map caches

To consider the randomness of process variations, we simulated 1000 chips and ran our algorithm on all of them. Die-to-die variations do not change the saving percentage (see Section 3) and were not modeled in these experiments. Benchmarks were compiled with no compiler optimization option and were simulated using M32R instruction-set simulator to obtain cache-residence and cache-line usage statistics for 1 million instructions (FIR ran up to completion).

Fig. 7 shows the average leakage powers (corresponding to an industrial 90nm process) before and after applying our leakage-saving techniques, obtained over 1000 8KB direct-mapped caches with 16-byte cache-line size. Each bar is composed of two parts: the leakage power dissipated by the cache-lines that were used during application execution, and those that were never used. Our rescheduling algorithm reduces the former, while the cache-initialization technique suppresses the latter.

Table 2 gives the individual average and maximum savings obtained by each technique over the above 1000 chips; note that the values in *rescheduling* and *initializing* columns respectively correspond to the leakage savings *only in used* and *only in unused* cache-lines. The rescheduling and register-renaming technique saves up to 31.31% of power for FIR while savings by the cache-initialization technique reaches 58.36% for JPEG benchmark. Average saving obtained by cache-initialization is 54.51% for all benchmarks since we assumed that before initialization, SRAM cells in the unused cache-lines randomly contain 0 or 1 values.

Table 2. Average and maximum leakage savings by our techniques

Benchmark	Average saving (%)			Maximum saving (%)		
	rescheduling	initializing	Together	rescheduling	initializing	Together
MPEG2	20.10	54.51	26.78	21.67	56.16	28.25
FFT	20.50	54.51	36.28	22.43	55.7	37.36
JPEG	16.70	54.51	17.96	17.91	58.36	19.26
Compress	19.74	54.51	48.15	23.95	55.32	48.92
FIR	20.04	54.51	53.52	31.31	55.19	54.18
DCT	19.31	54.51	39.09	21.49	55.61	40.13

Different cache-sizes result in different number of unused cache-lines, and hence, affect saving results. Fig. 8 depicts the savings for 16KB, 8KB, and 4KB direct-map caches with 16-byte line-size. As the figure shows, in general, the leakage saving reduces in smaller caches proportional to the reduction in the number of unused cache-lines. This, however, does not affect the results of the rescheduling and register-renaming techniques, and hence, increases their share in total leakage-reduction (see Fig. 8). Consequently, when finally all cache-lines are used by the application in a small cache, the leakage reduction reaches its minimum (as in MPEG2 and JPEG cases in Fig. 8), which is equal to the saving achieved by the rescheduling and register-renaming technique alone (compare MPEG2 and JPEG in Fig. 8 to their corresponding rows in Table 2 under *rescheduling* column).

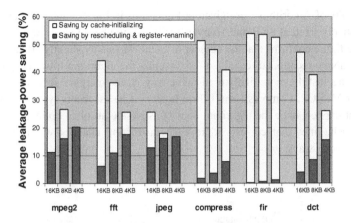

Fig. 8. Effect of cache-size on average leakage-saving results

Set-associative caches take better advantage of the available cache-lines and reduce the number of unused ones. Fig. 9 shows the leakage savings in an 8KB cache when the number of ways changes from 1 (direct-map) to 8. The leakage-saving by cache-initialization reduces in caches with higher associativity, and finally total saving reduces to that obtained by the rescheduling and register-renaming technique as is again the case for MPEG2 and JPEG in Fig. 9.

Furthermore, in set-associative caches, the location of each instruction in the cache cannot be precisely determined since there are multiple cache-lines in the cache-set that corresponds to the address of the instruction. This uncertainty is expected to decrease the saving results of the rescheduling algorithm, however, our cache simulator gives separate per-way residence-times for each instruction so as to direct the matching process toward the cache-ways with higher probability of hosting the instruction.

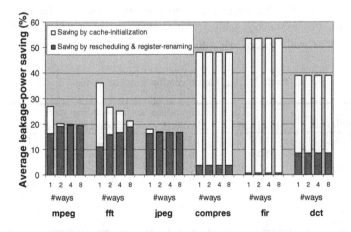

Fig. 9. Effect of set-associative caches on total leakage saving

Saving results of Algorithm 1 are given in Fig. 10; as in Fig. 9, cache size and line-size are respectively fixed at 8KB and 16-bytes while the number of cache-ways varies from 1 to 8. The figure confirms that the number of cache-ways only slightly affects the results due to the above-mentioned technique for directing the algorithm towards matching the instruction against the more likely used cache-way. Some marginal increases are seen in Fig. 10 for MPEG2, Compress, and FIR at higher cache associativity; these are random effects that happen since the algorithm does not give the absolute optimal schedule and also the cache-lines that correspond to each instruction changes when changing the number of cache-ways.

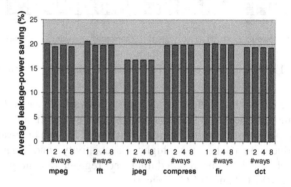

Fig. 10. Effect of set-associative caches on rescheduling algorithm

Execution-times of the rescheduling algorithm for the above caches are given in Table 3; values are measured on a Xeon 3.8GHz processor with 3.5GB memory. The execution time increases with the number of cache-ways, since more calculations are necessary, but it remains reasonably low to be practical.

Fig. 3 suggests that the achievable energy saving rises with the increase in V_{th} variation caused by technology scaling. We repeated the experiments for 8KB, 512-set direct-map cache with $\sigma_{Vth\text{-}intra}$ varying from 20 to 100mv (with mean-Vth=320mv

Table 3. Algorithm execution-time (in seconds)

Benchmark	Cache configuration (sets×ways×line_size)			
	512×1×16	256×2×16	128×4×16	64×8×16
MPEG2	0.15	0.33	0.55	1.04
FFT	0.08	0.19	0.31	0.60
JPEG	0.18	0.40	0.70	1.35
Compress	0.05	0.10	0.15	0.26
FIR	0.01	0.01	0.02	0.04
DCT	0.03	0.06	0.12	0.23
Average	0.08	0.18	0.31	0.59

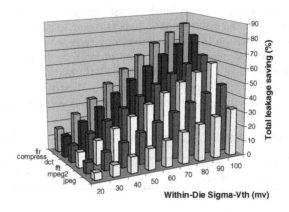

Fig. 11. Saving improvement with technology scaling

in all cases). Fig. 11 shows the trend in saving results which confirm the increasing significance of the approach in future technologies where random within-die V_{th} variation is expected to increase [20] due to random dopant fluctuation which is rising when further approaching atomic sizes in nanometer processes.

Costs of Intra-BB Rescheduling and Register-Renaming. Register-renaming imposes absolutely no penalty. Instruction-rescheduling has no impact on instruction-cache but may in rare cases marginally affect data-cache: since the order and address of basic-blocks do not change, instruction cache performance is kept intact. In data cache, however, reordering of instructions may change the sequence of accesses to data elements, and hence, may change cache behavior. If a miss-causing instruction is moved, the hit-ratio is kept, but residence-times (and hence leakage power) of the evicted and fetched data items change negligibly. In addition, if two instructions that access cache-conflicting data elements change their relative order, the cache hit-ratio changes if the originally-first one was to be a hit. This case may also change the data that finally remains in the cache after basic-block execution, and hence, potentially affects leakage power of the data cache. It is, however, very unlikely to happen when noting that due to locality of reference, two conflicting data accesses are unlikely to follow closely in time (and in a single BB). In our experiments data cache power and performance varied no more than 1%.

Cost of Cache Initialization. As explained in Section 3, the cache-initialization technique consumes some dynamic power to execute the cache-management instructions before it can save leakage power. Our implementation of M32R processor with two separate 8KB instruction and data caches on a 0.18μ process technology consumes 200mW at 50MHz clock frequency. This gives, on average, 4nJ per clock cycle or pessimistically 20nJ per instruction in the 5-stage pipelined M32R processor. Assuming all 512 cache-lines of the instruction cache are to be initialized, 10.24μJ is consumed for cache-initialization. T_{viable} can now be calculated using the power-saving values obtained by cache-initialization (Fig. 7). Results are given in Table 4 which confirm that most often a small fraction of a second is enough to make the initialization technique viable. Even for the worst benchmark, JPEG, a few seconds is enough. Assumptions in the estimations were pessimistic to not overestimate benefits: *(i)* processor implementation in a finer technology (e.g. 90nm) would consume less dynamic power, *(ii)* more than one instruction is often in the processor pipeline so average power per instruction would be less than 20nJ, *(iii)* not all cache-lines need to be initialized (e.g. for JPEG, only 14 cache-lines remain unused and should be initialized). Thus, values in Table 4 should be considered as upper bounds for T_{viable}.

Table 4. Estimated T_{viable} upper bounds for different applications

	MPEG2	FFT	JPEG	Compress	FIR	DCT
T_{viable} (s)	0.590	0.238	3.281	0.117	0.093	0.182

6 Conclusion

Our contributions here are *(i)* observing and analyzing a new opportunity for reducing cache leakage in nanometer technologies enabled by the reducing V_{th} and the increasing V_{th}-variation in such processes, and *(ii)* presenting first techniques that take advantage of this opportunity and reduce leakage up to 54.18% (36.96% on average) with negligible impact on system performance. It is important to note that our techniques *(i)* become more effective with technology scaling, *(ii)* reduce leakage also in the normal mode of system operation (in addition to standby mode) even when the cache-lines are actively in use, and *(iii)* are orthogonal to other techniques for leakage reduction such as body- and source-biasing. As future work, we are investigating techniques similar to garbage-collection so as to invalidate the cache-lines that won't soon have a hit and to store the less-leaky values in them.

Acknowledgments. This work is supported by VDEC, The University of Tokyo with collaboration of STARC, Panasonic, NEC Electronics, Renesas Technology, and Toshiba. This work is also supported by CREST project of Japan Science and Technology Corporation (JST). We are grateful for their support.

References

1. Moshnyaga, V.G., Inoue, K.: Low-Power Cache Design. In: Piguet, C. (ed.) Low-Power Electronics Design, CRC Press, Boca Raton (2005)
2. Roy, K., et al.: Leakage Current Mechanisms and Leakage Reduction Techniques in Deep-Submicron CMOS Circuits. In: Proc. IEEE (2003)
3. Taur, Y., Ning, T.H.: Fundamentals of Modern VLSI Devices. Cambridge University Press, Cambridge (1998)
4. Kao, J.T., Chandrakasan, A.P.: Dual-Threshold Voltage Techniques for Low-Power Digital Circuits. IEEE J. of Solid State Circuits 35, 1009–1018 (2000)
5. Fallah, F., Pedram, M.: Circuit and System Level Power Management. In: Pedram, M., Rabaey, J. (eds.) Power Aware Design Methodologies, pp. 373–412. Kluwer, Dordrecht (2002)

6. De, V., Borkar, S.: Low Power and High Performance Design Challenge in Future Technologies. In: Great Lake Symposium on VLSI (2000)

7. Kuroda, T., Fujita, T., Hatori, F., Sakurai, T.: Variable Threshold-Voltage CMOS Technology. IEICE Trans. on Fund. of Elec., Comm. and Comp. Sci. E83-C (2000)

8. Powell, M.D., et al.: Gated-Vdd: a Circuit Technique to Reduce Leakage in Cache Memories. In: Int'l Symp. Low Power Electronics and Design (2000)

9. Kaxiras, S., Hu, Z., Martonosi, M.: Cache Decay: Exploiting Generational Behavior to Reduce Cache Leakage Power. In: Int'l Symp. on Computer Architecture, pp. 240–251 (2001)

10. Flautner, K., et al.: Drowsy Caches: Simple Techniques for Reducing Leakage Power. In: Int'l Symp. on Computer Architecture (2002)

11. Meng, K., Joseph, R.: Process Variation Aware Cache Leakage Management. In: Int'l Symp. on Low Power Electronics and Design (2006)

12. Abdollahi, A., Fallah, F., Pedram, M.: Leakage Current Reduction in CMOS VLSI Circuits by Input Vector Control. IEEE Trans. VLSI 12(2), 140–154 (2004)

13. Clark, L., De, V.: Techniques for Power and Process Variation Minimization. In: Piguet, C. (ed.) Low-Power Electronics Design, CRC Press, Boca Raton (2005)

14. M32R Family 32-bit RISC Microcomputers, http://www.renesas.com

15. CACTI Integrated Cache Access Time, Cycle Time, Area, Leakage, and Dynamic Power Model, HP Labs, http://www.hpl.hp.com/personal/Norman_Jouppi/cacti4.html

16. Agarwal, A., Paul, B.C., Mahmoodi, H., Datta, A., Roy, K.: A Process-Tolerant Cache Architecture for Improved Yield in Nanoscale Technologies. IEEE Trans. VLSI 13(1) (2005)

17. Luo, J., Sinha, S., Su, Q., Kawa, J., Chiang, C.: An IC Manufacturing Yield Model Considering Intra-Die Variations. In: Design Automation Conference, pp. 749–754 (2006)

18. Agarwal, K., Nassif, S.: Statistical Analysis of SRAM Cell Stability. In: Design Automation Conference (2006)

19. Toyoda, E.: DFM: Device & Circuit Design Challenges. In: Int'l Forum on Semiconductor Technology (2004)

20. International Technology Roadmap for Semiconductors—Design, Update (2006), http:// www.itrs.net/Links/2006Update/2006UpdateFinal.htm

21. Hill, S.: The ARM 10 Family of Embedded Advanced Microprocessor Cores. In: HOT-Chips (2001)

22. Suzuki, K., Arai, T., Kouhei, N., Kuroda, I.: V830R/AV: Embedded Multimedia Superscalar RISC Processor. IEEE Micro 18(2), 36–47 (1998)

23. Hamdioui, S.: Testing Static Random Access Memories: Defects, Fault Models and Test Patterns. Kluwer, Dordrecht (2004)

24. Thibeault, C.: On the Comparison of Delta IDDQ and IDDQ Testing. In: VLSI Test Symp., pp. 143–150 (1999)

25. DSM-8104 Ammeter, http://www.nihonkaikeisoku.co.jp/densi/toadkk_zetuenteikou_dsm8104.htm

Part V

High-Performance Processors

The Significance of Affectors and Affectees Correlations for Branch Prediction

Yiannakis Sazeides[1], Andreas Moustakas[2,*], Kypros Constantinides[2,*],
and Marios Kleanthous[1]

[1] University of Cyprus, Nicosia, Cyprus
[2] University of Michigan, Ann Arbor, USA

Abstract. This work investigates the potential of *direction*-correlations to improve branch prediction. There are two types of *direction*-correlation: *affectors* and *affectees*. This work considers for the first time their implications at a basic level. These correlations are determined based on dataflow graph information and are used to select the subset of global branch history bits used for prediction. If this subset is small then *affectors* and *affectees* can be useful to cut down learning time, and reduce aliasing in prediction tables. This paper extends previous work explaining why and how correlation-based predictors work by analyzing the properties of *direction*-correlations. It also shows that branch history selected using oracle knowledge of *direction*-correlations improves the accuracy of the limit and realistic conditional branch predictors, that won at the recent branch prediction contest, by up to 30% and 17% respectively. The findings in this paper call for the investigation of predictors that can learn efficiently correlations from long branch history that may be non-consecutive with holes between them.

1 Introduction

The ever growing demand for higher performance and technological constraints drive for many years the computer industry toward processors with higher clock rates and more recently to multiple cores per chip. Both of these approaches can improve performance but at the same time can increase the cycle latency to resolve an instruction, the former due to deeper pipelines and the latter due to inter-core contention for shared on-chip resources. Longer resolution latency renders highly accurate conditional branch prediction a necessity because branch instructions are very frequent in programs and need to be resolved as soon as they are fetched in a processor to ensure continuous instruction supply.

Today, after many years of branch prediction research and the two recent branch prediction championship contests [1,2], the accuracies of the state of the art predictors are high but far from perfect. For many benchmarks the GTL predictor[1] [3] has more than five misses per thousand instructions. Such a rate

---

* The author contributed to this work while at the University of Cyprus.
[1] The winner predictor of the limit track of the 2006 branch prediction contest.

P. Stenström et al. (Eds.): HiPEAC 2008, LNCS 4917, pp. 243–257, 2008.

of misprediction, depending on the average branch resolution latency and other execution overheads, can correspond to a substantial part of the total execution time of a program. Consequently, we believe there is still a need to further improve prediction accuracy. The challenge is to determine how to achieve such an improvement.

In the seminal work by Evers et al. [4] it is shown that choosing more selectively the correlation information can be conducive for improving branch prediction. In particular, using an exhaustive search is determined for a gshare [5] predictor that only a few, not necessarily consecutive, of the most recent branches are sufficient to achieve best prediction accuracy. Furthermore, is demonstrated that a correlation may exist between branches that are far apart. The same work, introduces two reasons for why global history correlation exists between branches: *direction* and *in-path* correlation, and divides *direction*-correlations into *affectors* and *affectees*.[2] These various types of correlations can mainly be derived by considering the data and control flow properties of branches. These causes of correlation are only discussed qualitatively in [4] to explain what makes two-level branch predictors work, no measurements of their frequency or quantification of their importance are given.

The work by [4] motivated subsequent prediction research with goal the selective correlation from longer global history. One of the most notable is perceptron based prediction [7] that identifies, through training, the important history bits that a branch correlates on. The success of perceptron based prediction provides a partial justification for the claims by [4] for the importance of selective correlation. However, it was never established that the dominant perceptron correlations correspond to *direction* or *in-path* correlation and therefore remains uncertain if indeed such correlations are important or whether predictors exploit them efficiently.

One other interesting work by [6] investigated the usefulness of *affectors* branches, one of the types of *direction*-correlation introduced by [4] . In [6] the affector branches are selected dynamically from the global history using data dependence information and are used to train an overriding tagged predictor when a baseline predictor performs poorly. The experimental analysis, for specific microarchitectural configurations and baseline predictors, show that this idea can potentially improve both prediction accuracy and performance. This work also provides the first concrete evidence that the *direction*-correlation is an important information for prediction. However, [6] did not examine the importance of *affectees*.

In this paper we investigate the significance for improving branch prediction accuracy using the two types of *direction*-correlation: affectors and affectees. Our analysis is done at a basic level because we assume oracle knowledge of affectors and affectees with different degrees of precision for detecting the correlations and without regard to implementation issues. The primary objectives of this paper is to establish the extent that state of the art predictors learn *direction*-correlations,

---

[2] In [6] the two types of *direction*-correlation are referred to as affectors and forerunners.

and determine how precise the selection of *direction*-correlations needs to be for best accuracy. Our evaluation uses the two winning predictors of the limit and realistic track of the recent championship prediction [2] and considers their accuracy when they use the global history as is versus the global history packed [6] to "ignore" the positions with no *direction*-correlation.

Contributions

The key contributions and findings of this paper are:

- A framework that explains why some branches are more important than others to correlate on. The framework can be used to precisely determine these branches based on architectural properties.
- An experimental analysis of the potential of *direction*-correlations for branch prediction based on oracle knowledge of the correlations.
- An investigation of the position and the number of *direction*-correlations reveals that their behavior varies across programs. Also, is very typical for programs to have branches with the number of correlations ranging from few branches to several hundreds. The correlations can be clustered together but also be very far apart, i.e. correlations may not be consecutive and can have holes between them. Affectees are found to be more frequent than affectors.
- Demonstrate that for best accuracy both affectors and affectees correlations are needed. Their use can provide accuracy improvements of up to 30% for the limit predictor, and 17% for the realistic predictor
- Show that it is crucial to consider *direction*-correlations that are detectable by tracking dependences through memory.
- Establish a need to further study predictors that can learn correlation patterns with and without holes from long branch history.

The remaining of the paper is organized as follows. Section 2 defines what affectors and affectees correlations are and discusses parameters that influence the classification of a branch as correlating. Section 3 presents the experimental framework. Section 4 discusses the experimental results of this study and establishes the significance of affectors and affectees. Section 5 discusses related work. Finally, Section 6 concludes the paper and provides directions for future work.

2   Affectors and Affectees

This section defines what affector and affectee branches are and provides intuition as to why these are important branches to select for correlation. It also discusses how the treatment of memory instructions influence the classification of a branch as an affector or affectee of another branch. Finally, a discussion is presented on how this correlation information can be used for prediction. Part of this discussion is based on earlier work [4,6].

2.1   Definitions and Intuition

Affectors: A dynamic branch, A, is an affector for a subsequent dynamic branch, B, if the outcome of A affects information (data) used by the subsequent branch B.

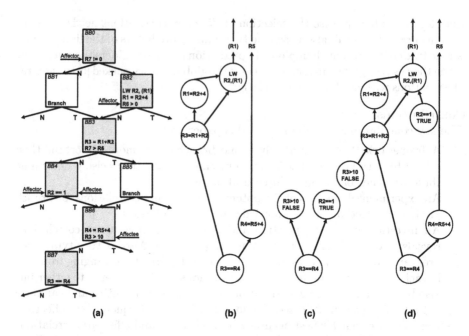

Fig. 1. (a) Example control flow graph, (b) affector graph, (c) affectee graph and (d) affector plus affectee graph

Affectors are illustrated using the example control flow graph in Fig. 1.a. Assume that the (predicted) program order follows the shaded basic blocks and we need to predict the branch in the basic block 7. The affector branches are all those branches that steer the control flow to the basic blocks that contain instructions that the branch, in basic block 7, has direct or indirect data dependence. Effectively, the selected affector branches can be thought of as an encoding of the data flow graph leading to the branch to be predicted (this affector data flow graph is shown in Fig. 1.b). Predictors may benefit by learning affector correlations because when branches repeat with the same data flow graph they will likely go the same direction. Furthermore, affector correlations use a more concise branch history to capture the data flow graph leading to a branch and thus reduce learning time and table pressure for training a predictor.

Affectees: A dynamic branch, A, is affectee of a subsequent dynamic branch, B, if A is testing the outcome of an instruction C that can trace a data dependence to an instruction D in the data flow graph leading to B.[3] The direction of an affectee branch encodes, usually in a lossy manner, the value produced or yet to be produced by D. In the example in Fig. 1.a there are two affectees. One of the affectees is also an affector. In effect, affectees provide an encoding for values consumed or produced in the dataflow graph leading to the branch to be predicted. For example, the affectee branch in BB 4 tell us whether or not

---

[3] C and D can be the same instruction.

the value loaded from memory in BB2 is 1. The affectee data flow graph for the example in Fig. 1.a is shown in Fig. 1.c.

Combo: It is evident that the combination of affectors and affectees can be more powerful than either correlation alone since affectees can help differentiate between branches with the same data affector data flow graphs but different input values. Similarly, affectors can help distinguish between same affectee graphs that correspond to different affector graphs. The combined affector and affectee data flow graph of our running example is shown in Fig. 1.d.

Section 4 investigates how the above types of correlations affect branch prediction accuracy. We believe that existing predictor schemes are able to learn data flow graphs, as those shown in Fig. 1, but they do this inefficiently using more history bits than needed. Therefore, they may suffer from cold effects and more table pressure/aliasing. Our analysis will establish how much room there is to improve them.

2.2   Memory Instructions

An important issue that influences whether a branch is classified as having a *direct*-correlation to another branch is the handling of memory instructions. For precise knowledge of the direct-correlations data dependences need to be tracked through memory. That way a branch that has a dependence to a load instruction can detect correlation to other branches through the memory dependence. Although, tracking dependences through memory is important for developing a better understanding for the potential and properties of affectors and affectees correlations, it may be useful to know the extent that such precise knowledge is necessary. Thus may be interesting to determine how well predictors will work if memory dependences correlations are approximated or completely ignored.

We consider two approximations of memory dependences. The one tracks dependence of address operands ignoring the dependence for the data. And the other does not consider any dependences past a load instruction, i.e. limiting a branch to correlations emanating from the most recent load instructions leading to the branch. These two approximations of memory dependences need to track register dependences whereas the precise scheme requires maintaining dependences between stores and load through memory. We will refer to the precise scheme of tracking dependences as *Memory*, and to the two approximations as *Address*, and *NoMemory*. In Section 4 we will compare the prediction accuracy of the various schemes to determine the importance of tracking accurately correlations through memory.

For the *Memory* scheme we found that is better to not include the address dependences of a load when a data dependence to a store is found (analysis not presented due to limited space). This is reasonable because the correlations of the data encode directly the information affecting the branch whereas the address correlations are indirect and possibly superfluous

Recall that our detection algorithm of correlations is oracle. It is based on analysis of the dynamic data dependence graph of a program. The intention of this work is to establish if there is potential from using more selective correlation.

2.3 How to Use Affectors and Affectees for Prediction

Based on the findings of this paper one can attempt to design a predictor grounds-up that exploits the properties exhibited by affectors and affectees correlations. That is also our ultimate goal and hopefully this paper will serve as a stepping stone in that direction. This is however may be a non-trivial task and before engaging in such a task may be useful to know if it is a worthwhile effort.

Therefore, in this paper we decided to determine the potential of affectors and affectees using unmodified existing predictors. We simply feed these predictors with the complete global history and with the history selected using our oracle affectors and affectees analysis and compare their prediction accuracy. If this analysis reveals that the selective correlations have consistently and substantially better accuracy then may be worthwhile to design a new predictor.

The only predictor design space option we have is how to represent the selected bits in the global history register. In [6] they were confronted with a similar problem and proposed the use of *zeroing* and *packing*. Zeroing means set a history bit to zero if it is not selected while branches retain their original position in the history register. Packing moves all the selected bits to the least significant part of the history register while other bits are set to zero. Therefore, in packing selected branches lose their original position but retain their order. Our experimental data (not shown due to space constraints) revealed that packing had on average the best accuracy and is the representation we used for the results reported in Section 4.

Our methodology for finding the potential of affectors and affectees may be suboptimal because it uses an existing predictor without considering the properties exhibited in the global history patterns after selection. Another possible limitation of our study has to do with our definition of affectors and affectees. Alternative definitions may lead to even more selective and accurate correlations. For instance by considering only affectees that trace dependences to load instructions. These and other limitations to be found may lead to increased potential and thus the findings of this study should be view as the potential under the assumptions and constraints used in the paper.

3 Experimental Framework

To determine the potential of affectors and affectees to increase branch prediction accuracy we used a functional simulation methodology using a simplescalar [8] derived simulator. A subset of SPEC2000 and SPEC95 benchmarks, listed in Table 1, are used for our analysis. For the SPEC2000 benchmarks the early regions identified by sim-point [9] are used, whereas for SPEC95 complete runs of modified reference inputs are executed.

The eight integer benchmarks were chosen because they exhibited the higher misprediction rates in the two suites for a 32KB L-Tage predictor. We did not include the *gzip* benchmark because the memory requirements of this benchmark to track dependences, affectors and affectees were very large. The FP benchmarks are included as typical representatives of benchmarks with low misprediction

Table 1. Benchmarks

SPECINT CPU2000	bzip200, crafty00, mcf00, twolf00, vpr00
SPECFP CPU2000	ammp00, fma3d00, mesa00
SPECINT CPU95	gcc95, go95, ijpeg95

rates to ensure that selective correlations does not hurt these benchmarks and to analyze if their correlation patterns are any different from integer or more difficult to predict benchmarks.

Two predictors are used in the experimentation: a 32KB L-TAGE [10] predictor with maximum history length of 400 bits, and the GTL [3] predictor with 400 maximum history length for the GEHL component and 100000 maximum history length for the TAGE component.

For the experiments where selective correlation is used, the selection is applied to the 400 bit global history of the L-TAGE predictor and to the 400 bit history used to access the GEHL component of the GTL predictor. Selection was not used for the TAGE component of GTL because the memory requirements required to track affectors and affectees for a 100000 global history were extremely large and beyond the memory capacities of todays servers.

The detection of affectors and affectees is oracle using the dynamic data flow graph of a program. For memory instructions, unless stated otherwise, the default policy is to track correlations past memory dependences.

The algorithm used to determine affectors is the simple approximation proposed in [6]. A dynamic branch is an affector, of a branch to be predicted, if it is the last, in the dynamic program order, branch that executed before an instruction in the dataflow graph of the branch to be predicted. The algorithm used for detecting affectees is not presented due to space limitations.

4   Results

We present three sets of results, the first analyzes the properties of affectors and affectees, the second discusses the accuracy of the GTL predictor, and the third shows the accuracy of the L-TAGE predictor

4.1   Characterization of Affectors and Affectees

Fig. 2 and 3 show the cumulative distribution of dynamic branches according to the number of affector and affectee correlations they have. The number of correlations can not exceed 400 since we consider only correlations from the 400 most recent branches. We decided to analyze the behavior for the 400 most recent branches since the two predictors used in the study use a 400 entry global branch history register.

The results reveal that branches usually have much fewer affectors than affectees. For most benchmarks 90% of the branches have at most 30 affectors. According to the definition of affectors, this means that the computation that

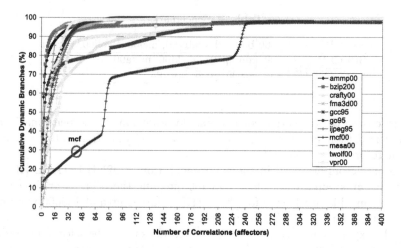

Fig. 2. Affectors distribution

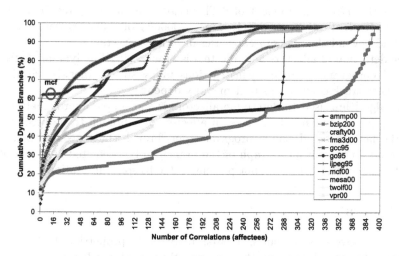

Fig. 3. Affectees distribution

determines the outcome of a branch can be found in less than 30 out of the most recent 400 basic blocks preceded by a conditional branch. The outlier is *mcf* where many branches have large number of affectors. The data about affectees correlations show clearly that for most programs 50% of the branches have 30 or more affectees. This means that a branch frequently checks information that partially or fully has been tested by at least 30 other out of the 400 most recent branches. The data also show few benchmarks, *bzip, ijpeg, vpr* to have 300 or more affectee correlations. It is noteworthy that *mcf00*, that has branches with many affectors, has also many branches, about 50%, with 0 affectees. This occurs because *mcf* loads and tests data from many memory locations where no correlation to the producers can be found within the least 400 branches. The

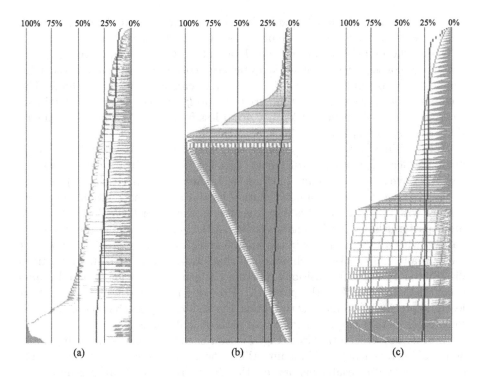

Fig. 4. Most frequent correlation patterns for (a)twolf00, (b)bzip00 and (c)ammp00

graph (not shown due to space) for the distribution of the branches when we consider both affectors and affectees is very similar to the one for the affectees.

Overall the data show that for *ALL* benchmarks there are many branches that have much less than maximum number correlations. Provided: (a) affectors and affectees are the dominant types of correlation that predictors need to learn, and (b) existing predictors are unable to use only the relevant part of history, then these data suggest that there may be room for improving prediction.

In Fig. 4 we attempt to give more insight by presenting the dominant patterns of correlation when we consider the combination of affectors and affectees. The figure shows for three benchmarks, *twolf, bzip* and *ammp* what are the most frequent 1000 patterns of correlations. To help the reader we present these top patterns sorted from top to bottom according to the oldest position with a correlation (i.e. the most recent correlation position is to the right). The curve that cut-across each graph represents from top to bottom the cumulative branch distribution of the patterns. This line is not reaching 100% since we only display the top 1000 patterns. A given pattern has a gray and white part representing the bit positions with and without correlations. To help the reader we present patterns with 100 positions where each position corresponds to 4 bits (a position is set to one if any of its corresponding four bits is set). These three graphs are representative of 10 of the 11 benchmarks we considered in this paper. Benchmark *twolf* is representative of *crafty, vpr, mesa, gcc and go, bzip* of *mcf and ijpeg*, and both *ammp* and *fma3d* have distinct behaviors. We define the length of a correlation pattern to be the oldest position with a correlation.

One of the main observation from these data is that branch correlations are not always consecutive, there are *holes* between correlated branches. These holes can be of any size and a given correlation pattern can have one or more holes. The hole behavior varies across benchmarks, for *twolf* like benchmarks is dominant whereas for *bzip* like benchmarks they occur less frequently. Within a benchmark there can be both sparse and dense patterns.

More specifically, the results indicate that virtually always correlation patterns include at least few of the most recent branches (for each benchmark almost all patterns have at the right end - most recent branches - few positions set). Also, it is observed across almost all benchmarks that for a given correlation length the pattern with all positions set is very frequent. However, for *twolf* like benchmarks many patterns have correlations that occur at the beginning and at the end of the pattern with all the branches in the middle being uncorrelated. Another remark for *bzip* and *ammp* like benchmarks, is that many branches with correlations distributed over all 100 positions (bottom pattern in Fig. 4 for *bzip* and *ammp* accounts for over 40% of the patterns). Provided it is important to predict by learning precisely the above correlations, the results suggest that there is a need for predictors that can learn efficiently patterns with holes.

Another key observation from Fig. 4 is that correlation patterns occur usually across all history lengths. These underlines the need for predictors to be capable of predicting with variable history length. The distribution of patterns according to length (not shown due to space limitations) is similar to the affectees distribution in Fig. 3 with a slight shift toward the bottom right corner. Assuming is important to learn precisely the correlation patterns, the exponential like cumulative distributions of correlation lengths, for most benchmarks, suggests that most prediction resources should be devoted to capture correlations with short history length and incrementally use less resources for longer correlations. This observation clearly supports the use of geometric history length predictors [11].

The above observations may represent a call for predictors that can handle both geometric history length and holes. As far as we know no such predictor exists today. In the next section we attempt to establish the potential of such a predictor using two existing geometric history length predictors that are accessed with selected history, with holes, using oracle affectors and affectees correlations.

4.2   GTL Results

Fig. 5 shows the accuracy of the GTL predictor when accessed with full global history, only with affectors correlations, only with affectees, and with the combination of affectors and affectees. The data show that the combination of affectors and affectees provides the best performance. It is always the same or better than GTL and almost always better than each correlation separately. The exception is *vpr00* where the combination does slightly worse than using only affectors. This can happen when the one type of correlation is sufficient to capture the program behavior and the use of additional information is detrimental. The improvement

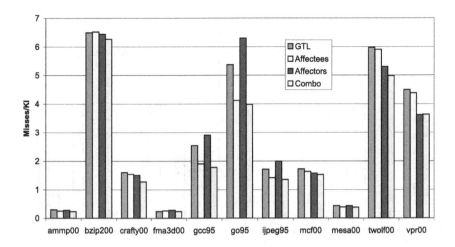

Fig. 5. GTL accuracy with selective correlation

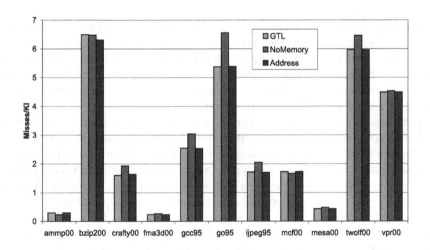

Fig. 6. Significance of memory dependence

provided by combining affectors and affectees is substantial for several bench-marks and in particular for *crafty, gcc, go, ijpeg, twolf, and vpr* it ranges from 15% to 30%. For the remaining paper we present results for experiments that combine affectors and affectees since they provide the best overall accuracy.

The data clearly support the claim by [4] that *direction*-correlation is one of the basic types of correlations in programs that predictors need to capture.

Fig. 6 shows the prediction accuracy when we combine affectors and affectees but with no correlations through memory. For each benchmark we present three results, the GTL predictor with full history, the affectors and affectees with no correlations past load instructions (NoMemory), and with correlations past load

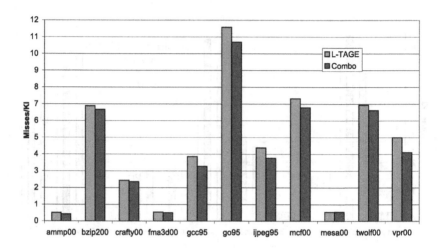

Fig. 7. L-TAGE accuracy with selective correlation

instructions using their address dependences (Address). The data show that there is very little improvement to be gain when we do not consider correlations through memory dependences. The data indicate that an approximation of memory dependences using addresses dependences offers very little improvement. This underlines that important correlations from the data predecessors of load instructions are needed for improved accuracy.

The data show that selective correlation using the combination of affectors and affectees can provide substantial improvement in prediction accuracy. The results also show that correlations past memory instructions are important and that address dependences provide a poor approximations of the data dependence correlations. Overall, we believe the data suggest that may be worthwhile investigating the development of a predictor that is capable of learning correlations from long history with holes. These conclusions are true for GTL an unrealistically large predictor that demonstrate that the improvements are not mere accident but due to basic enhancements in the prediction process. However, we are interested to know if these observations hold for a realistic predictor. Next we consider selective correlation for a 32KB L-TAGE predictor.

4.3 L-TAGE Results

Fig. 7 shows the prediction accuracy for a 32KB L-TAGE when accessed using the complete global history (L-TAGE) and with selective history using the combination of affectors and affectees (Combo). The results show that selective correlation with affectors and affectees can also improve the accuracy of the L-TAGE predictor at a realistic size. The amount of improvement is significant for several benchmarks. In particular, for *gcc, ijpeg, and vpr* is above 15% (for vpr 17%). We believe that these improvements call for the design of a predictor that can exploit *direct*-correlations.

The amount of improvements for L-TAGE are smaller as compared to GTL. However, one should recall that GTL is a completely different predictor not simply a bigger L-TAGE predictor. We also performed analysis of the importance of correlations through memory and the data suggest, similarly to GTL, that it is necessary to include such correlations for better accuracy.

5   Related Work

Since Smith [12] proposed the first dynamic table based branch predictor, innovation in the field of prediction has been sporadic but steady. Some of the key milestones are: correlation-based prediction [13] that exploits the global and or local correlation between branches, hybrid prediction [5] that combines different predictors to capture distinct branch behavior, variable history length [14] that adjusts the amount of global history used depending on program behavior, the use of perceptrons [7] to learn correlations from long history, geometric history length prediction [11] that employs different history lengths that follow a geometric series to index the various tables of a predictor, and partial tagging [15] of predictor table entries to better manage their allocation and deallocation. The above innovations have one main theme in common: the correlation information used to predict a branch is becoming increasingly more selective. This facilitates both faster predictor training time and less destructive aliasing. Our paper extends this line of work and shows that there is room for further improvement if we could select correlations with holes out of long history.

In two recently organized branch prediction championships [1,2] researchers established the state of the art in branch prediction. In 2006, the L-TAGE global history predictor [10] was the winner for a 32KB budget. L-TAGE is a multi-table predictor with partial tagging and geometric history lengths that also includes a loop predictor. In the 2006 championship limit contest the GTL predictor [3] provided the best accuracy. GTL combines GEHL [11] and L-TAGE predictors using a meta-predictor. The GEHL global history predictor [11] employs multiple components indexed with geometric history length. Our paper uses the L-TAGE and GTL predictors to examine our ideas to ensure that observations made are not accidental but based on basic principles. The use of longer history is central to these two predictors and the analysis in this paper confirmed the need and usefulness for learning geometrically longer history correlations.

Several previous paper explored the idea of improving prediction by encoding the data flow graphs leading to instructions to be predicted. They use information from instructions in the data flow graph [16,17,18,19,20], such as opcodes, immediate values, and register names, to train a predictor. Effectively these papers are implementing variations of predictors that correlate on affector branches. In [20], they consider using the live in values of the dataflow graphs when they become available and in [17] they examined the possibility of predicting such values. The inclusion of actual or predicted live-in values is analogous to the correlation on affectee branches of such values, since the predicted or actual outcome of affectee branches represents an encoding of the live-in values.

Mahlke and Natarajan [21] use static dataflow information to determine variables that may influence the outcome of a branch and then performed profiling analysis on these variable to determine simple correlation functions between the values of the variables and the branch outcome. Instructions are inserted in the code to compute the branch direction. In our view, this work also attempts to implement a variation of affectors and affectees correlation since a function supplies analogous information to what can be provided by affectee branches.

A return-history-stack [22] is a method that can introduce holes in the branch history. In broad terms, a return history stack pushes in a stack the branch history register on a call and recovers it on a return, thus introducing holes in the history. A return history stack was shown to be useful for a trace predictor [22] and offered modest improvements for a direction branch predictor [23]. This suggests that there are many cases where branches executed in a function are often no significant correlators to branches executed after the function return.

6   Conclusions and Future Work

In this paper we investigate the potential of selective correlation using affectors and affectees branches to improve branch prediction. Experimental analysis of affectors and affectees revealed that many branches have few correlations and often the correlations have holes between them. Prediction using selective correlation, based on oracle selection of affectors and affectees, is shown to have significant potential to improve accuracy for a both a limit and a realistic predictor. The analysis also shows that correlations past memory instruction are needed for best accuracy. Overall, our study suggests that may be worthwhile to consider the design of a realistic predictor that can exploit the properties exhibited by affectors and affectees correlation patterns by learning correlations with and without holes from long history. Another possible direction of future work, is to apply the findings of this paper to static branch prediction, and to other types of predictors, such as values and dependences.

Acknowledgments. This work is partially supported by an Intel research grant.

References

1. Wilkerson, C., Stark, J.: Introduction to JILP's Special Edition for Finalists of the Championship Branch Prediction (CBP1) Competition. Journal of Instruction-Level Parallelism 7 (2005)
2. Jiménez, D.A.: The Second Championship Branch Prediction Competition. Journal of Instruction-Level Parallelism 9 (2007)
3. Seznec, A.: The Idealistic GTL Predictor. Journal of Instruction-Level Parallelism 9 (2007)
4. Evers, M., Patel, S.J., Chappel, R.S., Patt, Y.N.: An Analysis of Correlation and Predictability: What Makes Two-Level Branch Predictors Work. In: 25th International Symposium on Computer Architecture (June 1998)

5. McFarling, S.: Combining Branch Predictors. Technical Report DEC WRL TN-36, Digital Western Research Laboratory (June 1993)
6. Thomas, R., Franklin, M., Wilkerson, C., Stark, J.: Improving Branch Prediction by Dynamic Dataflow-based Identification of Correlated Branches from a Large Global History. In: 30th International Symposium on Computer Architecture, pp. 314–323 (June 2003)
7. Jimenez, D.A., Lin, C.: Dynamic Branch Prediction with Perceptrons. In: 7th International Symposium on High Performance Computer Architecture (February 2001)
8. Burger, D., Austin, T.M., Bennett, S.: Evaluating Future Microprocessors: The SimpleScalar Tool Set. Technical Report CS-TR-96-1308, University of Wisconsin-Madison (July 1996)
9. Perelman, E., Hamerly, G., Biesbrouck, M.V., Sherwood, T., Calder, B.: Using SimPoint for Accurate and Efficient Simulation. In: International Conference on Measurement and Modeling of Computer Systems (2003)
10. Seznec, A.: The L-TAGE Branch Predictor. Journal of Instruction-Level Parallelism 9 (2007)
11. Seznec, A.: Analysis of the O-GEometric History Length branch predictor. In: 32nd International Symposium on Computer Architecture (2005)
12. Smith, J.E.: A Study of Branch Prediction Strategies. In: 8th International Symposium on Computer Architecture, pp. 135–148 (May 1981)
13. Yeh, T.Y., Patt, Y.N.: Two-Level Adaptive Branch Prediction. In: 24th International Symposium on Microarchitecture, pp. 51–61 (November 1991)
14. Juan, T., Sanjeevan, S., Navarro, J.J.: Dynamic History-Length Fitting: A third level of adaptivity for branch prediction. In: 25th International Symposium on Computer Architecture, pp. 155–166 (June 1998)
15. Michaud, P.: A PPM-like, Tag-based Predictor. Journal of Instruction-Level Parallelism 7 (2005)
16. Farcy, A., Temam, O., Espasa, R., Juan, T.: Dataflow analysis of branch mispredictions and its application to early resolution of branch outcomes. In: 31st International Symposium on Microarchitecture, pp. 59–68 (December 1998)
17. Thomas, R., Franklin, M.: Using Dataflow Based Context for Accurate Value Prediction. In: 2001 International Conference on Parallel Architectures and Compilation Techniques, pp. 107–117 (September 2001)
18. Sazeides, Y.: Dependence Based Value Prediction. Technical Report CS-TR-02-00, University of Cyprus (February 2002)
19. Constantinidis, K., Sazeides, Y.: A Hardware Based Method for Dynamically Detecting Instruction Isomorphism and its Application to Branch Prediction. In: 2nd Value Prediction Workshop (2004)
20. Chen, L., Dropsho, S., Albonesi, D.H.: Dynamic Data Dependence Tracking and its Application to Branch Prediction. In: 9th International Symposium on High Performance Computer Architecture, pp. 65–76 (February 2003)
21. Mahlke, S., Natarajan, B.: Compiler Synthesized Dynamic Branch Prediction. In: 29th International Symposium on Microarchitecture, pp. 153–164 (December 1996)
22. Jacobson, Q., Rottenberg, E., Smith, J.E.: Path-Based Next Trace Prediction. In: 30th International Symposium on Microarchitecture, pp. 14–23 (December 1997)
23. Gao, F., Sair, S.: Exploiting Intra-function Correlation with the Global History. In: Hämäläinen, T.D., Pimentel, A.D., Takala, J., Vassiliadis, S. (eds.) SAMOS 2005. LNCS, vol. 3553, Springer, Heidelberg (2005)

Turbo-ROB: A Low Cost Checkpoint/Restore Accelerator

Patrick Akl and Andreas Moshovos

University of Toronto, Canada

Abstract. Modern processors use speculative execution to improve performance. However, speculative execution requires a checkpoint/restore mechanism to repair the machine's state whenever speculation fails. Existing checkpoint/restore mechanisms do not scale well for processors with relatively large windows (i.e., 128 or more). This work presents Turbo-ROB, a checkpoint/restore recovery accelerator that can complement or replace existing checkpoint/restore mechanisms. We show that the Turbo-ROB improves performance and reduces resource requirements compared to a conventional Re-order Buffer mechanism. For example, on the average, a 64-entry TROB matches the performance of a 512-entry ROB, while a 128- and a 512-entry TROB outperform the 512-entry ROB by 6.8% and 9.1% respectively. We also demonstrate that the TROB improves performance with register alias table checkpoints effectively reducing the need from more checkpoints and the latency and energy increase these would imply.

1 Introduction

Modern processors use control flow speculation to improve performance. The processor does not wait until the target of a control flow instruction is calculated. Instead, it predicts a possible target and speculatively executes instructions at that target. To preserve correctness, recovery mechanisms restore the machine's state on mispeculation. Recovery involves reversing any changes done by the incorrectly executed instructions and resuming execution at the correct target instruction. Modern processors utilize two such recovery mechanisms. The first is the reorder buffer (ROB) which allows recovery at any instruction in addition to mispeculated branches. Recovering from the ROB amounts to *squashing*, i.e., reversing the effects of each mispeculated instruction, a process that requires time proportional to the number of squashed instructions. The second recovery mechanism uses a number of global checkpoints (GCs) that are allocated prior to executing a branch and in program order. A GC contains a complete snapshot of all relevant processor state. Recovery at an instruction with a GC is "instantaneous", i.e., it requires a fixed, low latency. GCs are typically embedded into the Register Alias Table (RAT) since virtually all other processor structures do not need a checkpoint/restore mechanism for most of their resources (they maintain a complete record of all in-flight instructions and thus recovery is possible by simply discarding all erroneous entries).

P. Stenström et al. (Eds.): HiPEAC 2008, LNCS 4917, pp. 258–272, 2008.

Ideally, a GC would be allocated at every instruction such that the recovery latency is always constant. In practice, because the RAT is a performance critical structure only a limited number of GCs can be implemented without impacting the clock cycle significantly and thus reducing overall performance. For example, RAT latency increases respectively by 1.6%, 5%, and 14.4% when four, eight, and 16 GCs are used relative to a RAT with no GCs for a 512-entry window 4-way superscalar processor with 64 architectural registers and for a 130nm CMOS commercial technology [12]. Recent work suggested using selective GC allocation to reduce the number of GCs necessary to maintain high performance [2,1,5,11]. Even with these advances, at least eight and often 16 GCs are needed to maintain performance within 2% of that possible with an infinite number of checkpoints allocated at all branches with a 256-entry or larger window processor. These GCs increase RAT latency and the clock cycle and thus reduce performance. Moreover, RAT GCs increase RAT energy consumption. This is undesirable as the RAT exhibits high energy density. Accordingly, methods for reducing the number of GCs or for eliminating the need for GCs altogether would lead to improved performance and avoid an increase in power density in the RAT.

This work proposes *Turbo-ROB*, or *TROB*, a checkpoint recovery accelerator that can complement or replace the ROB and the GCs. The TROB is off the critical path and as a result its latency and energy can be tuned with greater flexibility. The Turbo-ROB is similar to the ROB but it requires a lot fewer entries since the TROB only stores information necessary to recover at a few selected branches, called *repair points*. Specifically, the TROB stores recovery information for the first update to each register after a repair point. Because programs tend to reuse registers often, many instructions are ignored by the TROB. In contrast, the ROB stores information for all instructions because it allows recovery at *any* instruction. While the ROB is a general mechanism that treats all recoveries as equal, the TROB is optimized for the common case of branch-related recoveries. The TROB can be used to accelerate recovery in conjunction with a ROB or GCs, or it can be used as a complete replacement for the ROB and the GCs. Unlike previous proposals for reducing the recovery latency, the Turbo-ROB does not require modifications to the RAT.

This paper makes the following contributions: (1) It proposes "Turbo-ROB", a ROB-like recovery mechanism that requires less resources than the ROB and allows faster recovery on the frequent case of control flow mis-speculations. Given that the TROB is off the critical path it alleviates some of the pressure to scale the register alias table and the re-order buffer. (2) It shows that the TROB can be used to improve performance over a ROB-only recovery mechanism. (3) It shows that the TROB can replace a ROB offering performance that is close to that possible with few GCs. Eliminating the ROB is desirable since it is an energy and latency inefficient structure [2]. (4) It shows that the TROB improves performance even when used with a GC-based recovery mechanism. More importantly, the TROB reduces GC pressure allowing implementations that use very few GCs. For example, the results of this paper demonstrate that

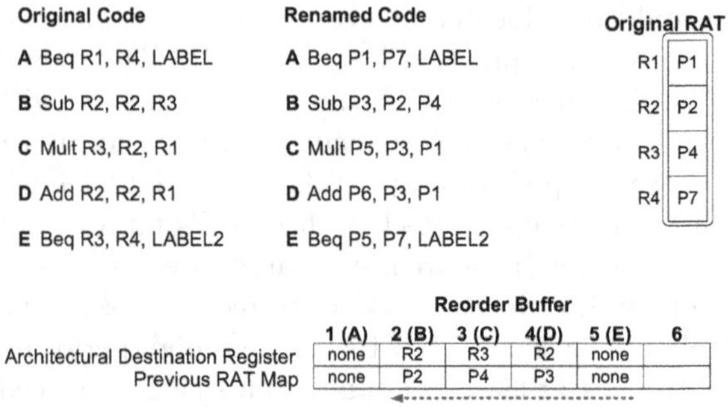

Original Code	Renamed Code	Original RAT
A Beq R1, R4, LABEL	A Beq P1, P7, LABEL	R1 P1
B Sub R2, R2, R3	B Sub P3, P2, P4	R2 P2
C Mult R3, R2, R1	C Mult P5, P3, P1	R3 P4
D Add R2, R2, R1	D Add P6, P3, P1	R4 P7
E Beq R3, R4, LABEL2	E Beq P5, P7, LABEL2	

Reorder Buffer

	1 (A)	2 (B)	3 (C)	4(D)	5 (E)	6
Architectural Destination Register	none	R2	R3	R2	none	
Previous RAT Map	none	P2	P4	P3	none	

Fig. 1. Given an instruction to recover at, it is not always necessary to process all subsequent instructions recorded in the ROB

a TROB with one GC performs as well as an implementation that uses four GCs. A single GC RAT implementation is simpler than one that uses more GCs.

The rest of this paper is organized as follows: Section 2 presents the TROB design. Section 3 reviews related work. Section 4 presents the experimental analysis of TROB. Finally, Section 5 concludes this work. In this paper we restrict our attention to recovery from control flow mispeculation. However, the TROB can also be used to recover from other exceptions such as page faults. In the workloads we study these exceptions are very infrequent. We also focus on relatively large processors with up to 512-entry instruction windows. However, we do demonstrate that the TROB is beneficial even for smaller window processors that are more representative of today's processor designs. We note, however, that as architects are revisiting the design of large window processor simplifying the underlying structures and as multithreading becomes commonplace it is likely that future processors will use larger windows.

2   Turbo-ROB Recovery

For clarity, we initially restrict our attention to using the TROB to complement a ROB recovery mechanism. In Sections 2.4 and 2.5 we discuss how the TROB can be used without a ROB or with GCs respectively. The motivation for Turbo-ROB is that not all instructions inserted in the ROB are needed for every recovery. We motivate the Turbo-ROB design by first reviewing how ROB recovery works.

The ROB maintains a log of all changes in program order. Existing ROB designs allocate one entry per instruction in the window. Each ROB entry contains sufficient information to reverse the effects of the corresponding instruction. For the RAT it is sufficient to keep the architectural register name and the previous physical register it mapped to. On a mis-speculation, *all* ROB entries for the wrong path instructions are traversed in reverse program order. While the ROB design allows recovery at *any* instruction, given a specific instruction to recover at, not all ROB entries need to be traversed. Specifically, for every RAT entry, only the first corresponding ROB entry after the mispredicted branch is needed.

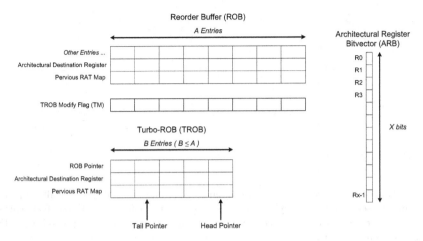

Fig. 2. Turbo-ROB organization. This figure assumes that the Turbo-ROB complements a ROB.

Moreover, branch instructions occupy ROB entries but do not modify the RAT. Figure 1 illustrates via an example these two points. The branch instruction *A* is mispredicted and the wrong path instructions *B* to *E* are fetched and decoded before the misprediction is discovered. The ROB-only recovery mechanism traverses the ROB entries *5* to *2* in reverse order updating the RAT. However, traversing just the entries *3* and *2* is sufficient: Entry *5* contains no state information since it corresponds to a branch; entry *4* corresponding to *R2* at instruction *D* can be ignored because the correct previous mapping (*P2*) is preserved by entry *2*. A mechanism that exploits these observations can reduce recovery latency and hence improve performance. The TROB mechanism presented next, exploits this observation. To do so, it allows recovery only on branches and relies on the ROB or in re-execution as in [2] to handle other exceptions.

2.1 Mechanism: Structure and Operation

We propose TROB, a ROB-like structure that requires fewer resources. TROB is optimized for the common case and thus allows recovery at *some* instructions, which we call *repair points*. The TROB records a subset of the information recorded in the ROB. Specifically, given a repair point *B*, the TROB contains at most one entry per architectural register corresponding to the first update to that register after *B*. Recoveries using the TROB are thus potentially faster than ROB-only recoveries. To ensure that recovery is still possible at all instructions (for handling exceptions), a normal ROB is used as a backup.

Figure 2 shows that the TROB is an array of entries that are allocated and released in program order. Each entry contains an architectural register identifier and a previous RAT map. Thus, for an architecture with X architectural registers and Y physical registers, each TROB entry contains $\log_2 X + \log_2 Y$ bits. A mechanism for associating TROB entries with the corresponding instructions

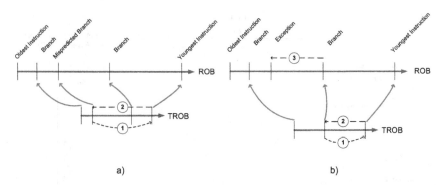

Fig. 3. Turbo-ROB recovery scenarios when repair points are initiated at all branches. a) Common scenario: recovery at any mispredicted branch uses only the fast Turbo-ROB. b) Infrequent scenario: recovery at any other instruction is supported using the Turbo-ROB and the ROB.

is needed. In one possible implementation, each TROB entry contains a ROB pointer. Thus an extra $\log_2 A$ bits per TROB entry are needed for an architecture with an A-entry reorder buffer. Detection of the first update to each register after a repair point is performed via the help of a single "Architectural Register Bitvector" (ARB) of size equal to the number of architectural registers (X bits). A "TROB modify" (TM) bit array with as many bits as the number of ROB entries is used to track which instructions in the ROB allocated a TROB entry. This is needed to keep the TROB in a consistent state.

Updating the Turbo-ROB: In our baseline design, repair points are initiated at all branches. Following a repair point, we keep track of the nearest subsequent *previous RAT map* for every RAT entry in the TROB. The ARB records which architectural registers have had their mapping in the RAT changed since the last repair point. The ARB is reset to all-zeros at every repair point and every time a TROB entry is created the corresponding ARB bit is set. TROB entries are created only when the corresponding ARB is zero. Finally, the corresponding TM is set, indicating that the corresponding instruction in the ROB modified the TROB. The TM facilitates in-order TROB deallocation whenever an instruction commits or is squashed. If the TROB has less entries than the ROB, it is possible to run out of free TROB entries. The base implementation stalls decode in this case.

Recovery: There are two recovery scenarios with the TROB: Figure 3(a) shows the first scenario where we recover at an instruction with a repair point. RAT recovery proceeds by traversing the TROB in reverse order while updating the RAT with the previous mappings. Figure 3(b) shows the second recovery scenario where we recover at an instruction without a repair point. In the base design that allocates repair points for all branches, this scenario is not possible for branches and applies only to other exceptions. Accordingly, this will happen infrequently. We first quickly recover the RAT partially at the closest subsequent TROB repair

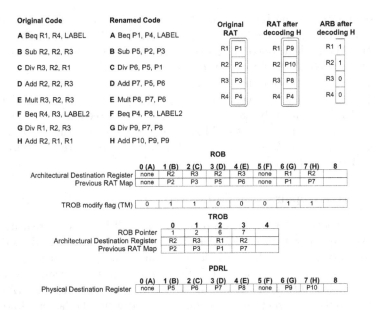

Fig. 4. Example of recovery using the Turbo-ROB: repair points are initiated at instructions **A** and **F**. Recovering at **A** requires traversing entries **3** to **0** in the TROB. The physical register free list is recovered by traversing entries **7** to **0** in the PDRL.

point. We then complete the recovery using the ROB, starting at the instruction corresponding to the repair point at which partial recovery took place. If no such repair point is found, we rely solely the ROB for recovery.

Reclaiming Physical Registers: Since the TROB contains only first updates, it can't be used to free all the physical registers allocated by wrong path instructions. We assume that the free register list (FRL) contains embedded checkpoints which are allocated at repair points. The free register list is typically implemented as a bit vector with one bit per register. Accordingly, checkpoints similar to those used for the RAT can be used here also. Since the FRL is a unidimensional structure embedding checkpoints does not impact its latency greatly as it does in the RAT. Upon commit, an instruction freeing a register, must mark it as free in the current FRL and in all active checkpoints by clearing all corresponding bits. Assuming that these bits are organized in a single SRAM column, clearing them requires extending the per column reset signal over the whole column plus a pull-down transistor per bit.

2.2 Recovery Example

Figure 4 illustrates an example of recovery using the TROB. Following the decode of branch *A*, instructions *B* and *C* perform first updates of RAT entries *R2* and *R3* and allocate TROB entries *0* and *1*. The ARB is reset at instruction *F* and new TROB entries are allocated for instructions *G* and *H*, which perform new first updates to the RAT entries *R1* and *R2*. If branch *A* is mispredicted, recovery proceeds in reverse order starting from the TROB head (entry *3*) and until entry *0* is reached. Recovering via the ROB would require traversing seven entries as opposed to the four required by the TROB. If branch *F* was mispredicted, recovery would only use TROB entries *3* and *2*. If instruction *C* raised an exception, recovery proceeds using the ROB by traversing entries *7* to *3* in reverse order. Alternatively, we could recover by first recovering at the closest subsequent repair point using the TROB (recovering at instruction *F* by using the TROB entries *3* and *2*) and then use the ROB to complete the recovery (by using ROB entries *4* to *3*).

2.3   Selective Repair Point Initiation

Our baseline mechanism initiates repair points at all branches. Creating repair points less frequently reduces the space requirements for the TROB and makes TROB recovery faster. In the example shown in Figure 4, not creating a TROB repair point at branch *F* reduces TROB pressure since instruction *H* would not be saved. Since TROB entry *3* would not be utilized, repairing the RAT state using the TROB if instruction *A* was mispredicted would be faster. However, if *F* was mis-speculated then we would have to use the slower ROB to recover. To balance between decreasing the utilization and the recovery latency of the TROB on one side, and increasing the rate of slow recoveries that do not utilize solely the TROB on the other side, we can selectively create repair points at branches that are highly likely to be mispredicted. Confidence estimators dynamically identify such branches. Zero-cost confidence estimation has been show to work well with selective RAT checkpoint allocation [11]. In the rest of this study, we refer to the method that uses selective repair point initiation as *sTROB*.

2.4   Eliminating the ROB

The TROB can be used as a complete replacement for the ROB. In one design, the TROB replaces the ROB and repair points are initiated at every branch. In this case, recovery is possible via the TROB at every branch. Other exceptions can be handled using re-execution and a copy of the RAT that is updated at commit time. This policy was suggested by Akkary et al. [2] for a design that used only GCs and no ROB. To guarantee that every branch gets a repair point we stall decode whenever the TROB is full and a new entry is needed. This design artificially restricts the instruction window. However, as we show experimentally, this rarely affects performance. Alternatively, we can allow some branches to proceed without a repair point, or to abandon the current repair point and rely instead on re-execution as done for other exceptions.

In another design, the TROB replaces the ROB but repair points are initiated only on weak branches as predicted via a confidence estimation mechanism. In this design, it is not always possible to recover via the TROB. Whenever no repair point exists, we rely instead on re-execution from an earlier repair point or from the beginning of the window.

2.5 TROB and In-RAT Global Checkpoints

Finally, the TROB can be used in conjunction with GCs with or without a ROB. If a ROB is available, recovery proceeds first at the nearest subsequent GC or repair point via the GCs or the TROB respectively. Then, recovery completes via the ROB. If no ROB is available, recovery first proceeds to the nearest earlier GC or repair point. Recovery completes by re-executing the intervening instructions as in [2]. In this paper we study the design that combines a TROB with few GCs and a ROB.

3 Related Work

Mispeculation recovery has been extensively studied in the literature. Related work can be classified into the following categories: 1) Reducing the mispeculation recovery latency, 2) Confidence estimation for speculation control, and 3) Multipath execution and instruction reuse. Due to space limitations, we restrict our attention to the first two categories noting that in principle the TROB is complementary to techniques in the third category.

Reducing the Mispeculation Recovery Latency: Aragon et al. analyzed the causes of performance loss due to branch mispredictions [3] and found that the *pipeline-fill* penalty is a significant source of performance loss due to mispredictions. The TROB reduces a significant component of this latency.

The Reorder Buffer, originally proposed by Smith and Pleszkun, is the traditional checkpointing mechanism used to recover the machine state on mispredictions or exceptions [13]. As previous studies have shown, recovering solely using the reorder buffer incurs significant penalties as the processor window increases [2,1,11,16]. To alleviate this concern, non-selective in-RAT checkpointing has been implemented in the MIPS R10000 processor [15]. Moshovos proposed an architecture where the reorder buffer is complemented with GCs taken selectively at hard-to-predict branches to reduce the GC requirements for large instruction window processors [11]. Akkary et al. proposed an architecture that does not utilize a reorder buffer and instead creates GCs at low confidence branches [2,1]. Recovery at branches without a GC proceeds by recovering at an earlier GC and re-executing instruction up until the mis-speculated branch. As we show in this paper, the TROB can be used in conjunction with in-RAT checkpointing. Modern checkpoint/recovery mechanisms have evolved out of earlier proposals for supporting speculative execution [7,13,14].

Zhou et al. proposed Eager Misprediction Recovery (EMR), which allows some instructions whose input registers' map were not corrupted to be renamed in parallel with RAT recovery [16]. While the idea is attractive, the implementation complexity has not been shown to be low. While Turbo-ROB can in principle be used with this approach also, this investigation is left for future work.

Confidence Estimation for Speculation Control: Turbo-ROB relies on a confidence estimator for identifying weak branches. Manne et al. propose throttling the pipeline's front end whenever too many hard-to-predict branches are simultaneously in-flight for energy reduction [10]. Moshovos proposed used a similar estimator based on the bias information from existing branch predictors, for selective GC allocation [11]. Jacobsen et al. proposed a more accurate confidence estimator whose implementation requires explicit resources [8]. This confidence estimator was used by Akkary et al. for GC prediction [2,1] and by Manne et al. for speculation control [10]. Jimenez and Lin studied composite confidence estimators [9].

4   Experimental Results

Section 4.1 discusses our experimental methodology and Section 4.2 discusses the performance metric used throughout the evaluation. Section 4.3 demonstrates that TROB can completely replace the ROB offering superior performance with less resources. Section 4.4 studies the performance of a TROB with a backing ROB. Finally, Section 4.5 demonstrates that TROB improves performance with a GC-based configuration. For the most part we focus on a 512-entry instruction window configuration. We do so since this configuration places much higher pressure on the checkpoint/recovery mechanism. However, since most commercial vendors today are focusing on smaller windows we also show that TROB is useful even for smaller window processors.

4.1   Methodology

We used Simplescalar v3.0 [4] to simulate the out-of-order superscalar processor detailed in Table 1. We used most of the benchmarks from the SPEC CPU 2000 which we compiled for the Alpha 21264 architecture using HP's compilers and for the Digital Unix V4.0F using the SPEC suggested default flags for peak optimization. All benchmarks were run using a reference input data set. It was not possible to simulate some of the benchmarks due to insufficient memory resources. To obtain reasonable simulation times, samples were taken for one billion committed instructions per benchmark. To skip the initialization section in order to obtain representative results, we collected statistics after skipping two billion committed instructions for all benchmarks.

4.2   Performance Metric

We report performance results relative to an oracle checkpoint/restore mechanism where it is always possible to recover in one cycle. We refer to this unrealizable design as *PERF*. PERF represents the upper bound on performance for checkpoint/restore mechanisms if we ignore performance side-effects from mispeculated instructions (e.g., prefetching). Accordingly, in most cases we report performance *deterioration* compared to PERF. The lower the deterioration the better the overall performance. Practical designs can perform at best as well as PERF and in most cases they will perform worse.

Table 1. Base processor configuration

Branch Predictor	Fetch Unit
8K-entry GShare and 8K-entry bi-modal 16K Selector 2 branches per cycle	Up to 4 or 8 instr. per cycle 64-entry Fetch Buffer Non-blocking I-Cache
Issue/Decode/Commit	**Scheduler**
Up to 4 instr. per cycle	128-, 256- or 512-entry/half size LSQ
Functional Unit Latencies	**Main Memory**
Default simplescalar values	Infinite, 200 cycles
L1D/L1I Cache Geometry	**UL2 Cache Geometry**
64KBytes, 4-way set-associative with 64-byte blocks	1MByte, 8-way set-associative with 64-byte blocks
L1D/L1I/L2 Cache Latencies	**Cache Replacement**
3/3/16 Cycles	LRU
Fetch/Decode/Commit Latencies	
4 cycles + cache latency for fetch	

4.3 TROB as a ROB Replacement

In this section we study the performance of a design that replaces the ROB with a TROB. In this design repair points are initiated at every branch so that it is always possible to recover from a control flow mis-speculation using the TROB. Other exceptions are handled by re-executing from a preceding repair point similar to what was proposed in [1]. Whenever a new entry must be written into the TROB and the TROB is full, decode stalls until a TROB entry becomes available.

Figure 5 shows the per-benchmark and average performance deterioration relative to PERF with TROB as a function of the number of TROB entries. The first bar per benchmark represents the deterioration with ROB-only recovery. Lower deterioration implies higher performance. On the average, the 512-entry TROB outperforms the similarly sized ROB by 9.1%. As we decrease the number of TROB entries, performance deteriorates since decode occasionally stalls. However, on the average, even a 64-entry TROB performs slightly better than the 512-entry ROB. With a 128-entry TROB performance is just 2.5% short of that of a 512-entry TROB and 6.8% better than the ROB.

Per-benchmark behavior varies. For many programs, such as *gzip* and *vpr*, a 32-entry TROB performs better than a 512-entry ROB. In this case, the TROB reduces the number of cycles that are needed for recovery. By comparison, a 32-entry ROB reduces performance by more than 50% on the average. However, *swim*, *mgrid*, *applu* and *lucas* suffer when using a TROB with less than 256 entries. In these programs the instruction window is at full capacity most of the time because they exhibit a low rate of branches and nearly perfect prediction accuracy. Moreover, these benchmarks tend to utilize most of the registers most of the time. As a result, a smaller TROB artificially restricts the instruction window. While not shown on the figure, a 384-entry TROB eliminates this

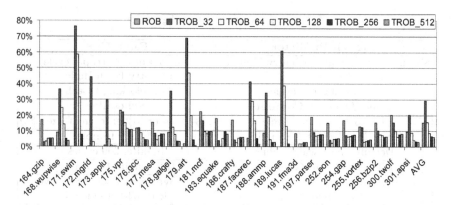

Fig. 5. Per-benchmark and average performance deterioration relative to PERF with ROB-only recovery and TROB-only recovery as a function of the number of the TROB entries

problem for all programs. Thus, TROB always outperforms the ROB even while requiring fewer resources. Since mis-speculations are virtually non-existent for these benchmarks we expect that selective repair point allocation coupled with re-execution recovery as in [1] will be sufficient to avoid performance degradation for these benchmarks even with a smaller TROB. However, due to time limitations this study is left for future work.

The results of this section demonstrate that TROB-only recovery can improve performance significantly over ROB-only recovery. When TROB is given the same entries as ROB it always performs better. A 384-entry TROB that requires 25% less resources performs better or as well as a 512-entry ROB. With half the resources, TROB performs significantly better than ROB for most benchmarks and virtually identically for those that exhibit very low misprediction rates. With just 25% the resources of ROB, TROB achieves an average performance deterioration of 7.5% compared to PERF which is significantly lower than the 17% deterioration observed with the 512-entry ROB.

Smaller Window Processors: Figures 6 and 7 report performance for TROB for processors with 128- and 256-entry instruction windows. The trends are similar to those observed for the 512-entry window processor, however, in absolute terms the differences are smaller. In either case, a TROB that has half the entries than the ROB it replaces is sufficient to improve performance. These results demonstrate that TROB is a viable ROB replacement for today's processors also.

4.4   Selective Repair Point Initiation

In this section we complement a ROB with an sTROB which is a TROB that uses selective repair point initiation. In this case, the sTROB acts as a recovery accelerator. This design requires more resources than the ROB-only recovery mechanism, however, these resources are off the critical path. Recovery at a

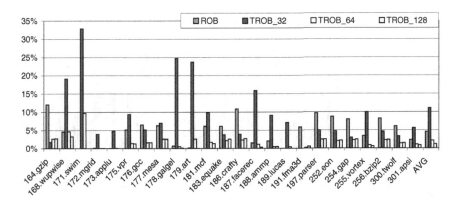

Fig. 6. Per-benchmark and average performance deterioration relative to PERF with ROB-only recovery and TROB-only recovery as a function of the number of the TROB entries for a **128-entry window processor**

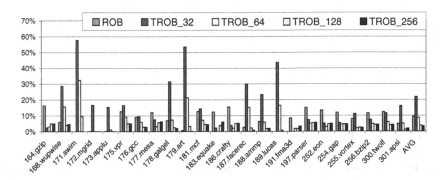

Fig. 7. Per-benchmark and average performance deterioration relative to PERF with ROB-only recovery and TROB-only recovery as a function of the number of the TROB entries for a **256-entry window processor**

branch with a repair point proceeds via the TROB only, otherwise, it is necessary to use both the ROB and the sTROB. In the latter case, recovery proceeds first at the nearest subsequent repair point via the sTROB. It takes a single cycle to locate this repair point if it exists provided that we keep a small ordered list of all repair points at decode. Recovery completes via the ROB for the remaining instructions if any. Whenever the TROB is full, decode is not stalled but the current repair point if any is marked as invalid. This repair point and any preceding ones can no longer be used for recovery. Figure 8 shows the per-benchmark and average performance deterioration for sTROB recovery as a function of the number of sTROB entries. We use a 1K-entry table of 4-bit resetting counters to identify low confidence branches [8]. Very similar results were obtained with the zero-cost, anyweak estimator [11]. Average performance improves even with a 32-entry sTROB. These results demonstrate that the TROB can be used as

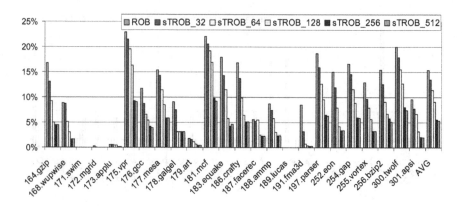

Fig. 8. Per-benchmark and average performance deterioration relative to PERF with ROB-only recovery and sTROB recovery as a function of the number of sTROB entries

a recovery accelerator on top of a conventional ROB. Comparing with the results of the next section, it can be seen that sTROB offers performance that is comparable to that possible with RAT checkpointing.

4.5   Turbo-ROB with GCs

This section demonstrates that the TROB successfully improves performance even when used with a state-of-the-art GC-based recovery mechanism [2,1,11]. In this design, the TROB complements both a ROB and in-RAT GCs. The TROB accelerates recoveries for those branches that could not get a GC. Recent work has demonstrated that including additional GCs in the RAT (as it is required to maintain high performance for processors with 128 or more instructions in their window) greatly increases RAT latency and hence reduces the clock cycle. Accordingly, in this case the TROB reduces the need for additional RAT GCs offering a high performance solution without the impact on clock cycle. The TROB is off the critical path and it does not impact RAT latency as GCs do.

Figure 9 shows the per-benchmark and average performance deterioration relative to PERF with (1) GC-based recovery (with one or four GCs), (2) sTROB, and (3) sTROB with GC-based recovery (sTROB with one or four GCs). We use a 1K-entry table of 4-bit resetting counters to identify low confidence branches [8]. A low confidence branch is given a GC if one is available, otherwise, a repair point is initiated for it in the TROB. If the TROB is full, decode stalls until space becomes available. In this experiments we use a 256-entry sTROB. On average, the sTROB with only one GC outperforms the GC-based only mechanism that utilizes four GCs. When four GCs are used with the sTROB, performance deterioration is 0.99% as opposed to 2.39% when only four GCs are used. This represents a 59% reduction in recovery cost. These results demonstrate that the TROB is useful even with in RAT GC checkpointing.

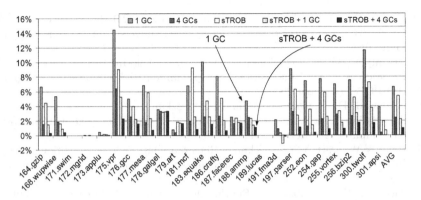

Fig. 9. Per-benchmark and average performance deterioration relative to PERF with GC-based recovery (one or four GCs), sTROB, and sTROB with GC-based recovery (sTROB with one or four GCs)

5 Conclusions

In this work, we presented "Turbo-ROB", a recovery accelerator that can complement or replace existing checkpoint/restore mechanisms. The TROB is a novel low cost and complexity structure that can be used to reduce the negative performance effects of checkpointing and restore in modern architectures. We have shown that TROB can completely replace a ROB and studied its performance assuming that repair points are initiated at every branch. We have also shown that the TROB can complement a conventional ROB acting as an accelerator. Additional benefits were possible with larger TROBs. Finally, we have shown that TROB can reduce the pressure for global checkpoints in the RAT.

Acknowledgements

We would like to thank the anonymous reviewers for their time and comments. This work was supported by an NSERC Discovery Grant, an equipment grant from the Canada Foundation for Innovation and from an equipment donation from Intel Corporation.

References

[1] Akkary, H., Rajwar, R., Srinivasan, S.: An Analysis of Resource Efficient Checkpoint Architecture. ACM Transactions on Architecture and Code Optimization (TACO) 1(4) (December 2004)

[2] Akkary, H., Rajwar, R., Srinivasan, S.: Checkpoint Processing and Recovery: Towards Scalable Instruction Window Processors. In: Proceedings of the 36th Annual IEEE/ACM International Symposium on Microarchitecture (November 2003)

[3] Aragon, J.L., Gonzalez, J., Gonzalez, A., Smith, J.E.: Dual Path Instruction Processing. In: Proceedings of the 16th International Conference on Supercomputing, pp. 220–229 (June 2002)

[4] Burger, D., Austin, T.: The Simplescalar Tool Set v2.0, Technical Report UW-CS-97-1342., Computer Sciences Department, University of Wisconsin-Madison (June 1997)

[5] Cristal, A., Ortega, D., Llosa, J., Valero, M.: Kilo-Instruction Processors. In: Proceedings The 5th International Symposium on High Performance Computing (ISHPC-V) (October 2003)

[6] Grunwald, D., Klauser, A., Manne, S., Pleszkun, A.: Confidence Estimation for Speculation Control. In: Proceedings of the 25th Annual International Symposium on Computer Architecture (June 1998)

[7] Hwu, W.W., Patt, Y.N.: Checkpoint Repair for Out-of-Order Execution Machines. In: Proceedings of the 14th Annual Symposium on Computer Architecture (June 1987)

[8] Jacobsen, E., Rotenberg, E., Smith, J.E.: Assigning Confidence to Conditional Branch Predictions. In: Proceedings of the 29th Annual International Symposium on Microarchitecture (Decmber 1996)

[9] Jimenez, D.A., Lin, C.: Composite Confidence Estimators for Enhanced Speculation Control, Technical Report TR-02-14, Department of Computer Sciences, The University of Texas at Austin (January 2002)

[10] Manne, S., Klauser, A., Grunwald, D.: Pipeline Gating: Speculation Control for Energy Reduction. In: Proceedings of the 25th Annual International Symposium on Computer Architecture (June 1998)

[11] Moshovos, A.: Checkpointing Alternatives for High Performance, Power-Aware Processors. In: Proceedings of the IEEE International Symposium Low Power Electronic Devices and Design (ISLPED) (August 2003)

[12] Safi, E., Akl, P., Moshovos, A., Veneris, A., Arapoyianni, A.: On the Latency, Energy and Area of Superscalar Renaming Tables. In: Proceedings of the IEEE/ACM International Symposium on Low Power Electronics and Devices (August 2007)

[13] Smith, J., Pleszkun, A.: Implementing Precise Interrupts in Pipelined Processors. IEEE Transactions on Computers 37(5) (May 1988)

[14] Sohi, G.S.: Instruction Issue Logic for High-Performance, Interruptible, Multiple Functional Unit, Pipelined Computers. IEEE Transactions on Computers (March 1990)

[15] Yeager, K.C.: The MIPS R10000 Superscalar Microprocessor. IEEE MICRO (1996)

[16] Zhou, P., Onder, S., Carr, S.: Fast Branch Misprediction Recovery in Out-of-Order Superscalar Processors. In: Proceedings of the International Conference on Supercomputing (June 2005)

LPA: A First Approach to the Loop Processor Architecture

Alejandro García[1], Oliverio J. Santana[2], Enrique Fernández[2], Pedro Medina[2], and Mateo Valero[13]

[1] Universitat Politècnica de Catalunya, Spain
{juanaleg,mateo}@ac.upc.edu
[2] Universidad de Las Palmas de Gran Canaria, Spain
{ojsantana,efernandez,pmedina}@dis.ulpgc.es
[3] Barcelona Supercomputing Center, Spain

Abstract. Current processors frequently run applications containing loop structures. However, traditional processor designs do not take into account the semantic information of the executed loops, failing to exploit an important opportunity. In this paper, we take our first step toward a loop-conscious processor architecture that has great potential to achieve high performance and relatively low energy consumption.

In particular, we propose to store simple dynamic loops in a buffer, namely the loop window. Loop instructions are kept in the loop window along with all the information needed to build the rename mapping. Therefore, the loop window can directly feed the execution back-end queues with instructions, avoiding the need for using the prediction, fetch, decode, and rename stages of the normal processor pipeline. Our results show that the loop window is a worthwhile complexity-effective alternative for processor design that reduces front-end activity by 14% for SPECint benchmarks and by 45% for SPECfp benchmarks.

1 Introduction

Recent years have witnessed an enormous growth of the distance between the memory and the ALUs, that is, the distance between where the instructions are stored and where computation actually happens. In order to overcome this gap, current superscalar processors try to exploit as much instruction-level parallelism (ILP) as possible by increasing the number of instructions executed per cycle.

Increasing the amount of ILP available to standard superscalar processor designs involves increasing both the number of pipeline stages and the complexity of the logic required to complete instruction execution. The search for mechanisms that reduce design complexity without loosing the ability of exploiting ILP is always an interesting research field for computer architects.

In this paper, we focus on high-level loop structures. It is well known that most applications execute just 10% of their static instructions during 90% of their run time [1]. This fact is mainly due to the presence of loop structures. However, although loops are frequent entities in program execution, standard superscalar

P. Stenström et al. (Eds.): HiPEAC 2008, LNCS 4917, pp. 273–287, 2008.

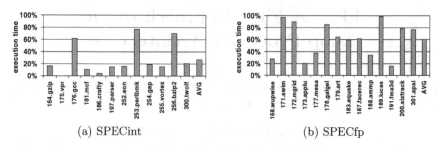

Fig. 1. Percentage of time executing simple dynamic loops

processors do not have any information about whether or not the individual instructions executed belong to a loop. Indeed, when an instruction reaches the execution engine of the processor after being fetched, decoded, and renamed, it retains little or none algorithmic semantic information. Each instruction only remembers its program order, kept in a structure like the reorder buffer (ROB), as well as the basic block it belongs to support speculation.

Our objective is to introduce the semantic information of high-level loop structures into the processor. A loop-conscious architecture would be able to exploit ILP in a more complexity-effective way, also enabling the possibility of rescheduling instructions and optimizing code dynamically. However, this is not an easy design task and must be developed step by step. Our first approach to design the Loop Processor Architecture (LPA) is to capture and store already renamed instructions in a buffer that we call the loop window.

In order to simplify the design of our proposal, we take into account just simple dynamic loops that execute a single control path, that is, the loop body does not contain any branch instruction whose direction changes during loop execution. We have found that simple dynamic loops are frequent structures in our benchmark programs. Figure 1 shows the percentage of simple dynamic loops in the SPECint2000 and SPECfp2000 programs. On average, they are responsible for 28% and 60% of the execution time respectively.

The execution of a simple dynamic loop implies the repetitive execution of the same group of instructions (loop instructions) during each loop iteration. In a conventional processor design, the same loop branch is predicted as taken once per iteration. Any existing branch inside the loop body will be predicted to have the same behavior in all iterations. Furthermore, loop instructions are fetched, decoded, and renamed once and again up to all loop iterations complete. Such a repetitive process involves a great waste of energy, since the structures responsible for these tasks cause a great part of the overall processor energy consumption. For instance, the first level instruction cache is responsible for 10%–20% [2], the branch predictor is responsible for 10% or more [3], and the rename logic is responsible for 15% [4].

The main objective of the initial LPA design presented in this paper is to avoid this energy waste. Since the instructions are stored in the loop window, there is no need to use the branch predictor, the instruction cache, and the decoding logic. Furthermore, the loop window contains enough information to build the

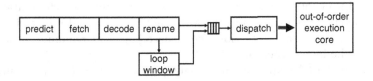

Fig. 2. LPA Architecture

rename mapping of each loop iteration, and thus there is no need to access the rename mapping table and the dependence detection and resolution circuitry.

According to our results, the loop window is able to greatly reduce the processor energy consumption. On average, the activity of the processor front-end is reduced by 14% for SPECint benchmarks and by 45% for SPECfp benchmarks. In addition, the loop window is able to fetch instructions at a faster rate than the normal front-end pipeline because it is not limited by taken branches or instruction alignment in memory. However, our results show that the performance gain achievable is limited due to the size of the main back-end structures in current processor designs. Consequently, we evaluate the potential of our loop window approach in a large instruction window processor [5] with virtually unbounded structures, showing that up to 40% performance speedup is achievable.

2   The LPA Architecture

The objective of our first approach to LPA is to replace the functionality of the prediction, fetch, decode, and rename stages during the execution of simple loop structures, as shown in Figure 2. To do this, the renamed instructions that belong to a simple loop structure are stored in a buffer that we call *loop window*. Once all the loop information required is stored in the loop window, it is able to feed the dispatch logic with already decoded and renamed instructions, making unnecessary all previous pipeline stages.

The loop window has very simple control logic, so the implementation of this scheme has little impact on the processor hardware cost. When a backward branch is predicted taken, LPA starts loop detection. All the decoded and renamed instructions after this point are then stored in the loop window during the second iteration of the loop. If the same backward branch is found and it is taken again, then LPA has effectively stored the loop. The detection of data dependences is done during the third iteration of the loop. When the backward branch is taken by the third time, LPA contains all the information it needs about the loop structure.

From this point onwards, LPA is able to fetch the instructions belonging to the loop from the loop window, and thus the branch predictor and the instruction cache are not used. Since these instructions are already decoded, there is no need to use the decoding logic. Moreover, the loop window stores enough information to build the register rename map, and thus there is no need to access the rename mapping table and the dependence detection and resolution circuitry. Therefore, whenever LPA captures a loop, the instructions belonging to each iteration of the loop are fetched from the loop window already decoded and renamed, avoiding the need for using the prediction, fetch, decoding, and renaming logic during almost all the loop execution.

Our current LPA implementation only supports simple loop structures having a single control path inside. The appearance of an alternative path will be detected when a branch inside the loop body causes a misprediction. Therefore, the loop window is flushed at branch mispredictions, regardless the loop is still being stored or it is already being fetched from the loop window. After flushing the loop window contents, execution starts again using the normal prediction, fetch, decoding, and renaming logic.

2.1 The Renaming Mechanism

The objective of the renaming logic is to remove data dependences between instructions by providing multiple storage locations (physical registers) for the same logical register. The target register of each renamed instruction receives a physical register that is used both to keep track of data dependences and to store the value produced by the instruction. The association between logical and physical registers is kept in a structure called rename table.

Our loop window proposal is orthogonal to any prediction, fetch, and decode scheme, but it requires to decouple register renaming from physical register allocation. Instead of assigning a physical register to every renamed instruction, our architecture assigns a tag as done by virtual register [6]. This association is kept in a table that we call LVM (Logical-to-Virtual Map table). In this way, dependence tracking is effectively decoupled from value storage. Virtual tags are enough to keep track of data dependences, and thus physical register assignment is delayed until instructions are issued for execution, optimizing the usage of the available physical registers.

The LVM is a direct mapped table indexed by the logical register number, that is, it has as many entries as logical registers exist in the processor ISA. Each entry contains the virtual tag associated to the corresponding logical register. When an instruction is renamed, the LVM is looked up to obtain the virtual tags associated to the logical source registers (a maximum of two read accesses per instruction). In addition, the target register receives a virtual tag from a list of free tags. The LVM is updated with the new association between the target register and the virtual tag to allow subsequent instructions getting the correct mapping (a maximum of one update access per instruction).

Our virtual tags are actually divided into two subtags: the root virtual tag (rVT) and the iteration-dependent virtual tag (iVT). When a virtual tag is assigned to a logical register, the rVT field in the corresponding entry of the LVM receives the appropriate value from the list of free virtual tags, while the iVT field is initialized to zero. The instructions that do not belong to a captured loop will keep iVT to zero during all their execution, using just rVT for tracking dependences.

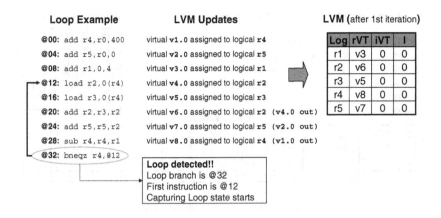

Fig. 3. Loop detection after the execution of its first iteration

The transparency of this process is an important advantage of LPA: there is no need for functional changes in the processor design beyond introducing the loop window and the two-component virtual tag renaming scheme. The out-of-order superscalar execution core will behave in the same way regardless it receives instructions from the normal pipeline or from the loop window.

2.2 Loop Detection and Storage

When a backward branch is predicted taken, LPA enters in the Capturing Loop state. Figure 3 shows an example of a loop structure that is detected by LPA at the end of its first iteration, that is, when the branch instruction finalizing the loop body is predicted taken. The backward branch is considered the loop branch and its target address is considered the first instruction of the loop body. Therefore, the loop body starts at instruction @12 and finalizes at the loop branch @32.

During the Capturing Loop state, the instructions belonging to the loop body are stored in the loop window. Data dependences between these instructions are resolved using the renaming mechanism. Figure 3 shows a snapshot of the LVM contents after the first loop iteration. We assume that there are just five logical registers in order to simplify the graph. Instructions are renamed in program order. Each instruction receives a virtual tag that is stored in the corresponding rVT field, while the iVT field is initialized to zero.

In addition, each LVM entry contains a bit (I) that indicates whether a logical register is inside a loop body and is iteration dependent. The I bit is always initialized to zero. The value of the I bit is only set to one for those logical registers that receive a new virtual register during the Capturing Loop state. An I bit set to one indicates that the associated logical register is iteration-dependent, that is, it is defined inside the loop body and thus its value is produced by an instruction from the current or the previous iteration.

Loop Example

→ @12: load r2,0(r4)   virtual **v9.0** assigned to logical **r2** (v6.0 out)
@16: load r3,0(r4)   virtual **v10.0** assigned to logical **r3** (v5.0 out)
@20: add r2,r3,r2   virtual **v11.0** assigned to logical **r2** (v9.0 out)
@24: add r5,r5,r2   virtual **v12.0** assigned to logical **r5** (v7.0 out)
@28: sub r4,r4,r1   virtual **v13.0** assigned to logical **r4** (v8.0 out)
└─ @32: bneqz r4,@12

LVM Updates

LVM (after 2nd iteration)

Log	rVT	iVT	I
r1	v3	0	0
r2	v11	0	1
r3	v10	0	1
r4	v13	0	1
r5	v12	0	1

Loop Window

Instruction	@12				@16				@20				@24				@28				@32			
Operand #1	r4	v8	0	0	r4	v8	0	0	r3	v10	0	1	r5	v7	0	0	r4	v8	0	0	r4	v13	0	1
Operand #2	x	x	x	x	x	x	x	x	r2	v9	0	1	r2	v11	0	1	r1	v3	0	0	x	x	x	x
Target	r2	v9	0	1	r3	v10	0	1	r2	v11	0	1	r5	v12	0	1	r4	v13	0	1	x	x	x	x
	Log	rVP	iVP	I	Log	rVP	iVP	I	Log	rVP	iVP	I	Log	rVP	iVP	I	Log	rVP	iVP	I	Log	rVP	iVP	I

Fig. 4. Loop storage during its second iteration

Loop Example

→ @12: load r2,0(r4)   virtual **v9.1** assigned to logical **r2** (v11.0 out)
@16: load r3,0(r4)   virtual **v10.1** assigned to logical **r3** (v10.0 out)
@20: add r2,r3,r2   virtual **v11.1** assigned to logical **r2** (v9.1 out)
@24: add r5,r5,r2   virtual **v12.1** assigned to logical **r5** (v12.0 out)
@28: sub r4,r4,r1   virtual **v13.1** assigned to logical **r4** (v13.0 out)
└─ @32: bneqz r4,@12

LVM Updates

LVM (after 3rd iteration)

Log	rVT	iVT	I
r1	v3	0	0
r2	v11	1	1
r3	v10	1	1
r4	v13	1	1
r5	v12	1	1

Loop Window

Instruction	@12				@16				@20				@24				@28				@32			
Operand #1	r4	v13	0	1	r4	v13	0	1	r3	v10	1	1	r5	v12	0	1	r4	v13	0	1	r4	v13	1	1
Operand #2	x	x	x	x	x	x	x	x	r2	v9	1	1	r2	v11	1	1	r1	v3	0	0	x	x	x	x
Target	r2	v9	1	1	r3	v10	1	1	r2	v11	1	1	r5	v12	1	1	r4	v13	1	1	x	x	x	x
	Log	rVP	iVP	I	Log	rVP	iVP	I	Log	rVP	iVP	I	Log	rVP	iVP	I	Log	rVP	iVP	I	Log	rVP	iVP	I

Fig. 5. Removal of dependences during the third loop iteration

Figure 4 shows a snapshot of the LVM at the end of the second iteration of our loop example, as well as the state of the loop window. All the instructions belonging to the loop body are stored in order in this buffer. Since the instructions are already decoded, the loop window should contain the instruction PC and the operation code. It should also contain the source registers, the target register, and any immediate value provided by the original instruction. In addition, each entry of the loop window should contain the renaming data for the source and target registers of the corresponding instruction, that is, the values of the rVT, iVT, and I fields of the corresponding LVM entries at the moment in which the instruction was renamed.

When the second iteration of the loop finishes and the taken backward branch is found again, then the full loop body has been stored in the loop window. However, there is not yet enough information in the loop window to allow LPA providing renamed instructions. For instance, take a look at the example in Figure 4. Instruction @32 reads the logical register $r4$. The loop window states that the value contained by this register is written by instruction @28 (virtual tag $v13.0$). This dependence is correct, since it will remain the same during all iterations of the loop. In the next iteration of the loop, instruction @12 will also read logical register $r4$. However, the loop window does not contain the correct virtual tag value ($v9.0$ instead of $v13.0$). It happens because the loop window states that the register value depends on an instruction outside the captured loop, which was true for that iteration but not for the subsequent ones.

In order to correctly capture dependences between the instructions inside the loop body, it is necessary to execute a third iteration of the loop. Therefore, when the second iteration finishes, LPA exits the Capturing Loop state and enters the Capturing Dependences state. LPA remains in the Capturing Dependences state during the third iteration of the loop. The source operands of the instructions are renamed as usual, checking the corresponding entries of the LVM. As happened during the previous iteration, the contents of the LVM entries are also stored in the loop window. However, when the target register of an instruction requires a new virtual tag, the rVT component of the tag does not change. New virtual tags are generated increasing the value of the iVT component by one.

Figure 5 shows a snapshot of the LVM at the end of the third iteration of our loop example, as well as the state of the loop window. Now, the dependence between instruction @28 and instruction @12 is correctly stored. Instruction @28 in the second iteration generates a value that is associated to virtual tag @13.0 (Figure 4). In the current iteration, instruction @12 reads the value associated to virtual tag @13.0, while the new instance of instruction @28 generates a new value that is associated to virtual tag @13.1 and later read by instruction @32. Extending this mapping for the next iteration is straightforward, since it is only necessary to increment the iVT field by one. During the fourth iteration, instruction @12 will read the value associated to virtual tag $v13.1$ and instruction @28 will generate a value that will be associated to virtual tag $v13.2$ and later read by instruction @32.

2.3 Fetching from the Loop Window

After the third iteration finishes, the loop window contains enough information to feed the dispatch logic with instructions that are already decoded and renamed. Figure 6 shows how to generalize the information stored during previous loop iterations. Let i be the current loop iteration. The rVT values assigned to all registers remain equal during the whole loop execution. The instructions that store a value in a register during current iteration get the value i for the iVT component of the virtual tag associated to its target. Those instructions that read a value defined in the previous iteration will get the value $i - 1$ for the iVT component, while those instructions that read a value defined in the current iteration will get the value i for the iVT component. Instructions that read a value defined outside the loop body will get the value 0 for the iVT component.

When an instruction is fetched from the loop window, the rVT value stored in the loop window is maintained for both the source operands and the target register. For each of these registers that has the I bit set to one, the iVT value stored in the loop window is increased by one to generate the new virtual tag that will be used in the next loop iteration. The iVT value is not increased if the

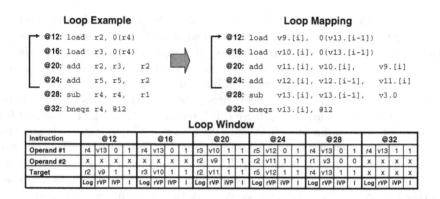

Fig. 6. Generalization of the rename map obtained by LPA for our loop example

I bit value is zero, since it indicates that the value is not iteration-dependent, that is, it has been defined by an instruction outside the loop body and remains the same during all the loop execution.

For example, Figure 6 shows the state of the loop window after the third loop iteration. All the values generated during this iteration are associated to virtual tags whose iVT component value is one. During the fourth iteration, instructions @12 and @16 increment the iVT value of their source register in order to generate the correct virtual tag ($v13.1$) that allows accessing the correct value generated by instruction @28 in the previous iteration. In addition, instructions @12 and @16 store this tag in the loop window. At the end of the fourth iteration, instruction @28 generates a new value that is associated to the virtual tag obtained from increasing the iVT value stored for its target register. In the fifth iteration, instructions @12 and @16 increase again the iVT value to access the correct target of instruction @28 ($v13.2$) and so on. Meanwhile, instruction @28 always read the same value for its source register $r1$, since its I bit value is zero, and thus it does not vary during the loop execution ($v3.0$). From this point onwards, there is no change in the normal behavior of the processor shown in Figure 2. Physical registers are assigned at the dispatch stage, regardless the instructions come from the loop window or the original pipeline, and then the instructions are submitted for execution to the out-of-order superscalar back-end. In other words, LPA is orthogonal to the dispatch logic and the out-of-order superscalar execution core.

3   Experimental Methodology

The results in this paper have been obtained using trace driven simulation of a superscalar processor. Our simulator uses a static basic block dictionary to allow simulating the effect of wrong path execution. This model includes the simulation of wrong speculative predictor history updates, as well as the possible interference and prefetching effects on the instruction cache.

Table 1. Configuration of the simulated processor

fetch, rename, and commit width	6 instructions
int and fp issue width	6 instructions
load/store issue width	6 instructions
int, fp, and load/store issue queues	64 entries
reorder buffer	256 entries
int and fp point registers	160 registers
conditional branch predictor	64K-entry gshare
branch target buffer	1024-entry 4-way
RAS	32-entry
L1 instruction cache	64 KB, 2-way associative, 64 byte block
L1 data cache	64 KB, 2-way associative, 64 byte block
L2 unified cache	1 MB, 4-way associative, 128 byte block
main memory latency	100 cycles

Our simulator models a 10-stage processor pipeline. In order to provide results representative of current superscalar processor designs, we have configured the simulator as a 6-instruction wide processor. Table 1 shows the main values of our simulation setup. The processor pipeline is modeled as described in the previous section. We have evaluated a wide range of loop-window setups and chosen a 128-instruction loop window because it is able to capture most simple dynamic loops. Larger loop windows would only provide marginal benefits that do not compensate the increased implementation cost.

We feed our simulator with traces of 300 million instructions collected from the SPEC2000 integer and floating point benchmarks using the *reference* input set. Benchmarks were compiled on a DEC Alpha AXP 21264 [7] processor with Digital UNIX V4.0 using the standard DEC C V5.9-011, Compaq C++ V6.2-024, and Compaq Fortran V5.3-915 compilers with -O2 optimization level. To find the most representative execution segment we have analyzed the distribution of basic blocks as described in [8].

4   LPA Evaluation

In this section, we evaluate our loop window approach. We show that the loop window is able to provide great reductions in the processor front-end activity. We also show that the performance gains achievable are limited by the size of the main back-end structures. However, if an unbounded back-end is available, the loop window can provide important performance speedups.

4.1   Front-End Activity

The loop window replaces the functionality of the prediction, fetch, decode, and rename pipeline stages, allowing to reduce their activity. Figure 7 shows the activity reduction achieved for both SPECint and SPECfp 2000 benchmarks. On average, the loop window reduces the front-end activity by 14% for SPECint

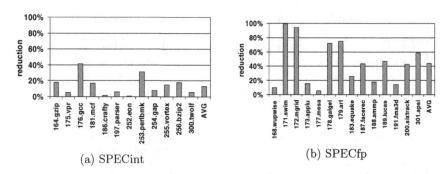

Fig. 7. Reduction in the activity of the prediction, fetch, decode, and rename stages

benchmarks. This reduction ranges from less than 2% in *186.crafty* and *252.eon* up to more than 40% in *176.gcc*. The reduction is higher for the SPECfp benchmarks, since they have more simple dynamic loops. On average, SPECfp achieve 45% activity reduction, ranging from 6% in *177.mesa* to more than 95% in *171.swim* and *172.mgrid*.

This activity reduction involves saving processor energy consumption. Reducing the total number of branch predictions involves reducing the number of accesses to the branch prediction mechanism. Reducing the number of instructions processed by the front-end involves reducing the number of accesses to the instruction cache, the decoding logic, the LVM, and the dependence check and resolution circuitry.

Although we are currently working on modeling the actual energy consumption of the processor front-end and the loop window, we are not ready yet to provide insight about this topic. Nevertheless, we are confident that the high reduction achieved in the processor front-end activity will more than compensate the additional consumption of the loop window itself, showing that the loop window is a valuable complexity-effective alternative for the design of high-performance superscalar processors.

4.2   Performance Evaluation

The loop window is able to improve processor performance because, unlike the normal front-end pipeline, it is not limited by taken branches and by the alignment of instructions in cache lines. Consequently, the loop window is able to provide instructions to the dispatch logic at a faster rate. This faster speed makes it possible to reduce the width of the processor front-end, and thus reduce its design complexity.

In this section, we evaluate the impact on performance caused by reducing the width of the processor front-end. Figure 8 shows the IPC speedup achieved by a 6-instruction wide superscalar processor (right bar) over a similar processor whose front-end is limited to just 4-instructions. As expected, increasing the front-end width from 4 to 6 instructions improves overall performance. On average, SPECint benchmarks achieve 3.3% speedup and SPECfp benchmarks

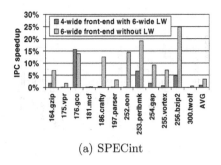

(a) SPECint

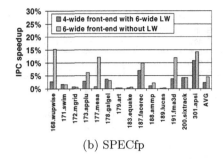

(b) SPECfp

Fig. 8. Performance speedup over a 4-wide front-end processor (back-end is always 6-wide)

achieve 4.5% speedup. The improvement is larger for SPECfp benchmarks because branch instructions are better predicted, and thus it is possible to extract more ILP.

The left bar shows the speedup achieved when the front-end is still limited to 4 instructions, but a loop window able to fetch up to 6 instructions per cycle is included. This loop window allows reducing the front-end activity. In addition, a 4-instruction wide front-end is less complex than a 6-wide one. However, it becomes clear from these results that adding a loop window is not enough for the 4-wide front-end to achieve the performance of the 6-wide front-end. It only achieves comparable performance in a few benchmarks like *176.gcc*, *200.sixtrack*, and *301.apsi*. On average, SPECint benchmarks achieve 1% IPC speedup and SPECfp achieve 2.3% speedup.

The loop window is not able to reach the performance of a wider processor front-end because the most important back-end structures are completely full most of the time, that is, back-end saturation is limiting the potential benefit of our proposal. Figure 9 shows performance speedup for the same setups previously shown in Figure 8, but using an unbounded back-end, that is, the ROB, the issue queues, and the register file are scaled to infinite.

The loop window achieves higher performance speedups for SPECint and especially SPECfp benchmarks. Furthermore, the loop window using a 4-wide front-end achieves better performance than the 6-wide front-end in several benchmarks: *176.gcc* (SPECint), *172.mgrid*, *178 galgel*, and *179.art*. Those benchmarks have a high amount of simple dynamic loops, enabling the loop window to fetch instructions at a faster rate than normal front-end most of time.

5   Related Work

To exploit instruction level parallelism, it is essential to have a large window of candidate instructions available to issue. Reusing loop instructions is a well-known technique in this field, since the temporal locality present in loops provides a good opportunity for loop caching. Loop buffers were developed in the sixties for the CDC 6600/6700 series [9] to minimize the time wasted due to conditional

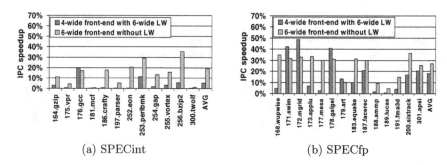

(a) SPECint   (b) SPECfp

Fig. 9. Performance speedup over a 4-wide front-end processor using an unbounded 6-wide back-end

branches, which could severely limit performance in programs composed of short loops. The IBM/360 model 91 introduced the loop mode execution as a way of reducing the effective fetch bandwidth requirements [10,11]. When a loop is detected in an 8-word prefetch buffer, the loop mode activates. Instruction fetch from memory is stalled and all branch instructions are predicted to be taken. On average, the loop mode was active 30% of the execution time.

Nowadays, hardware-based loop caching has been mainly used in embedded systems to reduce the energy consumption of the processor fetch engine. Lee et al. [12] describe a buffering scheme for simple dynamic loops with a single execution path. It is based on detecting backward branches (loop branches) and capturing the loop instruction in a direct-mapped array (loop buffer). In this way, the instruction fetch energy consumption is reduced. In addition, a loop buffer dynamic controller (LDC) avoids penalties due to loop cache misses. Although this LDC only captures simple dynamic loops, it was recently improved [13] to detect and capture nested loops, loops with complex internal control-flow, and portions of loops that are too large to fit completely in a loop cache. This loop controller is a finite machine that provides more sophisticated utilization of the loop cache.

Unlike the techniques mentioned above, our mechanism is not only focused on reducing the energy consumption of the fetch engine. The main contribution of LPA is our novel rename mapping building algorithm, which makes it possible for our proposal to reduce the consumption of the rename logic, which is one of the hot spots in processor designs. However, there is still room for improvement. The implementation presented in this paper only captures loops with a single execution path. However, in general-purpose applications, 50% of the loops has variable-dependent trip counts and/or contains conditional branches in their bodies. Therefore, future research effort should be devoted to enhance our renaming model for capturing more complex structures in the loop window.

Although our mechanism is based on capturing simple loops that are mostly predictable by traditional branch predictors, improving loop branch prediction would be beneficial for some benchmarks with loop branches that are not so predictable. In addition, advanced loop prediction would be very useful to enable LPA to capture more complex loop patterns. Many mechanisms have been developed to predict the behavior of loops. Sherwood et al. [14] use a Loop Termination Buffer (LTB) to predict patterns of loop branches (backward branches). The LTB stores the number of times that a loop branch is taken and a loop iteration counter is used to store the current iteration of the loop. Alba and Kaeli [15] use a mechanism to predict several loop characteristics: internal control flow, number of loop visits, number of iterations per loop visit, dynamic loop body size, and patterns leading up to the loop visit. Any of these techniques can be used in conjunction with our loop window to improve its efficiency.

Regarding our rename map building algorithm, there are other architectural proposals that try to remove instruction dependences without using a traditional renaming logic. Dynamic Vectorization [16,17] detects and captures loop structures like LPA does. This architecture saves fetch and decode power by fetching already decoded instructions from the loop storage. Rename information is also reused but it relies on a trace-processor implementation to achieve this goal. Those registers that are local to loops are renamed to special-purpose register queues, avoiding the need for renaming them in the subsequent iterations. However, only local registers take advantage of this mechanism. The live-on-entry and live-on-exit registers are still renamed once per iteration, since they are hold on a global register file using global mapping tables.

The Execution Cache Microarchitecture [18] is a more recent proposal that has some resemblance with Dynamic Vectorization. This architecture stores and reuses dynamic traces, but they are later executed using a traditional superscalar processor core instead of a trace-processor. Rename information is also reused by this architecture. However, like Dynamic Vectorization, it does not use a traditional register file but a rotating register scheme that assigns each renamed register to a register queue.

The main advantage of LPA is that it does not require such a specialized architecture. LPA can be applied to any traditional register file design. Therefore, the design and implementation cost of our proposal would be lower. In addition, all the optimization techniques developed for previous architectures like Dynamic Vectorization can be applied orthogonally. This will be an important research line to improve the performance-power features of LPA in a near future.

6   Conclusions

The Loop Processor Architecture (LPA) is focused on capturing the semantic information of high-level loop structures and using it for optimizing program execution. Our initial LPA design uses a buffer, namely the loop window, to dynamically detect and store the instructions belonging to simple dynamic loops with a single execution path. The loop window stores enough information to build the rename mapping, and thus it can feed directly the instruction queues of the processor, avoiding the need for using the prediction, fetch, decode, and rename stages of the normal processor front-end.

The LPA implementation presented in this paper reduces the front-end activity, on average, by 14% for the SPECint benchmarks and by 45% for the

SPECfp benchmarks. However, the performance gain achievable by the loop window is seriously limited by the size of the back-end structures in current processor designs. If an unbounded back-end with unlimited structures is available, the loop window achieves better performance than a traditional front-end design, even if this front-end is wider. The speedup achieved by some benchmarks like *171.swim*, *172.mgrid*, and *178.galgel* is over 40%, which suggests that the loop window could be a worthwhile contribution to the design of future large instruction window processors [5].

These results show that even the simple LPA approach presented in this paper can improve performance and, especially, reduce energy consumption. Furthermore, this is our first step towards a comprehensive LPA design that extracts all the possibilities of introducing the semantic information of loop structures into the processor. We plan to analyze loop prediction mechanisms and implement them in conjunction with the loop window. In addition, if the loop detection is guided by the branch predictor, the loop window can be managed in a more efficient way, reducing the number of insertions required and optimizing energy consumption.

The coverage of our proposal is another interesting topic for research. We only capture now simple dynamic loops with a single execution path, but we will extend our renaming scheme to enable capturing more complex loops that include hammock structures, that is, several execution paths. Increasing coverage will also benefit the possibility of applying dynamic optimization techniques to the instructions stored in the loop window, and especially those optimizations focused on loops, improving the processor performance. In general, we consider LPA is a worthwhile contribution for the computer architecture community, since our proposal has a great potential to improve processor performance and reduce energy consumption.

Acknowledgements

This work has been supported by the Ministry of Science and Technology of Spain under contract TIN2007-60625, the HiPEAC European Network of Excellence, and the Barcelona Supercomputing Center. We would like to thank the anonymous referees for their useful reviews that made it possible to improve our paper. We would also like to thank Adrián Cristal, Daniel Ortega, Francisco Cazorla, and Marco Antonio Ramírez for their comments and support.

References

1. de Alba, M.R., Kaeli, D.R.: Runtime predictability of loops. In: Proceedings of the 4th Workshop on Workload Characterization (2001)
2. Badulescu, A., Veidenbaum, A.: Energy efficient instruction cache for wide-issue processors. In: Proceedings of the International Workshop on Innovative Architecture (2001)

3. Parikh, D., Skadron, K., Zhang, Y., Barcella, M., Stan, M.: Power issues related to branch prediction. In: Proceedings of the 8th International Symposium on High-Performance Computer Architecture (2002)
4. Folegnani, D., González, A.: Energy-effective issue logic. In: Proceedings of the 28th International Symposium on Computer Architecture (2001)
5. Cristal, A., Santana, O., Cazorla, F., Galluzzi, M., Ramírez, T., Pericàs, M., Valero, M.: Kilo-instruction processors: Overcoming the memory wall. IEEE Micro 25(3) (2005)
6. Monreal, T., González, J., González, A., Valero, M., Viñals, V.: Late allocation and early release of physical registers. IEEE Transactions on Computers 53(10) (2004)
7. Gwennap, L.: Digital 21264 sets new standard. Microprocessor Report 10(14) (1996)
8. Sherwood, T., Perelman, E., Calder, B.: Basic block distribution analysis to find periodic behavior and simulation points in applications. In: Proceedings of the 15th International Conference on Parallel Architectures and Compilation Techniques (2001)
9. Thornton, J.E.: Parallel operation in the Control Data 6600. In: Proceedings of the AFIPS Fall Joint Computer Conference (1964)
10. Tomasulo, R.M.: An efficient algorithm for exploiting multiple arithmetic units. IBM Journal of Research and Development 11(1) (1967)
11. Anderson, D.W., Sparacio, F.J., Tomasulo, R.M.: The IBM System/360 model 91: Machine philosophy and instruction-handling. IBM Journal of Research and Development 11(1) (1967)
12. Lee, L.H., Moyer, W., Arends, J.: Instruction fetch energy reduction using loop caches for embedded applications with small tight loops. In: International Symposium on Low Power Electronics and Design (1999)
13. Rivers, J.A., Asaad, S., Wellman, J.D., Moreno, J.H.: Reducing instruction fetch energy with backward branch control information and buffering. In: International Symposium on Low Power Electronics and Design (2003)
14. Sherwood, T., Calder, B.: Loop termination prediction. In: Proceedings of the 3rd International Symposium on High Performance Computing (2000)
15. de Alba, M.R., Kaeli, D.R.: Path-based hardware loop prediction. In: Proceedings of the International Conference on Control, Virtual Instrumentation and Digital Systems (2002)
16. Vajapeyam, S., Mitra, T.: Improving superscalar instruction dispatch and issue by exploiting dynamic code sequences. In: Proceedings of the 24th International Symposium on Computer Architecture (1997)
17. Vajapeyam, S., Joseph, P.J., Mitra, T.: Dynamic vectorization: A mechanism for exploiting far-flung ILP in ordinary programs. In: Proceedings of the 24th International Symposium on Computer Architecture (1999)
18. Talpes, E., Marculescu, D.: Execution cache-based microarchitectures for power-efficient superscalar processors. IEEE Transactions on Very Large Scale Integration (VLSI) Systems 13(1) (2005)

Part VI

Profiles: Collection and Analysis

Complementing Missing and Inaccurate Profiling Using a Minimum Cost Circulation Algorithm

Roy Levin[1], Ilan Newman[2], and Gadi Haber[3]

[1] University of Haifa, Haifa, Israel
royl@dpolls.com
[2] University of Haifa, Haifa, Israel
ilan@cs.haifa.ac.il
[3] IBM Haifa Labs University Campus, Haifa, Israel
haber@il.ibm.com

Abstract. Edge profiling is a very common means for providing feedback on program behavior that can be used statically by an optimizer to produce highly optimized binaries. However collecting full edge profile carries a significant runtime overhead. This overhead creates addition problems for real-time applications, as it may prevent the system from meeting runtime deadlines and thus alter its behavior. In this paper we show how a low overhead sampling technique can be used to collect inaccurate profile which is later used to approximate the full edge profile using a novel technique based on the Minimum Cost Circulation Problem. The outcome is a machine independent profile gathering scheme that creates a slowdown of only 2%-3% during the training set, and produces an optimized binary which is only 0.6% less than a fully optimized one.

Keywords: Control Flow, Sampling, Profiling, Real-time, Circulations, Flow network.

1 Introduction

Control flow profiling is the determination of the number of time each edge/vertex is traversed in the flow graph of a program, when running a 'typical' input. Such profile can be obtained by adding instrumentation code or by using external sampling, and are extremely useful as they provide empirical information about the application such as determining performance critical areas in the code and deducing probabilities of conditional branches to be taken. Indeed, such methods have been used since the 70s. Profile driven optimizations are supported today in most modern compilers and post-link optimizers [6 – 13]. Profile-directed compilation uses information gathered in several ways: Run-time profiling which is mainly used today by dynamic optimizers such as the Java Just In Time (JIT) compiler, in which profile is collected at run-time. The problem with this approach is that it requires additional system resources at runtime, which may be undesirable in high performance low resource embedded applications, especially if they carry real time constraints. Another method for profile-driven optimization uses pre-selected representative workload which trains the program

P. Stenström et al. (Eds.): HiPEAC 2008, LNCS 4917, pp. 291–304, 2008.

on typical workloads and then uses this data to produce a highly optimized version. Finally, static profiling can be used by compilers as a method for predicting program's control flow, but such methods are not as effective as the previously mentioned options [4].

Collecting full edge profile requires creating instrumented code with edge counters that will increment upon execution and persist this data, typically by mapping it to some file. Thomas Ball and James R. Larus suggest algorithms for optimally inserting monitoring code to profile and trace programs and they report a slowdown of between 9% to 105% when comparing the original binary to the instrumented one [1]. Due to this slowdown, along with the extra build step which is required for instrumentation which also increases the complexity of the compilation/build process, many consider alternative approaches such as low overhead profiling [2]. In real time embedded applications another problem arises, as intrusive instrumentation code may alter real-time application behavior as a result of deadlines in the real time program that may be missed [21]. Therefore collecting profile for real-time applications calls for less intrusive profile collection techniques, such as low rate sampling, selective instrumentation or running the instrumented binary in a machine which is significantly stronger than target machine. However, using sampling techniques or selective instrumentation will produce both inaccurate and lacking profile information which may result in sub-optimal performance of an application optimized according to this profile.

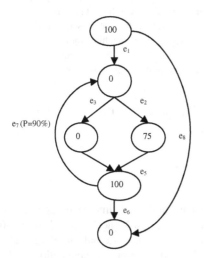

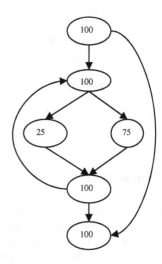

Fig. 1. – Partial vertex profile   **Fig. 2.** – The complete vertex profile

In this work, we present a new edge profile estimation algorithm based on given partial and possibly inaccurate vertex counts with costs attached to the edges and vertices. Our edge profile estimation is translated to the Minimum Cost Circulation Problem [5], which infuses a legal circulation in a flow network while keeping the weighted flow-costs on the edges at a minimum. The assumption is that by creating a legal network flow, while minimizing some criteria for the amount of global change

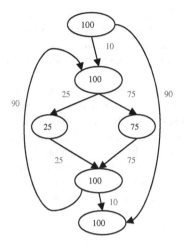

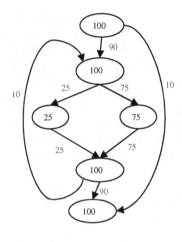

Fig. 2a. - Possible edge estimation 1   **Fig. 2b.** - Possible edge estimation 2

done to the given flow, it will provide a better estimate for the actual flow. We provide empirical proof for this assumption in the experimental results which appear in section 6. Let us consider the problem of filling in missing profile data. As an example, consider the control flow graph shown in figure 1 which includes partial vertex profiling collected by sampling the Instruction Complete hardware event (the numbers represent the execution counts for each vertex). From the given example, it is clear that the complete vertex counters which a zero value should be fixed as shown in figure 2.

However, determining the edge profile from the vertex counters alone is not always possible. In this example, the control flow graph shown in figure 2 has two possible edge profile estimates as shown in figures 2a and 2b.

Both optional estimates adhere to the flow conservation constraints but the differences between the edge weights may be very significant. The freedom to choose weight for edges e_1, e_6, e_7, e_8 may yield very different results. As one would expect, Youfeng Wu and James R. Larus [4], show that loop back edges have a very high probability to be taken. Keeping this in mind, we can determine that optional estimation 1 (from figure 2a), that infuses much more flow on edge e_7 has a much higher chance of achieving a better approximation of the actual flow. Any attempt to infuse flow on the graph's edges will have to be made aware of the probabilities on the edges to be taken. However, examining the probabilities locally is not optimal since if one decides to infuse a count of 50 on e_1 and on e_8 (as the probabilities on them may be equal) then that will determine a count of 50 on e_6 and on e_7 as well. This is undesirable, since we would want to infuse most of the flow through e_7 which is a back edge with high probability to be taken. Therefore, in order for a complementing algorithm to be successful it should have some global view of the edge probabilities. Indeed, in this example, the high probability of 90% for e_7, shown in figure 1, will guide our proposed algorithm's global view to prefer the 2nd estimated profile edge.

We know how to find optimal solution with respect to several cost functions. However, in order to test the applicability of our method for real life applications we, heuristically, tried several different cost functions that were assigned to a profile gathered by low-rate sampling profiling. This will be thoroughly explained in section 3, where we formulate the problem.

The paper is arranged in the following manner: section 2 describes additional related work on profile gathering techniques. Section 3 formulates the problem of complementing the missing profiling information to the Minimum Circulation problem. Section 4 and 5 describes the proposed algorithm for fixing the missing graph. The complete proof of the algorithm correctness has been taken out due to size limitations. Section 6 provides experimental results which were obtained by implementing the algorithm into FDPR post-link optimizer and running it on AIX POWER 5 SPEC INT 2000 suite. Finally, future directions are discussed in section 7 followed by a summary section.

2   Related Work for Profiling Techniques

Many papers have been written on techniques for collecting profile information. The issue is of major importance since the collected profile is very useful at guiding optimizing both static and dynamic compilers and post-link optimizers while the collection of the profile carries a significant overhead. The goal is therefore to collect accurate profile while keeping the runtime overhead of the profile collection to minimum.

J. Anderson et al present a method for collecting profile samples at a high rate and with low overhead [2]. To describe performance at the instruction level, they address two issues: how long each instruction stalls and the reasons for each stall. To determine stall latencies, an average CPI is computed for each instruction, using estimated execution frequencies. Accurate frequency estimates are recovered from profile data by a set of heuristics that use a detailed model of the processor pipeline and the constraints imposed by program control flow graphs to correlate sample counts for different instructions. The processor pipeline model explains static stalls; dynamic stalls are explained using a "guilty until proven innocent" approach that reports each possible cause not eliminated through careful analysis. In section 6.1.4 they refer to their Local Propagation algorithm and add a note that they are experimenting with a global constraint solver.

Additional papers suggest ways to collect profile information while reducing the overhead of the profile collection and attempting to keep the profile accuracy high at the same time. Matthew Arnold and Barbara G. Ryder [15] propose a framework that performs code duplication and uses compiler inserted counter-based sampling to switch between instrumented and non-instrumented code in a controlled fine-grained manner. Thomas Ball and James R. Larus suggest algorithms for optimally inserting monitoring code to profile and trace programs [1]. The algorithms optimize the placement of counting/tracing code with respect to the expected or measured frequency of each block or edge in a program's control-flow graph. Their idea is to find the lowest cost set of instrumentation points, when given a flow network and costs.

The technique proposed in our paper attempts to suggest a general, and global algorithm that can address filling in missing or inaccurate profile information, such as that which occurs when performing sampling but not limited to. For filling in, and fixing, the profile for the sampling case, we use an *instruction complete* event counter instead of sampling the program counter and then estimating the basic block frequencies using machine dependant heuristics.

3 Formulating the Problem

Our method is based on the assumption that by creating a legal network flow, while minimizing some criteria for the amount of weighted change done to the given flow, we can provide a better estimate to the actual flow that occurred. So the problem can be generalized and viewed as follows:

Given a directed graph $G = (V, E)$ with (integer) measured flow, $w(v)$, $w(e)$ for each vertex v and each edge e, the measured flows are assumed to be derived from inaccurate flow measurements in a given flow network. The inaccuracies may manifest themselves as discrepancies in the given flow network which break the flow conservation rule stating that for every $v \in V \setminus (S \cup T)$ the following should hold:

$$\sum_{e_{in} \in in(v)} w(e_{in}) = \sum_{e_{out} \in out(v)} w(e_{out}) = w(v) \tag{1}$$

S,T here are arbitrary given (possibly empty) subsets of V (of sources and sinks respectively) for which flow conservation is not demanded. In the application, these sets correspond to entry/ exit points in the control graph.   These can be the prologue/epilogue basic blocks if our control flow graph represents a single procedure, or entry points and exit points of a program if our control flow graph refers to the entire program. We refer to (1) as the *generalized flow conservation rule*.

The idea is that by fixing the flow to adhere to the *generalized flow conservation rule* while limiting the amount of weighted change to a minimum we will achieve a near approximation to the actual flow. Thus, a feasible solution to the problem is a *fixup vector*, ($\Delta(o): o \in V \cup E$), namely a vector of changes, one per each edge and vertex, for which the corrected flow $w^*(o) = w(o) + \Delta(o)$ yields a legal flow that satisfies the *generalized flow conservation* (1). We rank different feasible solutions by a cost function associated with each fixup vector and that is formally part of the input (in application this would be a heuristically chosen function as will be explained in the next section). Indeed our experimental results show that such optimal (or high rank) feasible solutions are a good approximation to the profiling problem.

Our algorithms can find optimal solution to the above formal problem for a wide variety of costs. Linear cost functions are theoretically easy to deal with, while not very practical, as it would imply that for each edge / vertex, either increasing the flow by an infinite amount, or decreasing it by an infinite amount is beneficial. A class of reasonable cost functions would be of the form:

$$\cos t(\Delta) = \sum_{o \in V \cup E} \cos t(\Delta(o)) = \sum_{o \in V \cup E} cp(o) \cdot |\Delta(o)| \tag{2}$$

Where $cp(o)$ is a non negative vector of coefficients. Such functions are monotone with the absolute amount of change for each edge/ vertex and are referred as *weighted* l_1 *costs*. Such functions give the ability, by chosing the right weights, to prefer changes to some edges than to others (e.g due to some a-priory knowledge of the reliability of the measurements at different sites). We can, however, do a bit more. Weighted l_1 costs do not distinguish between increasing and decreasing the flow at a site. It might be important for some edges to charge more for decreasing the flow than for increasing it (again, due to some prior knowledge on the flow). Thus we define:

$$\cos t(\Delta) = \sum_{o \in V \cup E} \cos t(\Delta(o)) = \sum_{o \in V \cup E} cp(o, \Delta) \cdot |\Delta(o)| \qquad (3)$$

Where the coefficient $cp(o,\Delta) = k^+(o)$ if $\Delta > 0$ and $cp(o,\Delta) = k^-(o)$ if $\Delta < 0$. These coefficients are called the *confidence constants*. Clearly such cost function generalizes weighted l_1 costs and will be referred to as *generalized* l_1.

In the following we solve the problem optimally for generalized l_1. Indeed we show in the experimental results that such functions can be used to obtain good practical results. We elaborate on other possible cost functions in the future directions section.

4 Polynomial Algorithm for Finding the Optimal Fixup Vector

To find the optimal generalized l_1 solution we use a reduction to minimum-cost circulation algorithm [5] which we apply on a transformed graph we call the fixup graph (see section 4.1). A circulation is a generalization of flow in a network in the sense that there is no source and sink, and thus flow conservation must be maintained for each and every vertex in the graph. A minimum-cost circulation is a circulation that satisfies the flow conservation for every vertex in the graph while keeping the weighted cost of the flow at a minimum (here the cost is a simple linear function, that is, for a circulation c=(c(e)) for every edge e, its cost is $\cos t(c) = \sum_{e \in E} k(e) \cdot c(e)$,

where k(e) is a non-negative weight for each edge e. The reduction is composed of two steps. In the first step, denoted as *vertex transformation*, we stay in the optimum flow fixup problem, but get rid of vertex flows and their corresponding costs. This is done by applying a standard vertex transformation which splits each vertex v into two vertices v' and v'', while distributing the incoming and outgoing edges respectively to v' and v''. The two resulting vertices, v' and v'', are then connected by an edge e^v, outgoing from v' and incoming to v''. We define the weight and cost functions for this new edge to be $w(e^v) \equiv w(v)$ and $k^{\pm}(e^v) \equiv k^{\pm}(v)$ so that $cp(e^v) = cp(v)$. Clearly this first step does not change the cost, thus we will assume in what follows that we only have edge folws and costs. In addition, we may assume that the set of sources is a singleton, that is S={s}, as other wise we just add a new source s' and connect it to every original source is S with an edge of cost 0. Thus original sources will conserve flow automatically with no additional costs while moving the surplus flow to the single source s'. Similarly, we may assume that there is a single sink t' by an analogue argument. Finally, we may insert a new directed edge of cost 0 from the single sink t to the single source s. This will turn any feasible flow to a circulation of the same cost. Thus we may assume that in fact $S=T=\varnothing$.

4.1 Constructing the Fixup Graph

Given a graph $G = (V, E)$ and its measured flow $w(v)$ and $w(e)$ for the vertices and edges respectively, as input for the optimal flow fixup, we wish to create a new graph $G' = (V', E')$ with given minimal and maximal capacity constraints (b, c) for each edge, herein the *fixup graph*. This transformation is formally defined below.

Input:

- $G_t = (V_t, E_t)$ denotes the original graph after applying the vertex transformation.

- $w(e)$ denotes the initial flow estimation for every edge $e \in E_t$ (this is thoroughly explained in section 5 under "**setting the constants**").

- $k^{\pm}(e)$ denotes the negative/positive *confidence constants* on any $e \in E_t$ (see section 3).

- Let $D(v) \equiv \sum_{e_l \in out(v)}(w(e_l)) - \sum_{e_k \in in(v)}(w(e_k))$ for every $v \in V_t$.

Output:

- $G' = (V', E')$ the *fixup graph*

- $b(e'), c(e')$ minimum/maximum capacities for flow on every edge $e' \in E'$

- $k(e')$ *positive confidence constant* for any $e' \in E'$ (note that infusing negative flow is not possible so here we do not need a *negative confidence constants*)

The output graph for the circulation problem is defined as follows:

1. $s' \leftarrow$ new Vertex, $t' \leftarrow$ new Vertex
2. $b(\langle t', s' \rangle) \leftarrow 0, c(\langle t', s' \rangle) \leftarrow \infty$
3. $cp(\langle t', s' \rangle) \leftarrow 0$
4. $E_r \leftarrow \phi, L \leftarrow \phi$
5. foreach $e \in E_t$ do:
    a. $b(e) \leftarrow 0, c(e) \leftarrow \infty, k'(e) \leftarrow k^{+}(e)$
6. foreach $e = \langle v, u \rangle \in E_t$ such that $\langle u, v \rangle \notin E_t$ do:
    a. $E_r \leftarrow E_r \cup \langle u, v \rangle$
    b. $k'(\langle u, v \rangle) \leftarrow k^{-}(\langle v, u \rangle), b(\langle u, v \rangle) \leftarrow 0, c(\langle u, v \rangle) \leftarrow w(e)$

7.   foreach $v \in V_t$ do:

    a.   if $D(v) > 0$ then

        i. $L \leftarrow L \cup \{\langle v, t' \rangle\}, b(\langle v, t' \rangle) \leftarrow D(v), c(\langle v, t' \rangle) \leftarrow D(v)$

    b.   if $D(v) < 0$ then

        i. $L \leftarrow L \cup \{\langle s', v \rangle\}, b(\langle s', v \rangle) \leftarrow -D(v), c(\langle s', v \rangle) \leftarrow -D(v)$

8. $V' \leftarrow V \cup \{s', t'\}$

9. $E' \leftarrow E \cup E_r \cup L \cup \langle t', s' \rangle$

Note that in the final phase of the construction we add an edge from t to s to create a circulation problem rather than a flow problem.

Any solution to the circulation problem is a flow function for each edge in E'. For each edge in the original graph, $e = \langle v, u \rangle \in E$ we then calculate the fixup vector,

$\Delta(e)$ as follows: $\Delta(e) = \begin{cases} f(v,u) & f(v,u) \geq 0 \\ -f(u,v) & f(u,v) < 0 \end{cases}$. By mapping back the edges

which were derived from the vertices when we applied the vertex transformation (the vertex splitting at the beginning of this section) we can determine the values of $\Delta(v)$ for each v in V as well.

4.2 Complexity of the Algorithm

Goldberg & Tarjan [5], present an algorithm for the circulation problem. Theoretically the worst running time of this algorithm is:

$$O\left(|V|^2 \cdot |E|^2 \cdot \min\left(\log(|V| \cdot C), |E| \cdot \log(|V|)\right)\right) \tag{4}$$

Note that C is the maximum absolute value of an arc cost. Despite this frightening worst case complexity we found that in practice the algorithm performed very well on the benchmarks from SPECint which we used for our analysis, and the algorithm's runtime was not an issue worth addressing when we applied it in procedure granularity (thus applying it on control flow graphs derived from procedures). Even as some of the control flow graphs which correspond to procedures from SPECint benchmarks contained thousands of vertices and edges.

5 Estimating Vertex and Edge Frequencies

After gathering many experimental results and studying several *cost coefficient* functions we choose to define the *cost coefficient* function for the vertices and edges as follows:

$$cp(o) = \frac{k'(\Delta(o))}{\ln(w(o)+2)}, \ k'(\Delta(o)) = \begin{cases} \Delta(o) \geq 0 & k_o^+ \\ \Delta(o) < 0 & k_o^- \end{cases} \tag{5}$$

Let us examine the terms in $cp(o)$:

- The *confidence constants* k_o^+ / k_o^-, represent the confidence we have in the measurement of a vertex or edge. k_o^+ / k_o^- effect the cost of increasing/decreasing the flow on $o \in V \cup E$ (thus setting positive/negative values to $\Delta(o)$). Note that the higher the confidence we have in the measurement the higher the cost to change its measured value will be.
- $w(o)$ represents an initial flow estimation on $o \in V \cup E$, this is explained thoroughly in section 5, but for now it is sufficient to think of it as the inaccurate flow as measured on $o \in V \cup E$.
- The *ln* function is used to normalize the weight of the edge/vertex which is in the denominator of the cost function, thus creating a denser distribution of costs.

For any application of the technique for filling in the missing/inaccurate gathered profile information we limit ourselves to filling in intra-procedural (local) missing frequencies.

The algorithm for applying the **intra-procedural** fixes is as follows:

1. foreach *f* in the list of functions do
   a. build control flow graph *g* for *f*
   b. foreach $o \in V \cup E$ in *G* assign values to the *confidence constants* $k^\pm(o)$ and the weight function $w(o)$ (see *Setting the constants* ahead)
   c. Build a fixup graph *G'* (see section 4)
   d. apply the minimum cost circulation algorithm to *G'* to find the minimum flow function *f*
   e. Retrieve the *fixup vector* Δ from *f* as explained in section 4.

Setting the constants: $k^\pm(o), w(o)$

Setting $w(o)$: Youfeng Wu and James R. Larus suggest techniques to estimate edge probabilities [4]. We determine the probability for each edge $p(\langle u, v \rangle)$ by using static profile techniques as suggested in their paper. The weight for each edge is then set as follows: $w(\langle v, u \rangle) = w(v) \cdot p(\langle v, u \rangle)$

Setting $k^\pm(o)$: we set the value for the *confidence constants* as follows:

$$k_o^\pm = a^\pm \cdot b; \; a^+ = 1, a^- = 50, b = \sqrt{avg\_vertex\_weight(cfg)} \qquad (6)$$

Note that the *b* parameter is just for normalization so it's not very important. Setting a^+ and a^- as shown above, worked well because it made the cost of decreasing flow on a vertex/edge significantly larger than that of increasing the flow on it. If we would have given a^+ and a^- similar values we would end up with a *fixup vector* that cancels most of the measured flow, as the trivial solution that cancels all the flow on the edges may is very appealing. On the other hand setting them farther apart caused edges and vertices with $w=0$ to increase dramatically which is also undesirable.

6 Experimental Results

To evaluate the effectiveness of our profile fixup technique, we applied our algorithm on benchmarks from the SPECint2000 suite and measured the accuracy using a criterion called degree of overlap. The comparison was done between the fixed dynamic control flow graph of the program and the actual dynamic control flow graph collected using full edge instrumentation and profile collection on the ref input. In order to gather complete edge profiling we used the IBM post-link optimizer FDPR-Pro [8] which can statically instrument a given executable and generate an instrumented version which produces an accurate edge profile file when run. We also measured the performance impact on each of the SPECint2000 benchmarks when applying FDPR-Pro –O3 optimizations when using as profile input the low-rate sampling profiling fixed by our technique versus full accurate profiling gathered by FDPR-Pro instrumentation. In addition we also refer to an addition measure called *degree of overlap*. The degree of overlap metric is used to compare the completeness of one control flow graph with respect to another, and has been used in several other research papers [15, 16, 17, 18]. The definition is as follows:

$$overlap(cfg1, cfg2) = \sum_{e \in E(cfg1) \cap E(cfg2)} \min(pw(e, cfg1), pw(e, cfg2)) \qquad (7)$$

Where $pw(e,cfg)$ is defined as the percentage of cfg's total edge weights represented by the edge weight on e. Only edges on both CCT1 and CCT2 are counted, in our specific problem there edge sets of cfg1 and cfg2 are identical so that $E(cfg1) \cap E(cfg2) = E(cfg1) \cup E(cfg2)$. The degree of overlap indicates how cfg2 overlaps with cfg1 or how cfg2 is covered by cfg1. The degree of overlap range is from 0% to 100%. The experiments were conducted on the IBM AIX POWER 5 platform with SPECint2000 benchmarks compiled for 32bit. The SPECint2000 or CPU2000 suite is primarily used to measure workstation performance but was designed to run on a broad range of processors as stated in [20]: "SPEC designed CPU2000 to provide a comparative measure of compute intensive performance across the widest practical range of hardware". Although it may be hard to imagine that applications such as gcc (C compiler), vpr (circuit placement), or twolf (circuit simulation) running on hand held devices, others such as gzip (compression), parser (word processing), and eon (visualization) are sure to be. The sampling data was collected using the IBM AIX *tprof* command which samples running applications and makes use of the POWER 5 hardware counters. The cell Oprofile tool provides similar capabilities for the cell embedded processor [22, 23]. For collecting the sampled frequency for the SPECint2000 programs we sampled the Instruction Complete hardware counter (PM_INST_CMPL) every ~1,000,000 instructions. This created a relatively small overhead of 2% - 3% on the runtime of each sampled program.

6.1 Filling Edge Profile from Vertex Profile

We first began by using FDPR-Pro to collect basic block profile alone, on the SPECint2000 benchmarks and then apply our technique to fill in the missing edge profile. Our measurements show, that when using our technique in such a way that the *confidence constants* for changing counts on basic blocks are set to ∞, and costs for changing costs on edges is set using the heuristics proposed by Youfeng Wu and James R. Larus [4], we reach an average degree of overlap that is higher than 99%, which obviously yields a negligible immeasurable performance delta when comparing to using full edge profile collected by FDPR-Pro. The conclusion is therefore, that when using our proposed method for filling in the missing edge profile, vertex profile is as good as edge profile for any practical purpose.

6.2 Approximating Dynamic Control Flow for External Sampling

A more challenging problem is creating an approximation for full edge profile when only partial, external sampling information exists. For this purpose we used tprof, which is an AIX tool for externally collecting hardware events using sampling. We used tprof to collect instruction complete events once every 1,000,003 events. Collecting the profile at such a low rate reduces the run-time of the SPECint2000 applications by 2-3%. Note that selecting a prime number as the event counter is advised since it reduces the chance for synchronization in a loop. If, for example, a trace containing 100 instructions occurs many millions of times sequentially and we would sample every 1,000,000 events we would hit the same instruction every time, and this would yield a false view on the counts in that trace of instructions.

The initial flow estimate $w(v)$ is set as follows:

$$w(v) = \frac{\sum_{ins \in V} sampled(ins)}{num\_of\_instrs(v) \cdot sample\_rate} \tag{8}$$

To measure the effectiveness of our technique we compared the degree of overlap and the performance gain with the full edge profile collected by FDPR-Pro and compared it to the degree of overlap and performance gain that was achieved without applying our method, which uses the calculated $w(o)$ (see above) for each $o \in V \bigcup U$. The results of our measurements are presented in tables 1, 2 and in figure 3.

Table 1. Degree of overlap comparison

Benchmark	degree of overlap: Sampled profile vs. Full profile	degree of overlap: fixed Sampled profile vs. Full profile
Parser	72%	81%
Bzip	70%	80%
Crafty	53%	62%
Gap	66%	92%
Gzip	72%	93%
Gcc	65%	78%
Mcf	83%	89%
Twolf	66%	82%
Vpr	71%	83%
Average	69%	82%

Table 2. Runtime comparison

Bench-mark	Runtime after FDPR O3 using sampled	Runtime after FDPR O3 using fixed sampled	Runtime after FDPR O3 using full profile
parser	5.2%	6.6%	7.2%
bzip	3.8%	5%	5%
crafty	4.1%	4.5%	6%
gap	8.5%	13.5%	13.2%
gzip	12%	16.5%	16.5%
gcc	4.35%	3.4%	4.4%
mcf	8%	8.5%	8.5%
twolf	10.25%	12.25%	14.1%
vpr	8.2%	8.8%	9.3%

Note: The percentages above refer to performance improvement compared to the base runtime.

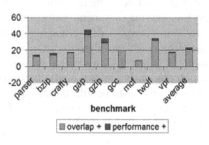

Fig. 3. fixed vs. unfixed sampling

The average degree of overlap, using our technique, calculated on SPECint2000 is 82% compared to 62% without using the fix. The average performance gain is only 0.6% less than when using the full edge profile, while without using the suggested fix, the average performance gain is 2.2% less than the full edge profile. Finally, the average improvement in degree of overlap is 21% and we reach a 1.8% average improvement in performance when compared to not using our fixup algorithm.

7 Future Directions

Our fixup technique can be used for a wide variety of profiling problems. Collection of inaccurate or lacking profile information may be due to several reasons, other than those addressed in the paper, such as the following:

- After applying several optimizations, such as function cloning, inlining, or after applying optimizations such as constant/value-range propagation which may eliminate edges in the control flow graph, the original profile information becomes inconsistent and needs to be corrected. In most cases, re-running the profiling phase on the modified program is not desirable.
- When profiling a multithreaded or multiprocessed application some counter promotions may be missing as a result of multiple threads/processes incrementing the same counter without synchronization. Adding synchronization to each vertex's/edge's counter may be undesirable due to additional runtime overhead and additional memory to be used as a mutex for each basic block/edge.
- When reusing profile information from older versions of the program.

Another future direction can be fining the optimal flow-fix, our *fixup vector*, with respect to different cost types such as minimizing L_∞ or L_2 (the least mean squares) and the weighted version of each. The weighted L_∞ can be minimized by using linear program along with a form of binary search. The weighted L_2 can be minimized by convex optimization using interior-point methods, Lagrange methods and several others.

8 Summary

We defined a technique for effectively fixing inaccurate and incomplete control flow profile information. This allows using non-intrusive low overhead profile techniques to collect profile for real-time embedded applications and then effectively using our technique to enhance the profile data and make it reasonably accurate. We implemented our technique and measured how well it performs when filling in edge profile from vertex profile and from *instruction complete* event counter run on a set of representative benchmarks. We showed that when applying over vertex profile, edge profile can be derived almost perfectly and when applying over the suggested sampling technique, we may reach an average overlap degree of 82%. When applying our technique into a post-link optimizer called FDPR-Pro, we reach an average performance gain which is only 0.6% less than when using full, accurate edge profile gathered using edge instrumentation. More generally, this suggests a platform independent, low overhead profiling scheme (2-3% overhead) with a high degree of accuracy. In addition we also show that when applying our technique over vertex profile we can fill in the missing edge profile with almost perfect overlap.

References

1. Ball, T., Larus, J.R.: Optimally profiling and tracing programs. ACM Transactions on Programming Languages and Systems (July 1994)
2. Anderson, J., Bert, L.M., Dean, J., Ghemawat, S., Henzinger, M.R., Leung, S.-T., Sites, R.L., Vandevoorde, M.T., Waldspurger, C.A., Weihl, W.E.: Continuous profiling: Where have all the cycles gone? In: Proceedings of the 16th Symposium on Operating Systems Principles (October 1997)
3. Reps, T., Ball, T., Das, M., Larus, J.: The use of program profiling for software maintenance with applications to the Year 2000 Problem. In: Jazayeri, M. (ed.) ESEC 1997 and ESEC-FSE 1997. LNCS, vol. 1301, pp. 432–449. Springer, Heidelberg (1997)
4. Wu, Y., Larus, J.R.: Static Branch Frequency and Program Profile Analysis. In: 27th IEEE/ACM InterÕl Symposium on Microarchitecture (MICRO-27) (November 1994)
5. Goldberg, V., Tarjan, R.E.: Finding minimum-cost circulations by canceling negative cycles. J. ACM 36, 873–886 (1989) Preliminary version appeared In: Proceedings of the 20th Annual ACM Symposium on Theory of Computing, pp. 388–397 (1987)
6. Haber, G., Henis, E.A., Eisenberg, V.: Reliable Post-link Optimizations Based on Partial Information. In: Proceedings of the 3rd Workshop on Feedback Directed and Dynamic Optimizations (December 2000)
7. Henis, E.A., Haber, G., Klausner, M., Warshavsky, A.: Feedback Based Post-link Optimization for Large Subsystems. In: Second Workshop on Feedback Directed Optimization, Haifa, Israel, pp. 13–20 (November 1999)

8. Nahshon, Bernstein, D.: FDPR - A Post-Pass Object Code Optimization Tool. In: Proc. Poster Session of the International Conference on Compiler Construction, pp. 97–104 (April 1996)

9. Romer, T., Voelker, G., Lee, D., Wolman, A., Wong, W., Levy, H., Bershad, B., Chen, B.: Instrumentation and Optimization of Win32/Intel Executables Using Etch. In: Proceedings of the USENIX Windows NT Workshop, pp. 1–7 (August 1997)

10. Schwarz, B., Debray, S., Andrews, G., Legendre, M.: PLTO: A link-Time Optimizer for the Intel IA-32 Architecture. In: Proceedings of Workshop on Binary Rewriting (September 2001)

11. Cohn, R., Goodwin, D., Lowney, P.G.: Optimizing Alpha Executables on Windows NT with Spike. Digital Technical Journal, Digital Equipment Corporation 9(4), 3–20 (1997)

12. Muth, R., Debray, S., Watterson, S.: alto: A Link-Time Optimizer for the Compaq Alpha, Technical Report 98-14, Dept. of Computer Science, The University of Arizona (December 1998)

13. Chang, P., et al.: Using Profile Information to Assist Classic Code Optimizations. Software-Practice and Experience 21(12), 1301–1321 (1991)

14. Ball, T., Larus, J.R.: Optimally Profiling and Tracing Programs. ACM Transactions on Programming Languages and Systems 16(4), 1319–1360 (1994)

15. Arnold, M., Ryder, B.: A framework for reducing the cost of instrumented code. In: SIGPLAN Conference on Programming Language Design and Implementation, pp. 168–179 (2001)

16. Arnold, M., Sweeney, P.F.: Approximating the calling context tree via sampling. IBM Research Report (July 2000)

17. Feller, P.T.: Value profiling for instructions and memory locations. Masters Thesis CS98-581, University of California San Diego (April 1998)

18. Zhuang, X., Serrano, M.J., Cain, H.W.: Accurate, Efficient, and Adaptive Calling Context Profiling. In: PLDI 2006 (2006)

19. Knuth, D.E., Stevenson, F.R.: Optimal measurement points for program frequency counts. BIT 13, 313–322 (1973)

20. SPEC CPU2000, http://www.spec.org/cpu2000

21. Spezialetti, M., Gupta, R.: Timed Perturbation Analysis: An Approach for Non-Intrusive Monitoring of Real-Time Computations. In: ACM SIGPLAN Workshop on Language, Compiler, and Tool Support for Real-Time Systems, Orlando, Florida (June 1994)

22. Cell SPE Oprofile patch, http://patchwork.ozlabs.org/linuxppc/patch?id=9627

23. Cell alphaworks SDK, http://www.alphaworks.ibm.com/topics/cell

Using Dynamic Binary Instrumentation to Generate Multi-platform SimPoints: Methodology and Accuracy

Vincent M. Weaver and Sally A. McKee

School of Electrical and Computer Engineering
Cornell University
{vince,sam}@csl.cornell.edu

Abstract. Modern benchmark suites (e.g., SPEC CPU2006) take months to simulate. Researchers and practitioners thus use partial simulation techniques for efficiency, and hope to avoid sacrificing accuracy. SimPoint is a popular method of choosing representative parts that approximate an application's entire behavior. The approach breaks an application into intervals, generates a Basic Block Vector (BBV) to represent instructions executed in each interval, clusters the BBVs according to similarity, and chooses a representative interval from the most important clusters. Unfortunately, tools to generate BBVs efficiently have heretofore been widely unavailable for many architectures, especially embedded ones.

We develop plugins for both the Qemu and Valgrind dynamic binary instrumentation (DBI) tools, and compare results to those generated by the PinPoints utility. All three methods can deliver under 6% average CPI error on both the SPEC CPU2000 and CPU2006 benchmarks while running under 0.4% of the total applications. Our tools increase the number of architectures for which BBVs can be generated efficiently and easily; they enable simulation points that include operating system activity; and they allow cross-platform collection of BBV information (e.g., generating MIPS SimPoints on IA32). We validate our tools via hardware performance counters on nine 32-bit Intel Linux platforms.

1 Introduction

Cycle-accurate simulators are slow. Using one to run a modern benchmark suite such as SPEC CPU2006 [16] can take months to complete when full reference inputs are used. This prohibitive slowdown prevents most modelers from using the full reference inputs. Yi et al. [18] investigate the six most common ways of speeding up simulations:

- Representative sampling (SimPoint [13]),
- Statistics based sampling (SMARTS [17]),
- Reduced input sets (MinneSPEC [6]),
- Simulating the first X Million instructions,
- Fast-forwarding Y Million instructions and simulating X Million, and
- Fast-forwarding Y Million, performing architectural warmup, then simulating X Million.

P. Stenström et al. (Eds.): HiPEAC 2008, LNCS 4917, pp. 305–319, 2008.
© Springer-Verlag Berlin Heidelberg 2008

They conclude that SimPoint and SMARTS give the most accurate results. Over 70% of the previous 10 years of HPCA, ISCA, and MICRO papers (ending in 2005) use reduced simulation methods that are less accurate. Most remaining papers use full input sets. Sampling is thus an under-utilized technique that can greatly increase the breadth and accuracy of computer architecture research.

Collecting data needed by SimPoint is difficult and time consuming; we present two tools to more easily generate the Basic Block Vectors (BBVs) that SimPoint needs. Our tools greatly expand the platforms for which BBVs can be generated, including a number of embedded platforms. We implement the tools using dynamic binary instrumentation (DBI), a technique that generates BBVs much faster than simulation. DBI tools are easier to use than simulators, removing many barriers to wider SimPoint use. Features inherent in the tools we extend make it possible to collect data that previous tools cannot.This includes creating cross-platform BBV files (e.g., generating MIPS BBVs from MIPS binaries on an IA32 host), as well as collecting BBVs that include operating system information along with normal user-space information.

We validate the generated BBVs and compare them against the PinPoint [10] BBVs generated by the Pin utility. We validate all three methods using hardware performance counters while running the SPEC CPU2000 [15] and SPEC CPU2006 [16] benchmark suites on a variety of 32-bit Intel Linux system. Our website contains source code for our Qemu and Valgrind modifications.

2   Generating Simulation Points

SimPoint exploits phase behavior in programs. Many applications exhibit cyclic behavior: code executing at one point in time behaves similarly to code running at some other point. Entire program behavior can be approximated by modeling only a representative set of intervals (in our case, *simulation points* or SimPoints).

Figures 1, 2, and 3 show examples of program phase behavior at a granularity of 100M instructions; these are captured using hardware performance counters on the CPU2000 benchmarks. Each figure shows two metrics: the top is L1 D-Cache miss rate, and the bottom is cycles per instruction (CPI). Figure 1 shows twolf, which exhibits almost completely uniform behavior. For this type of program, one interval is enough to approximate whole-program behavior. Figure 2 shows the mcf benchmark, which has more complex behavior. Periodic behavior is evident: representative intervals from the various phases can be used to approximate total behavior. The last example, Figure 3, shows the extremely complex behavior of gcc running the 200.i input set. Few patterns are apparent; this type of program is difficult to approximate with the SimPoint methodology (smaller phase intervals are needed to recognize patterns, and variable-size phases are possible, but choosing appropriate interval lengths is non-trivial). We run the CPU2000 benchmarks on nine implementations of architectures running the IA32 ISA, finding that phase behavior is consistent across all platforms when using the same binaries, despite large differences in hardware process and design.

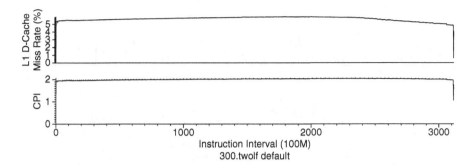

Fig. 1. L1 Data Cache and CPI behavior for `twolf`: behavior is uniform throughout, with one phase representing the entire program

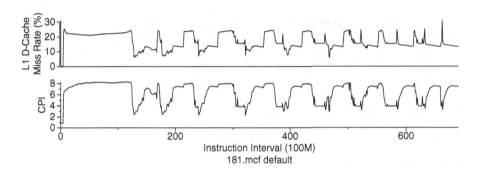

Fig. 2. L1 Data Cache and CPI behavior for `mcf`: several recurring phases are evident

To generate the simulation points for a program, the SimPoint tool needs a Basic Block Vector (BBV) describing the code's execution. Dynamic execution is split into intervals (often fixed size, although that is not strictly necessary). Interval size is measured by number of committed instructions, usually 1M-300M instructions. Smaller sizes enable finer grained phase detection; larger sizes mitigate warmup error when fast-forwarding (without explicit state warmup) in a simulator. We use 100M instruction intervals, which is a common compromise.

During execution, a list is kept of all basic blocks executed, along with a count of how many times each block is executed. The block count is weighted by the number of instructions in each block to ensure that instructions in smaller basic blocks are not given disproportionate significance. When total instruction count reaches the interval size, the basic block list and frequency count are appended to the BBV file. The SimPoint methodology uses the BBV file to find simulation points of interest by K-means clustering. The algorithm selects one representative interval from each phase identified by clustering. Number of phases can be specified directly, or the tool can search within a given range for an appropriate number of phases. The final step in using SimPoint is to gather statistics for all chosen simulation points. For multiple simulation points, the SimPoint tools

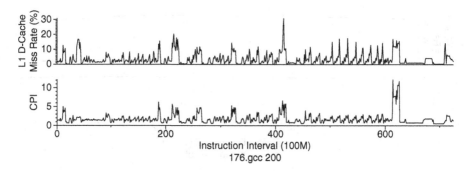

Fig. 3. L1 Data Cache and CPI behavior for `gcc.200`: this program exhibits complex behavior that is hard to capture with phase detection

generate weights to apply to the intervals (and several SimPoints must be modeled for accurate results). By scaling the statistics by the corresponding weights, an accurate approximation of entire program behavior can be estimated quickly (within a small fraction of whole-application simulation time).

2.1   BBV Generation

The BBV file format looks like:

```
T:45:1024 :189:99343
T:11:78573 :15:1353 :56:1
T:18:45 :12:135353 :56:78 314:4324263
```

A T signifies the start of an interval, and is followed by a series of colon separated pairs; the first is a unique number specifying a basic block, and the second is the scaled frequency count. There are many methods for gathering information needed to create such BBV files. Requirements are that the tool count the number of committed instructions and track entries into every basic block. The SimPoint website only provides BBV generation tools using ATOM [14] and SimpleScalar [1] sim-alpha. These are useful for experiments involving the Alpha processor, but that architecture has declined in significance. There remains a need for tools to generate BBVs on a wider range of platforms.

Our first attempt used DynInst [3], which supports many platforms, operating systems, and architectures. Unfortunately, the tool is not designed for generating BBVs, and memory overhead for instrumenting some of the benchmarks exceeds 4GB. Furthermore, the tool works with dynamically linked applications. We hope to use future versions, and work with the DynInst developers to generate BBVs without undue overheads. In contrast, Qemu [2] and Valgrind [9] already provide capabilities needed with acceptable overhead, and we modify these two DBI tools to generate BBVs. To validate our methods, we compare results to those from the Pin [7] tool. Figure 4 shows architectures supported for each tool; since all run on Intel platforms, we use them as a common reference.

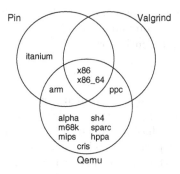

Fig. 4. Architectures supported by Pin, Qemu, and Valgrind: IA32 is the ideal platform for comparison, as it is supported by all of three tools

2.2 Pin

Pin [7] is a dynamic binary instrumentation tool that runs on Intel architectures (including IA32, Intel 64, Itanium, and Xscale), and it supports Linux, Windows, and Macintosh OSX operating systems. We use the PinPoint [10] BBV generation tool bundled with version pin-2.0-10520-gcc.4.0.0-ia32-linux. Pin analysis routines are written in C++, and the instrumentation happens just-in-time, with the resulting instrumented code cached for performance. The core of Pin is proprietary, so internals must be treated as a black box. PinPoint analyses run from 1.5 (**swim**) to 20 (**vortex**) times slower than the binary run on native hardware.

2.3 Qemu

Qemu [2] is a portable dynamic translator. It is commonly used to run a full operating system under hardware emulation, but it also has a Linux user-space emulator that runs stand-alone Linux binaries using system-call translation. Qemu supports the Alpha, SPARC, PowerPC, sh4, IA32, AMD64, MIPS, m68k, and ARM architectures. The user-mode translation we use is currently supported on Linux. Ongoing work will support more operating systems. Qemu uses gcc to compile code corresponding to each intermediate language micro-operation. At translation time, these pre-compiled micro-operations are chained together to create translated basic blocks that are cached.

Qemu is not designed for DBI. Using it for our purposes requires intrusive changes to Qemu source. Our code is a patch applied on top of the Qemu 0.9.0 release. We add a unique identifier field to the internal *TargetBlock* basic block structure, which is set the first time a BB is translated. At translation time, we instrument every instruction to call our BBV tracking routine to update BBV counts and total instruction count. Once the interval size is reached, the BBV file is updated, and all counters are reset. Qemu runs from between 4 (**art**) to 40 (**vortex**) times slower than native execution. This makes it slower than Pin but faster than our Valgrind implementation.

Note that `gcc` uses an extremely large stack. By default Qemu only emulates a 512KB stack, but the `-s` command-line option enables at least 8MB of stack space, which allows all `gcc` benchmarks to run to completion.

2.4 Valgrind

Valgrind [9] is a dynamic binary instrumentation tool for the PowerPC, IA32, and AMD64 architectures. It was originally designed to detect application memory allocation errors, but it has developed into a generic and flexible DBI utility. Valgrind translates native processor code into a RISC-like intermediate code. Instrumentation occurs on this intermediate code, which is then recompiled back to the native instruction set. Translated blocks are cached.

Our BBV generation code is a plugin to Valgrind 3.2.3. By default, Valgrind instruments at a *super-block* level rather than the basic block level. A super-block only has one entrance, but can have multiple exit points. We use the `--vex-guest-chase-thresh=0` option to force Valgrind to use basic blocks, although our experiments show that using super-blocks yields similar results. Valgrind implements just-in-time translation of the program being run. We instrument every instruction to call our BBV generation routine. It would be more efficient to call only the routine once per block, but in order to work around some problems with the "rep" instruction prefix (described later) we must instrument every instruction. When calling our instruction routine, we look up the current basic block in a hash table to find a data structure that holds the relevant statistics. We increment the basic block counter and the total instruction count. If we finish an interval by overflowing the committed instruction count, we update BBV information and clear all counts. Valgrind runs from 5 (`art`) to 114 (`vortex`) times slower than native execution, making it the slowest of the tools we evaluate.

3 Evaluation

To evaluate the BBV generation tools, we use the SPEC CPU2000 [15] and CPU2006 [16] benchmarks with full reference inputs. We compile the benchmarks on SuSE Linux 10.2 with gcc 4.1 and "-O2" optimization (except for `vortex`, which we compile without optimization because it crashes, otherwise). We link binaries statically to avoid library differences on the machines we use to gather data. The choice to use static linking is not due to tool dependencies; all three handle both dynamic and static executables.

We choose IA32 as our test platform because it is widely used and because all three tools support it. We use the Perfmon2 [5] interface to gather hardware performance counter results for the platforms described in Table 1.

The performance counters are set to write out the the relevant statistics every 100M instructions. The data collected are used in conjunction with simulation points and weights generated by SimPoint to calculate estimated CPI. We calculate actual CPI for the benchmarks by using the performance counter data, and use this as a basis for our error calculations. Note that calculated statistics

Table 1. Machines used

machine	processor	memory	L1 I/D	L2/L3 Cache	performance counters used
nestle	400MHz Pentium II	256MB	16KB/16KB	512KB	inst_retired, cpu_clk_unhalted
spruengli	550MHz Pentium III	512MB	16KB/16KB	512KB	inst_retired, cpu_clk_unhalted
itanium	800MHz Itanium	1GB	16KB/16KB	96KB/3MB	ia32_inst_retired, cpu_cycles
chocovic	1.66GHz Core Duo	1GB	32KB/32KB	1MB	instructions_retired, unhalted_core_cycles
milka	1.733MHz Athlon MP	512MB	64KB/64KB	256KB	retired_instructions, cpu_clk_unhalted
gallais	1.8GHz Pentium 4	256MB	12Kμ/16KB	256KB	instr_retired:nbogusntag, global_power_events:running
jennifer	2GHz Athlon64 X2	1GB	64KB/64KB	512KB	retired_instructions, cpu_clk_unhalted
sampaka12	2.8GHz Pentium 4	2GB	12Kμ/16KB	512KB	instr_retired:nbogusntag, global_power_events:running
domori25	3.46GHz Pentium D	4GB	12Kμ/16KB	2MB	instr_retired:nbogusntag, global_power_events:running

are ideal, with full warmup. If we were analyzing via a simulation, the results would likely vary in accuracy depending on how architectural state is warmed up after fast-forwarding between simulation points. We use SimPoint version 3.2, the newest version from the SimPoint website, to generate our simulation points.

3.1   The Rep Prefix

When validating against actual hardware, total retired instruction counts closely match Pin results, but Qemu and Valgrind results diverge on certain benchmarks. We find the cause of this problem to be the IA32 `rep` prefix. This prefix appears before string instructions (which typically implement a memory operation followed by a pointer auto-increment). The prefix causes the string instruction to repeat, decrementing the `ecx` register until it reaches zero. A naive implementation of the `rep` prefix treats each *repetition* as a committed instruction. In actual hardware, this instruction is grouped in multiples of 4096, so only every 4096th repetition counts as one committed instruction. The performance counters and Pin both show this behavior. Our Valgrind and Qemu plugins are modified to compensate for this, so that we achieve consistent committed instruction counts across all of the BBV generators and actual hardware.

3.2   The Art Benchmark

Under Valgrind, the `art` floating point benchmark finishes with half the number of instructions committed by actual hardware. Valgrind uses 64-bit floating point arithmetic for portability reasons, but by default on Linux IA32, programs use 80-bit floating point operations. The `art` benchmark unwisely uses the "==" C operator to compare two floating point numbers, and due to rounding errors between the 80-bit and 64-bit versions, the 64-bit version can finish early, while still generating the proper reference output.

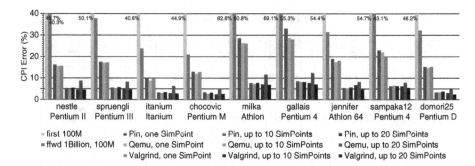

Fig. 5. Average CPI error for CPU2000 when using first, blind fast-forward, and Sim-Point selected intervals on various IA32 machines: when using up to 10 simulation points per benchmark, average error is 5.3% for Pin, 5.0% for Qemu, and 5.4% for Valgrind

Having vastly different numbers of completed instructions interferes with simulation point generation, since it limits SimPoint intervals to only part of the complete execution. In order to have the benchmark finish with the same number of instructions, we modify `art` to execute an IA32 assembly instruction to force the FPU to use 64-bit arithmetic. This small change makes the performance counter, Pin, and Valgrind results match. Unfortunately, this does not work for Qemu, which ignores the settings and always uses 80-bit operations.

There are solutions to this problem. One is to use the `-msse2` option of `gcc` to use the 64-bit SSE2 unit instead of the 80-bit x87 floating point unit. Not all of our machines support SSE2, so that workaround is not available. Another option is to use another compiler, such as the Intel C Compiler, which has specific compiler options to enable 64-bit floating point. This does not work with Qemu, which uses 80-bit operations regardless. Therefore we modify the benchmark, and let Qemu generate skewed results.

4   Results

Figure 5 shows results for the SPEC CPU2000 benchmarks. When allowing SimPoint to choose up to 10 simulation points per benchmark, the average error across all machines for CPI is 5.32% for Pin, 5.04% for Qemu, and 5.38% for Valgrind. Pin chooses 354 SimPoints, Qemu 363, and Valgrind 346; this represents only 0.4% of the total execution length, making the simulations finish 250 times faster than if run to completion. It is reassuring that all three BBV methods pick a similar number of intervals, and in many cases they pick the same intervals.

Figure 5 also shows results when SimPoint is allowed to pick up to 20 simulation points. The results are better: error is 4.96% for Pin, 8.00% for Qemu, and 4.45% for Valgrind. This requires less than twice as much simulation — around 0.7% of the total execution length. The increase in error for Qemu is due to poor SimPoint choices in the `gcc` benchmark with the `166.i` input: on many of the architectures, chosen intervals give over 100% error.

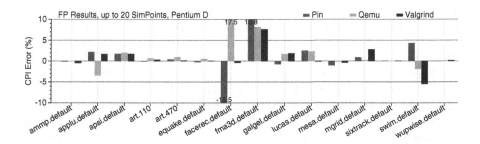

Fig. 6. Percent error in CPI on a Pentium D when using up to 20 SimPoints on CPU2000 FP: the error with `facerec` and `fma3d` is due to extreme swings in the phase behavior that SimPoint has trouble capturing

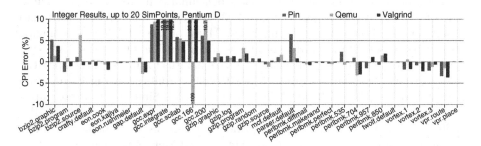

Fig. 7. Percent error in CPI on a Pentium D when using up to 20 SimPoints on CPU2000 INT: the large error with the `gcc` benchmarks is due to spikes in the phase behavior that SimPoint does not capture well

In addition to the degree of error when using multiple simulation points, Figure 5 shows error for other common methods of interval selection. The first column shows error when running only the first 100M instructions from each benchmark. This method of picking points is poor: error averages around 54% for CPI. Another common method is fast-forwarding 1B instructions and then simulating an interval beginning there (this is equivalent to always choosing the 10th interval as a single SimPoint). This produces better results than using the first interval, but at 37%, the error is still large. Using SimPoint analysis but only choosing one representative interval is a way to use the same amount of simulation time as the previous two methods, but attempts to make a more intelligent choice of which interval to run. As the graph shows, this behaves much better than the blind methods, but the error is twice as large as that from using up to 10 SimPoints.

Figures 6 and 7 show the CPI error for the individual benchmarks on the Pentium D system. For floating point applications, `facerec` and `fma3d` have significantly more error than the others. This is because those programs feature phases which exhibit extreme shifts in CPI from interval to interval, a behavior often has trouble capturing. The integer benchmarks have the biggest source of error, which is the gcc benchmarks. The reason gcc behaves so poorly is that there are intervals during its execution where the CPI and other metrics spike. These huge spikes do not repeat, and only happen for one interval; because of this, SimPoint does not weight them as being important, and they therefore are omitted from the chosen simulation points. These high peaks are what cause the actual average results to be much higher than what is predicted by SimPoint. It might be possible to work around this problem by choosing a smaller interval size, which would break the problematic intervals into multiple smaller ones that would be more easily seen by SimPoint.

We also use our BBV tools on the SPEC CPU2006 benchmarks. These runs use the same tools as for CPU2000, without any modifications. These tools yield good results without requiring any special knowledge of the newer benchmarks. We do not have results for the zeusmp benchmark: it would not run under any of the DBI tools. Unlike the CPU2000 results, we only have performance counter data from four of the machines. Many of the CPU2006 benchmarks have working sets of over 1GB, and many of our machines have less RAM than that. On those machines the benchmarks take months to run, with the operating system paging constantly to disk. The CPU2006 results shown in Figure 8 are as favorable as the CPU2000 results. When allowing SimPoint to choose up to 10 simulation points per benchmark, the average error for CPI is 5.58% for Pin, 5.30% for Qemu and 5.28% for Valgrind. Pin chooses 420 simulation points, Qemu 433, and Valgrind. This would require simulating only 0.056% of the total benchmark suite. This is an impressive speedup, considering the long running time of these benchmarks. Figure 8 also shows the results when SimPoint is allowed to pick up to 20 simulation points, which requires simulating only 0.1% of the total benchmarks. Average error for CPI is 3.39% for Pin, 4.04% for Qemu, and 3.68% for Valgrind.

Error when simulating the first 100M instructions averages 102%, showing that this continues to be a poor way to choose simulation intervals. Fast-forwarding 1B instructions and then simulating 100M produces an average error of 31%. Using only a single simulation point again has error over twice that of using up to 10 SimPoints. Figures 9 and 10 show CPI errors for individual benchmarks on the Pentium D machine. For floating point applications, there are outlying results for cactusADM, dealII, and GemsFDTD. For these benchmarks, total number of committed instructions measured by the DBI tools differs from that measured with the performance counters. Improving the BBV tools should fix these outliers.

As with the CPU2000 results, the biggest source of error is from gcc in the integer benchmarks. The reasons are the same as described previously: Sim-Point cannot handle the spikes in the phase behavior. The bzip2 benchmarks in CPU2006 exhibit the same problem that gcc has. Inputs used in CPU2006 have spiky behavior that the CPU2000 inputs do not. The other outliers, perlbench and astar require further investigation.

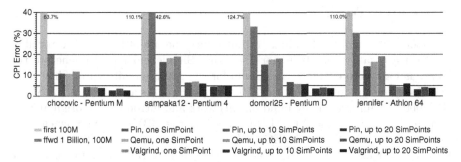

Fig. 8. Average CPI error for CPU2006 on a selection of IA32 machines when using first, blind fast-forward, and SimPoint selected intervals: when using up to 10 simulation points per benchmark, average error is 5.6% for Pin, 5.30% for Qemu, and 5.3% for Valgrind

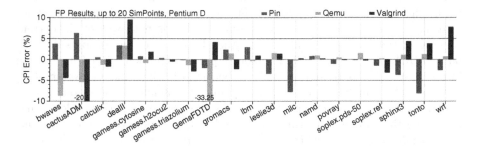

Fig. 9. Percent error in CPI on a Pentium D when using up to 20 SimPoints on CPU 2006 FP: the large variation in results for *cactusADM*, *dealII* and *GemsFDRD* are due to unresolved inaccuracies in the way the tools count instructions

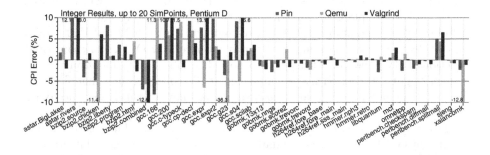

Fig. 10. Percent error in CPI on a Pentium D when using up to 20 SimPoints on CPU 2006 INT: the large error with the `gcc` and `bzip2` benchmarks is due to spikes in the phase behavior not captured by SimPoint

5   Related Work

Sherwood, Perelman, and Calder [12] introduce the use of basic block distribution to investigate phase behavior. They use SimpleScalar [4] to generate the BBVs, as well as to evaluate the results for the Alpha architecture. They show preliminary results for three of the SPEC95 benchmarks and three of the SPEC CPU2000 benchmarks. They build on this work and introduce the original Sim-Point tool [13]. They use ATOM [14] to collect the BBVs and SimpleScalar to evaluate the results for the SPEC CPU2000 benchmark suite. They use an interval of 10M instructions, and find an average 18% IPC error for using one simulation point for each benchmark, and 3% IPC error using between 6 to 10 simulation points. These results roughly match ours. The benchmarks that require the most simulation points are *ammp* and *bzip2*, which is different from the *gcc* bottleneck we find on the IA32 architecture. This is most likely due to the different ISAs, as well as differences in the memory hierarchy.

Perelman, Hamerly and Calder [11] investigate finding "early" simulation points that can minimize fast-forwarding in the simulator. This paper does not investigate early points because that functionality is not available in current versions of the SimPoint utility. When they look at a configuration similar to ours, with 43 of the SPEC2000 reference input combinations, 100M instruction intervals, and up to 10 simulations per benchmark, they find an average CPI error of 2.6%. This is better than our results, but again this was done on the Alpha architecture, which apparently lacks the *gcc* benchmark problems that appear on the IA32 architectures. They collect BBVs and evaluate results with SimpleScalar, showing that the results on one architectural configuration track the results on other configurations while using the same simulation points. We also find this to be true, but in our case we compare the results from various real hardware platforms.

While many people use SimPoint in their research, often no mention is made of how the BBV files are collected. If not specified, it is usually assumed that the original method described by Sherwood et al. [13] is used, which involves ATOM [14] or SimpleScalar [4]. Alternatively, the SimPoint website has a known set of simulation points provided for pre-compiled Alpha SPEC CPU2000 binaries, so that recalculating using SimPoint is not necessary. Other work sometimes mentions BBV generation briefly, with no indication of any validation. For example, Nagpurkar and Krintz [8] implement BBV collection in a modified Java Virtual Machine in order to analyze Java phase behavior, but do not specify the accuracy of the resulting phase detection.

Patil et al.'s work on PinPoints [10] is most similar to ours. They use the Pin [7] tool to gather BBVs, and then validate the results on the Itanium architecture using performance counters. This work predates the existence of Pin for IA32, so no IA32 results are shown. Their results show that 95% of the SPEC CPU2000 benchmarks have under 8% CPI error when using up to ten 250M instruction intervals. All their benchmarks complete with under 12% error, which is more accurate than our results. One reason for this is that they use much longer simulation points, so they are simulating more of each benchmark. They also investigate commercial benchmarks, and find that the results are not as accurate as the SPEC results. These Itanium results, as in other previous studies, do not suffer from the huge errors we find in the *gcc* benchmarks. This is probably due to the vastly different architectures and memory hierarchies. Even for the minimally configured machine they use, the cache is much larger than on most of our test machines. The benefit of our study is that we investigate three different methods of BBV generation, whereas they only look at Itanium results generated with Pin.

6   Conclusions and Future Work

We have develop two new BBV generation tools and show that they deliver similar performance to that of existing BBV generation methods. Our Valgrind and Qemu code can provide an average of under 6% CPI error while only running 0.4% of the total SPEC CPU2000 suite on full reference inputs. This is similar to results from the existing PinPoints tool. Our code generates under 6% CPI error when running under 0.06% of SPEC CPU2006 (excepting zeusmp) with full reference inputs. The CPU2006 results are obtained without any special tuning for those benchmarks, which indicates that these methods should be adaptable to other benchmark workloads.

We show that our results are better than those obtained with other common sampling methods, such as simulating the beginning of a program, simulating after fast-forwarding 1B instructions, or only simulating one simulation point. All of our results are validated with performance counters on a range of IA32 Linux systems. In addition, our work vastly increases the number of architectures for which efficient BBV generation is now available. With Valgrind, we can generate PowerPC BBVs. Qemu makes it possible to generate BBVs for m68k, MIPS, sh4, CRIS, SPARC, and HPPA architectures. This means that many embedded platforms can now make use of SimPoint methodologies.

The potential benefits of Qemu should be further explored, since it can simulate entire operating systems. This enables collection of BBVs that include full-system effects, not just user-space activity. Furthermore, Qemu enables simulation of binaries from one architecture directly on top of another. This allows gathering BBVs for architectures where actual hardware is not available or is excessively slow, and for experimental ISAs that do not exist yet in hardware.

Valgrind has explicit support for profiling MPI applications. It would be interesting to investigate whether this can be extended to generate BBVs for parallel programs, and to attempt to use SimPoint to speed up parallel workload design studies. Note that we would have to omit synchronization activity from the BBVs in order to capture true phase behavior.

The poor results for gcc indicate that some benchmarks lack sufficient phase behavior for SimPoint to generate useful simulation points. It might be necessary to simulate these particular benchmarks fully in order to obtain sufficiently accurate results, or to decrease the interval size. Determining why the poor results only occur on IA32, and do not occur on Alpha and Itanium architectures, requires further investigation.

Overall, these tools show great promise in encouraging use of SimPoint for architectural studies. Our tools make generating simulation points fast and easy, and will help others in generating more accurate results in their experiments.

Acknowledgments

This material is based upon work supported by the National Science Foundation under Grants 0509406, 0444413, and 0325536.

References

1. Austin, T.: Simplescalar 4.0 release note http://www.simplescalar.com/
2. Bellard, F.: Qemu, a fast and portable dynamic translator. In: Proc. 2005 USENIX Annual Technical Conference, FREENIX Track, pp. 41–46 (April 2005)
3. Buck, B., Hollingsworth, J.: An API for runtime code patching. The International Journal of High Performance Computing Applications 14(4), 317–329 (2000)
4. Burger, D., Austin, T.: The simplescalar toolset, version 2.0. Technical Report 1342, University of Wisconsin (June 1997)
5. Eranian, S.: Perfmon2: A flexible performance monitoring interface for Linux. In: Proc. of the 2006 Ottawa Linux Symposium, pp. 269–288 (July 2006)
6. KleinOsowski, A., Lilja, D.: MinneSPEC: A new SPEC benchmark workload for simulation-based computer architecture research. Computer Architecture Letters 1 (June 2002)
7. Luk, C.-K., Cohn, R., Muth, R., Patil, H., Klauser, A., Lowney, G., Wallace, S., Reddi, V., Hazelwood, K.: Pin: Building customized program analysis tools with dynamic instrumentation. In: Proc. ACM SIGPLAN Conference on Programming Language Design and Implementation, pp. 190–200 (June 2005)
8. Nagpurkar, P., Krintz, C.: Visualization and analysis of phased behavior in Java programs. In: Proc. ACM 3rd international symposium on Principles and practice of programming in Java, pp. 27–33 (2004)
9. Nethercote, N., Seward, J.: Valgrind: A framework for heavyweight dynamic binary instrumentation. In: Proc. ACM SIGPLAN Conference on Programming Language Design and Implementation, pp. 89–100 (June 2007)
10. Patil, H., Cohn, R., Charney, M., Kapoor, R., Sun, A., Karunanidhi, A.: Pinpointing representative portions of large Intel Itanium programs with dynamic instrumentation. In: Proc. IEEE/ACM 37th Annual International Symposium on Microarchitecture, pp. 81–93 (December 2004)
11. Perelman, E., Hamerly, G., Calder, B.: Picking statistically valid and early simulation points. In: Proc. IEEE/ACM International Conference on Parallel Architectures and Compilation Techniques, pp. 244–256 (September 2003)
12. Sherwood, T., Perelman, E., Calder, B.: Basic block distribution analysis to find periodic behavior and simulation points in applications. In: Proc. IEEE/ACM International Conference on Parallel Architectures and Compilation Techniques, pp. 3–14 (September 2001)
13. Sherwood, T., Perelman, E., Hamerly, G., Calder, B.: Automatically characterizing large scale program behavior. In: Proc. 10th ACM Symposium on Architectural Support for Programming Languages and Operating Systems, pp. 45–57 (October 2002)

14. Srivastava, A., Eustace, A.: ATOM: A system for building customized program analysis tools. In: Proc. ACM SIGPLAN Conference on Programming Language Design and Implementation, pp. 196–205 (June 1994)
15. Standard Performance Evaluation Corporation. SPEC CPU benchmark suite (2000), http://www.specbench.org/osg/cpu2000/
16. Standard Performance Evaluation Corporation. SPEC CPU benchmark suite (2006), http://www.specbench.org/osg/cpu2006/
17. Wunderlich, R., Wenish, T., Falsafi, B., Hoe, J.: SMARTS: Accelerating microarchitecture simulation via rigorous statistical sampling. In: Proc. 30th IEEE/ACM International Symposium on Computer Architecture, pp. 84–95 (June 2003)
18. Yi, J., Kodakara, S., Sendag, R., Lilja, D., Hawkins, D.: Characterizing and comparing prevailing simulation techniques. In: Proc. 11th IEEE Symposium on High Performance Computer Architecture, pp. 266–277 (February 2005)

Phase Complexity Surfaces:
Characterizing Time-Varying Program Behavior

Frederik Vandeputte and Lieven Eeckhout

ELIS Department, Ghent University
Sint-Pietersnieuwstraat 41, B-9000 Gent, Belgium
{fgvdeput,leeckhou}@elis.UGent.be

Abstract. It is well known that a program execution exhibits time-varying behavior, i.e., a program typically goes through a number of phases during its execution with each phase exhibiting relatively homogeneous behavior within a phase and distinct behavior across phases. In fact, several recent research studies have been exploiting this time-varying behavior for various purposes.

This paper proposes phase complexity surfaces to characterize a computer program's phase behavior across various time scales in an intuitive manner. The phase complexity surfaces incorporate metrics that characterize phase behavior in terms of the number of phases, its predictability, the degree of variability within and across phases, and the phase behavior's dependence on the time scale granularity.

1   Introduction

Understanding program behavior is at the foundation of computer system design and optimization. Deep insight into inherent program properties drive software and hardware research and development. A program property that has gained increased interest over the past few years, is time-varying program behavior. Time-varying program behavior refers to the observation that a computer program typically goes through a number of phases at run-time with relatively stable behavior within a phase and distinct behavior across phases. Various research studies have been done towards exploiting program phase behavior, for example for simulation acceleration [9,26], hardware adaptation for energy consumption reduction [1,6,7,27], program profiling and optimization [11,21], etc.

This paper concerns characterizing a program's phase behavior. To identify phases, we divide a program execution into non-overlapping intervals. An *interval* is a contiguous sequence of instructions from a program's dynamic instruction stream. A *phase* is a set of intervals within a program's execution that exhibit similar behavior irrespective of temporal adjacency, i.e., a program execution may go through the same phase multiple times.

Basically, there are four properties that characterize a program's phase behavior.

- The first property is the *time scale* at which time-varying program behavior is being observed. Some programs exhibit phase behavior at a small time granularity while other programs only exhibit phase behavior at a coarse granularity; and yet other

P. Stenström et al. (Eds.): HiPEAC 2008, LNCS 4917, pp. 320–334, 2008.

programs may exhibit phase behavior at various time scales, and the phase behavior may be hierarchical, i.e., a phase at one time scale may consist of multiple phases at a finer time scale.

- The second property is the *number of phases* a program goes through at run-time. Some programs repeatedly stay in the same phase, for example when executing the same piece of code over and over again; other programs may go through many distinct phases.
- The third property concerns the *variability* within phases versus the variability across phases. The premise of phase behavior is that there is less variability within a phase than across phases, i.e., the variability in behavior for intervals belonging to a given phase is fairly small compared to intervals belonging to different phases.
- The fourth and final property relates to the *predictability* of the program phase behavior. For some programs, its time-varying behavior is very regular and by consequence very predictable. For other programs on the other hand, time-varying behavior is rather complex, irregular and hard to predict.

Obviously, all four properties are related to each other. More in particular, the time scale determines the number of phases to be found with a given degree of homogeneity within each phase; the phases found, in their turn, affect the predictability of the phase behavior. By consequence, getting a good understanding of a program's phase behavior requires all four properties be characterized simultaneously.

This paper presents *phase complexity surfaces* as a way to characterize program phase behavior. The important benefit over prior work in characterizing program phase behavior is that phase complexity surfaces capture *all* of the four properties mentioned above in a unified and intuitive way while enabling the reasoning in terms of these four properties individually.

As a subsequent step, we use these phase complexity surfaces to characterize and classify programs in terms of their phase behavior. Within SPEC CPU2000 we identify a number of prominent groups of programs with similar phase behavior. Researchers can use this classification to select benchmarks for their studies in exploiting program phase behavior.

2   Related Work

There exists a large body of related work on program phase behavior. In this section, we only discuss the issues covered in prior work that relate most closely to this paper.

Granularity. The granularity at which time-varying behavior is studied and exploited varies widely. Some researchers look for program phase behavior at the 100K instruction interval size [1,6,7]; others look for program phase behavior at the 1M or 10M instruction interval granilarity [23]; and yet others identify phase behavior at yet a larger granularity of 100M or even 1B instructions [22,26]. The granularity chosen obviously depends on the purpose of the phase-level optimization. The advantage of a small time scale is that the optimization can potentially achieve better performance because the optimization can be applied more aggressively. A larger time scale on the other hand has the advantage that the overhead of exploiting the phase behavior can be amortized more easily.

Some researchers study phase behavior at different time scales simultaneously. Wavelets for example provide a natural way of characterizing phase behavior at various time scales [4,13,24], and Lau et al. [17] identify a hierarchy of phase behavior.

Fixed-length versus variable-length phases. Various researchers aim at detecting phase behavior by looking into fixed-length instruction intervals [1,6,7]. The potential problem with the fixed-length interval approach though is that in some cases it may be hard to identify phase behavior because of the effect of dissonance between the fixed-length interval and the natural period of the phase behavior. In case the length of the fixed-length interval is slightly smaller or bigger than the period of the phase behavior, the observation made will be out of sync with the natural phase behavior. To address this issue, some researchers advocate identifying phases using variable-length intervals. Lau et al. [17] use pattern matching to find variable-length intervals, and in their follow-on work [16] they identify program phases by looking into a program's control flow structure consisting of loops, and methods calls and returns. Huang et al. [12] detect (variable-length) phases at method entry and exit points by tracking method calls via a call stack.

Microarchitecture-dependent versus microarchitecture-independent characterization. Identifying phases can be done in a number of ways. Some identify program phase behavior by inspecting microarchitecture-dependent program behavior, i.e., they infer phase behavior from inspecting time-varying microarchitecture performance numbers. For example, Balasubramonian et al. [1] collect CPI and cache miss rates. Duesterwald et al. [8] collect IPC numbers, cache miss rates and branch misprediction rates. Isci and Martonosi [14] infer phase behavior from power vectors. A concern with microarchitecture-dependent based phase detection is that once phase behavior is being exploited, it may affect the microarchitecture-dependent metrics being measured; this potentially leads to the problem where it is unclear whether the observed time-varying behavior is a result of natural program behavior or is a consequence of exploiting the observed phase behavior.

An alternative approach is to measure microarchitecture-independent metrics to infer phase behavior from. Dhodapkar and Smith [7,6] for example keep track of a program's working set; when the working set changes, they infer that the program transitions to another phase. Sherwood et al. [26] use Basic Block Vectors (BBVs) to keep track of the basic blocks executed — BBVs are shown to correlate well with performance in [18]. Other microarchitecture-independent metrics are for example memory addresses [13] and data reuse distances [24], a program's control flow structure such as loops and methods [11,12,16], a collection of program characteristics such as instruction mix, ILP, memory access patterns, etc. [9,19].

Phase classification. Different researchers have come up with different approaches to partitioning instruction intervals into phases. Some use threshold clustering [6,7,27]; others use machine learning techniques such as k-means clustering [26], pattern matching [17,24]; yet others use frequency analysis through wavelets [4,5,13,24].

Phase prediction. An important aspect to exploiting phase behavior is to be able to predict and anticipate future phase behavior. Sherwood et al. [27] proposed last phase, RLE and Markov phase predictors. In their follow-on work [20], they added confidence counters to the phase predictors. Vandeputte et al. [28] proposed conditional update which only updates the phase predictor at the lowest confidence level.

Relation to this paper. In this paper, we characterize program phase behavior at different time scale granularities. To this end, we consider fixed-length intervals, use BBVs to identify phase behavior, use threshold clustering for phase classification, and use a theoretical predictor to study phase predictability. We will go in more detail about our phase characterization approach in the next section.

The important difference between this paper compared to prior work is that the explicit goal of this paper is to *characterize* the complexity of a program's phase behavior in an intuitively understandable way. Most of this prior work on the other hand concerned *exploiting* program phase behavior. The work mostly closely related to this paper probably is the work done by Cho and Li [4,5]. They use wavelets to characterize the complexity of a program's phase behavior by looking at different time scales. This complexity measure intermingles the four phase behavior properties mentioned in the introduction; phase complexity surfaces on the other hand provide a more intuitive view on a program's phase behavior by factoring out all four properties.

3 Phase Complexity Surfaces

As mentioned in the introduction, there are four properties that characterize the program's overall phase behavior: (i) the time scale, (ii) the number of phases, (iii) the within and across phase variability, and (iv) phase sequence and transition predictability. The phase behavior characterization surfaces proposed in this paper capture all four properties in a unified way. There are three forms of surfaces: the phase count surface, the phase predictability surface and the phase complexity surface. This section discusses all three surfaces which give an overall view of the complexity of a program's time-varying behavior. Before doing so, we first need to define a Basic Block Vector (BBV) and discuss how to classify instruction intervals into phases using BBVs.

3.1 Basic Block Vector (BBV)

In this paper, we use the Basic Block Vector (BBV) proposed by Sherwood et al. [25] to capture a program's time-varying behavior. A basic block is a linear sequence of instructions with one entry and one exit point. A Basic Block Vector (BBV) is a one-dimensional array with one element per static basic block in the program binary. Each BBV element captures how many times its corresponding basic block has been executed. This is done on an interval basis, i.e., we compute one BBV per interval. Each BBV element is also multiplied with the number of instructions in the corresponding basic block. This gives a higher weight to basic blocks containing more instructions. A BBV thus provides a picture of what portions of code are executed and also how frequently those portions of code are executed.

We use a BBV to identify a program's time-varying behavior because it is a microarchitecture-independent metric and by consequence gives an accurate picture of a program's time-varying behavior across microarchitectures. Previous work by Lau et al. [18] has shown that there exists a strong correlation between the code being executed — this is what a BBV captures — and actual performance. The intuition is that if two instruction intervals execute roughly the same code, and if the frequency of the portions of code executed is roughly the same, these two intervals should exhibit roughly the same performance.

3.2 Phase Classification

Once we have a BBV per instruction interval, we now need to classify intervals into phases. As suggested above, and intuitively speaking, this is done by comparing BBVs to find similarities. Intervals with similar BBVs are considered belonging to the same program phase.

Classifying instruction intervals into phases can be done in a number of ways. We view it as a clustering problem. There exist a number of clustering algorithms, such as linkage clustering, k-means clustering, threshold clustering, and many others. In this paper, we use threshold clustering because it provides a natural way of bounding the variability within a phase. As will become clear later, the advantage of using threshold clustering is that, by construction, it builds phases for which the variability (in terms of BBV behavior) is limited to a threshold θ. Classifying intervals into phases using threshold clustering works in an iterative way. It selects an instruction interval as a cluster center and then computes the distance with all the other instruction intervals. If the distance measure is smaller than a given threshold θ, the instruction interval is considered to be part of the same cluster/phase. Out of all remaining instruction intervals (not part of previously formed clusters), another interval is selected as a cluster center and the above process is repeated. This iterative process continues until all instruction intervals are assigned to a cluster/phase.

In our clustering approach we scan all instruction intervals once from the beginning until the end of the dynamic instruction stream. This means that the clustering algorithm has a complexity of $O(kN)$ with N the number of instruction intervals and k clusters ($k \ll N$), which is much more efficient than the iterative approach as described above which has an $O(N^2)$ computational complexity.

We use the Manhattan distance as our distance metric between two BBVs:

$$d = \sum_{i=1}^{D} \|A_i - B_i\|,$$

with A and B being two BBVs and A_i being the i-th element of BBV A; the dimensionality of the BBV, or the number of basic blocks in the program binary, equals D. The advantage of the Manhattan distance over the Euclidean distance is that it weighs differences more heavily. Assuming that the BBVs are normalized — the sum over all BBV elements equals one — the Manhattan distance varies between 0 (both BBVs are identical) and 2 (maximum possible difference between two BBVs). The θ threshold is expressed as a percentage of the maximum possible Manhattan distance between two instruction intervals.

After having applied threshold clustering, there are typically a number of clusters that represent only a small fraction of the total program execution, i.e., clusters with a small number of cluster members. We group all the smallest clusters to form a single cluster, the so called transition phase [20]. The transition phase accounts for no more than 5% of the total program execution.

3.3   Phase Count Surfaces

Having discussed how to measure behavioral similarity across instruction intervals using BBVs and how to group similar instruction intervals into phases through threshold clustering, we can now describe what a phase count surface looks like. A *phase count surface* shows the number of program phases as a function of intra-phase variability across different time scales, i.e., each point on a phase count surface shows the number of program phases at a given time scale at a given intra-phase variability threshold. The time scale is represented as the instruction interval length, and the per-phase variability is represented by θ used to drive the threshold clustering.

3.4   Phase Predictability Surfaces

As a result of the threshold clustering step discussed in the previous section, we can now assign phase IDs to all the instruction intervals. In other words, the dynamic instruction stream can be represented as a sequence of phase IDs with one phase ID per instruction interval in the dynamic instruction stream. We are now concerned with the regularity or predictability of the phase ID sequence. This is what a phase predictability surface characterizes.

Prediction by Partial Matching. We use the Prediction by Partial Matching (PPM) technique proposed by Chen et al. [3] to characterize phase predictability. The reason for choosing the PPM predictor is that it is a universal compression/prediction technique which presents a theoretical basis for phase prediction, and is not tied to a particular implementation.

A PPM predictor is built on the notion of a Markov predictor. A Markov predictor of order k predicts the next phase ID based upon k preceding phase IDs. Each entry in the Markov predictor records the number of phase IDs for the given history. To predict the next phase ID, the Markov predictor outputs the most likely phase ID for the given k-length history. An m-order PPM predictor consists of $(m+1)$ Markov predictors of orders 0 up to m. The PPM predictor uses the m-bit history to index the mth order Markov predictor. If the search succeeds, i.e., the history of phase IDs occurred previously, the PPM predictor outputs the prediction by the mth order Markov predictor. If the search does not succeed, the PPM predictor uses the $(m-1)$-bit history to index the $(m-1)$th order Markov predictor. In case the search misses again, the PPM predictor indexes the $(m-2)$th order Markov predictor, etc. Updating the PPM predictor is done by updating the Markov predictor that makes the prediction and all its higher order Markov predictors. In our setup, we consider a 32-order PPM phase predictor.

Predictability surfaces. A *phase predictability surface* shows the relationship between phase predictability and intra-phase variability across different time scales. Each point on a phase predictability surface shows the phase predictability as a function of time scale (quantified by the instruction interval granularity) and intra-phase variability (quantified by the θ parameter used during threshold clustering). Phase predictability itself is measured through the PPM predictor, i.e., for a given θ threshold and a given time scale, we report the prediction accuracy by the PPM predictor to predict phase IDs.

3.5   Phase Complexity Surfaces

Having discussed both the phase count surface as well as the phase predictability surface, we can now combine both surfaces to form a so called *phase complexity surface*. A phase complexity surface shows phase count versus phase predictability across different time scales. A phase complexity surface is easily derived from the phase count and predictability surfaces by factoring out the θ threshold. In other words, each point on the phase complexity surface corresponds to a particular θ threshold which determines phase count and predictability at a given time scale. The motivation for the phase complexity surface is to represent an easy-to-grasp intuitive view on a program's phase behavior through a single graph.

3.6   Discussion

Time complexity. The time complexity for computing phase complexity surfaces is linear as all of the four steps have a linear-time complexity. The first step computes the BBVs at the smallest interval granularity of interest. This requires a functional simulation or instrumentation run of the complete benchmark execution; the overhead is limited though. The second step computes BBVs at larger interval granularities by aggregating the BBVs from the previous step. This step is linear in the number of smallest-granularity intervals. The third step applies threshold clustering at all interval granularities. As mentioned in the paper, the basic approach to threshold clustering is an iterative process, our approach though makes a linear scan over the BBVs. Once the phase IDs are determined through the clustering step, the fourth step then determines the phase predictability by predicting next phase IDs — again, this is linear-time complexity.

Applications. The phase complexity surfaces provide a number of potential applications. One is to select representative benchmarks for performance analysis based on their inherent program phase behavior. A set of benchmarks that represent diverse phase behaviors can capture a representative picture of the benchmark suite's phase behavior; this will be illustrated further in section 6. Second, phase complexity surfaces are also useful in determining an appropriate interval size for optimization. For example, reducing energy consumption can be done by downscaling hardware resources on a per-phase basis [1,6,7,27]. An important criterion for good energy saving and limited performance penalty, is to limit the number of phases (in order to limit the training time at run time of finding a good per-phase hardware setting) and to achieve good phase predictability (in order to limit the number of phase mispredictions which may be costly in terms of missed energy saving opportunities and/or performance penalty).

4   Experimental Setup

We use all the SPEC CPU2000 integer and floating-point benchmarks, use reference inputs for all benchmarks and run all benchmarks to completion. We use the SimpleScalar Tool Set [2] for collecting BBVs on an interval basis.

5 Program Phase Characterization

Due to space constraints, it is impossible to present phase complexity curves for all benchmarks. Instead we present and discuss typical example phase complexity surfaces that we observed during our study. Example surfaces are shown in Figures 1 and 2: Figure 1 shows phase count and predictability surfaces for gcc-scilab, gzip-program, eon-kajiya and equake, and Figure 2 shows surfaces for bzip2-graphic, lucas, fma3d and gap. As mentioned before, a phase count surface shows the (logarithm of the) number of phases on the Z-axis versus the clustering threshold (which is a measure for intra-phase variability) and the interval size (which is a measure of time granularity) on the X and Y axes; the phase predictability surface shows phase predictability on the Z-axis versus clustering threshold and interval size. The θ clustering threshold is varied from 0.05 up to 0.5 in 0.05 increments — the smaller the threshold, the smaller the intra-phase variability; interval size is varied from 1M up to 1G — note the labels are shown as log_2 of the interval size.

There are basically two types of phase count surfaces. The first type shows a decreasing number of program phases at larger time granularities. This is illustrated in Figure 1. The second type shows an increasing number of program phases at larger time granularities and a decreasing number of program phases at a yet larger time granularity, see Figure 2.

The first type of phase count surface can be explained by the observation that phase behavior at a small time granularity gets averaged out at a larger time granularity. As a result, more and more portions of the program execution start looking similar which is reflected in a decreasing number of program phases. The second type of phase count surface appears for programs with obvious phase behavior, however, this obvious phase behavior seems to be difficult to capture over a range of time scales. This can occur in case the period of the inherent phase behavior is not a multiple of a given time granularity. For the purpose of illustration, consider the following example of a phase ID sequence: 'AAABBAAABBAAABB...' with 'A' and 'B' being phase IDs. The number of phases at time granularity 1 equals 2, namely 'A' and 'B'. At the time granularity of 2, there are 3 phases observed, namely 'AA', 'AB' (or 'BA') and 'BB'. At the time granularity of 4, there are only 2 phases observed: 'AAAB' and 'AABB'. In some sense this could be viewed of as a consequence of our choice for fixed-length intervals in our phase-level characterization, however, we observe the large number of phases across a range of time granularities. This seems to suggest that this phase behavior has a fairly long period, and that variable-length intervals (which are tied to some notion of time granularity as well) may not completely solve the problem.

It is also interesting to observe that for both types of phase count surfaces, phase predictability can be high or low. For example, the predictability is low for gcc-scilab, gzip-program and bzip2-graphic and is very high for equake, fma3d and lucas. For some benchmarks, phase predictability correlates inversely with the number of phases, see for example gzip-program: for a given clustering threshold, the higher the number of phases, the lower the predictability. For other benchmarks on the other hand, the opposite seems to be true: for a given clustering threshold, phase predictability decreases with a decreasing number of phases, see for example gcc-scilab.

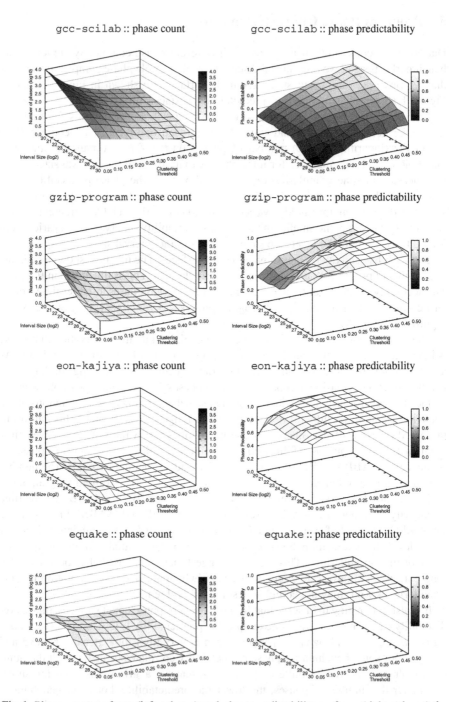

Fig. 1. Phase count surfaces (left column) and phase predictability surfaces (right column) for gcc-scilab, gzip-program, eon-kajiya and equake

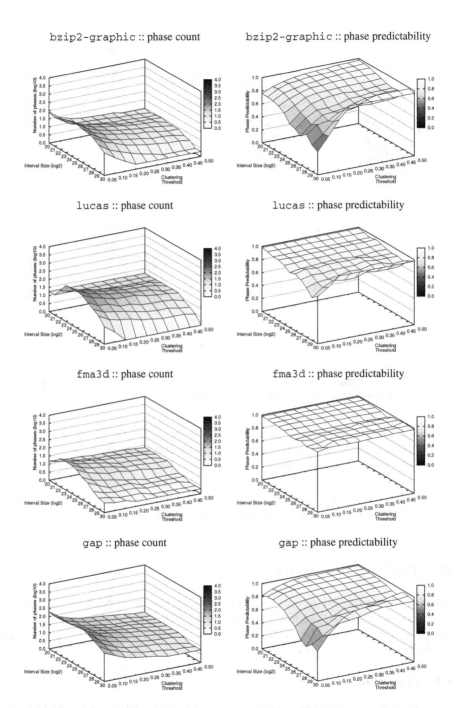

Fig. 2. Phase count surfaces (left column) and phase predictability surfaces (right column) for bzip2-graphic, lucas, fma3d and gap

gcc-scilab   eon-kajiya

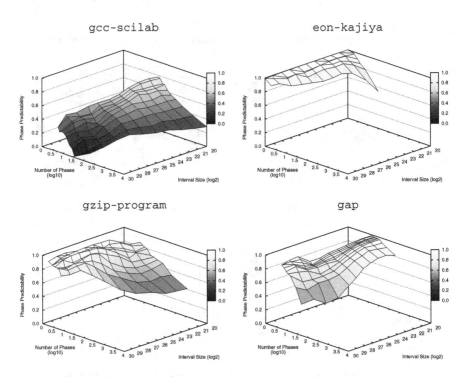

Fig. 3. Phase complexity surfaces for gcc-scilab (top left), eon-kajiya (top right), gzip-program (bottom left) and gap (bottom right)

Figure 3 shows the phase complexity surfaces for gcc-scilab, eon-kajiya, gzip-program and gap which combine the phase count and predictability surfaces. These examples clearly show two extreme phase behaviors. The phase behavior for eon-kajiya is much less complex than for gcc-scilab: eon-kajiya has fewer program phases and shows very good phase predictability; gcc-scilab on the other hand, exhibits a large number of phases and in addition, phase predictability is very poor.

6   Classifying Benchmarks

Having characterized all the benchmarks in terms of their phase behavior using phase complexity surfaces, we can now categorize benchmarks according to their phase behavior. To this end we employ the methodology proposed by Eeckhout et al. [10] to find similarities across benchmarks.

6.1   Methodology

As input to this methodology we provide a number of characteristics per benchmark: we provide phase predictability and (the logarithm of) the number of phases at three threshold values ($\theta = 5\%$, $\theta = 10\%$ and $\theta = 25\%$) at four time scales (1M, 8M, 64M and 512M) — there are 24 characteristics in total. Intuitively speaking, we sample the phase complexity surface. This yields a data matrix with the rows being the benchmark-input pairs and the columns being the 24 phase characteristics.

This data matrix serves as input to Principal Components Analysis (PCA) [15] — the goal of PCA is (i) to remove corand a given clustering threshold, relation from the data set and (ii) to reduce the dimensionality. PCA computes new dimensions, called *principal components*, which are *linear combinations* of the original phase characteristics. In other words, PCA tranforms the $p = 24$ phase characteristics $X_1, X_2, \ldots, X_p$ into p principal components $Z_1, Z_2, \ldots, Z_p$ with $Z_i = \sum_{j=1}^{p} a_{ij} X_j$. This transformation has the properties (i) $Var[Z_1] \geq Var[Z_2] \geq \ldots \geq Var[Z_p]$ — this means Z_1 contains the most information and Z_p the least; and (ii) $Cov[Z_i, Z_j] = 0, \forall i \neq j$ — this means there is no information overlap between the principal components. Some principal components have a higher variance than others. By removing the principal components with the lowest variance from the analysis, we reduce the dimensionality of the data set while controlling the amount of information that is thrown away. On our data set we retain 3 principal components that collectively explain 87.4% of the total variance in the original data set. Note that prior to PCA we normalize the data matrix (the columns have a zero mean and variance of one) to put all characteristics on a common scale; also after PCA, we normalize the principal components to give equal weight to the underlying mechanisms extracted by PCA.

We now have a reduced data matrix, i.e., we are left with three principal component values for all benchmark-input pairs. This reduced data set now serves as input to cluster analysis which groups benchmark-input pairs that exhibit similar phase behavior. We use linkage clustering here because it allows to visualize the clustering through a dendrogram. Linkage clustering starts with a matrix of distances between the benchmarks. As a starting point for the algorithm, each benchmark is considered as a group. In each iteration of the algorithm, groups that are closest to each other are merged and groups are gradually merged until we are left with a single group. This can be represented in a so called *dendrogram*, which graphically represents the linkage distance for each group merge at each iteration of the algorithm. Having obtained a dendrogram, it is up to the user to decide how many clusters to take. This decision can be made based on the linkage distance. Indeed, small linkage distances imply strong clustering while large linkage distances imply weak clustering. There exist several methods for calculating the distance between clusters. In this paper we use the weighted pair-group average method which computes the distance between two clusters as the weighted average distance between all pairs of program-input points in the two different clusters. The weighting of the average is done by considering the cluster size, i.e., the number of program-input points in the cluster.

6.2 Results

Figure 4 shows the dendrogram obtained from clustering the benchmarks based on their phase behavior. Classifying the benchmarks using this dendrogram with a critical threshold of 2.5, results in four major clusters representing the most diverse phase behaviors across the SPEC CPU2000 benchmarks, see also Table 1. Note that in case a more fine-grained distinction needs to be made among the benchmarks in terms of their

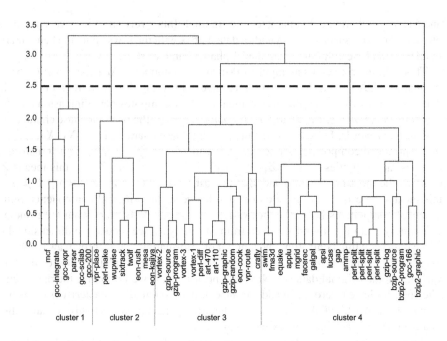

Fig. 4. Dendrogram visualizing the clustering

Table 1. Classifying benchmarks in terms of their phase behavior; cluster representatives are shown in bold

ID	benchmarks
1	gcc-200, **gcc-scilab**, gcc-expr, gcc-integrate, parser, mcf
2	**eon-kajiya**, eon-rush, mesa, twolf, sixtrack, wupwise, perl-make, vpr-place
3	crafty, vpr-route, eon-cook, **gzip-program**, gzip-source, gzip-graphic, gzip-random,art, perl-diff, vortex
4	bzip2, gcc-166, gzip-log, perl-split, ammp, **gap**, lucas, apsi, galgel, facerec, mgrid, applu, equake, fma3d, swim

phase behavior, the critical threshold should be made smaller; this will result in more fine-grained types of phase behavior. We observe the following key phase characteristics in each of the four major clusters:

- cluster 1 :: very poor phase predictability and a very large number of phases
- cluster 2 :: very small number of phases and very good phase predictability;
- cluster 3 :: a relatively poor predictability and a high number of phases at small time granularities, in combination with relatively better predictability and relatively fewer phases at large time granularities;
- cluster 4 :: a moderate number of phases across all time granularities, and mostly good to excellent predictability.

In summary, cluster 2 exhibits the simplest phase behavior. Clusters 3 and 4 show moderately complex phase behaviors, with cluster 3 showing poorer phase predictability at small time granularities. Cluster 1 represents the most complex phase behaviors observed across the SPEC CPU2000 benchmark suite. Referring back to Figure 3, the phase complexity surfaces shown represent an example benchmark from each of these groups: `eon-kajiya` as an example for the simple phase behavior in cluster 2; `gzip-program` and `gap` as examples for the moderately complex phase behaviors in clusters 3 and 4, respectively; and `gcc-scilab` as an example for the very complex phase behavior in cluster 1.

7   Conclusion

Program phase behavior is a well-known program characteristic that is subject to many optimizations both in software and hardware. In order to get a good understanding in a program's phase behavior, it is important to have a way of characterizing a program's time-varying behavior. This paper proposed phase complexity surfaces which characterize a program's phase behavior in terms of its four key properties: time scale, number of phases, phase predictability and intra- versus inter-phase predictability. Phase complexity surfaces provide a good intuitive and unified view of a program's phase behavior. These complexity surfaces can be used to classify benchmarks in terms of their inherent phase behavior.

Acknowledgements

We would like to thank the reviewers for their valuable comments. Frederik Vandeputte and Lieven Eeckhout are supported by the Fund for Scientific Research in Flanders (Belgium) (FWO-Vlaanderen). Additional support is provided by the FWO project G.0160.02, and the HiPEAC European Network-of-Excellence.

References

1. Balasubramonian, R., Albonesi, D., Buyuktosunoglu, A., Dwarkadas, S.: Memory hierarchy reconfiguration for energy and performance in general-purpose processor architectures. In: MICRO (December 2000)
2. Burger, D.C., Austin, T.M.: The SimpleScalar Tool Set. Computer Architecture News (1997), http://www.simplescalar.com
3. Chen, I.K., Coffey, J.T., Mudge, T.N.: Analysis of branch prediction via data compression. In: ASPLOS, pp. 128–137 (October 1996)
4. Cho, C.-B., Li, T.: Complexity-based program phase analysis and classification. In: PACT, pp. 105–113 (September 2006)
5. Cho, C.-B., Li, T.: Using wavelet domain workload execution characteristics to improve accuracy, scalability and robustness in program phase analysis. In: ISPASS (March 2007)
6. Dhodapkar, A., Smith, J.E.: Dynamic microarchitecture adaptation via co-designed virtual machines. In: International Solid State Circuits Conference (February 2002)
7. Dhodapkar, A., Smith, J.E.: Managing multi-configuration hardware via dynamic working set analysis. In: ISCA (May 2002)

8. Duesterwald, E., Cascaval, C., Dwarkadas, S.: Characterizing and predicting program behavior and its variability. In: Malyshkin, V. (ed.) PaCT 2003. LNCS, vol. 2763, Springer, Heidelberg (2003)
9. Eeckhout, L., Sampson, J., Calder, B.: Exploiting program microarchitecture independent characteristics and phase behavior for reduced benchmark suite simulation. In: IISWC, pp. 2–12 (October 2005)
10. Eeckhout, L., Vandierendonck, H., De Bosschere, K.: Workload design: Selecting representative program-input pairs. In: PACT, pp. 83–94 (September 2002)
11. Georges, A., Buytaert, D., Eeckhout, L., De Bosschere, K.: Method-level phase behavior in Java workloads. In: OOPSLA, pp. 270–287 (October 2004)
12. Huang, M., Renau, J., Torrellas, J.: Positional adaptation of processors: Application to energy reduction. In: ISCA (June 2003)
13. Huffmire, T., Sherwood, T.: Wavelet-based phase classification. In: PACT, pp. 95–104 (September 2006)
14. Isci, C., Martonosi, M.: Identifying program power phase behavior using power vectors. In: WWC (September 2003)
15. Johnson, R.A., Wichern, D.W.: Applied Multivariate Statistical Analysis, 5th edn. Prentice Hall, Englewood Cliffs (2002)
16. Lau, J., Perelman, E., Calder, B.: Selecting software phase markers with code structure analysis. In: CGO, pp. 135–146 (March 2006)
17. Lau, J., Perelman, E., Hamerly, G., Sherwood, T., Calder, B.: Motivation for variable length intervals and hierarchical phase behavior. In: ISPASS, pp. 135–146 (March 2005)
18. Lau, J., Sampson, J., Perelman, E., Hamerly, G., Calder, B.: The strong correlation between code signatures and performance. In: ISPASS (March 2005)
19. Lau, J., Schoenmackers, S., Calder, B.: Structures for phase classification. In: ISPASS, pp. 57–67 (March 2004)
20. Lau, J., Schoenmackers, S., Calder, B.: Transition phase classification and prediction. In: HPCA, pp. 278–289 (February 2005)
21. Nagpurkar, P., Krintz, C., Sherwood, T.: Phase-aware remote profiling. In: CGO, pp. 191–202 (March 2005)
22. Patil, H., Cohn, R., Charney, M., Kapoor, R., Sun, A., Karunanidhi, A.: Pinpointing representative portions of larhe Intel Itanium programs with dynamic instrumentation. In: MICRO, pp. 81–93 (December 2004)
23. Perelman, E., Hamerly, G., Calder, B.: Picking statistically valid and early simulation points. In: Malyshkin, V. (ed.) PaCT 2003. LNCS, vol. 2763, pp. 244–256. Springer, Heidelberg (2003)
24. Shen, X., Zhong, Y., Ding, C.: Locality phase prediction. In: ASPLOS (October 2004)
25. Sherwood, T., Perelman, E., Calder, B.: Basic block distribution analysis to find periodic behavior and simulation points in applications. In: Malyshkin, V. (ed.) PaCT 2001. LNCS, vol. 2127, pp. 3–14. Springer, Heidelberg (2001)
26. Sherwood, T., Perelman, E., Hamerly, G., Calder, B.: Automatically characterizing large scale program behavior. In: ASPLOS, pp. 45–57 (October 2002)
27. Sherwood, T., Sair, S., Calder, B.: Phase tracking and prediction. In: ISCA, pp. 336–347 (June 2003)
28. Vandeputte, F., Eeckhout, L., De Bosschere, K.: A detailed study on phase predictors. In: Cunha, J.C., Medeiros, P.D. (eds.) Euro-Par 2005. LNCS, vol. 3648, pp. 571–581. Springer, Heidelberg (2005)

Part VII

Optimizing Memory Performance

MLP-Aware Dynamic Cache Partitioning

Miquel Moreto[1], Francisco J. Cazorla[2], Alex Ramirez[1,2], and Mateo Valero[1,2]

[1] Universitat Politècnica de Catalunya, DAC, Barcelona, Spain
HiPEAC European Network of Excellence
[2] Barcelona Supercomputing Center – Centro Nacional de Supercomputación, Spain
{mmoreto,aramirez,mateo}@ac.upc.edu, francisco.cazorla@bsc.es

Abstract. Dynamic partitioning of shared caches has been proposed to improve performance of traditional eviction policies in modern multi-threaded architectures. All existing Dynamic Cache Partitioning (DCP) algorithms work on the number of misses caused by each thread and treat all misses equally. However, it has been shown that cache misses cause different impact in performance depending on the distribution of the Memory Level Parallelism (MLP) of the application L2 misses: clustered misses share their miss penalty as they can be served in parallel, while isolated misses have a greater impact as the memory latency is not shared with other misses.

We take this fact into account and propose a new DCP algorithm that considers misses differently depending on their influence in throughput. Our proposal obtains improvements over traditional traditional eviction policies up to 63.9% (10.6% on average) and it also outperforms previous DCP proposals by up to 15.4% (4.1% on average) in a four-core architecture. Finally, we give a practical implementation with a hardware cost under 1% of the total L2 cache size.

1 Introduction

The limitation imposed by instruction-level parallelism (ILP) has motivated the use of thread-level parallelism (TLP) as a common strategy for improving processor performance. TLP paradigms such as simultaneous multithreading (SMT) [1, 2], chip multiprocessor (CMP) [3] and combinations of both offer the opportunity to obtain higher throughputs. However, they also have to face the challenge of sharing resources of the architecture. Simply avoiding any resource control can lead to undesired situations where one thread is monopolizing all the resources and harming the other threads. Some studies deal with the resource sharing problem in SMTs at core level resources like issue queues, registers, etc. [4]. In CMPs, resource sharing is focused on the cache hierarchy.

Some applications present low reuse of their data and pollute caches with data streams, such as multimedia, communications or streaming applications, or have many compulsory misses that cannot be solved by assigning more cache space to the application. Traditional eviction policies such as Least Recently Used (LRU), pseudo LRU or random are demand-driven, that is, they tend to give more space to the application that has more accesses to the cache hierarchy.

P. Stenström et al. (Eds.): HiPEAC 2008, LNCS 4917, pp. 337–352, 2008.

As a consequence, some threads can suffer a severe degradation in performance. Previous work has tried to solve this problem by using static and dynamic partitioning algorithms that monitor the L2 cache accesses and decide a partition for a fixed amount of cycles in order to maximize throughput [5, 6, 7] or fairness [8]. Basically, these proposals predict the number of misses per application for each possible cache partition. Then, they use the cache partition that leads to the minimum number of misses for the next interval.

A common characteristic of these proposals is that they treat all L2 misses equally. However, it has been shown that L2 misses affect performance differently depending on how clustered they are. An isolated L2 miss has approximately the same miss penalty than a cluster of L2 misses, as they can be served in parallel if they all fit in the reorder buffer (ROB) [9]. In Figure 1 we can see this behavior. We have represented an *ideal* IPC curve that is constant until an L2 miss occurs. After some cycles, commit stops. When the cache line comes from main memory, commit ramps up to its steady state value. As a consequence, an isolated L2 miss has a higher impact on performance than a miss in a burst of misses as the memory latency is shared by all clustered misses.

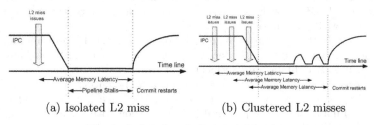

(a) Isolated L2 miss   (b) Clustered L2 misses

Fig. 1. Isolated and clustered L2 misses

Based on this fact, we propose a new DCP algorithm that gives a cost to each L2 access according to its impact in final performance. We detect isolated and clustered misses and assign a higher cost to isolated misses. Then, our algorithm determines the partition that minimizes the total cost for all threads, which is used in the next interval. Our results show that differentiating between clustered and isolated L2 misses leads to cache partitions with higher performance than previous proposals. The main contributions of this work are the following.

1) A runtime mechanism to dynamically partition shared L2 caches in a CMP scenario that takes into account the MLP of each L2 access. We obtain improvements over LRU up to 63.9% (10.6% on average) and over previous proposals up to 15.4% (4.1% on average) in a four-core architecture.

2) We extend previous workloads classifications for CMP architectures with more than two cores. Results can be better analyzed in every workload group.

3) We give a sampling technique that reduces the hardware cost in terms of storage under 1% of the total L2 cache size with an average throughput degradation of 0.76% (compared to the throughput obtained without sampling).

The rest of this paper is structured as follows. In Section 2 we introduce the methods that have been previously proposed to decide L2 cache partitions and related work. Next, in Section 3 we explain our MLP-aware DCP algorithm. In Section 4 we describe the experimetal environment and in Section 5 we discuss simulation results. Finally, we conclude with Section 6.

2   Prior Work in Dynamic Cache Partitioning

Stack Distance Histogram. Mattson et al. introduce the concept of stack distance to study the behavior of storage hierarchies [10]. Common eviction policies such as LRU have the *stack property*. Thus, each set in a cache can be seen as an LRU stack, where lines are sorted by their last access cycle. In that way, the first line of the LRU stack is the Most Recently Used (MRU) line while the last line is the LRU line. The position that a line has in the LRU stack when it is accessed again is defined as the *stack distance* of the access. As an example, we can see in Table 1(a) a stream of accesses to the same set with their corresponding stack distances.

Table 1. Stack Distance Histogram

(a) Stream of accesses to a given cache set

# Reference	1	2	3	4	5	6	7	8
Cache Line	A	B	C	C	A	D	B	D
Stack Distance	-	-	-	1	3	-	4	2

(b) SDH example

Stack Distance	1	2	3	4	>4
# Accesses	60	20	10	5	5

For a K-way associative cache with LRU replacement algorithm, we need $K + 1$ counters to build SDHs, denoted $C_1, C_2, \ldots, C_K, C_{>K}$. On each cache access, one of the counters is incremented. If it is a cache access to a line in the ith position in the LRU stack of the set, C_i is incremented. If it is a cache miss, the line is not found in the LRU stack and, as a result, we increment the miss counter $C_{>K}$. SDH can be obtained during execution by running the thread alone in the system [5] or by adding some hardware counters that profile this information [6,7]. A characteristic of these histograms is that the number of cache misses for a smaller cache with the same number of sets can be easily computed. For example, for a K'-way associative cache, where $K' < K$, the new number of misses can be computed as $misses = C_{>K} + \sum_{i=K'+1}^{K} C_i$.

As an example, in Table 1(b) we show a SDH for a set with 4 ways. Here, we have 5 cache misses. However, if we reduce the number of ways to 2 (keeping the number of sets constant), we will experience 20 misses (5 + 5 + 10).

Minimizing Total Misses. Using the SDHs of N applications, we can derive the L2 cache partition that minimizes the total number of misses: this last number corresponds to the sum of the number of misses of each thread with the assigned number of ways. The optimal partition in the last period of time is a suitable candidate to become the future optimal partition. Partitions are decided periodically after a fixed amount of cycles. In this scenario, partitions are decided at a *way granularity*. This mechanism is used in order to minimize the total number of misses and try to maximize throughput. A first approach proposed a static partitioning of the L2 cache using profiling information [5]. Then, a dynamic approach estimated SDHs with information inside the cache [7]. Finally, Qureshi et al. presented a suitable and scalable circuit to measure SDHs using sampling and obtained performance gains with just 0.2% extra space in the L2 cache [6]. Throughout this paper, we will call this last policy *MinMisses*.

Fair Partitioning. In some situations, *MinMisses* can lead to unfair partitions that assign nearly all the resources to one thread while harming the others [8]. For that reason, the authors propose considering fairness when deciding new partitions. In that way, instead of minimizing the total number of misses, they try to equalize the statistic $X_i = \frac{misses_{shared_i}}{misses_{alone_i}}$ of each thread i. They desire to force all threads to have the same increase in percentage of misses. Partitions are decided periodically using an iterative method. The thread with largest X_i receives a way from the thread with smallest X_i until all threads have a similar value of X_i. Throughout this paper, we will call this policy *Fair*.

Table 2. Different Partitioning Proposals

Paper	Partitioning	Objective	Decision	Algorithm	Eviction Policy
[5]	Static	Minimize Misses	Programmer	–	Column Caching
[7]	Dynamic	Minimize Misses	Architecture	Marginal Gain	Augmented LRU
[6]	Dynamic	Maximize Utility	Architecture	Lookahead	Augmented LRU
[8]	Dynamic	Fairness	Architecture	Equalize X_1^i	Augmented LRU
[11]	Dyn./Static	Configurable	Operating System	Configurable	Augmented LRU

Other Related Work. Several papers propose different DCP algorithms in a multithreaded scenario. In Table 2 we summarize these proposals with their most significant characteristics. Rafique et al. propose to manage shared caches with a hardware cache quota enforcement mechanism and an interface between the architecture and the OS to let the latter decide quotas [11]. We have to note that this mechanism is completely orthogonal to our proposal and, in fact, they are compatible as we can let the OS decide quotas according to our scheme. Hsu et al. evaluate different cache policies in a CMP scenario [12]. They show that none of them is optimal among all benchmarks and that the best cache policy varies depending on the performance metric being used. Thus, they propose to use a thread-aware cache resource allocation. In fact, their results reinforce the motivation of our paper: if we do not consider the impact of each L2 miss in performance, we can decide suboptimal L2 partitions in terms of throughput.

Cache partitions at a way granularity can be implemented with *column caching* [5], which uses a bit mask to mark reserved ways, or by augmenting the LRU policy with counters that keep track of the number of lines in a set belonging to a thread [7]. The evicted line will be the LRU line among its owned lines or other threads lines depending on wether it reaches its quota or not.

In [13] a new eviction policy for *private* caches was proposed in single-threaded architectures. This policy gives a weight to each L2 miss according to its MLP when the block is filled from memory. Eviction is decided using the LRU counters and this weight. This idea was proposed for a different scenario as it focus on single-threaded architectures.

3   MLP-Aware Dynamic Cache Partitioning

3.1   Algorithm Overview

The algorithm steps to decide dynamic cache partitions according to the MLP of each L2 access can be seen in Algorithm 1. When we start executing different applications in our CMP architecture, we have to decide an initial partition of the L2 cache. As we have no prior knowledge of the applications, we choose to assign $\frac{Associativity}{Number\ of\ Cores}$ ways to each core.

Step 1: Establish an initial even partition for each core ;
Step 2: Run threads and collect data for the MLP-aware SDHs ;
Step 3: Decide new partition ;
Step 4: Update MLP-aware SDHs ;
Step 5: Go back to Step 2 ;

Algorithm 1. MLP-Aware dynamic cache partitioning algorithm

Afterwards, we begin a period of measuring the total MLP cost of each application. We denote MLP-aware SDH the histogram of each thread containing the total MLP cost for each possible partition. For small values of this period, DCP algorithms react quicker to phase changes. However, the overhead of this method also increases. Small performance variations are obtained for different periods from 10^5 to 10^8 cycles, with a peak for a period of 5 million cycles.

When this interval ends, MLP-aware SDHs are analyzed and a new partition is decided for the next interval. We assume that we will have a similar pattern of L2 accesses in the next measuring period. Thus, the optimal partition for the last period will be chosen for the following period. Evaluating all possible combinations gives the optimal partition. However, this algorithm does not scale adequately when associativity and the number of cores is raised. If we have a K-way associativity L2 cache shared by N cores, the number of possible partitions without considering the order is $\binom{N+K-1}{K}$. For example, for 8 cores and 16 ways, we have 245157 possible combinations. Several heuristics have been proposed to reduce the number of cycles required to decide the new partition [6,7], which can be used in our situation. These proposals bound the decision period by 10000 cycles. This overhead is very low compared to 5 million cycles (under 0.2%).

Since characteristics of applications dynamically change, MLP-aware SDHs should reflect these changes. However, we also wish to maintain some history of the past MLP-aware SDHs to make new decisions. Thus, after a new partition is decided, we multiply all the values of the MLP-aware SDHs times $\rho \in [0,1]$. Large values of ρ have larger reaction times to phase changes, while small values of ρ quickly adapt to phase changes but tend to forget the behavior of the application. Small performance variations are obtained for different values of ρ ranging from 0 to 1, with a peak for $\rho = 0.5$. Furthermore, this value is very convenient as we can use a shifter to update histograms. Next, a new period of measuring MLP-aware SDHs begins. The key contribution of this paper is the method to obtain MLP-aware SDHs that we explain in the following Subsection.

3.2   MLP-Aware Stack Distance Histogram

As previously stated, *MinMisses* assumes that all L2 accesses are equally important in terms of performance. However, this is not always true. Cache misses affect differently the performance of applications, even inside the same application. As was said in [9], an isolated L2 data miss has a penalty cost that can be approximated by the average memory latency. In the case of a burst of L2 data misses that fit in the ROB, the penalty cost is shared among misses as L2 misses can be served in parallel. In case of L2 instruction misses, they are serialized as fetch stops. Thus, L2 instruction misses have a constant miss penalty and MLP.

We want to assign a cost to each L2 access according to its effect on performance. In [13] a similar idea was used to modify LRU eviction policy for single core and single threaded architectures. In our situation, we have a CMP scenario where the shared L2 cache has a number of reserved ways for each core. At the end of a measuring period, we can decide to continue with the same partition or change it. If we decide to modify the partition, a core i that had w_i reserved ways will receive $w_i' \neq w_i$. If $w_i < w_i'$, the thread receives more ways and, as a consequence, some misses in the old configuration will become hits. Conversely, if $w_i > w_i'$, the thread receives less ways and some hits in the old configuration will become misses. Thus, we want to have an estimation of the performance effects when misses are converted into hits and vice versa. Throughout this paper, we will call this impact on performance *MLP_cost*. All accesses are treated as if they were in the correct path until the branch prediction is checked. All misses on the wrong path are not considered as accesses in flight.

MLP_cost of L2 misses. If we force an L2 configuration that assigns exactly $w_i' = d_i$ ways to thread i with $w_i' > w_i$, some of the L2 misses of this thread will

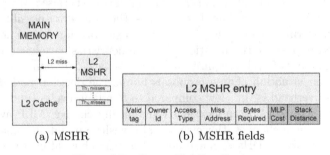

(a) MSHR   (b) MSHR fields

Fig. 2. Miss Status Holding Register

become hits, while other will remain misses, depending on their stack distance. In order to track the stack distance and MLP_cost of each L2 miss, we have modified the L2 Miss Status Holding Registers (MSHR) [14]. This structure is similar to an L2 miss buffer and is used to hold information about any load that has missed in the L2 cache. The modified L2 MSHR has one extra field that contains the MLP_cost of the miss as can be seen in Figure 2(b). It is also necessary to store the stack distance of each access in the MSHR. In Figure 2(a) we show the MSHR in the cache hierarchy.

When the L2 cache is accessed and an L2 miss is determined, we assign an MSHR entry to the miss and wait until the data comes from Main Memory. We initialize the MLP_cost field to zero when the entry is assigned. We store the access stack distance together with the identificator of the owner core. Every cycle, we obtain N, the number of L2 accesses with stack distance greater or equal to d_i. We have a hardware counter that tracks this number for each possible number of d_i, which means a total of *Associativity* counters. If we have N L2 misses that are being served in parallel, the miss penalty is shared. Thus, we assign an equal share of $\frac{1}{N}$ to each miss. The value of the MLP_cost is updated until the data comes from Main Memory and fills the L2. At this moment we can free the MSHR entry.

MLP_cost of L2 hits. Next, we want to estimate the MLP_cost of an L2 hit with stack distance d_i when it becomes a miss. If we forced an L2 configuration that assigned exactly $w_i' = d_i$ ways to the thread i with $w_i' < w_i$, some of the L2 hits of this thread would become misses, while L2 misses would remain as misses. The hits that would become misses are the ones with stack distance greater or equal to d_i. Thus, we count the total number of accesses with stack distance greater or equal to d_i (including L2 hits and misses) to estimate the length of the cluster of L2 misses in this configuration.

Deciding the moment to free the entry used by an L2 hit is more complex than in the case of the MSHR. As it was said in [9], in a balanced architecture, L2 data misses can be served in parallel if they all fit in the ROB. Equivalently, we say that L2 data misses can be served in parallel if they are at ROB distance smaller than the ROB size. Thus, we should free the entry if the number of committed instructions since the access has reached the ROB size or if the number of cycles since the hit has reached the average latency to memory. The first condition is clear as we have said that L2 misses can overlap if their ROB distance is less than the ROB size. The second condition is also necessary as it can occur that no L2 access is done for a period of time. To obtain the average latency to memory, we add a specific hardware that counts and averages the number of cycles that a given entry is in the MSHR.

We use new hardware to obtain the MLP_cost of L2 hits. We denote this hardware Hit Status Holding Registers (HSHR) as it is similar to the MSHR. However, the HSHR is private for each core. In each entry, the HSHR needs an identificator of the ROB entry of the access, the address accessed by the L2 hit, the stack distance value and a field with the corresponding MLP_cost as can be seen in Figure 3(b). In Figure 3(a) we show the HSHR in the cache hierarchy.

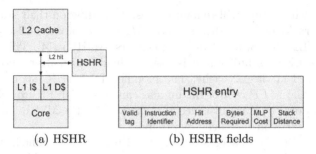

(a) HSHR   (b) HSHR fields

Fig. 3. Hit Status Holding Register

When the L2 cache is accessed and an L2 hit is determined, we assign an HSHR entry to the L2 hit. We init the fields of the entry as in the case of the MSHR. We have a stack distance d_i and we want to update the MLP_cost field in every cycle. With this objective, we need to know the number of active entries with stack distance greater or equal to d_i in the HSHR, which can be tracked with one hardware counter per core. We also need a ROB entry identificator for each L2 access. Every cycle, we obtain N, the number of L2 accesses with stack distance greater or equal to d_i as in the L2 MSHR case. We have a hardware counter that tracks this number for each possible number of d_i, which means a total of *Associativity* counters.

In order to avoid array conflicts, we need as many entries in the HSHR as possible L2 accesses in flight. This number is equal to the L1 MSHR size. In our scenario, we have 32 L1 MSHR entries, which means a maximum of 32 in flight L2 accesses per core. However, we have checked that we have enough with 24 entries to ensure that we have an available slot 95% of the time in an architecture with a ROB of 256 entries. If there are no available slots, we simply assign the minimum weight to the L2 access as there are many L2 accesses in flight.

Quantification of MLP_cost. Dealing with values of MLP_cost between 0 and the memory latency (or even greater) can represent a significant hardware cost. Instead, we decide to quantify this MLP_cost with an integer value between 0 and 7 as was done in [13]. For a memory latency of 300 cycles, we can see in Table 3 how to quantify the MLP_cost. We have splitted the interval $[0; 300]$ with 7 intervals of equal length.

Finally, when we have to update the corresponding MLP-aware SDH, we add the quantified value of MLP_cost. Thus, isolated L2 misses will have a weight

Table 3. MLP_cost quantification

MLP_cost	Quantification	MLP_cost	Quantification
From 0 to 42 cycles	0	From 171 to 213 cycles	4
From 43 to 85 cycles	1	From 214 to 246 cycles	5
From 86 to 128 cycles	2	From 247 to 300 cycles	6
From 129 to 170 cycles	3	300 or more cycles	7

of 7, while two overlapped L2 misses will have a weight of 3 in the MLP-aware SDH. In contrast, *MinMisses* always adds one to its histograms.

3.3   Obtaining Stack Distance Histograms

Normally, L2 caches have two separate parts that store data and address tags to know if the access is a hit. Basically, our prediction mechanism needs to track every L2 access and store a separated copy of the L2 tags information in an *Auxiliary Tag Directory* (ATD), together with the LRU counters [6]. We need an ATD for each core that keeps track of the L2 accesses for any possible cache configuration. Independently of the number of ways assigned to each core, we store the tags and LRU counters of the last K accesses of the thread, where K is the L2 associativity. As we have explained in Section 2, an access with stack distance d_i corresponds to a cache miss in any configuration that assigns less than d_i ways to the thread. Thus, with this ATD we can determine whether an L2 access would be a miss or a hit in all possible cache configurations.

3.4   Putting All Together

In Figure 4 we can see a sketch of the hardware implementation of our proposal. When we have an L2 access, the ATD is used to determine its stack distance d_i. Depending on whether it is a miss or a hit, either the MSHR or the HSHR is used to compute the *MLP_cost* of the access. Using the quantification process we obtain the final *MLP_cost*. This number estimates how performance is affected when the applications has exactly $w_i' = d_i$ assigned ways. If $w_i' > w_i$, we are estimating the performance benefit of converting this L2 miss into a hit. In case $w_i' < w_i$, we are estimating the performance degradation of converting this L2 hit into a miss. Finally, using the stack distance, the *MLP_cost* and the core identifier, we can update the corresponding MLP-aware SDH.

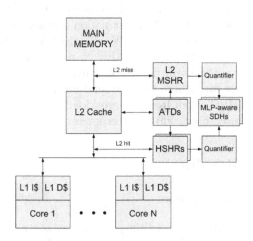

Fig. 4. Hardware implementation

We have used two different partitionig algorithms. The first one, that we denote *MLP-DCP* (standing for MLP-aware Dynamic Cache Partitioning), decides the optimal partition according to the MLP_cost of each way. We define the total MLP_cost of a thread i that uses w_i ways as $TMLP(i, w_i) = MLP\_SDH_{i,>K} + \sum_{j=w_i}^{K} MLP\_SDH_{i,j}$. We denote the total MLP_cost of all accesses of thread i with stack distance j as $MLP\_SDH_{i,j}$. Thus, we have to minimize the expression $\sum_{i=1}^{N} TMLP(i, w_i)$, where $\sum_{i=1}^{N} w_i = $ Associativity.

The second one consists in assigning a weight to each total MLP_cost using the IPC of the application in core i, IPC_i. In this situation, we are giving priority to threads with higher IPC. This point will give better results in throughput at the cost of being less fair. IPC_i is measured at runtime with a hardware counter per core. We denote this proposal *MLPIPC-DCP*, which consists in minimizing the expression $\sum_{i=1}^{N} IPC_i \cdot TMLP(i, w_i)$, where $\sum_{i=1}^{N} w_i = $ Associativity.

4   Experimental Environment

We target this study to the case of a CMP with two and four cores with their respective own data and instruction L1 caches and a unified L2 cache shared among threads as in previous studies [8, 6, 7]. Each core is single-threaded and fetches up to 8 instructions each cycle. It has 6 integer (I), 3 floating point (FP), and 4 load/store functional units and 32-entry I, load/store, and FP instruction queues. Each thread has a 256-entry ROB and 256 physical registers. We use a two-level cache hierarchy with 64B lines with separate 16KB, 4-way associative data and instruction caches, and a unified L2 cache that is shared among all cores. We have used two different L2 caches, one of size 1MB and 16-way associativity, and the second one of size 2MB and 32-way associativity. Latency from L1 to L2 is 15 cycles, and from L2 to memory 300 cycles. We use a 32B width bus to access L2 and a multibanked L2 of 16 banks with 3 cycles of access time.

We extended the SMTSim simulator [2] to make it CMP. We collected traces of the most representative 300 million instruction segment of each program, following the SimPoint methodology [15]. We use the FAME simulation methodology [16] with a Maximum Allowable IPC Variance of 5%. This evaluation methodology measures the performance of multithreaded processors by reexecuting all threads in a multithreaded workload until all of them are fairly represented in the final IPC taken from the workload. As performance metrics we have used the IPC throughput, which corresponds to the sum of individual IPCs.

5   Evaluation Results

5.1   Workload Classification

In [17] two metrics are used to model the performance of a partitioning algorithm like *MinMisses* for pairings of benchmarks in the SPEC CPU 2000 benchmark suite. Here, we extend this classification for architectures with more cores.

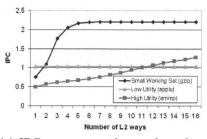

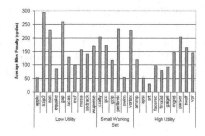

(a) IPC as we vary the number of assigned ways of a 1MB 16-way L2 cache

(b) Average miss penalty of an L2 miss with a 1MB 16-way L2 cache

Fig. 5. Benchmark classification

Metric 1. The $w_{P\%}(B)$ metric measures the number of ways needed by a benchmark B to obtain at least a given percentage $P\%$ of its maximum IPC (when it uses all L2 ways).

The intuition behind this metric is to classify benchmarks depending on their cache utilization. Using $P = 90\%$ we can classify benchmarks into three groups: *Low utility* (L), *Small working set* or *saturated utility* (S) and *High utility* (H). L benchmarks have $1 \leq w_{90\%} \leq \frac{K}{8}$ where K is the L2 associativity. L benchmarks are not affected by L2 cache space because nearly all L2 accesses are misses. S benchmarks have $\frac{K}{8} < w_{90\%} \leq \frac{K}{2}$ and just need some ways to have maximum throughput as they fit in the L2 cache. Finally, H benchmarks have $w_{90\%} > \frac{K}{2}$ and always improve IPC as the number of ways given to them is increased. Clear representatives of these three groups are `applu` (L), `gzip` (S) and `ammp` (H) in Figure 5(a). In Table 4 we give $w_{90\%}$ for all SPEC CPU 2000 benchmarks.

Table 4. Benchmark characterization

Bench	$w_{90\%}$	APTC	IPC	Bench	$w_{90\%}$	APTC	IPC	Bench	$w_{90\%}$	APTC	IPC
ammp	14	23.63	1.27	applu	1	16.83	1.03	apsi	10	21.14	2.17
art	10	46.04	0.52	bzip2	1	1.18	2.62	crafty	4	7.66	1.71
eon	3	7.09	2.31	equake	1	18.6	0.27	facerec	11	10.96	1.16
fma3d	9	15.1	0.11	galgel	15	18.9	1.14	gap	1	2.68	0.96
gcc	3	6.97	1.64	gzip	4	21.5	2.20	lucas	1	7.60	0.35
mcf	1	9.12	0.06	mesa	2	3.98	3.04	mgrid	11	9.52	0.71
parser	11	9.09	0.89	perl	5	3.82	2.68	sixtrack	1	1.34	2.02
swim	1	28.0	0.40	twolf	15	12.0	0.81	vortex	7	9.65	1.35
vpr	14	11.9	0.97	wupw	1	5.99	1.32				

The average miss penalty of an L2 miss for the whole SPEC CPU 2000 benchmark suite is shown in Figure 5(b). We note that this average miss penalty varies a lot, even inside each group of benchmarks, ranging from 30 to 294 cycles. This Figure reinforces the main motivation of the paper, as it proves that the clustering level of L2 misses changes for different applications.

Metric 2. The $w_{LRU}(th_i)$ metric measures the number of ways given by LRU to each thread th_i in a workload composed of N threads. This can be done simulating all benchmarks alone and using the frequency of L2 accesses for each thread [18]. We denote the number of L2 Accesses in a Period of one Thousand Cycles for thread i as $APTC_i$. In Table 4 we list these values for each benchmark.

$$w_{LRU}(th_i) = \frac{APTC_i}{\sum_{j=1}^{N} APTC_j} \cdot Associativity$$

Next, we use these two metrics to extend previous classifications [17] for workloads with more than two benchmarks.

Case 1. When $w_{90\%}(th_i) \leq w_{LRU}(th_i)$ for all threads. In this situation LRU attains 90% of each benchmark performance. Thus, it is intuitive that in this situation there is very little room for improvement.

Case 2. When there exists two threads A and B such that $w_{90\%}(th_A) > w_{LRU}(th_A)$ and $w_{90\%}(th_B) < w_{LRU}(th_B)$. In this situation, LRU is harming the performance of thread A, because it gives more ways than necessary to thread B. Thus, in this situation LRU is assigning some shared resources to a thread that does not need them, while the other thread could benefit from these resources.

Case 3. Finally, the third case is obtained when $w_{90\%}(th_i) > w_{LRU}(th_i)$ for all threads. In this situation, our L2 cache configuration is not big enough to assure that all benchmarks will have at least a 90% of their peak performance. In [17] it was observed that pairings belonging to this group showed worse results when the value of $|w_{90\%}(th_1) - w_{90\%}(th_2)|$ grows. In this case, we have a thread that requires much less L2 cache space than the other to attain 90% of its peak IPC. LRU treats threads equally and manages to satisfy the less demanding thread necessities. In case of *MinMisses*, it assumes that all misses are equally important for throughput and tends to give more space to the thread with higher L2 cache necessity, while harming the less demanding thread. This is a problem due to *MinMisses* algorithm. We will show in next Subsections that MLP-aware partitioning policies are available to overcome this situation.

Table 5. Workloads belonging to each case for two different shared L2 caches

#cores	1MB 16-way			2MB 32-way		
	Case 1	Case 2	Case 3	Case 1	Case 2	Case 3
2	155 (48%)	135 (41%)	35 (11%)	159 (49%)	146 (45%)	20 (6.2%)
4	624 (4%)	12785 (86%)	1541 (10%)	286 (1.9%)	12914 (86%)	1750 (12%)
6	306 (0.1%)	219790 (95%)	10134 (5%)	57 (0.02%)	212384 (92%)	17789 (7.7%)

In Table 5 we show the total number of workloads that belong to each case for different configurations. We have generated all possible combinations without repeating benchmarks. The order of benchmarks is not important. In the case of a 1MB 16-way L2, we note that Case 2 becomes the dominant case as the number of cores increases. The same trend is observed for L2 caches with larger associativity. In Table 5 we can also see the total number of workloads that belong to each case as the number of cores increases for a 32-way 2MB L2 cache. Note that with different L2 cache configurations, the value of $w_{90\%}$ and $APTC_i$ will change for each benchmark. An important conclusion from Table 5 is that as we increase the number of cores, there are more combinations that belong to the second case, which is the one with more improvement possibilities.

To evaluate our proposals, we randomly generate 16 workloads belonging to each group for three different configurations. We denote these configurations $2C$ (2 cores and 1MB 16-way L2), $4C$-1 (4 cores and 1MB 16-way L2) and $4C$-2 (4 cores and 2MB 32-way L2). We have also used a 2MB 32-way L2 cache as future CMP architectures will continue scaling L2 size and associativity. For example, the IBM Power5 [19] has a 10-way 1.875MB L2 cache and the Niagara 2 has a 16-way 4MB L2. Average improvements do consider the distribution of workloads among the three groups. We denote this mean *weighted mean*, as we assign a weight to the speed up of each case depending on the distribution of workloads from Table 5. For example, for the $2C$ configuration, we compute the weighted mean improvement as $0.48 \cdot x_1 + 0.41 \cdot x_2 + 0.11 \cdot x_3$, where x_i is the average improvement in Case i.

5.2 Performance Results

Throughput. The first experiment consists in comparing throughput for different DCP algorithms, using LRU policy as the baseline. We simulate *MinMisses* and our two proposals with the 48 workloads that were selected in the previous Subsection. We can see in Figure 6(a) the average speed up over LRU for these mechanisms. *MLPIPC-DCP* systematically obtains the best average results, nearly doubling the performance benefits of *MinMisses* over LRU in the four-core configurations. In configuration $4C$-1, *MLPIPC-DCP* outperforms *MinMisses* by 4.1%. *MLP-DCP* always improves *MinMisses* but obtains worse results than *MLPIPC-DCP*.

All algorithms have similar results in Case 1. This is intuitive as in this situation there is little room for improvement. In Case 2, *MinMisses* obtains a

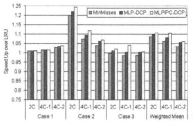

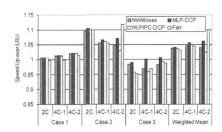

(a) Throughput speed up over LRU   (b) Fairness speed up over LRU

Fig. 6. Average performance speed ups over LRU

relevant improvement over LRU in configuration *2C*. *MLP-DCP* and *MLPIPC-DCP* achieve an extra 2.5% and 5% improvement, respectively. In the other configurations, *MLP-DCP* and *MLPIPC-DCP* still outperform MinMisses by a 2.1% and 3.6%. In Case 3, *MinMisses* presents larger performance degradation as the asymmetry between the necessities of the two cores increases. As a consequence, it has worse average throughput than LRU. Assigning an appropiate weight to each L2 access gives the possibility to obtain better results than LRU using *MLP-DCP* and *MLPIPC-DCP*.

Fairness. We have used the harmonic mean of relative IPCs [20] to measure fairness. The relative IPC is computed as $\frac{IPC_{shared}}{IPC_{alone}}$. In Figure 6(b) we show the average speed up over LRU of the harmonic mean of relative IPCs. *Fair* stands for the policy explained in Section 2. We can see that in all situations, *MLP-DCP* always improves over both *MinMisses* and LRU (except in Case 3 for two cores). It even obtains better results than *Fair* in configurations *2C* and *4C-1*. *MLPIPC-DCP* is a variant of the *MLP-DCP* algorithm optimized for throughput. As a consequence, it obtains worse results in fairness than *MLP-DCP*.

5.3 Hardware Cost

We have used the hardware implementation of Figure 4 to estimate the hardware cost of our proposal. In this Subsection, we focus our attention on the configuration *2C*. We suppose a 40-bit physical address space. Each entry in the ATD needs 29 bits (1 valid bit + 24-bit tag + 4-bit for LRU counter). Each set has 16 ways, so we have an overhead of 58 Bytes (B) for each set. As we have 1024 sets, we have a total cost of 58KB per core.

The hardware cost that corresponds to the extra fields of each entry in the L2 MSHR is 5 bits for the stack distance and 2B for the *MLP_cost*. As we have 32 entries, we have a total of 84B. HSHR entries need 1 valid bit, 8 bits to identify the ROB entry, 34 bits for the address, 5 bits for the stack distance and 2B for the *MLP_cost*. In total we need 64 bits per entry. As we have 24 entries in each HSHR, we have a total of 192B per core. Finally, we need 17 counters of 4B for each MLP-Aware SDH, which supposes a total of 68B per core. In addition to the storage bits, we also need an adder for incrementing MLP-aware SDHs and a shifter to halve the hit counters after each partitioning interval.

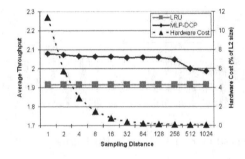

Fig. 7. Throughput and hardware cost depending on d_s in a two-core CMP

Sampled ATD. The main contribution to hardware cost corresponds to the ATD. Instead of monitoring every cache set, we can decide to track accesses from a reduced number of sets. This idea was also used in [6] with *MinMisses* in a CMP environment. Here, we use it in a different situation, say to estimate MLP-aware SDHs with a sampled number of sets. We define a *sampling distance* d_s that gives the distance between tracked sets. For example, if $d_s = 1$, we are tracking all the sets. If $d_s = 2$, we track half of the sets, and so on. Sampling reduces the size of the ATD at the expense of less accuracy in MLP-aware SDHs predictions as some accesses are not tracked, Figure 7 shows throughput degradation in a 2 cores scenario as the d_s increases. This curve is measured on the left y-axis. We also show the storage overhead in percentage of the total L2 cache size, measured on the right y-axis. Thanks to the sampling technique, storage overhead drastically decreases. Thus, with a sampling distance of 16 we obtain average throughput degradations of 0.76% and a storage overhead of 0.77% of the L2 cache size. We think that this is an interesting point of design.

6 Conclusions

In this paper we propose a new DCP algorithm that gives a cost to each L2 access according to its impact in final performance: isolated misses receive higher costs than clustered misses. Next, our algorithm decides the L2 cache partition that minimizes the total cost for all running threads. Furthermore, we have classified workloads for multiple cores into three groups and shown that the dominant situation is precisely the one that offers room for improvement.

We shown that our proposal reaches high throughput for two- and four-core architectures. In all evaluated configurations, *MLP-DCP* and *MLPIPC-DCP* systematically outperform both LRU and *MinMisses*, reaching a speed up of 63.9% (10.6% on average) and 15.4% (4.1% on average) over LRU and *MinMisses*, respectively. Finally, we have used a sampling technique to propose a practical implementation with a hardware cost in terms of storage under 1% of the total L2 cache size with nearly no performance degradation.

Acknowledgments. This work has been supported by the Ministry of Education and Science of Spain under contracts TIN2004-07739, TIN2007-60625 and grant AP-2005-3318, and by SARC European Project. The authors would like to thank C. Acosta, A. Falcon, D. Ortega, J. Vermoulen and O. J. Santana for their work in the simulation tool and the reviewers for their helpful comments.

References

1. Serrano, M.J., Wood, R., Nemirovsky, M.: A study on multistreamed superscalar processors, Technical Report 93-05, University of California Santa Barbara (1993)
2. Tullsen, D.M., Eggers, S.J., Levy, H.M.: Simultaneous multithreading: Maximizing on-chip parallelism. In: ISCA (1995)
3. Hammond, L., Nayfeh, B.A., Olukotun, K.: A single-chip multiprocessor. Computer 30(9), 79–85 (1997)

4. Cazorla, F.J., Ramirez, A., Valero, M., Fernandez, E.: Dynamically controlled resource allocation in SMT processors. In: MICRO (2004)
5. Chiou, D., Jain, P., Devadas, S., Rudolph, L.: Dynamic cache partitioning via columnization. In: Design Automation Conference (2000)
6. Qureshi, M.K., Patt, Y.N.: Utility-based cache partitioning: A low-overhead, high-performance, runtime mechanism to partition shared caches. In: MICRO (2006)
7. Suh, G.E., Devadas, S., Rudolph, L.: A new memory monitoring scheme for memory-aware scheduling and partitioning. In: HPCA (2002)
8. Kim, S., Chandra, D., Solihin, Y.: Fair cache sharing and partitioning in a chip multiprocessor architecture. In: PACT (2004)
9. Karkhanis, T.S., Smith, J.E.: A first-order superscalar processor model. In: ISCA (2004)
10. Mattson, R.L., Gecsei, J., Slutz, D.R., Traiger, I.L.: Evaluation techniques for storage hierarchies. IBM Systems Journal 9(2), 78–117 (1970)
11. Rafique, N., Lim, W.T., Thottethodi, M.: Architectural support for operating system-driven CMP cache management. In: PACT (2006)
12. Hsu, L.R., Reinhardt, S.K., Iyer, R., Makineni, S.: Communist, utilitarian, and capitalist cache policies on CMPs: Caches as a shared resource. In: PACT (2006)
13. Qureshi, M.K., Lynch, D.N., Mutlu, O., Patt, Y.N.: A case for MLP-aware cache replacement. In: ISCA (2006)
14. Kroft, D.: Lockup-free instruction fetch/prefetch cache organization. In: ISCA (1981)
15. Sherwood, T., Perelman, E., Hamerly, G., Sair, S., Calder, B.: Discovering and exploiting program phases. IEEE Micro (2003)
16. Vera, J., Cazorla, F.J., Pajuelo, A., Santana, O.J., Fernandez, E., Valero, M.: FAME: Fairly measuring multithreaded architectures. In: PACT (2007)
17. Moreto, M., Cazorla, F.J., Ramirez, A., Valero, M.: Explaining dynamic cache partitioning speed ups. IEEE CAL (2007)
18. Chandra, D., Guo, F., Kim, S., Solihin, Y.: Predicting inter-thread cache contention on a chip multi-processor architecture. In: HPCA (2005)
19. Sinharoy, B., Kalla, R.N., Tendler, J.M., Eickemeyer, R.J., Joyner, J.B.: Power5 system microarchitecture. IBM J. Res. Dev. 49(4/5), 505–521 (2005)
20. Luo, K., Gummaraju, J., Franklin, M.: Balancing throughput and fairness in SMT processors. In: ISPASS (2001)

Compiler Techniques for Reducing Data Cache Miss Rate on a Multithreaded Architecture

Subhradyuti Sarkar and Dean M. Tullsen

Department of Computer Science and Engineering
University Of California, San Diego

Abstract. High performance embedded architectures will in some cases combine simple caches and multithreading, two techniques that increase energy efficiency and performance at the same time. However, that combination can produce high and unpredictable cache miss rates, even when the compiler optimizes the data layout of each program for the cache.

This paper examines data-cache aware compilation for multithreaded architectures. Data-cache aware compilation finds a layout for data objects which minimizes inter-object conflict misses. This research extends and adapts prior cache-conscious data layout optimizations to the much more difficult environment of multithreaded architectures. Solutions are presented for two computing scenarios: (1) the more general case where any application can be scheduled along with other applications, and (2) the case where the co-scheduled working set is more precisely known.

1 Introduction

High performance embedded architectures seek to accelerate performance in the most energy-efficient and complexity-effective manner. Two technologies that improve performance and energy efficiency at the same time are caches and multithreading. However, when used in combination, these techniques can be in conflict, as unpredictable interactions between threads can result in high conflict miss rates. It has been shown that in large and highly associative caches, these interactions are not large; however, embedded architectures are more likely to combine multithreading with smaller, simpler caches. The techniques in this paper allow the architecture to maintain these simpler caches, solving the problem in software via the compiler, rather than necessitating more complex and power-hungry caches.

Cache-conscious Data Placement (CCDP) [1] is a technique which finds an intelligent layout for the data objects of an application, so that at runtime objects which are accessed in an interleaved pattern are not mapped to the same cache blocks. On a processor core with a single execution context, this technique has been shown to significantly reduce the cache conflict miss rate and improve performance over a wide set of benchmarks.

However, CCDP loses much of its benefit in a multithreaded environment, such as simultaneous multithreading (SMT) [2,3]. In an SMT processor multiple threads run concurrently in separate hardware contexts. This architecture has

P. Stenström et al. (Eds.): HiPEAC 2008, LNCS 4917, pp. 353–368, 2008.

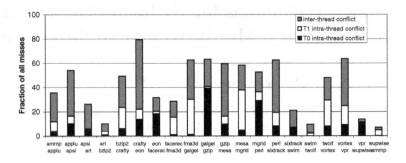

Fig. 1. Percentage of data cache misses that are due to conflict. The cache is 32 KB direct-mapped, shared by two contexts in an SMT processor.

been shown to be a much more energy efficient approach to accelerate processor performance than other traditional performance optimizations [4,5], and thus is a strong candidate for inclusion in high performance embedded architectures. In a simultaneous multithreading processor with shared caches, however, objects from different threads compete for the same cache lines – resulting in potentially expensive inter-thread conflict misses. These conflicts cannot be analyzed in the same manner that was applied successfully by prior work on intra-thread conflicts. This is because inter-thread conflicts are not deterministic.

Figure 1, which gives the percentage of conflict misses for various pairs of co-scheduled threads, shows two important trends. First, inter-thread conflict misses are just as prevalent as intra-thread conflicts (26% vs. 21% of all misses). Second, the infusion of these new conflict misses significantly increases the overall importance of conflict misses, relative to other types of misses.

This phenomenon extends beyond multithreaded processors. Multi-core architectures may share on-chip L2 caches, or possibly even L1 caches [6,7]. However, in this work we focus in particular on multithreaded architectures, because they interact and share caches at the lowest level.

In this paper, we develop new techniques that allow the ideas of CCDP to be extended to multithreaded architectures, and be effective. We consider the following compilation scenarios:

(1) First we solve the most general case, where we cannot assume we know which applications will be co-scheduled. This may occur, even in an embedded processor, if we have a set of applications that can run in various combinations.

(2) In more specialized embedded applications, we will be able to more precisely exploit specific knowledge about the applications and how they will be run. We may have *a priori* knowledge about application sets to be co-scheduled in the multithreaded processor. In these situations, it should be feasible to co-compile, or at least cooperatively compile, these concurrently running applications.

This paper makes the following contributions: (1) We show that traditional multithreading-oblivious cache-conscious data placement is not effective in a multithreading architecture. In some cases, it does more harm than good. (2) We propose two extensions to CCDP that can identify and eliminate most of the inter-thread conflict misses for each of the above mentioned scenarios. We have seen as much as a 26% average reduction in misses after our placement optimization. (3) We show that even for applications with many objects and interleavings, temporal relationship graphs of reasonable size can be maintained without sacrificing performance and quality of placement. (4) We present several new mechanisms that improve the performance and realizability of cache conscious data placement (whether multithreaded or not). These include object and edge filtering for the temporal relationship graph. (5) We show that these algorithms work across different cache configurations, even for set-associative caches. Previous CCDP algorithms have targeted direct-mapped caches – we show that they do not translate easily to set-associative caches. We present a new mechanism that eliminates set-associative conflict misses much more effectively.

2   Related Work

Direct-mapped caches, although faster, more power-efficient, and simpler than set-associative caches, are prone to conflict misses. Consequently, much research has been directed toward reducing conflicts in a direct-mapped cache. Several papers [8,9,10] explore unconventional line-placement policies to reduce conflict misses. Lynch, et al. [11] demonstrate that careful virtual to physical translation (page-coloring) can reduce the number of cache misses in a physically-indexed cache. Rivera and Tseng [12] predict cache conflicts in a large linear data structure by computing expected conflict distances, then use intra- and inter-variable padding to eliminate those conflicts.   The Split Cache [13] is a technique to virtually partition the cache through special hardware instructions, which the compiler can exploit to put potentially conflicting data structures in isolated virtual partitions.

In a simultaneous multithreading architecture [2,3],various threads share execution and memory system resources on a fine-grained basis. Sharing of the L1 cache by multiple threads usually increases inter-thread conflict misses [2,14,15]. Until now, few studies have been conducted which try to improve cache performance in an SMT processor, particularly without significant hardware support. It has been shown [16] that partitioning the cache into per-thread local regions and a common global region can avoid some inter-thread conflict misses.   Traditional code transformation techniques (tiling, copying and block data layout) have been applied, along with a dynamic conflict detection mechanism to achieve significant performance improvement [17]; however, these transformations yield good results only for regular loop structures. Lopez, et al. [18] also look at the interaction between caches and simultaneous multithreading in embedded architectures. However, their solutions also require dynamically reconfigurable caches to adapt to the behavior of the co-scheduled threads.

This research builds on the profile-driven data placement proposed by Calder, et al. [1]. The goal of this technique is to model temporal relationships between data objects through profiling. The temporal relationships are captured in a *Temporal Relationship Graph* (TRG), where each node represents an object and edges represent the degree of temporal conflict between objects. Hence, if objects P and Q are connected by a heavily weighted edge in the TRG, then placing them in overlapping cache blocks is likely to cause many conflict misses.

We have extended this technique to SMT processors and set associative caches. Also, we have introduced the concept of object and edge trimming - which significantly reduces the time and space complexity of our placement algorithm. Kumar and Tullsen [19] describe techniques, some similar to this paper, to minimize instruction cache conflicts on an SMT processor. However, the dynamic nature of the sizes, access patterns, and lifetimes of memory objects makes the data cache problem significantly more complex.

3   Simulation Environment and Benchmarks

We run our simulations on SMTSIM [20], which simulates an SMT processor. The detailed configuration of the simulated processor is given in Table 1. For most portions of the paper, we assume the processor has a 32 KB, direct-mapped data cache with 64 byte blocks. We also model the effects on set associative caches in Section 6, but we focus on a direct-mapped cache both because the effects of inter-thread conflicts is more severe, and because direct mapped caches continue to be an attractive design point for many embedded designs. We assume the address mappings resulting from the compiler and dynamic allocator are preserved in the cache. This would be the case if the system did not use virtual to physical translation, if the cache is virtually indexed, or if the operating system uses page coloring to ensure that our cache mappings are preserved.

The fetch unit in our simulator fetches from the available execution contexts based on the ICOUNT fetch policy [3] and the *flush* policy from [21], a performance optimization that reduces the overall cost of any individual miss.

It is important to note that a multithreaded processor tends to operate in one of two regions, in regards to its sensitivity to cache misses. If it is latency-limited (no part of the hierarchy becomes saturated, and the memory access time is dominated by device latencies), sensitivity to the cache miss rate is low, because of the latency tolerance of multithreaded architectures. However, if the processor is operating in bandwidth-limited mode (some part of the subsystem is saturated, and the memory access time is dominated by queuing delays), the multithreaded system then becomes very sensitive to changes in the miss rate. For the most part, we choose to model a system that has plenty of memory and cache bandwidth, and never enters the bandwidth-limited regions. This results in smaller observed performance gains for our placement optimizations, but we still see significant improvements. However, real processors will likely reach that saturation point with certain applications, and the expected gains from our techniques would be much greater in those cases.

Table 2 alphabetically lists the 20 SPEC2000 benchmarks that we have used. The SPEC benchmarks represent a more complex set of applications than represented in some of the embedded benchmark suites, with more dynamic memory usage; however, these characteristics do exist in real embedded applications. For

Table 1. SMT Processor Details

Parameter	Value
Fetch Bandwidth	2 Threads, 4 Instructions Total
Functional Units	4 Integer, 4 Load/Store, 3 FP
Instruction Queues	32 entry Integer, 32 entry FP
Instruction Cache	32 KB, 2-way set associative
Data Cache	32 KB, direct-mapped
L2 Cache	512 KB, 4-way set associative
L3 Cache	1024 KB, 4-way set associative
Miss Penalty	L1 15 cycles, L2 80 cycles, L3 500 cycles
Pipeline Depth	9 stages

Table 2. Simulated Benchmarks

ID	Benchmark	Type	Hit Rate(%)	ID	Benchmark	Type	Hit Rate(%)
1	*ammp*	FP	84.19	11	*gzip*	INT	95.41
2	*applu*	FP	83.07	12	*mesa*	FP	98.32
3	*apsi*	FP	96.54	13	*mgrid*	FP	88.56
4	*art*	FP	71.31	14	*perl*	INT	89.89
5	*bzip2*	INT	94.66	15	*sixtrack*	FP	92.38
6	*crafty*	INT	94.48	16	*swim*	FP	75.13
7	*eon*	INT	97.42	17	*twolf*	INT	88.63
8	*facerec*	FP	81.52	18	*vortex*	INT	95.74
9	*fma3d*	FP	94.54	19	*vpr*	INT	86.21
10	*galgel*	FP	83.01	20	*wupwise*	INT	51.29

our purposes, these benchmarks represent a more challenging environment to apply our techniques. In our experiments, we generated a k-threaded workload by picking each benchmark along with its $(k-1)$ successors (modulo the size of the table) as they appear in Table 2. Henceforth we shall refer to a workload by the ID of its first benchmark. For example, workload 10 (at two threads) would be the combination {*galgel gzip*}. Our experiments report results from a simulation window of two hundred million instructions; however, the benchmarks are fast-forwarded by ten billion dynamic instructions beforehand. Table 2 also lists the L1 hit rate of each application when they are run independently. All profiles are generated running the SPEC *train* inputs, and simulation and measurement with the *ref* inputs. We also profile and optimize for a larger portion of execution than we simulate.

This type of study represents a methodological challenge in accurately reporting performance results. In multithreaded experimentation, every run consists of a potentially different mix of instructions from each thread, making relative IPC a questionable metric. In this paper we use weighted speedup [21] to report our results. Weighted speedup much more accurately reflects system-level performance improvements, and makes it more difficult to create artificial speedups by changing the bias of the processor toward certain threads.

4   Independent Data Placement

In the next two sections, we consider two different execution scenarios. In this section, we solve the more general and difficult scenario, where the compiler actually does not know which applications will be scheduled together dynamically, or the set of co-scheduled threads changes frequently; however, we assume all applications will have been generated by our compiler. In this execution scenario, then, co-scheduling will be largely unpredictable and dynamic. However, we can still compile programs in such a way that conflict misses are minimized. Since all programs would essentially be compiled in the same way, some support from the operating system, runtime system, or the hardware is required to allow each co-scheduled program to be mapped onto the cache differently.

We have modified CCDP techniques to create an intentionally unbalanced utilization of the cache, mapping objects to a *hot* portion and a *cold* portion. This does not necessarily imply more intra-thread conflict misses. For example, the two most heavily accessed objects in the program can be mapped to the same cache index without a loss in performance, if they are not typically accessed in an interleaved pattern – this is the point of using the temporal relationship graph of interleavings to do the mapping, rather than just using reference counts. CCDP would typically create a more balanced distribution of accesses across the cache; however, it can be tuned to do just the opposite. This is a similar approach to that used in [19] for procedure placement, but applied here to the placement of data objects.

However, before we present the details of the object placement algorithm, we first describe the assumptions about hardware or OS support, how data objects are identified and analyzed, and some options that make the CCDP algorithms faster and more realizable.

4.1   Support from Operating System or Hardware

Our independent placement technique (henceforth referred to as IND) repositions the objects so that they have a *top-heavy* access pattern, i.e. most of the memory accesses are limited to the *top portion* of the cache. Now let us consider an SMT processor with two hardware contexts, and a shared L1 cache (whose size is at least twice the virtual-memory page size). If the architecture uses a virtual cache, the processor can xor the high bits of the cache index with a hardware context ID (e.g., one bit for 2 threads, 2 bits for 4 threads), which will then map the hot portions of the address space to different regions of the cache. In a physically indexed cache, we don't even need that hardware support. When the operating system loads two different applications in the processor, it ensures (by page coloring or otherwise) that heavily accessed virtual pages from the threads do not collide in the physically indexed cache.

For example, let us assume an architecture with a 32 KB data cache, 4 KB memory pages, and two threads. The OS or runtime allocates physical pages to virtual pages such that the three least significant bits of the page number are preserved for thread zero, and for thread one the same is done but with the third bit reversed. Thus, the mapping assumed by the compilers is preserved, but with each thread's "hot" area mapped to a different half of the cache. This is simply an application of page coloring, which is not an unusual OS function.

4.2 Analysis of Data Objects

To facilitate data layout, we consider the address space of an application as partitioned into several *objects*. An *object* is loosely defined as a contiguous region in the (virtual) address space that can be relocated with little help from the compiler and/or the runtime system. The compiler typically creates several objects in the code and data segment, the starting location and size of which can be found by scanning the symbol table. A section of memory allocated by a `malloc` call can be considered to be a single *dynamic object*, since it can easily be relocated using an instrumented front-end to `malloc`. However, since the same invocation of `malloc` can return different addresses in different runs of an application – we need some extra information to identify the dynamic objects (that is, to associate a profiled object with the same object at runtime). Similar to [1], we use an additional tag (henceforth referred to as `HeapTag`) to identify the dynamic objects. `HeapTag` is generated by xor-folding the top four addresses of the return stack and the call-site of `malloc`. We do not attempt to reorder stack objects. Instead the stack is treated as a single object.

After the objects have been identified, their reference count and lifetime information over the simulation window can be retrieved by instrumenting the application binary with a tool such as ATOM [22]. Also obtainable are the temporal relationships between the objects, which can be captured using a temporal relationship graph (henceforth referred to as `TRGSelect` graph). The `TRGSelect` graph contains nodes that represent objects (or portions of objects) and edges between nodes contain a weight which represents how many times the two objects were interleaved in the actual profiled execution.

Temporal relationships are collected at a finer granularity than full objects – mainly because some of the objects are much larger than others, and usually only a small portion of a *bigger* object has temporal association with the *smaller* one. It is more logical to partition the objects into fixed size chunks, and then record the temporal relationship between chunks. Though all the chunks belonging to an object are placed sequentially in their original order, having finer-grained temporal information helps us to make more informed decisions when two conflicting objects must be put in an overlapping cache region. We have set the chunk size equal to the block size of the targeted cache. This provides the best performance, as we now track conflicts at the exact same granularity that they occur in the cache.

4.3 Object and Edge Filtering

Profiling a typical SPEC2000 benchmark, even for a partial profile, involves tens of thousands of objects, and generates hundreds of millions of temporal relationship edges between objects. To make this analysis manageable, we must reduce both the number of nodes (the number of objects) as well as the number of edges (temporal relationships between objects) in the `TRGSelect` graph. We classify objects as unimportant if their reference count is zero, or the sum of the weights of incident edges is below a threshold.

If a `HeapTag` assigned to a heap object is non-unique, we mark all but the most frequently accessed object having that `HeapTag` as unimportant. Multiple objects usually have the same `HeapTag` when dynamic memory is being allocated in a loop and they usually have similar temporal relationship with other objects.

A similar problem exists for building the `TRGSelect` graph. Profiling creates a `TRGSelect` graph with a very large number of edges. Since it is desirable to store the entire `TRGSelect` graph in memory, keeping all these edges would not be practical. Fortunately, we have noted that in a typical profile more than 90% of all the edges are *light-weight*, having an edge weight less than one tenth of the heavier edges. We use the following epoch-based heuristic to periodically trim off the *potentially* light-weight edges, limiting the total number of edges to a preset maximum value. In a given epoch, edges with weight below a particular threshold are marked as *potentially light-weight*. In the next epoch, if the weight of an edge marked as *potentially light-weight* does not increase significantly from the previous epoch, it is deleted from the `TRGSelect` graph. The threshold is liberal when the total number of edges is low, but made more aggressive when the number of edges nears our preset limit on the number of edges.

In this algorithm, then, we prune the edges dynamically during profiling, and prune the objects after profiling, but before the placement phase. We find pruning has little impact on the quality of our results.

4.4   Placement Algorithm

For independent data placement, the cache blocks are partitioned into *native* and *foreign* sets. If we know the application is going to be executed on an SMT processor with k contexts, the top $\frac{1}{k}$ cache blocks are marked as *native*, and other cache blocks are marked as *foreign*. For any valid placement of an object in a native block, we define an associated cost. That cost is the sum of the costs for each chunk placed in the contiguous cache blocks. The cost of a chunk is the edge weight (interleaving factor) between that chunk and all chunks of other objects already placed in that cache block. If the cache block is marked as foreign, a bias is added to the overall cost to force the algorithm to only place an object or part of an object in the foreign section if there is no good placement in the native. The bias for an object is set to be λ times the maximum edge weight between a chunk belonging to this object and any other chunk in the `TRGSelect` graph. Varying this bias allows a tradeoff between combined cache performance, and uncompromised cache performance when running alone. Our basic placement heuristic is to order the objects and then place them each, in that order, into the cache where they incur minimal cost. Since some objects are fundamentally different in nature and size from others, we came up with a set of specialized placement strategies, each targetting one particular type of object. Specifically, we will separately consider constant objects, small global objects, important global objects, and heap objects.

An object which resides in the code segment is defined as a constant object. Constant objects are placed in their default location (altering the text segment might have adverse effects on the instruction cache). However when other objects are placed in cache, their temporal relationship with the constant objects is taken into consideration.

Small global objects are handled differently than larger objects, allowing us to transform potential conflicts into cache prefetch opportunities. A statically allocated object which resides in the data segment is defined as a global object. Furthermore, a global object is classified as *small* if its size is less than three-fourths of the block size. As in [1], we try to cluster the small global objects that have heavily-weighted edges in the TRG and place them in the same cache block. Accessing any of the objects in the cluster will prefetch the others, avoiding costly cache misses in the near future. Small global objects are clustered greedily, starting with the pair of objects with the highest edge weight between them.

After a cluster has been formed, nodes representing individual objects in the cluster are coalesced into a single node (in the TRGSelect graph). The cluster will be assigned a starting location along with other non-small objects in the next phase of the placement algorithm.

Next, we place the global objects. Our greedy placement algorithm is sensitive to the order in which the objects are placed. By experimentation, we have found the following approach to be effective. We build a TRGPlace graph from the TRGSelect graph, where chunks of individual objects are merged together into a single node (edge weights are adjusted accordingly). Next, the most heavily weighted edge is taken from the TRGPlace graph. The two objects connected by that edge are placed in the cache, and marked as placed; however, recall that the actual placement still uses the TRGSelect graph, which tracks accesses to the individual chunks.

In each subsequent iteration of the algorithm, an unplaced object is chosen which maximizes the sum of TRGPlace edge-weights between itself and the objects that have been already placed. In case of a tie, the object with a higher reference count is given preference.

Unimportant global objects are placed so as to fill holes in the address space created by the allocation of the important global objects.

Heap objects also reside in the data segment, however they are dynamically created and destroyed at runtime using malloc and free calls. Specifying a placement for heap objects is more difficult because a profiled heap object might not be created, or might have different memory requirements in a later execution of the same application with different input. Thus, we determine the placement assuming the object is the same size, but only indicate to our custom malloc the location of the first block of the desired mapping. The object gets placed there, even if the size differs from the profiled run.

During execution, our customized malloc first computes the HeapTag for the requested heap object. If the HeapTag matches any of the recorded HeapTags for which a customized allocation should be performed, malloc returns a suitably aligned address from the available memory. When the newly created heap

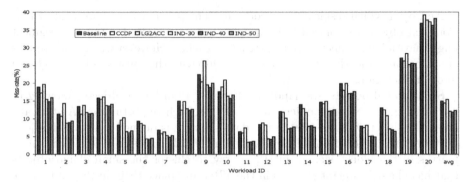

Fig. 2. Data Cache miss rate after Independent Placement (IND)

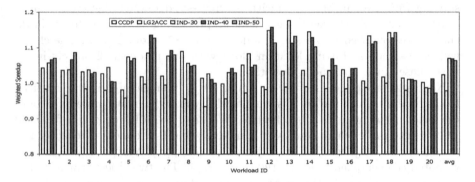

Fig. 3. Weighted Speedup after Independent Placement (IND)

object is brought in the cache, it occupies the blocks specified by the placement algorithm.

4.5 Independent Placement Results

The effects of data placement by IND on miss rate and weighted speedup are shown in Figure 2 and Figure 3 respectively. The Baseline series shows data cache miss rate without any type of placement optimization. CCDP shows the miss rate if traditional CCDP is performed on each of the applications. Since CCDP ignores inter-thread conflicts, for four workloads CCDP actually increases the miss rate over Baseline. LG2ACC shows the miss rate if L1 data cache is implemented as a *Double access local-global split cache* [16]. Split caches are designed to reduce conflicts in a multithreaded workload, though in our experiments the split cache was not overly effective. The final three series (IND-30, IND-40, IND-50) show the effect of co-ordinated data placement with λ (the placement bias) set to 0.30, 0.40 and 0.50 respectively. The figure shows that no single value of λ is universally better than others, though all of them yield improvement over traditional CCDP. For future work, it may be that setting λ individually for each application, based on number and size of objects, for example, will yield even better results. A careful comparison of Figure 2 and Figure 1 shows that the effectiveness of co-ordinated data placement is heavily correlated with the fraction of cache misses that are caused by conflicts. On workloads like {*crafty eon*} (workload 6) or {*gzip mesa*} (11), more than half of the cache misses are caused by conflicts, and IND-30 reduces the miss rate by 54.0% and 46.8%, respectively. On the other hand, only 6% of the cache misses in workload {*wupwise ammp*} (20) are caused by conflicts, and IND-30 achieves only a 1% gain.

On average, IND reduced overall miss rate by 19%, reduced total conflict misses by more than a factor of two, and achieved a 6.6% speedup. We also ran experiments with limited bandwidth to the L2 cache (where at most one pending L1 miss can be serviced in every two cycles), and in that case the performance tracked the miss rate gains somewhat more closely, achieving an average weighted speedup gain of 13.5%.

IND slightly increases intra-thread cache conflict (we still are applying cache-conscious layout, but the bias allows for some inefficiency from a single-thread standpoint). For example, the average miss rate of the applications, when run alone with no co-scheduled jobs increases from 12.9% to 14.3%, with λ set to 0.4. However, this result is heavily impacted by one application, *ammp* for which this mapping technique was largely ineffective due to the large number of heavily-accessed objects. If the algorithm was smart enough to just leave *ammp* alone, the average single-thread miss rate would be 13.8%. Unless we expect single-thread execution to be the common case, the much more significant impact on multithreaded miss rates makes this a good tradeoff.

5   Co-ordinated Data Placement

In many embedded environments, applications that are going to be co-scheduled are known in advance. In such a scenario, it might be more beneficial to co-compile those applications and lay out their data objects in unison. This approach provides more accurate information about the temporal interleavings of objects to the layout engine.

Our coordinated placement algorithm (henceforth referred to as CORD) is similar in many ways to IND. However, in CORD the cache is not split into *native* and *foreign* blocks, and thus there is no concept of *biasing*. In CORD, the TRGSelect graph from all the applications are merged together and important objects from all the applications are assigned a placement in a single pass.

5.1   Merging of TRGSelect Graphs

The TRGSelect graph generated by executing the instrumented binary of an application captures the temporal relationships between the objects of that application. However, when two applications are co-scheduled on an SMT processor, objects from different execution contexts will vie for the same cache blocks in the shared cache. We have modeled inter-thread conflicts by merging the TRGSelect graphs of the individual applications. It is important to note that we profile each application separately to generate two graphs, which are then merged probabilistically. While we may have the ability to profile the two threads running together and their interactions, there is typically little reason to believe the same interactions would occur in another run. The exception would be if the two threads communicate at a very fine granularity, in which case it would be better to consider them a single parallel application.

Assigning temporal relationship weights between two objects from different applications requires modeling interactions that are much less deterministic than interactions between objects in the same thread. We thus use a probabilistic model to quantify expected interactions between objects in different threads.

Two simplifying assumptions have been made for estimating the inter-thread temporal edge weights, which make it easier to quantify the expected interactions between objects in separate threads. (1) The relative execution speeds of the two threads is known a priori. Relative execution speed of co-scheduled threads typically remains fairly constant unless one of the threads undergoes a phase change – which can be discovered via profiling. (2) Within its lifetime, an object is accessed in a regular pattern, i.e. if the lifetime of an object o is k cycles, and the total reference count of o is n, then o is accessed once every $\frac{k}{n}$ cycles. Few objects have very skewed access pattern so this assumption gives a reasonable estimate of the number of references made to an object in a particular interval.

We use these assumptions to estimate the interleavings between two objects (in different threads). From the first assumption, along with the known lifetimes of objects, we can calculate the likelihood that two objects have overlapping lifetimes (and the expected duration). From the second assumption, we can estimate the number of references made to those objects during the overlap. The number of interleavings cannot be more than twice the lesser of the two (estimated) reference counts. We apply a scaling factor to translate this worst-case estimate of the interleavings during an interval, into an expected number of interleavings. This scaling factor is determined experimentally. To understand the point of the scaling factor, if the two objects are being accessed at an equal rate by the two threads, but we always observe a run of two accesses from one thread before the other thread issues an access, the scaling factor would be 0.50.

In our experiments we have found it sufficient to only put temporal edges between *important* objects of each application, which eliminates edge explosion.

5.2 Coordinated Placement Results

The miss-rate impact and weighted speedup achieved by CORD is shown in Figures 4 and 5. The three series CORD-60, CORD-70 and CORD-80 represents the result of independent data placement with scaling factor set to 0.6, 0.7 and 0.8 respectively. The scaling factor represents the degree of interleaving we expect between memory accesses from different threads accessing the same cache set.

In most of the workloads, the speedup is somewhat more than that obtained from independent placement, thus confirming our hypothesis that having access to more information about conflicting objects leads to better placement decisions. On the average CORD reduced miss rate by 26% and achieved 8.8%

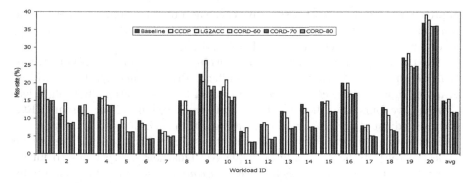

Fig. 4. Data Cache miss rate after Coordinated Placement (CORD)

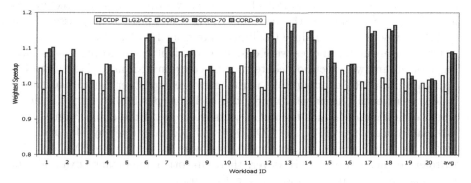

Fig. 5. Weighted Speedup after Coordinated Placement (CORD)

speedup. However, if one of these *optimized* applications is run alone (i.e. without its counterpart application) we do sacrifice single-thread performance slightly, but the effect is much less than the gain when co-scheduled. The amount of the single-thread loss depends somewhat on the scaling factor. The average Baseline miss rate was 12.9%. With coordinated placement, and a scaling factor of 0.7, the average single-thread miss rate goes up to 13.1%, but when the scaling factor is 0.8, the miss rate actually becomes 12.7%.

6   Exploring other Processor and Cache Configurations

We have demonstrated the effectiveness of our placement techniques for a single hardware configuration. We also did extensive sensitivity analysis, to understand how these techniques work as aspects of the architecture change. We lack space to show those results in detail, but include a brief summary here. We examined alternate cache sizes and organizations, different latencies, and different levels of threading.

Cache associativity is the most interesting alternative, in large part because proposed CCDP algorithms do not accommodate associative caches. The naive approach would model a set-associative cache as a direct-mapped cache with the same number of sets. It would over-state conflicts, but would hopefully produce a good mapping. In fact, we found that it did not.

Any mapping function that used our current TRGs would be an approximation, because we only capture 2-way conflicts. Profiling and creating a hypergraph to capture more complex conflicts would be computationally prohibitive. However, we found the following algorithm to work well, using our existing TRG. We have adjusted our default placement algorithm such that for a k-way set associative cache, an object incurs placement cost only if is placed in a set where at least k objects have already been placed. This new policy tends to fill up every set in the associative cache to its *maximum capacity* before potentially conflicting objects are put in the set that already contains more than k objects.

The actual results for set-associative caches are indicative of the low incidence of conflict misses for these workloads. However, we do see that our techniques are effective – we eliminate the vast majority of remaining conflict misses. For a 16 KB, 2-way cache, we reduce total miss rate from 15.8% to 13.8%.

Our placement techniques were designed to adapt easily to processors having more than two execution contexts. For co-ordinated data placement of k applications, k `TRGSelect` graphs must be merged together before placement. Independent data placement requires the cache be partitioned into k regions, where each region contains the *hot* objects from one of the applications. For a 4-thread processor, IND-30 and CORD-60 reduced miss rates by 14% and 22% on the average; however, the actual speedups were smaller, due to SMT's ability to tolerate cache latencies. However, there are other important advantages of reducing L1 miss rate, like lower power dissipation.

7   Conclusion

As we seek higher performance embedded processors, we will increasingly see architectures that feature caches and multiple thread contexts (either through multithreading or multiple cores), and thus we shall see greater incidence of threads competing for cache space. The more effectively each application is tuned to use the caches, the more interference we see between competing threads.

This paper demonstrates that it is possible to compile threads to share the data cache, to each thread's advantage. We specifically address two scenarios. Our first technique does not assume any prior knowledge of the threads which might be co-scheduled together, and hence is applicable to all general-purpose computing environments. Our second technique shows that when we do have more specific knowlege about which applications will run together, that knowledge can be exploited to enhance the quality of object placement even further. Our techniques demonstrated 26% improvement in miss rate and 9% improvement in performance, for a variety of workloads constructed from the SPEC2000 suite. It is also shown that our placement techniques scale effectively across different hardware configurations, including set-associative caches.

References

1. Calder, B., Krintz, C., John, S., Austin, T.: Cache-conscious data placement. In: Eighth International Conference on Architectural Support for Programming Languages and Operating Systems (1998)
2. Tullsen, D.M., Eggers, S., Levy, H.M.: Simultaneous multithreading: Maximizing on-chip parallelism. In: Proceedings of the 22nd Annual International Symposium on Computer Architecture (1995)
3. Tullsen, D.M., Eggers, S.J., Emer, J.S., Levy, H.M., Lo, J.L., Stamm, R.L.: Exploiting choice: Instruction fetch and issue on an implementable simultaneous multithreading processor. In: Proceedings of the 23rd Annual International Symposium on Computer Architecture (1996)
4. Li, Y., Brooks, D., Hu, Z., Skadron, K., Bose, P.: Understanding the energy efficiency of simultaneous multithreading. In: Intl. Symposium on Low Power Electronics and Design (2004)
5. Seng, J., Tullsen, D., Cai, G.: Power-sensitive multithreaded architecture. In: International Conference on Computer Design (September 2000)
6. Kumar, R., Jouppi, N., Tullsen, D.M.: Conjoined-core chip multiprocessing. In: 37th International Symposium on Microarchitecture (December 2004)
7. Dolbeau, R., Seznec, A.: Cash: Revisiting hardware sharing in single-chip parallel processor. In: IRISA Report 1491 (November 2002)
8. Agarwal, A., Pudar, S.: Column-associative caches: A technique for reducing the miss rate of direct-mapped caches. In: International Symposium On Computer Architecture (1993)
9. Topham, N., González, A.: Randomized cache placement for eliminating conflicts. IEEE Transactions on Computer 48(2) (1999)
10. Seznec, A., Bodin, F.: Skewed-associative caches. In: International Conference on Parallel Architectures and Languages, pp. 305–316 (1993)
11. Lynch, W.L., Bray, B.K., Flynn, M.J.: The effect of page allocation on caches. In: 25th Annual International Symposium on Microarchitecture (1992)
12. Rivera, G., Tseng, C.W.: Data transformations for eliminating conflict misses. In: SIGPLAN Conference on Programming Language Design and Implementation, pp. 38–49 (1998)
13. Juan, T., Royo, D.: Dynamic cache splitting. In: XV International Confernce of the Chilean Computational Society (1995)
14. Nemirovsky, M., Yamamoto, W.: Quantitative study on data caches on a multistreamed architecture. In: Workshop on Multithreaded Execution, Architecture and Compilation (1998)
15. Hily, S., Seznec, A.: Standard memory hierarchy does not fit simultaneous multithreading. In: Proceedings of the Workshop on Multithreaded Execution Architecture and Compilation (with HPCA-4) (1998)
16. Jos, M.G.: Data caches for multithreaded processors. In: Workshop on Multithreaded Execution, Architecture and Compilation (2000)
17. Nikolopoulos, D.S.: Code and data transformations for improving shared cache performance on SMT processors. In: International Symposium on High Performance Computing, pp. 54–69 (2003)
18. Lopez, S., Dropsho, S., Albonesi, D.H., Garnica, O., Lanchares, J.: Dynamic capacity-speed tradeoffs in smt processor caches. In: Intl. Conference on High Performance Embedded Architectures & Compilers (January 2007)

19. Kumar, R., Tullsen, D.M.: Compiling for instruction cache performance on a multithreaded architecture. In: 35th Annual International Symposium on Microarchitecture (2002)
20. Tullsen, D.M.: Simulation and modeling of a simultaneous multithreading processor. In: 22nd Annual Computer Measurement Group Conference (December 1996)
21. Tullsen, D.M., Brown, J.: Handling long-latency loads in a simultaneous multithreaded processor. In: 34th International Symposium on Microarchitecture (December 2001)
22. Srivastava, A., Eustace, A.: Atom: A system for building customized program analysis tools. In: SIGPLAN Notices, vol. 39, pp. 528–539 (2004)

Code Arrangement of Embedded Java Virtual Machine for NAND Flash Memory[*]

Chun-Chieh Lin and Chuen-Liang Chen

Department of Computer Science and Information Engineering,
National Taiwan University, Taipei,
10764, Taiwan
{d93020,clchen}@csie.ntu.edu.tw

Abstract. This paper proposed a systematic approach to optimize J2ME KVM running directly on NAND flash memories (XIP). The refined KVM generated cache misses 96% less than the original version did. The approach appended a post processor to the compiler. The post processor relocates and rewrites basic blocks within the VM interpreter using a unique mathematical model. This approach analyzed not only static control flow graph but also the pattern of bytecode instruction streams, since we found the input sequence drives the program flow of the VM interpreter. The proposed mathematical model is used to express the execution flows of Java instructions of real applications. Furthermore, we concluded the mathematical model is a kind of graph partition problem, and this finding helped the relocation process to move program blocks to proper NAND flash pages. The refinement approach dramatically improved the locality of the virtual machine thus reduced cache miss rates. Our technique can help J2ME-enabled devices to run faster and extend longer battery life. The approach also brings potential for designers to integrate the XIP function into System-on-Chip thanks to lower demand for cache memory.

Keywords: NAND flash memory, code placement, cache miss, Java virtual machine, interpreter, power-saving, memory management, embedded system.

1 Introduction

Java platform extensively exist in all kinds of embedded and mobile devices. It is no doubt that Java™ Platform, Micro Edition (Java ME) [1] has become a de facto standard platform of smart phone. The Java virtual machine (it is KVM in Java ME) is a key component that affects performance and power consumptions.

NAND flash memories come with serial bus interface. It does not allow random access and the CPU must read out the whole page at a time. This property leads a processor hardly to execute programs stored in NAND flash memories in "execute-in-place" (XIP) fashion. However, NAND flash memories are very fast in writing operation, and the most important of all, the technology has advantages in offering

---

[*] We acknowledge the support for this study through grants from National Science Council of Taiwan (NSC 95-2221-E-002 -137).

P. Stenström et al. (Eds.): HiPEAC 2008, LNCS 4917, pp. 369–383, 2008.

higher capacity than NOR flash technology does. As the applications of embedded devices become large and complicated, more mainstream devices adopt NAND flash memories to replace NOR flash memories.

In this paper, we tried to offer one of the answers to this question: can we speed up a Java-enabled device using NAND flash memories to store programs? We begin to construct our approach from considering the page-oriented access property of NAND flash memories; because the penalty of each access to the NAND flash memory is higher than accessing RAM. By the unique nature of the KVM interpreter, we found a special way to discover the locality of the KVM while execution, and implemented a post-processing program running behind the compiler code generation stage. The post-processing program refined machine code placement of KVM based on the graph that formalizes both Java instruction trace patterns and code size constraints. The tuned KVM dramatically reduced page accesses to NAND flash memories, thus saves more battery power as well.

2   Related Works

Park *et al.*, in [2], proposed a hardware module connecting with NAND flash to allow direct code execution from NAND flash memory. In this approach, program codes stored in NAND flash pages will be loaded into RAM cache on-demand instead of move entire contents into RAM. Their work is a universal hardware-based solution without considering application-specific characteristics.

Samsung Electronics offers a commercial product called "OneNAND" [3] based on the same concept of above approach. It is a single chip with a standard NOR flash interface. Actually, it contains a NAND flash memory array for data storage. The vendor was intent to provide a cost-effective alternative to NOR flash memories used in existing designs. The internal structure of OneNAND comprises a NAND flash memory, control logics, hardware ECC, and 5KB buffer RAM. The 5KB buffer RAM is comprised of three buffers: 1KB for boot RAM, and a pair of 2KB buffers used for bi-directional data buffers. Our approach is suitable for systems using this type of flash memories.

Park *et al.*, in [4], proposed yet another pure software approach to archive execute-in-place by using a customized compiler that inserts NAND flash reading operations into program code at proper place. Their compiler determines insertion points by sum up sizes of basic blocks along the calling tree. Although special hardware is no longer required, but it still need a tailor-made compiler in contrast to their previous work [2].

Conventional studies of refining code placement to minimize cache misses can apply to NAND flash cache system. Parameswaran *et al.*, in [5], used the bin-packing approach. It reorders the program codes by examining the execution frequency of basic blocks. Code segments with higher execution frequency are placed next to each other within the cache. Janapsatya *et al.*, in [6], proposed a pure software heuristic approach to reduce number of cache misses by relocating program sections in the main memory. Their approach was to analyze program flow graph, identify and pack basic blocks within the same loop. They have also created relations between cache miss and energy consumption. Although their approach can identify loops within a program, it is hard to break the interpreter of a virtual machine into individual loops because all the loops share the same starting point.

There are researches in improving program locality and optimizing code placement for either cache or virtual memory environment. Pettis [7] proposed a systematic approach using dynamic call graph to position procedures. They tried to wind up two procedures as close as possible if one of the procedure calls another frequently. The first step of Pettis' approach uses the profiling information to create weighted call graph. The second step iteratively merges vertexes connected by heaviest weight edges. The process repeats until the whole graph composed of one or more individual vertex without edges.

3 Background

3.1 XIP with NAND Flash

NOR flash memories are popular as code memories because of the XIP feature. To use a NAND flash memory as an alternative to a NOR flash memory, there were several approaches. Because NAND flash memory interface cannot connect to the CPU host bus, there has to be a memory interface controller helps to move data from NAND flash memories to RAM.

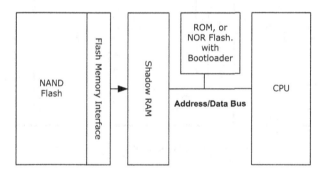

Fig. 1. Access NAND flash thru shadow RAM

In system-level view, Figure 1 shows a straightforward design which uses RAM as the shadow copy of NAND flash. The system treats NAND flash memories as secondary storage devices [8]. There should be a boot loader or RTOS resided in ROM or NOR flash memory. It copies program codes from NAND flash to RAM, then the processor executes program codes in RAM [9]. This approach offers best execution speed because the processor operates with RAM. The downside of this approach is it needs huge amount of RAM to mirror NAND flash. In embedded devices, RAM is a precious resource. For example, the Sony Ericsson T610 mobile phone [10] reserved 256KB RAM for Java heap. In contrast to using 256MB for mirroring NAND flash memory, all designers should agree that they would prefer to retain those RAM for Java applets rather than for mirroring. The second pitfall is the implementation takes longer time to boot because the system must copy contents to RAM prior to execution.

Figure 2 shows a demand paging approach uses limited amount of RAM as the cache of NAND flash. The "romized" program codes stay in NAND flash memory, and a MMU loads only portions of program codes which is about to be executed from NAND into the cache. The major advantage of this approach is it consumes less RAM. Several kilobytes of RAM are enough to cache a NAND flash memory. Using less RAM means it is easier to integrate CPU, MMU and cache into a single chip (The shadowed part in Figure 2). The startup latency is shorter since CPU is ready to run soon after the first NAND flash page is loaded into the cache. The material cost is relative lower than the previous approach. The realization of the MMU might be either hardware or software approach, which is not covered in this paper.

However, performance is the major drawback of this approach. The penalty of each cache miss is high, because loading contents from a NAND flash page is nearly 200 times slower than doing the same operation with RAM. Therefore reducing cache misses becomes a critical issue to such configuration.

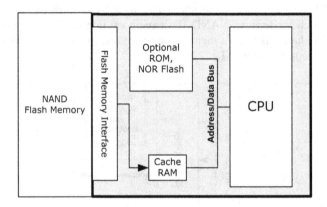

Fig. 2. Using cache unit to access NAND flash

3.2 KVM Internals

Source Level. In respect of functionality, the KVM can be broken down into several parts: startup, class files loading and constant pool resolving, interpreter, garbage collection, and KVM cleanup. Lafond *et al.*, in [11], have measured the energy consumptions of each part in the KVM. Their study showed that the interpreter consumed more than 50% of total energy. In our experiments running Embedded Caffeine Benchmark [12], the interpreter contributed 96% of total memory accesses. These evidences concluded that the interpreter is the performance bottleneck of the KVM, and they motivated us to focus on reducing the cache misses generated by the interpreter.

Figure 3 shows the program structure of the interpreter. It is a loop encloses a large switch-case dispatcher. The loop fetches bytecode instructions from Java application, and each "case" sub-clause, say bytecode handler, deals with one bytecode instruction. The control flow graph of the interpreter, as illustrated in Figure 4, is a flat and shallow spanning tree. There are three major steps in the interpreter,

(1) Rescheduling and Fetching. In this step, KVM prepares the execution context, stack frame. Then it fetches a bytecode instruction from Java programs.

(2) Dispatching and Execution. After reading a bytecode instruction from Java programs, the interpreter jumps to corresponding bytecode handlers through the big "switch...case..." statement. Each bytecode handler carries out the function of the corresponding bytecode instruction.

(3) Branching. The branch bytecode instructions may bring the Java program flow away from original track. In this step, the interpreter resolves the target address and modifies the program counter.

```
ReschedulePoint:
RESCHEDULE
opcode = FETCH_BYTECODE ( ProgramCounter );
switch ( opcode )
{
case ALOAD: /* do something */
        goto ReschedulePoint;
        case IADD: /* do something */
        ...
        case IFEQ: /* do something */
        goto BranchPoint;
        ...
}
BranchPoint:
        take care of program counter;
        goto ReschedulePoint;
```

Fig. 3. Pseudo code of KVM interpreter

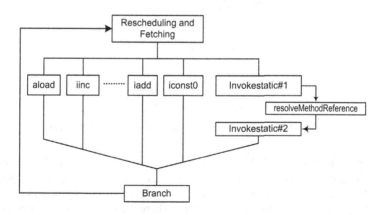

Fig. 4. Control flow graph of the interpreter

Assembly Level. Our finding explained the program structure of the VM interpreter is peculiar by observing its source files. Analyzing the code layout in the compiled executables of the interpreter helped this study to construct a code placement strategy. The assembly code analysis in this study was restricted to ARM and *gcc* for the sake of demonstration, but it is easy to apply our theory to other platforms and tools. Figure 5 illustrates the layout of the interpreter in assembly form (FastInterpret() in interp.c). The first trunk *BytecodeFetching* is the code block for rescheduling and fetching, it is exactly the first part in the original source code. The second trunk *LookupTable* is a large lookup table used in dispatching bytecode instructions. Each entry links to a bytecode handler. It is actually the translated result of the "switch...case...case" statement.

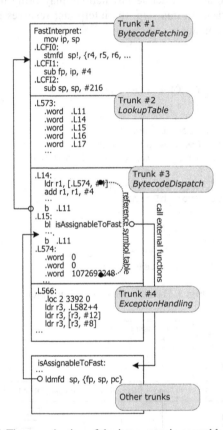

Fig. 5. The organization of the interpreter in assembly aspect

The third trunk *BytecodeDispatch* is the aggregation of more than a hundred bytecode handlers. Most bytecode handlers are self-contained which means a bytecode handler occupies a contiguous memory space in this trunk and it does not jump to program codes stored in other trunks. There are only a few exceptions which call functions stored in other trunks, such as "invokevirtual." Besides, there are several constant symbol tables spread over this trunk. These tables are referenced by the program codes within the *BytecodeDispatch* trunk.

The last trunk *ExceptionHandling* contains code fragments related with exception handling. Each trunk occupies a number of NAND flash pages. In fact, the total size of *BytecodeFetching* and *LookupTable* is about 1200 bytes (compiled with *arm-elf-gcc-3.4.3*), which is almost small enough to fit into two or three 512-bytes-page. Figure 8 showed the size distribution of bytecode handlers. The average size of a bytecode handler is 131 bytes, and there are 79 handlers smaller than 56 bytes. In the other words, a 512-bytes-page could gather 4 to 8 bytecode handlers. The intra-handler execution flow dominates the number of cache misses generated by the interpreter. This is the reason that our approach tried to rearrange bytecode handlers within the *BytecodeDispatch* trunk.

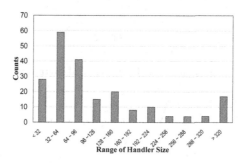

Fig. 6. Distribution of Bytecode Handler Size (compiled with *gcc-3.4.3*)

4 Analyzing Control Flow

4.1 Indirect Control Flow Graph

Typical approaches derive the code placement of a program from its control flow graph (CFG). However, the CFG of a VM interpreter is a special case, its CFG is a flat spanning tree enclosed by a loop. All bytecode handlers are always sibling code blocks in the aspect of CFG regardless of executed Java applications. Therefore, the CFG does not provide information to distinguish the temporal order between each bytecode handler. If someone wants to improve the program locality by observing the dynamic execution order of program blocks, and CFG is apparently not a good tool to this end. Therefore, we proposed a concept called "Indirect Control Flow Graph" (ICFG); it uses the dynamic instruction sequence to construct the dual CFG of the interpreter.

Consider a simplified virtual machine with 5 bytecode instructions: A, B, C, D, and E. Besides, take the following short alphabetic sequences as the input to the simplified virtual machine:

A-B-A-B-C-D-E-C

Each letter in the sequence represents a bytecode instruction. In Figure 7, the graph connected with the solid lines is the CFG of the simplified interpreter. Yet, this CFG cannot convey whether handler B will be called after handler A is executed. Therefore, we construct the ICFG by using the dashed directed lines to connect the bytecode handlers in the order of the input sequence. Actually, the Figure 8 expresses the ICFG in a readable way.

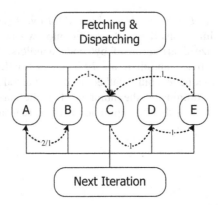

Fig. 7. The CFG of the simplified interpreter

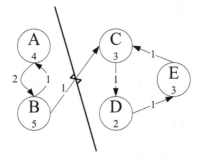

Fig. 8. An ICFG example. The number inside the circle represents the size of the handler.

4.2   Tracing the Locality of the Interpreter

Our study found that the Java applications that a KVM runs dominate the locality of the VM interrupter. Precisely speaking, the incoming Java instruction sequence dominates locality. The first step is to consider the bytecode sequences executed by KVM. Consider the previous sequences as an example. The order of accessed NAND flash pages is supposed to be:

[*BytecodeFetching*]-[*LookupTable*]-[A]-[*BytecodeFetching*]-[*LookupTable*]-[B]-
[*BytecodeFetching*]-[*LookupTable*]-[A]…

Obviously, NAND flash pages contained *BytecodeFetching* and *LookupTable* were much often to appear in the sequence than those contained *BytecodeDispatch*. As a result, pages belonging to *BytecodeFetching* and *LookupTable* are favorable to last in the cache. Pages holding bytecode handlers have to compete with each other to stay in the cache. Thus, we induced that the order of executed bytecode instructions is the key factor impacts cache misses.

Consider an extreme case: In a system with three cache blocks, pages of *BytecodeFetching* and *LookupTable* occupied two cache blocks, and then there is only one free cache block for swapping pages containing bytecode handlers. If all the bytecode handlers were located in distinct NAND flash pages, each bytecode instruction decoding operation would cause a cache miss. This is because the next-to-execute bytecode handler is always located in an uncached NAND flash page. In the other word, the sample sequence caused at least eight cache misses. Nevertheless, if both the handlers of A and B are grouped to the same page, cache misses will decline to 5 times, and the page access trace becomes:

fault-A-B-A-B-fault-C-fault-D-fault-E-fault-C

If we expand the group (A, B) to include the handler of C, the cache miss count would even drop to four times, and the page access trace looks like the following one:

fault-A-B-A-B-C-fault-D-fault-E-fault-C

Therefore, an effective code layout method should partition all bytecode instructions into disjoined sets based on their execution relevance. Each NAND flash page contains one set of bytecode handlers. Partitioning the ICFG can reach this goal.

Back to Figure 8, the directed edges represented the temporal order of the instruction sequence. The weight of an edge is the repetitious count that the bytecode instruction succeeded to the other in the instruction sequence. If we cut off edge (B, C), the ICFG is divided into two disjoined sets. That is, the bytecode handlers of A and B are placed in one page, and the bytecode handlers of C, D, and E are placed in the other. The page access trace became:

fault-A-B-A-B-fault-C-D-E-C

This placement would cause only two cache misses, which is 75% lower than the worst case! The next step is to transform the ICFG diagram to an undirected graph by merging opposite direction edges connected same vertices, and weight of the undirected edge is the sum of weights of those two directed edges. The consequence is actually a derivation of the classical MIN k-CUT problem. Formally speaking, given a graph $G(V, E)$, it can be modeled as:

- V_i – represent the i-th bytecode instruction.
- $E_{i,j}$ – the edge connect i-th and j-th bytecode instruction.
- $F_{i,j}$ – number of times that two bytecode instructions i and j executed after each other. It is the weight of edge $E_{i,j}$.
- K – number of expected partitions.
- $W_{x,y}$ – the intra-set weight. $x \neq y$, $W_{x,y} = \Sigma F_{i,j}$ where $V_i \in P_x$ and $V_j \in P_y$.
The goal is to model the problem as the following definition:

Definition 1. The MIN k-CUT problem is to divide G into K disjoined partitions $\{P_1, P_2,...,P_k\}$. Such that $\Sigma W_{i,j}$ is minimized.

4.3 The Mathematical Model

Yet there was another constraint on our program. Gathering bytecode instructions for partitions regardless of total size of handlers is impractical, since the size of each bytecode handler is distinct, and the total code size of a partition cannot exceed the size of a NAND flash page. Our aim is to distribute bytecode handlers into several disjoined partitions $\{P_1, P_2,...,P_k\}$. We defined the following notations:

- S_i – the code size of bytecode handler V_i.
- N – the size of one NAND flash page.
- $M(P_k)$ – the size of partition P_k. It is ΣS_m for all $V_m \in P_k$.
- $H(P_k)$ – the value of partition P_k. It is $\Sigma F_{i,j}$ for all V_i, $V_j \in P_k$.

Our goal was to construct partitions that satisfy the following constrains.

Definition 2. The problem is to divide G into K disjoined partitions $\{P_1, P_2,...,P_k\}$. For each P_k that $M(P_k) \leq N$. Such that $W_{i,j}$ is minimized. And maximize $\Sigma H(P_i)$ for all $P_i \in \{P_1, P_2,...,P_k\}$.

This rectified model is exactly an application of the graph partition problem, i.e., the size of each partition must satisfy the constraint (NAND flash page size), and the sum of intra-partition path weights is minimal. The graph partition problem is NP-complete [13]. However, the purpose of this paper was neither to create a new graph partition algorithm nor to discuss difference between existing algorithms. The experimental implementation just adopted the following algorithm to demonstrate our approach works. Other implementations based on this approach may choose another graph partition algorithm that satisfies specific requirements.

Partition (G)
    1. Find the edge with maximal weight $F_{i,j}$ among graph G, while the $S_i + S_j \leq N$. If there is no such an edge, go to step 4.
    2. Call *Merge (V_i, V_j)* to combine vertexes V_i and V_j.
    3. Remove both V_i and V_j from G. go to step 1.
    4. Find a pair of vertexes V_i and V_j in G such that $S_i + S_j \leq N$. If there isn't a pair satisfied the criteria, go to step 7.
    5. Call *Merge (V_i, V_j)* to combine vertexes V_i and V_j.
    6. Remove both V_i and V_j out of G. go to step 4.
    7. End.

The procedure of merging both vertexes V_i and V_j is:

Merge (V_i, V_j)
    1. Add a new vertex V_k. to G.
    2. Pickup an edge E connects V_t with either V_i or V_j. If there is no such an edge, then go to step 6.
    3. If there is already an edge F connects V_t to V_k,
    4.   Then, add the weight of E to F, and discard E.
    5.   Else, replace one end of E which is either V_i or V_j with V_k.
    6. End.

Finally, each vertex in G is an aggregation of several bytecode handlers. The refinement process is to collect bytecode handlers belong to the same vertex and place them into one NAND flash page.

5 Refinement Process

The implementation of the refinement process consisted of two steps. The refinement process acted as a post processor of the compiler. It parsed intermediate files generated by the compiler, rearranged blocks, and wrote optimized assembly codes as a substitution. Our implementation is inevitably compiler-dependent and CPU-dependent. Current implementation tightly integrated with *gcc* for ARM, but the approach is easy to apply to other platforms. Figure 9 illustrates the outline of the processing flow, entities, and relations between each entity. The following paragraphs explain the functions of each step.

A. Collecting dynamic bytecode instruction trace. The first step was to collect statistics from real Java applications or benchmarks, because the following steps will need these data for partitioning bytecode handlers. The modified KVM dumped the bytecode instruction trace while running Java applications. A special program called TRACER analyzed the trace dump to find the relevance of all instruction pairs.

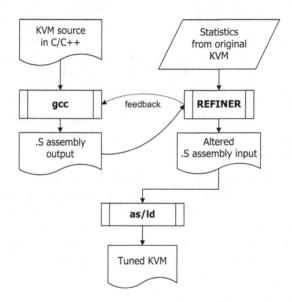

Fig. 9. Entities in the refinement process

B. Rearranging the KVM interpreter. This is the core step realized by a program called REFINER. It acted as a post processor of *gcc*. Its duty was to parse bytecode handlers expressed in the assembly code and re-assemble them into partitions. Each partition fit for one NAND flash page. The program consisted of several sub tasks described as follows.

(i) Parsing layout information of original KVM. The very first thing was to compile the original KVM. REFINER parsed the intermediate files generated by gcc. According to structure of the interpreter expressed in assembly code introduced in §3.2, REFINER analyzed the jumping table in the *LookupTable* trunk to find out the address and size of each bytecode handler.

(ii) Using the graph partition algorithm to group bytecode handlers into disjoined partitions. At this stage, REFINER constructed the ICFG with two key parameters: (1) the relevance statistics of bytecode instructions collected by TRACER; (2) the machine code layout information collected in the step A. It used the approximate algorithm described in §4.3 to divide the undirected ICFG into disjoined partitions.

(iii) Rewriting the assembly code. REFINER parsed and extracted assembly codes of all bytecode handlers. Then, it created a new assembly file and dumped all bytecode handlers partition by partition according to the result of (ii).

(iv) Propagating symbol tables to each partition. As described in §3.2, there are several symbol tables distributed in the *BytecodeDispatch* trunk. For most RISC processors like ARM or MIPS, an instruction is unable to carry arbitrary constants as operands because of limited instruction word length. The solution is to gather used constants into a symbol table and place this table near the instructions that will access those constants. Hence, the compiler generates instructions with relative addressing operands to load constants from the nearby symbol tables. Take ARM for example, its ABI defined two instructions called LDR and ADR for loading a constant from a symbol table to a register [14]. The ABI restricts the maximal distance between a LDR/ADR instruction and the referred symbol table to 4K bytes.

Besides, it would cause a cache miss if a machine instruction in page X loads a constant s_i from symbol table S_Y located in page Y. Our solution was to create a local symbol table S_x in page X and copy the value s_i to the new table. Therefore, the relative distance between s_i and the instruction never exceeds 4KB, and it is impossible to raise cache misses when the CPU tried to load s_i.

(v) Dumping contents in partitions to NAND flash pages. The aim is to map bytecode handlers to NAND flash pages. It re-assembled bytecode handlers belong to the same partition into one NAND flash page. After that, REFINER refreshed the address and size information of all bytecode handlers. The updated information helped REFINER to add padding to each partition and enforce the starting address of each partition to align to the boundary of a NAND flash page.

6   Experimental Result

Figure 10 shows the block diagram of our experimental setup. To mimic real embedded applications, we have implanted J2ME KVM to uClinux for ARM7 in the experiment. One of the reasons to use this platform is that uClinux supports FLAT executable file format which is perfect for supporting XIP. We ran KVM/uClinux on a customized *gdb*. This customized *gdb* dumped memory access trace and performance statistics to files. The experimental setup assumed there was a specialized hardware unit acted as the NAND flash memory controller which loads program codes from NAND flash pages to the cache. It also assumed all flash access operations worked transparently without the help from the operating system. In other words, it is not necessary to modify the OS kernel for the experiment. This experiment used "Embedded Caffeine Mark 3.0" [12] as the benchmark.

Embedded Caffeine Mark	J2ME API
K Virtual Machine (KVM) 1.1	
uClinux Kernel	

GDB 5.0/ARMulator
Windows/Cygwin

Java / RAM

ARM7 / FLASH

ARM7 / ROM

Intel X86

Title	Version
arm-elf-binutil	2.15
arm-elf-gcc	3.4.3
uClibc	0.9.18
J2ME (KVM)	CLDC 1.1
elf2flt	20040326

Fig. 10. Hierarchy of simulation environment

There are only two kinds of NAND flash commodities in the market: 512-bytes and 2048-bytes per page. In this experiment, we setup the cache simulator to meet the following conditions:

1. There were four NAND flash page size options: 512, 1024, 2048 and 4096.
2. The page replacement policy was full associative, and it is a FIFO cache.
3. The number of cache memory blocks varied from 2, 4... to 32.

We tuned four versions of KVM using the optimization process described in §5; each version suited to one kind of page size. All the experimental measurements are compared with those from the original KVM. Table 1 is the highlight of experimental results and shows the degrees of improvement of the optimized versions as well.

In the test case with 4KB/512-bytes per page, the cache miss rate of the tuned KVM dropped to less than 1%, but the cache miss rate of the original KVM is greater than 3% at the same condition. In the best case, the cache miss rate of the tuned KVM was 96% lower than the value from the original one. Besides, in the case with only two cache blocks (1KB/512-bytes per page), the improvement was about 50%. It means tuned KVMs outperformed on devices with limited cache blocks.

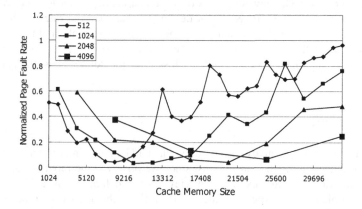

Fig. 11. The chart of normalized cache-miss rates. The x-axis is the total size of the cache memory (*number_of_blocks * block_size*).

Table 1. Experimental cache miss counts. Data of 21 to 32 blocks were omitted due to their miss rates are too low to read.

512 Bytes/Blk		Miss Count	
# Blks	Improve.	Original	Optimized
2	48.94%	52106472	25275914
4	50.49%	34747976	16345163
6	71.19%	26488191	7249424
8	80.12%	17709770	3294736
10	78.02%	12263183	2560674
12	89.61%	9993229	986256
14	95.19%	6151760	280894
16	95.63%	4934205	204975
18	94.37%	3300462	176634
20	90.48%	1734177	156914
Total Access		548980637	521571173

1024 Bytes/Blk		Miss Count	
# Blks	Improve.	Original	Optimized
2	38.64%	29760972	17350643
4	69.46%	21197760	6150007
6	78.15%	13547700	2812730
8	88.11%	8969062	1013010
10	96.72%	6354864	197996
12	96.02%	3924402	148376
14	92.97%	1735690	115991
16	90.64%	1169657	104048
18	75.11%	380285	89934
20	58.30%	122884	48679
Total Access		548980637	521571046

2048 Bytes/Blk		Miss Count	
# Blks	Improve.	Original	Optimized
2	40.74%	25616314	14421794
4	78.17%	14733164	3055373
6	80.10%	8284595	1566059
8	93.80%	4771986	281109
10	95.66%	2297323	94619
12	81.33%	458815	81395
14	54.22%	96955	42166
16	52.03%	62322	28403
18	24.00%	26778	19336
20	10.08%	18390	15710
Total Access		548980637	521570848

4096 Bytes/Blk		Miss Count	
# Blks	Improve.	Original	Optimized
2	62.32%	14480682	5183539
4	86.32%	7529472	978537
6	93.27%	2893864	185037
8	74.91%	359828	85762
10	33.39%	88641	56096
12	-89.68%	25067	45173
14	0.08%	16547	15708
16	-33.81%	7979	10144
18	-17.08%	5484	6100
20	-24.69%	3536	4189
Total Access		548980637	521570757

Figure 11 is the chart of the normalized miss rates (i.e., *optimized_miss_rate / original_miss_rate*.) The envelope lines of these charts are similar to concave curves. The cache miss rate of the tuned KVM declined faster than the rates of the original version in the cases that the amounts of cache blocks were small, and the curve goes downward. Once there were enough cache blocks to hold the working set of the original KVM, the tuned version gradually loss its competence. Thus, the curve turns upward.

7 Conclusion

Our refinement process analyzes not only the CFG of the interpreter but also the patterns of bytecode instruction streams, since we observed the input sequence drives the program flow. From this point of view, we concluded it is a kind of graph partition problem. Therefore, our technique utilized the theory to tune KVM for specific NAND flash page sizes. The experimental result proves that the refined KVM generates much lower cache misses than the unmodified version.

The most important of all, it performed well with limited cache memory blocks. Consider the case of 8KB/512-bytes per page, the cache miss rate of the tuned KVM is 0.6%. As compare with 3.2% from the original KVM, this is a significant improvement. Yes, if the cache is big, miss rate will not be an issue. However, our approach can ensure that the KVM generates lower misses at marginal conditions. This technique also enables SOC to integrate a small block of embedded SRAM as cache and still execute the KVM fast.

Virtual machine is a special kind of software. Their common practice is to have an interpreter with a wide span of instruction handlers. Therefore, the execution flow is determined by applications running on top of virtual machines. As a result, our tuning process should apply to other interpreters or virtual machines besides KVM.

References

1. Sun Microsystems. J2ME Building Blocks for Mobile Devices. Sun Microsystems, Inc. (May 19, 2000)
2. Park, C., Seo, J., Bae, S., Kim, H., Kim, S., Kim, B.: A Low-Cost Memory Architecture with NAND XIP for Mobile Embedded Systems. In: ISSS+CODES 2003: First IEEE/ACM/IFIP International conference on Hardware/Software Codesign and System Synthesis, ACM Press, New York (2003)
3. Samsung Electronics. OneNAND Features & Performance. Samsung Electronics (November 4, 2005)
4. Park, C., Lim, J., Kwon, K., Lee, J., Min, S.L.: Compiler Assisted Demand Paging for Embedded Systems with Flash Memory. In: EMSOFT 2004. Proceedings of the 4th ACM international conference on Embedded software, Pisa, Italy, September 27-29, 2004, pp. 114–124. ACM Press, New York (2004)
5. Parameswaran, S., Henkel, J.: I-CoPES: Fast Instruction Code Placement for Embedded Systems to Improve Performance and Energy Efficiency. In: Proceedings of the 2001 IEEE/ACM international conference on Computer-aided design, pp. 635–641. IEEE Press, Los Alamitos (2001)
6. Janapsatya, A., Parameswaran, S., Henkel, J.: REMcode: Relocating embedded code for improving system efficiency. IEE Proc. Comput. Digit. Tech., 151(6) (November 2004)
7. Pettis, K., Hansen, R.: Profile-guided code positioning. In: PLDI 1990. The Proceedings of the ACM SIGPLAN 1990 conference on Programming language design and implementation, vol. 25(6), pp. 16–27. ACM Press, New York (1990)
8. Santarini, M.: NAND versus NOR-Which flash is best for bootin' your next system? EDN October 2005. Reed Business Information, a division of Reed Elsevier Inc., pp. 41-48 (October 13, 2005)
9. Micron Technology, Inc. Boot-from-NAND Using Micron® MT29F1G08ABA NAND Flash with the Texas Instruments™ (TI) OMAP2420 Processor, Micron Technology, Inc. (2006)
10. Sony Ericsson. Java™ Support in Sony Ericsson Mobile Phones. Sony Ericsson Mobile Communications AB (2003)
11. Lafond, S., Lilius, J.: An Energy Consumption Model for Java Virtual Machine. In: Turku Centre for Computer Science TUCS Technical Report No 597, TUCS (March 2004)
12. CaffeineMark 3.0, Pendragon Software Corp., http://www.benchmarkhq.ru/cm30
13. Garey, M.R., Johnson, D.S.: Computer and Intractability - A Guide to the Theory of NP-Completeness. Bell Telephone Laboratories (1979)
14. Fuber, S.: ARM System-on-Chip Architecture, 2nd edn., pp. 49–72. Addison-Wesley, Reading (2000)

Aggressive Function Inlining: Preventing Loop Blockings in the Instruction Cache

Yosi Ben Asher, Omer Boehm, Daniel Citron,
Gadi Haber, Moshe Klausner, Roy Levin, and Yousef Shajrawi

IBM Research Lab in Haifa, Israel
Computer Science Department Haifa University, Haifa Israel
{omerb,citron,haber,klausner}@il.ibm.com

Abstract. Aggressive function inlining can lead to significant improvements in execution time. This potential is reduced by extensive instruction cache (Icache) misses caused by subsequent code expansion. It is very difficult to predict which inlinings cause Icache conflicts, as the exact location of code in the executable depends on completing the inlining first. In this work we propose a new method for selective inlining called "Icache Loop Blockings" (ILB). In ILB we only allow inlinings that do not create multiple inlined copies of the same function in hot execution cycles. This prevents any increase in the Icache footprint. This method is significantly more aggressive than previous ones, experiments show it is also better.

Results on a server level processor and on an embedded CPU, running SPEC CINT2000, show an improvement of 10% in the execution time of the ILB scheme in comparison to other inlining methods. This was achieved without bloating the size of the hot code executed at any single point of execution, which is crucial for the embedded processor domain.

We have also considered the synergy between code reordering and inlining focusing on how inlining can help code reordering. This aspect of inlining has not been studied in previous works.

1 Introduction

Function inlining [1] is a known optimization where the compiler or post link tool replaces a call to a function by its body, directly substituting the values passed as parameters. Function inlining can improve instruction scheduling as it increases the size of basic blocks. Other optimizations such as global scheduling, dead code elimination, constant propagation, and register allocation may also benefit from function inlining. In order to optimize the code that was generated by the inlining operation, inlining must be executed before most of the backend optimizations.

There is a special relation between inlining and embedded systems. Embedded CPUs have relatively small branch history tables compared to servers. Aggressive inlining can improve the branch prediction in embedded systems, compensating for their relatively small number of entries. The reason is that return instructions are implemented with branch-via-register instructions which are typically

P. Stenström et al. (Eds.): HiPEAC 2008, LNCS 4917, pp. 384–397, 2008.

responsible for most of the branch mis-predictions. Inlining eliminates many return instructions thus "freeing" significant amount of entries in the branch history tables.[1] Finally, eliminating the code of the function's prologue and epilogue may further reduce execution time.

In spite of these potentials, inlining is not used aggressively and is usually applied to restricted cases. The reason is that aggressive function inlining can cause code bloat and consequently instruction cache (Icache) conflicts; thus, degrading performance. In particular, different copies of the same function may compete for space in the Icache. If a function is frequently called from different call sites, duplicating it can cause more cache misses due to frequent references to these multiple copies or to code segments that are activated through them.

The main problem with inlining is that the final instructions' locations (addresses in the final executable) are determined only after inlining is completed. Consequently, it is not possible to determine which inlinings will eventually lead to Icache conflicts. Many optimizations that modify the code and change its location are applied after inlining (such as scheduling and constant propagation). An important optimization that dramatically alters code locations and is applied after inlining is code reordering [7]. Code reordering groups sequences of hot basic blocks (frequently executed) in ordered "chains" that are mapped to consecutive addresses in the Icache. Thus, code reordering can reduce or repair part of the damage caused by aggressive inlining decisions. However, it does not eliminate the need to carefully select the inlined function calls.

Even sophisticated versions [2] of code reordering that use cache coloring techniques can not repair the damage caused by excessive inlining. This inherent circular dependency leads compiler architects to use heuristics for function inlining. Current inlining methods use a combination of these basic methods and they differ only in the criterion/threshold of when to use a given basic method:

– inline only very small functions, basically preserving the original code size.
– inline a function if it only has a single caller. Thus, preserving or even reducing the original code size. This is extended to inlining only dominant calls, i.e., call sites that account for the majority of calls for a given function.
– inline only hot calls, not necessary the dominant ones.
– inline if a consecutive chain of basic blocks does not exceed the size of the L1 Icache.
– inline calls with constant parameters whose substitution followed by constant propagation and dead code elimination will improve performance. This criterion was proposed and used in [5] for the related optimization of function cloning, i.e., create a specialized clone of a function for a specific call site[2].

We have experimented with these rules in IBM's FDPR-Pro tool which is a post link optimizer [7] and discovered that they are too restrictive and can prevent many possible inlinings that could lead to significant code improvement.

---

[1] This is important in processors with deep pipelines or minor branch prediction support. The latter attribute is prevalent in leading high-end embedded processors.
[2] Cloning is less efficient than inlining since it does not increase the size of consecutive chains of hot basic blocks.

An "execution cycle" is a cycle in the joined call graph and control flow graph of all functions in a program. This graph contains explicit edges for all call and return instructions (forming an inter-procedural control flow graph). These cycles usually correspond to loops. ILB prevents any inlining that will create two or more copies of the same function in the same hot cycle/loop of this extended control flow graph. One reason for this criterion is that the Icache footprint of hot loops after ILB inlining does not increase (since each cycle can contain at most one inlined copy of the same function). Moreover, multiple copies of the same function can have a cascading effect, as follows: Let $f_0, \ldots f_k$ be a set of functions where each f_i $(i < k)$ has a hot loop with two hot calls to f_{i+1}. Aggressive inlining will lead to 2^{k-1} copies of f_k in the Icache footprint of f_0. Since all of these 2^{k-1} inlinings belong to a hot execution cycle, repeated Icache misses are likely to occur. The proposed criterion is called "Icache Loop Blockings" (ILB) referring to repeated Icache misses caused by loops as "Icache Blockings".

Figure 1 illustrates how ILB is applied to two cases of hot loops. The two-sided arrows in the figure represent call/return-edges, other arrows represent the control flow edges. For simplicity, a call to a function can appear as a single node in a loop or pointed by a two-sided arrow (e.g., $f1() \longleftrightarrow g()$). The loop shown in the left side has two distinct calls $f1(), f2()$ that can be safely inlined. However, the inlining of $g()$ in the inlined calls $f1(), f2()$ is not allowed since it will lead to two copies of $g()$ in the same hot execution cycle. Next, consider the two consecutive loops shown on the right side of figure 1. The calls to $f1(), f2()$ and $g()$ in the two loops can be safely inlined since each call belongs to a different execution cycle.

More complex examples of using the ILB method are illustrated in figure 2 that includes cases of "pseudo cycles". An execution cycle in the extended CFG is called a "pseudo cycle" if it returns from a different call node than the one it entered. Each loop of the left example of figure 2 contains two single calls to g and q (through $f1(), f2()$ respectively) forming hot cycles containing multiple

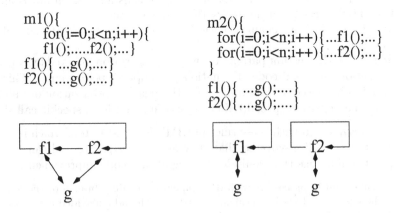

Fig. 1. Loop blocking (left) and pseudo loop Blocking (right)

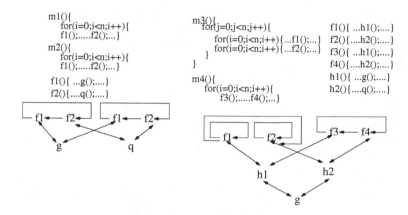

Fig. 2. Complex cases addressed by the ILB method

copies of $g()$ and $q()$. However, all these cycles are pseudo-cycles and hence full inlining is allowed by the ILB. Thus, care must be given to the detection of these pseudo-cycles. The right side of figure 2 is a combination of the two previous examples. The inlining of g in the right side of figure 2 is allowed only in the copies of $h1$ and $h2$, that have been inlined into $f1$ and $f2$ respectively, and not allowed inside $f3$ or $f4$. The maximal sequence of inlinings allowed by ILB in this example is therefore $f1 \Longleftarrow h1 \Longleftarrow g$, $f2 \Longleftarrow h2 \Longleftarrow g$, $f3 \Longleftarrow h1$, and $f4 \Longleftarrow h2$. Hence the algorithm for implementing ILB must be able to compute the right order in which the inlinings are made.

Next, the ILB optimization is followed by a code reordering pass creating a synergy between inlining and code reordering as follows:

- Code reordering rearranges basic blocks in consecutive hot chains, removing part of the Icache conflicts caused by aggressive inlining.
- Function inlining creates better opportunities for code reordering by extending its scope across function calls.

We include a separate discussion of this synergy and show in detail how code reordering can benefit from the aggressive inlining.

The proposed scheme relies on profile information to build and analyze the call graph and the joined/extended control flow graph of the program. Based on this profile information we consider functions and/or basic blocks as being 'hot' (frequently called) or 'cold' (infrequently called).

We conclude with some data on embedded CPUs supporting our claim regarding the special relation between inlining and embedded systems. Table 1 lists the leading high-end embedded processors and the number of entries in their branch direction (Branch History Table) and branch target predictors (Branch Target Buffer), and the number of entries in their return stacks. Many have little or no support for branch target predictions, in particular for return address predictions. This is opposed to high-end servers, such as the IBM Power4, which has a complex, two-tiered, direction predictor, a 32-entry function call cache,

Table 1. Dynamic branch predictors on leading high-end embedded processors

Processor	BHT	BTB	Return Stack	L1 I-cache
AMCC 440GX	1024	16	–	32KB, 32B, 64 ways
Broadcom BCM1250	1024	64	16	32KB, 32B, 4 ways
Cavium Octeon	256	–	4	32KB, 32B, 4 ways
IBM 750GX	512	64	–	32KB, 32B, 8 ways
FreeScale MPC7447A	2048	2	–	32KB, 32B, 8 ways
FreeScale MPC8560	512	512	–	32KB, 32B, 8 ways
PMC-Sierra RM9000x2GL	256	–	4	32KB, 32B, 4 ways

and 16-entry return address cache. On the other hand their L1 I-caches are in par with the aforementioned class of processors. The numbers demonstrate the importance of aggressive inlining techniques for embedded systems.

2   ILB Based Aggressive Function Inlining

Inlining decisions are based on the Call Graph (CG) of the program. Each edge of the graph is assigned a weight: the frequency of each function call according to the profile information collected. The *Average Heat ratio (AvgHeat)* is the sum of all the frequencies of all the executed (dynamic) instructions (DI) gathered during the profiling stage, divided by the total number of static instructions (SI) in the program:

$$AvgHeat = \frac{\sum_i^{DI} freq_i}{SI}$$

Cold edges are defined as any edge in the extended CFG whose weight is lower than some threshold (e.g., 10%) of *AvgHeat*. The algorithm implementing the ILB method is:

1. Based on edge profile information, create the call graph CG for the given program and attach a weight to each edge. The weight is its execution frequency.
2. Traverse CG and remove all cold edges. Section 2.2 elaborates on this.
3. Remove cyclic paths from CG by finding the smallest weighted set of edges in CG using the algorithm of Eades et. al. [6] for solving the feedback edge set problem. Section 3 elaborates on this.
4. Let EG be the extended control flow graph containing the control flow graph of each function and direct edges for call and return instructions. For each function f in the call graph CG, which is a candidate for inlining:
   (a) For every two incoming edges $e1$ and $e2$ to f in CG, let $caller1$ be the caller basic block ending with $e1$ and let $caller2$ be the caller basic block ending with $e2$ in EG. $fallthru1$ and $fallthru2$ are the basic blocks following $caller1$ and $caller2$ in EG respectively.
   (b) Traverse EG and search for directed paths from $fallthru1$ to $caller2$ and from $fallthru2$ to $caller1$.
   (c) If both paths exist, remove the $e1$ and $e2$ edges from CG.

5. Sort CG in topological order.
6. Traverse the sorted graph from the root in descending order. For each function f:
   (a) Duplicate the code of function f for each of the call sites that have an outgoing edge to f. All relevant information related to the copies of f $(f_1, f_2, ...)$, such as symbolic information, branch tables, traceback data, etc., are duplicated as well.
   (b) Update the selected call sites to f, to call its copies.
   (c) Update the weights of the edges in both the call graph and the control flow graphs of both f and its copies, to reflect the changes resulting from duplicating f. For example if a function f is called 100 times from g and 200 times from h then the weights of the edges in each copy of f should be divided by this ratio as well.
7. Traverse all the functions in CG starting from the leaf functions in ascending order. For each function f_i:
   Embed f_i into its calling function g while eliminating the save, restore, call, and return instructions.
8. Update CG and EG to reflect the changes resulting from inlining f.

2.1   ILB Experimental Results

We implemented the various inlining algorithms into IBM FDPR-Pro - a post-link optimization tool. Measurements were obtained on the SPEC CINT2000 benchmark running on platforms based on the following processors:

1. IBM Power4 that has a 64KB, direct mapped, L1 Instruction Cache with 128-byte lines.
2. AMCC 440GX that has a 32KB, 64-way associative, L1 Instruction Cache with 32-byte lines.

In both measurements, FDPR-Pro was also used to collect the profiling data by instrumenting the benchmarks and running them on the train workload. Performance measurements were collected using the reference input. The following graphs compare ILB versus four inlining methods:

all - all executed functions that were somewhat hot.
hot - all functions that are above the average heat.
dominant - call sites that make more than 80% of the executed calls to the function.
small - only small size functions.

This was also repeated for the embedded CPU. The results in Figure 3 show that ILB improves the execution time by 10% compared to the other four methods. Note that the ILB almost never degraded the performance compared to the "base" case, while there are cases where *small, hot* and *all* reduced the performance. Note that dominant calls are a subset of ILB since a hot call that is repeated in a hot cycle can not be dominant. This indicates that ILB is safer than

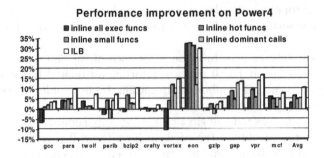

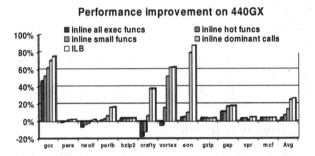

Fig. 3. Performance improvements on the Power4 (top) and 440GX (bottom)

inlining methods that are based on combinations of size and temperature. The improvements on the embedded CPU are smaller than those on the server. This can be explained by the fact that the Icache on the AMCC 440GX is highly associative. Therefore, conflicting inlinings on the Power4's direct-mapped Icache do not conflict on the 440GX's associative Icache.

Figure 4 depicts the number of function inlined by each method. Note that ILB inlined less functions than most of the other methods yet obtained a higher performance. This suggests that the ILB scheme inlines the "correct" set of functions. Moreover, there is a clear correlation between inlining to many functions and performance degradation, demonstrating the need for "precise" inlining methods.

2.2 Removing Cold Edges

Here we describe in detail how "cold" edges are removed from the call graph, and are not considered for inlining. The algorithm is based on a threshold that indicates which edges are considered cold. The experimental results verify that each program requires a different threshold in order to maximize the performance of aggressive inlining. This requires a normalization procedure of the profile information as follows:

Number of functions inlined

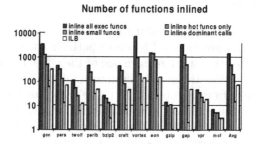

Fig. 4. Number of functions inlined per method

AvgHeat the average edge weight in the control flow graph of the entire program (defined above).

MaxHeat the maximal weight in the graph.

HT an input Heat Threshold percentage between 0 and 1.

NormHT the Normalized Heat Threshold calculated by the following formula:

$$NormHT = \begin{cases} 0 & \text{if } HT = 0 \\ MaxHeat + 1 & \text{if } HT = 1 \\ min(AvgHeat/\ln(1/HT^2), MaxHeat + 1) & \text{if } 0 < HT < 1 \end{cases}$$

The computed $NormHT$ formula is based on the distribution of the execution of the edges in the control flow graph. For heat (frequency) values below $AvgHeat$, $NormHT$ ascends very slowly. until it reaches the $AvgHeat$ threshold (at around $HT = 60\%$), when it suddenly ascends very quickly until reaching the $MaxHeat$ value where it remains constant. Figure 5 displays the function's behavior.

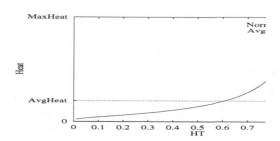

Fig. 5. Behavior of $NormHT$ as a function of HT

Every edge of the control flow graph that falls below $NormHT$ is removed from the graph. As a result, the higher the HT, the more aggressive the optimization. For $HT = 0$, all the edges in the call graph are removed completely, thus disabling the optimization. For $HT = 1$, the call graph is left unchanged, enabling the optimization for every non-cold edge that was left after applying Step 2 of the main algorithm.

3   Cyclic Paths

Given the call graph of the program, the proposed algorithm must handle recursive function calls that are reflected by cyclic paths in the call graph. To handle cyclic paths, the algorithm must remove one of the edges in the cycle.

Different inlining orders are created for different edges being removed from the graph, as can be seen from Figure 6. The figure shows an example of a cycle in the call graph of a given program, in which function f includes a call to function i that in turn calls j, which calls back to f. Different possible inlining chains are created by removing different edges (lower part of Figure 6). They are drawn according to the following rules:

1. If a function foo contains an embedded calling site to an inlined function bar, then bar is drawn beneath foo and slightly aligned to the right.
2. If bar is drawn directly beneath function foo, without being aligned to the right, then both foo and bar are inlined into some other function gal containing the two calling sites to foo and bar.

Figure 6 shows all possible inlining chains created by removing different edges in the $f - i - j$ cycle. For example, removing the $j - f$ edge, causes function j to be inlined into i, which in turn is inlined into f (as shown in Figure 6a). Therefore, it is important to search for the maximal directed acyclic graph representation of the given call graph. This problem is a variation of the feedback edge set problem [6] . The problem is NP-hard and the time complexity of the algorithm is exponential in respect to the number of edges in the largest strongly connected component of G. However, in practice, the number of recursive functions that participate in the creation of cycles in a call graph is usually very small. Thus, the time complexity is manageable.

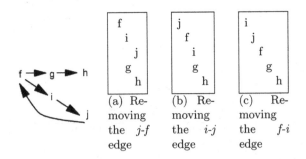

Fig. 6. Different inlining options for cycles in the call graph

4   The Synergy of Function Inlining and Global Code Reordering

One of the fundamental issues related to function inlining is the insertion of 'cold' (rarely executed) code next to 'hot' (frequently executed) code. This instruction

foo:(80 times)	foo:(80 times)	foo:(80 times)	foo:(80 times)
BB1: Call bar	BB1: Call bar	BB1: Call bar	BB5: CMP R6,R7
BB2: CMP R3,0	JMP BB2 (penalty)	BB2: CMP R3,0	JNE BB6
JEQ BB4	bar:	JNE BB3	BB2: CMP R3,0
BB3: ADD R3,12	BB5: CMP R6,R7	BB4: RET	JNE BB3
BB4: RET	JNE BB6	bar:	BB4: RET
	BB7: RET	BB5: CMP R6,R7	
bar:(90 times)	BB2: CMP R3,0	JNE BB6	BB6: ADD R6,9
BB5: CMP R6,R7	JNE BB3	BB7: RET	JMP BB4
JEQ BB7	BB4: RET		BB3: ADD R3,12
BB6: ADD R6,9		BB6: ADD R6,9	JMP BB4
BB7: RET	BB6: ADD R6,9	JMP BB7	
	JMP BB7	BB3: ADD R3,12	bar:(10 times)
	BB3: ADD R3,12	JMP BB4	BB5: CMP R6,R7
	JMP BB4		JEQ BB7
			BB6: ADD R6,9
			BB7: RET

(a) Before code reordering	(b) After code reordering (i)	(c) After code reordering (ii)	(d) After reordering and inlining

Fig. 7. Code reordering followed by function inlining

grouping increases the Icache miss rate by spreading the hot code over more cache lines. In addition it increases the amount of "mixed" Icache lines containing both hot and cold instructions. Thus, after inlining we apply code reordering to rearrange the code layout by grouping hot consecutive basic blocks into consecutive chains. Code reordering is the last phase of the optimization process and as such it can determine the final location of instructions. Hence, code reordering can rearrange code segments such that Icache misses are reduced.

Most previous works also used code reordering after inlining as will be explained in section 5, hence this aspect of code reordering is well known. In this section we focus on a different aspect of code reordering and inlining which is the way inlining can help improve code reordering's ability to group larger and more efficient code segments.

The code reordering algorithm for generating optimized sequences of basic blocks is based on the *tracing scheme* [11]. The algorithm starts with an entry point and grows a *trace* of basic blocks, based on profile information. A trace is a sequence of basic blocks that are executed serially. When the control flow to the next block in a trace reaches an indirect branch instruction (which usually indicates a function return) or falls below a certain frequency threshold, the algorithm stops growing a trace and starts a new one.

The example in Figure 7 exemplifies this scenario (hot basic blocks are boldfaced). Figure 7a shows the hot path within function foo that includes a hot call to function bar. There are two options to build the traces during code reordering:

1. Ideally, the best reordering trace starts with the hot basic block BB1 in foo, followed by the hot basic blocks BB5 and BB7 in bar itself, and finally the hot basic blocks BB2 and BB4 that follow the call instruction to bar in foo. This trace reordering is given in Figure 7b. Unfortunately, although this is the ideal reordering trace, there is an extra jump instruction to BB2 that we are forced to add immediately after the call instruction to bar. The extra jump instruction is necessary to maintain the original program correctness, so that the return instruction in bar will continue to BB2.

2. In order to avoid the extra jump instruction, it is possible to form two reordering traces. A trace consisting of the hot basic blocks in foo: BB1, BB2, and BB4, is followed by a second trace consisting of the hot basic blocks in bar: BB5 and BB7. The resulting code for this selection of reordering traces is shown in Figure 7c. Although this selection does not generate extra jumps for maintaining correctness, it does not reflect the true control flow of the program, as it avoids creating traces that can cross function boundaries.

Figure 7 shows that after inlining bar at the call site in foo, the code reordering creates the optimal hot path without the extra jump or return instructions, and by following the true control flow. Furthermore, function inlining increases the average size of each reordering trace. In Figure 7, the reordering trace size after function inlining includes six instructions, which is longer than each of the reordering traces BB1, BB2, BB3 or BB5, BB7, shown in Figure 7c.

The longer the traces produced by code reordering, the better the program locality. We assert that the average size of traces created before aggressive inlining vs. the average size after inlining can serve as a measure for the improvement to the reverse effect where inline helps code reordering. In general, the average size of traces increases due to function inlining: traces that started to grow in a certain function can now grow into the corresponding inlined callee functions.

4.1 Synergy Experimental Results

The following experimental results demonstrate this "reverse effect" and synergy between function inlining and code reordering on the Power4. The Power4 has an extensive set of Performance Counters (PMCs), that enable us to isolate the reasons for a program's behavior. These count the L1 Icache fetches and branch target mispredictions. Figure 8 shows the improvements of reduced L1 Icache fetches (percentage) comparing code reordering and the combination of inlining and code reordering (denoted as "aggressive inlining"). The average improvement due to inlining is from 16% to 24%. More significant results are presented in Figure 9, which shows the percentage of reduced branch target mispredictions. The code ordering scheme adds extra branches, which cause extra target mispredictions. Applying the aggressive inlining scheme removes many of these branches and reduces the number of target mispredictions for most applications. The direction mispredictions are reduced as well, albeit at a lower rate (3%) than the target mispredictions.

We have also tested the synergy between code reordering and inlining on the PowerPC 405 processor used for embedded systems. The PowerPC 405 is the core

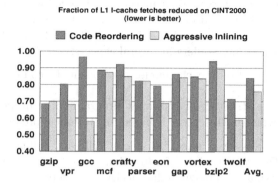

Fig. 8. Amount of L1 Icache fetches reduced on CINT2000 (lower is better)

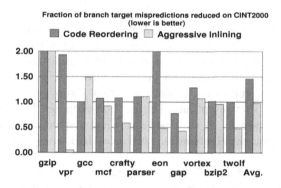

Fig. 9. Amount of branch target mispredictions reduced on CINT2000 (lower is better)

of the IBM PCIX Cryptographic Coprocessor. We tested the *csulcca* (Common Support Utility Linux Common Cryptographic Architecture) application and obtained 2% improvements over code reordering due to the use of inlining.

5   Related Work

Methods for selective inlining have been studied and implemented in the last 10 years. These works should be separated from the works in code reordering wherein inlining is only a pre-stage to code reordering. The goal of code reordering is to rearrange code segments to minimize Icache misses. As explained in Section 1 this differs from the the goal of selecting "safe" yet aggressive inlinings.

Scheifler [12] proposed to inline functions based on: a) function size, b) number of calls versus function size and c) dominant calls. Scheifler showed that computing optimal inlining is at least NP hard. Ball [4] proposed to inline functions based on their utility for constant propagation and other optimizations.

McFarling [9] describes a statistical method to predict which calls should be inlined. The method is based on the distribution of relative "hotness" of calls versus their size. This method refines the method of inlining "hot" functions. The method proposed here differs in several aspects:

- it does not depend on a cache model nor does it depend on the size of the inlined functions.
- it considers the structure of the input program (preventing duplication in hot cycles). whereas [9] scheme is based on statistical predictions.

[8] considers the issue of selecting among different "inlined versions" of a given function. Different versions of a function $f()$ are created during the inline processes as a result of different inline decisions of functions called from $f()$. For example, for $f()\{ ...; g(); h(); ...\}$ there are four immediate versions: the original $f()\{...\}$, $f()\{ ...; inlined\_g(); h(); ...\}$, $f()\{ ...; g(); inlined\_h(); ...\}$ and $f()\{ ...; inlined\_g(); inlined\_h(); ...\}$. Three methods are compared: cv- use maximally inlined version, ov- original version of the callee and current version of the caller and av- use any version. There is a correspondence between these methods and actual inlining systems such as the one used in GCC or in [12]. A probabilistic model to estimate the benefit of inlining given call sequences is devised. This model is based entirely on calling frequencies. Based on this model and experimental results the authors show that the ov- method is at least as powerful as the other two options. The method proposed here is orthogonal to the classification used in [8] as it is based on the structural properties of the call-graph and thus, any combination such as av-ILB, ov-ILP and cv-ILB can be devised.

Ayers et al. [3] and Das [5] found an analogy between the code expansion problem and the Knapsack problem. They used this analogy to help identify appropriate candidates for function inlining. Arnold et al. [1] tried to find the best candidates that fit a given code size budget for the Jalapeño dynamic optimizing compiler. Way et al. [15] suggest different inlining method that are based on the idea of *region-based* analysis. The use of regions is designed to enable the compiler to operate on reduced control flow graphs of inlined functions before applying the register allocation and scheduling algorithms. The formation of a region is guided by profiling information and is similar to the way the code reordering algorithm determines the new order of the basic blocks. Their heuristics reduce compilation complexity but are bound by code size limitations. For function inlining optimization, Way et al. [14] describe a new profile-based method for determining which functions to inline to avoid cases of code bloat, by collecting path profiling information on the call graph of the program. Another work in this direction is [16] introducing two heuristics for the ORC compiler called "adaptation" and "cycle density". Both methods are based on temperature and size, e.g, cycle density prevent inlining of hot functions whose calling frequency is low.

The post-link tools PLTO [13] and Alto [10] address the issue of code inlining as part of their post-link optimizations. PLTO uses a cache model for determining which functions to inline (similar to McFarling's [9]). We have also chosen to implement our techniques at post-link level using the FDPR tool [7]. However, in our work, we eliminate the restriction on the increase of code size by selecting only hot functions as candidates and by not duplicating them to call sites for which they are likely to cause cache conflicts.

References

1. Arnold, M., Fink, S., Sarkar, V., Sweeney, P.: A Comparative Study of Static and Profile-based Heuristics for Inlining. In: Proceedings of the ACM SIGPLAN Workshop on Dynamic and Adaptive Compilation and Optimization, pp. 52–64 (2000)
2. Aydin, H., Kaeli, D.: Using Cache Line Coloring to Perform Aggressive Procedure Inlining. SIGARCH Computer Architecture News 28(1), 62–71 (2000)
3. Ayers, A., Gottlieb, R., Schooler, R.: Aggressive Inlining. In: Proceedings of the 1997 ACM SIGPLAN Conference on Programming Language Design and Implementation, pp. 134–145 (June 1997)
4. Ball, J.E.: Program improvement by the selective integration of procedure calls. Technical report, PhD thesis, University of Rochester (1982)
5. Das, D.: Function Inlining versus Function Cloning. ACM SIGPLAN Notices 38(6), 23–29 (2003)
6. Eades, P., Lin, X., Smyth, W.F.: A fast and effective heuristic for the feedback arc set problem. Info. Proc. Letters 47, 319–323 (1993)
7. Haber, G., Klausner, M., Eisenberg, V., Mendelson, B., Gurevich, M.: Optimization Opportunities Created by Global Data Reordering. In: CGO 2003. First International Symposium on Code Generation and Optimization (March 2003)
8. Kaser, O., Ramakrishnan, C.R.: Evaluating inlining techniques. Computer Languages 24(2), 55–72 (1998)
9. McFarling, S.: Procedure merging with instruction caches. In: Proceedings of the SIGPLAN Conference on Programming Language Design and Implementation, pp. 71–79 (June 1991)
10. Muth, R., Debray, S., Watterson, S.: ALTO: A Link-Time Optimizer for the Compaq Alpha. Technical Report 98-14, Dept. of Computer Science, The University of Arizona (December 1998)
11. Nahshon, I., Bernstein, D.: FDPR - A Post-Pass Object Code Optimization Tool (April 1996)
12. Scheifler, R.W.: An analysis of inline substitution for a structured programming language. Communications of the ACM 20(9), 647–654 (1977)
13. Schwarz, B., Debray, S., Andrews, G., Legendre, M.: PLTO: A Link-Time Optimizer for the Intel IA-32 Architecture. In: Proceedings of Workshop on Binary Rewriting (September 2001)
14. Way, T., Breech, B., Du, W., Stoyanov, V., Pollock, L.: Using path-pectra-based cloning in regional-based optimization for instruction level parallelism. In: Proceedings of the 14th International Conference on Parallel and Distributed Computing Systems, pp. 83–90 (2001)
15. Way, T., Pollock, L.: Evaluation of a Region-based Partial Inlining Algorithm for an ILP Optimizing Compiler. In: IASTED International Conference on Parallel and Distributed Computing and Systems (November 2002)
16. Zhao, P., Amaral, J.N.: To inline or not to inline? enhanced inlining decisions (2003)

Author Index

Lecture Notes in Computer Science

Sublibrary 1: Theoretical Computer Science and General Issues

For information about Vols. 1– 4576
please contact your bookseller or Springer